THE ENTHUSIAST'S GUIDE TO PORTRAITURE

59 Photographic Principles You Need to Know

JEROD FOSTER

THE ENTHUSIAST'S GUIDE TO TO PORTRAITURE:
59 PHOTOGRAPHIC PRINCIPLES YOU NEED TO KNOW

Jerod Foster

Project editor: Maggie Yates
Project manager: Lisa Brazieal
Marketing manager: Jessica Tiernan
Layout and type: WolfsonDesign
Design system and front cover design: Area of Practice
Front cover image: Jerod Foster

ISBN: 978-1-68198-138-3
1st Edition (1st printing, November 2016)
© 2016 Jerod Foster
All images © Jerod Foster unless otherwise noted

Rocky Nook Inc.
1010 B Street, Suite 350
San Rafael, CA 94901
USA

www.rockynook.com

Distributed in the U.S. by Ingram Publisher Services
Distributed in the UK and Europe by Publishers Group UK

Library of Congress Control Number: 2016930703

To my students,
who keep pushing me as much as I push them.

ACKNOWLEDGEMENTS

IMMENSE THANKS goes out to many folks for helping put this book together. So many people gave their time and talents to ensure this project came off without a hitch.

First and foremost, I must thank my family. My wife, Amanda, and two daughters, Eva and Lola Mae, know the life of a traveling photographer all too well, and I'll never be able to repay them the time I've missed while out on the road chasing this dream and career. They are a continual source of inspiration and influence and the very definition of patience. I love you with all of my heart!

Great thanks goes out to the fine folks at Rocky Nook for allowing me to play an integral role in the development of the new Enthusiast's Guides. Thank you all for letting me be a part of the team! Thanks to Ted Waitt, who invited me to join Alan Hess and Khara Plicanic in writing these first books for the series. Also, many thanks to Maggie Yates, whose outstanding contribution to the project ensured the text and content you see in the following pages is both relevant and comprehensible. Finally, many thanks to Lisa Brazieal, whose book production management once again resulted in a great-looking text!

Additionally, thank you to my colleagues and administration at Texas Tech University. My time as a photography and electronic media professor at the College of Media and Communication has been one of excitement, challenge, and growth. I can't think of a more supportive group to push my work, both in and out of the classroom. Specifically, thanks goes to Drs. Rob Peaslee, Todd Chambers, and David Perlmutter for your guidance and encouragement through the years. I'm fortunate to call you colleagues and friends.

Lastly, I would like to thank my students and friends who have supported me and/or played a role in helping put this book together. I'm fortunate to play roles as an educator and a professional, and my students allow me great flexibility and openness in bringing the "real" world into the classroom. They are a great inspiration for many of the books I've written. Specifically, I would like to thank Simon Parmley, Torico Price, Laurie Tolboom, Anna Claire Beasley, Demi Cole, Abbie Burnett, Tate Leatherwood, Lynley Lewis, Alyssa Peden, Lauren Purser, Allison Reid, Hannah Turner, Hope Hancock, and Justin Rex. Many thanks for your integral contribution to the books. Photography, as individualistic as it seems on the surface, is indeed a collaborative effort.

CONTENTS

Introduction x

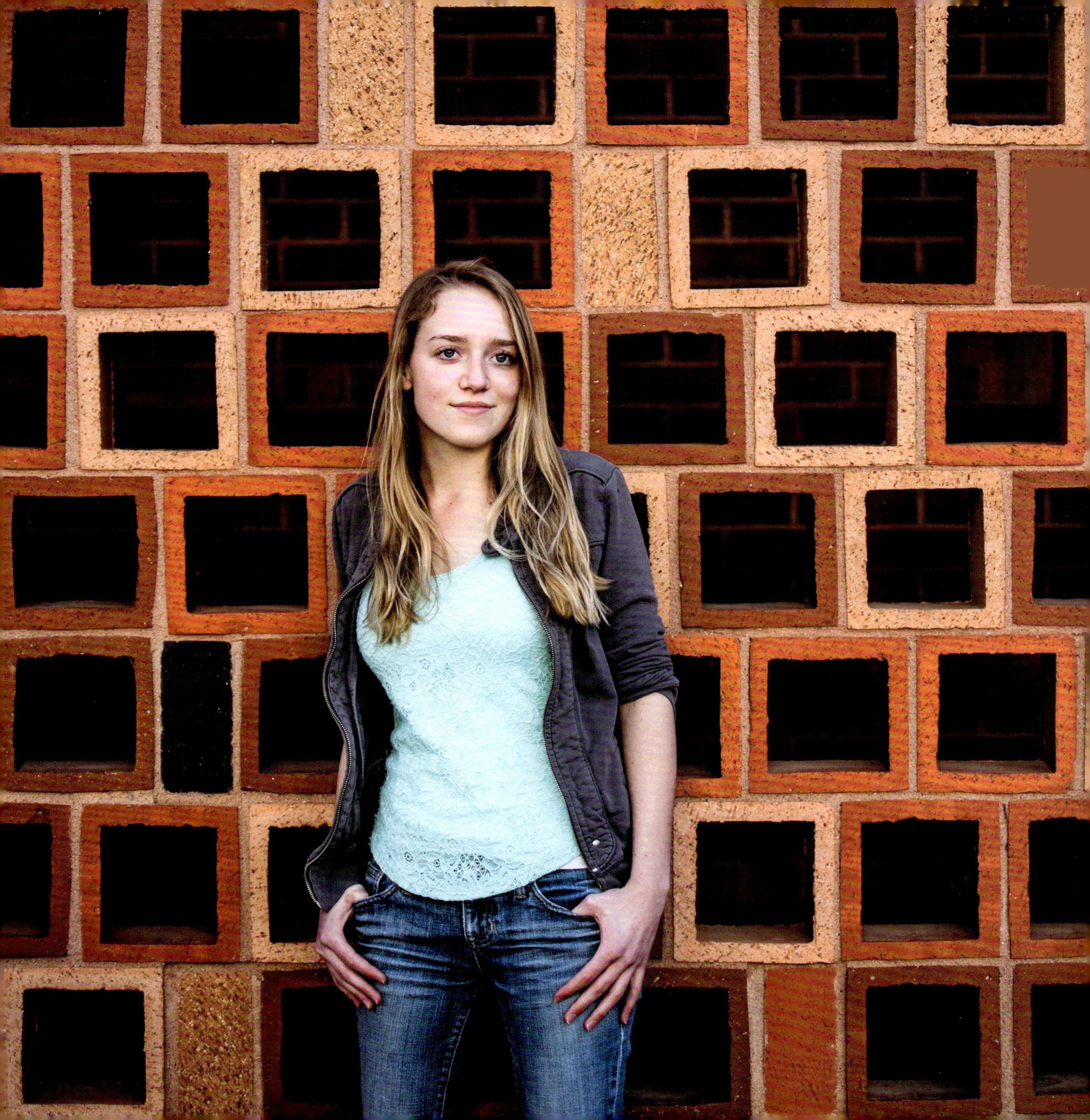

CONTENTS

INTRODUCTION

Portraiture is a large subject. It's a historical way of making art, and an enormous part of the modern photography industry. It's an important part of both photography and society in general. The fact that you've picked this book up is a testimony to how attractive making portraits can be, and I welcome you to this essential aspect of your craft and art as a photographer.

As part of the Enthusiast's Guide series of books from Rocky Nook, I want to highlight what this book is and what it is not. It is first and foremost a guide: it provides you useful, practical, take-to-the-bank tips, considerations, and best practices for your adventure into portrait photography. It is efficient, allowing you to study certain concepts or techniques briefly and quickly actualize them in your own work.

Finally, it *is* a starting point, a way of grounding your portraiture work—a platform from which you can grow your photographic creativity and proficiency. These are the pieces of information that I take with me every time I shoot a portrait, whether it's on assignment or at a family gathering, and I believe they can be useful for your work as well.

Conversely, this book *is not* a technical manual. Although one chapter is completely devoted to setting up your camera, and other chapters include technical details—aperture/depth of field considerations, focal length choice, and the like—it's not my goal to teach you about your camera (although I believe you'll pick up a thing or two). My goal is to move you beyond thinking about the camera more than thinking about the image you're making. It's helpful to have a fairly good understanding of your camera in order to put many of the following tips and techniques to practice for your portraiture.

Additionally, the book *is not* one centered on a specific type of portraiture. It does not look at only family portraiture, or wedding/engagement portraiture, or even editorial environmental portraiture. Instead, it highlights information that can be employed in all types of portraiture. You'll see a variety of portrait types represented in the following pages, but note that at any point, you can apply most, if not all, the information to your portraiture "brand" of choice.

Lastly, this book *is not* comprehensive. Looking for a completely exhaustive guide on all things portraiture? There isn't one. This subject is so large and so diverse that there is no way to contain all of the useful information about creating portraits in one single volume. This book contains a great many tips and techniques that I've picked up over the years as a photographer, some of which I've stumbled upon, many of which were learned from other photographers. Depending on your own experiences, you might be able to add a tip or two to this book.

OK! Now that we have laid the ground rules, I'll highlight my content approach, particularly the images that relate to the text. First, many, if not most, of the images you'll see are from when I was either on editorial or commercial assignment, or when I was hired to photograph portraits for an individual or a family. I believe in seeing how concepts and techniques are put together when the "heat is on," so to speak. Images that were not shot on assignment or commissioned were made for instructional purposes. You'll see a large number of these in the chapter focused on posture.

Second, you're going to see some duplication of portrait subjects (I dare you to count the number of cowboy hats in the book). This is intentional, and it is largely purposed with showing you how any number of techniques or concepts can be applied to a single portrait shoot.

Third, post-processing is kept to a minimum, even in the chapter about post-processing. There is a world of information and best practices regarding post-processing portraits, but this book focuses primarily on photographing your subject. Likewise, you'll only see full color or black-and-white images in the book. I believe in disallowing any given post-processing technique to override the portrait's content. It certainly is an integral part of your workflow, but let it be just that: a *part* of the workflow that contributes to your subject and your creative intention.

Bear in mind that your ability to put the information inside this book successfully into action positively correlates with the amount of intentional photography you create. Don't just read the book and look at the images. Go shoot! Create your own portraits and watch your skills develop over time. There is no, and will never be, substitute for experience!

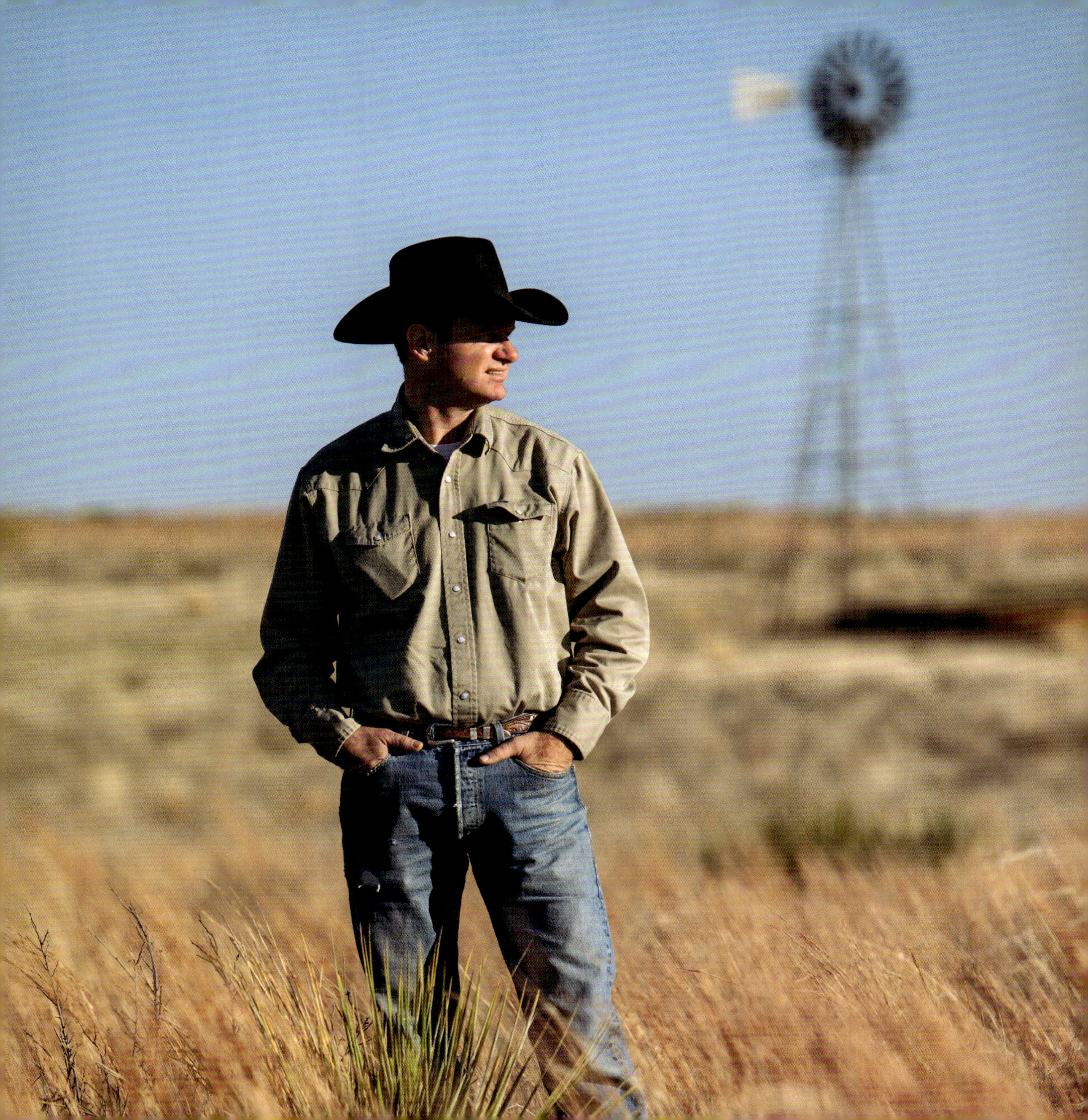

1

THE GENRE

Portraiture is arguably the most popular form or genre of photography. Almost every other genre of photography includes portraiture as a necessary element, with extremely traditional landscape and wildlife photography, and macro photography not included. Regardless of what type of photographer you are, it's wise to have the skills to make a good portrait on the off chance the opportunity to make one arises.

This chapter situates portraiture as a genre of photography and serves as a brief but sturdy launching pad for more specific discussions on practical application of the techniques discussed. Certainly, there are proprietary concerns and considerations, such as posing (if you need it) and how the light on your subject will be read. However, if you work with great fundamentals, chances are you will start seeing and shooting better portraits as you grow in your photography.

1. WHAT'S A PORTRAIT?

A PORTRAIT, LITERALLY, is a visual portrayal of a person. A more appropriate question is: What are we portraying? Typically, we shoot a portrait to showcase something characteristic about a subject, such as their personality, a physical characteristic or quality, a portion of the subject's narrative, or how others perceive them. Does this sound abstract? A bit heady? That may be because portraiture is a rather large topic, comprised of many concepts, techniques, and styles. Portraiture also has a vast history that extends much further back in time than photography, so humankind has a certain familiarity with portraiture due to its significance in society. From early paintings of monarchs to modern day photographic portraits, the portrait has remained a popular means of portraying a person to an audience. Portraiture is one of the most popular genres and industries within photography.

Defining something as big as portraiture can be rather daunting. A portrait is an *intentional* way of communicating your subject to an audience, whether that is an audience of one or of millions (**Figure 1.1**). Portraits are purposeful, both in their making and in their viewing.

One of the most compelling reasons to shoot portraits, and quite possibly the strongest argument for their existence, is their ability to connect people to each other (**Figure 1.2**). Portraits of political leaders or celebrities provide us a way to see people we've read or heard about, to relate to them more personally. For example, a portrait of a famous actor in their home garden might resonate well with fans that are also gardeners, and a portrait of the President of the United States with his family might relate extremely well to others that also have children. In both cases, the portraits help convey this very simple idea that the subjects—people that many of us will never have the opportunity to meet—are in many ways just like the rest of us. A more accessible example is photographing a graduating senior; the audience of family and friends will appreciate establishing a lasting connection with the subject by seeing them at that monumental moment in their life (**Figure 1.3**). All of this goes beyond the even more basic, primal connection we have with others through our eyes, which we'll discuss later in the book.

This broad definition will grow in specificity in the third section of this chapter, but it is vital to have a foundational understanding of what portraits are and why they are important. To grow as a photographer, one must see a purpose—creative, strategic, or otherwise—in their images. To that end, you should always ask yourself as it relates, "Am I really *shooting a portrait*?" Are you creating an image that portrays personality, narrative, or both? Are all of the technical and aesthetic characteristics of the image working in conjunction with the subject to actually "say" something about them? If so, then I imagine you are on the right track.

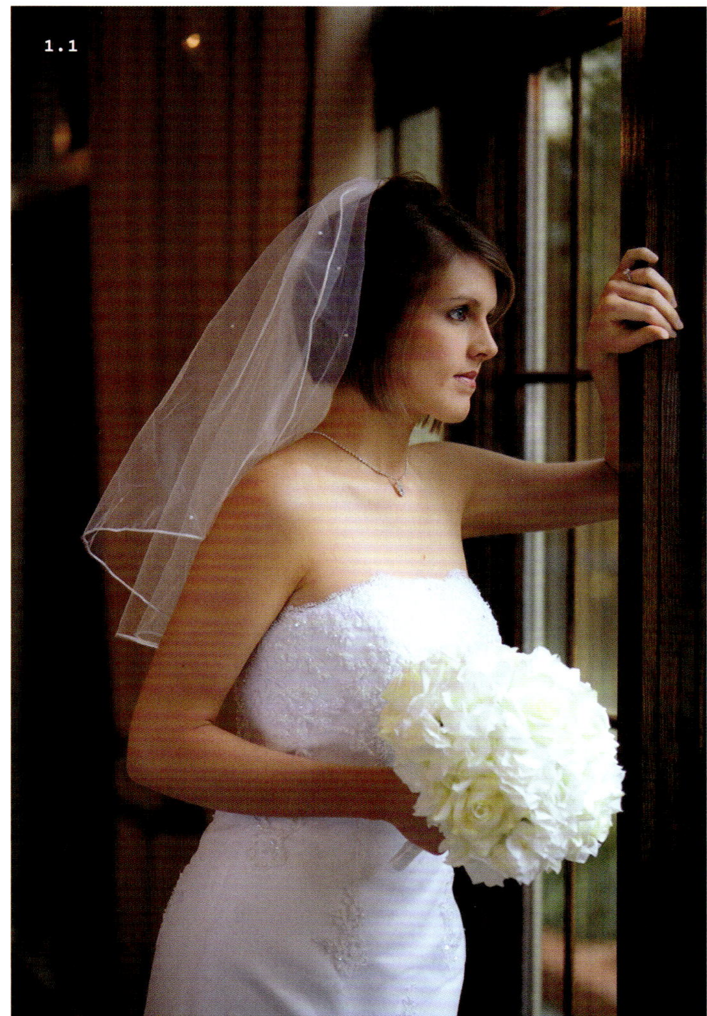

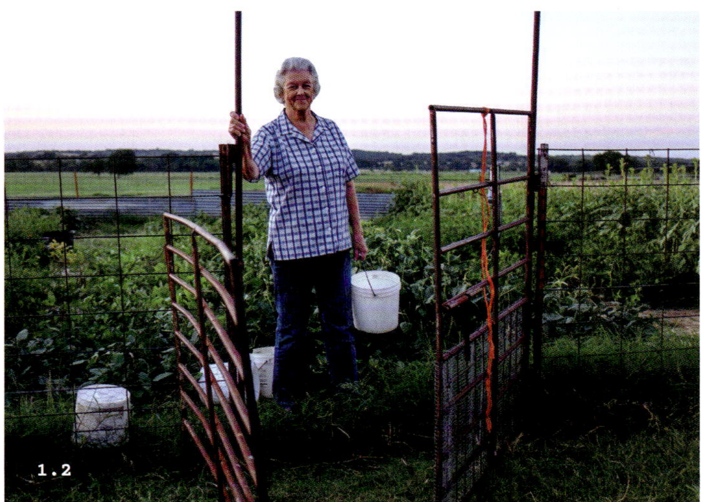

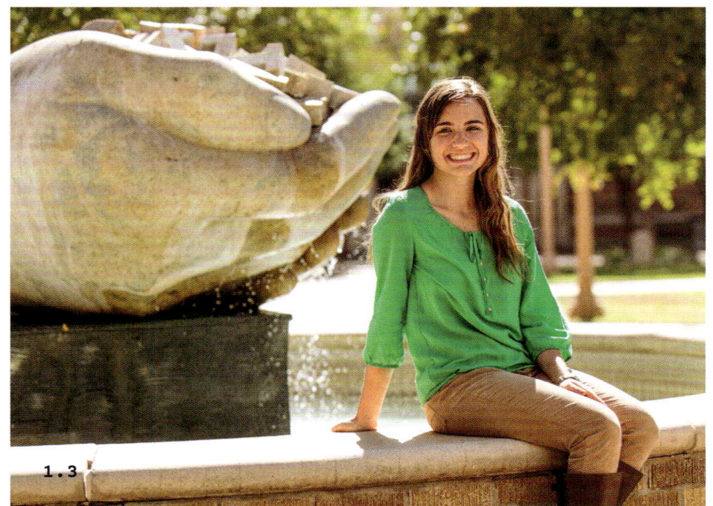

1.1 Everything about this bridal portrait was planned from the moment I spoke with the bride-to-be. The clean lighting and lines correspond well with her personality and classic style.
ISO 400; 1/80 sec.; f/2.8; 115mm

1.2 Environmental portraits do a better job than other types of photographs at connecting subject and audience. Not only does it highlight a facet of the subject's life, it also evokes relatability between subject and viewers.
ISO 200; 1/140 sec.; f/2; 23mm

1.3 Although a senior portrait might see a smaller audience than an environmental *portrait* published in *National Geographic*, it is nonetheless a popular way to represent an important aspect of the subject's life to her and her family.
ISO 100; 1/640 sec.; f/3.5; 93mm

2. THE PORTRAIT MOVEMENT

PORTRAITURE IS A large enough field that it's treated as its own genre. It is the inspiration for many new camera owners' ventures into the world of photography. It is also the one genre of photography that I believe every shooter needs to have a handle on.

My story in portraiture is similar to that of how other professionals became interested in photography. I started out primarily as a landscape and natural history magazine photographer. However, I quickly learned that in order to maintain freelance opportunities with many publications, I was going to have to learn how to photograph people. One day, I was offered an assignment to shoot 10 environmental portraits of academic researchers for a university alumni magazine (**Figure 2.1**). Although I had very little previous portrait experience, I accepted the assignment, dug into researching my subjects *and* the genre, and proceeded over the next week to make a series of portraits that truly cultivated a love for environmental portraits as they relate to the editorial world. I also gained a greater understanding of light and working with people. Since then, my abilitiy to make portraits has grown, and I never leave an assignment without making at least one or two.

The portrait movement is not new, but it has grown quite a bit since the birth of the digital camera. Many people would take up photography in the past as a means of exploring their surroundings—the land and cityscapes in which they lived and visited—yet, the explosion of digital technology has seen the emergence of many more photographers interested in shooting portraits, professionally or otherwise.

And the demand for good portraiture is there. At our most basic, humankind is a visual culture. As we grow more visual in the digital world, so will our demand for more images. Whether someone is seeking a portrait for a professional website or resume, a magazine needs a portrait made for an upcoming feature, or someone wants a few new portraits made for their personal social media presence, the demand for folks that know what they are doing behind the camera grows (**Figure 2.2**). Every time a new child is born, a couple becomes engaged and married, or a child graduates high school, a photographer is there to capture the moment. The portrait photographer holds a special place in society as someone that can provide quality and creative visual documentation of an individual or a group in important occasions. When it comes down to it, portrait photography may be the only type of photography that also cannot be superseded by massive stock image archives for generic photography use.

Speaking of which, it's also worth noting the business aspect of portrait photography—it can be a fairly lucrative professional endeavor. Someone that is recognized for their craft can do well as a full-time photographer, or even as a part-time weekend warrior. Your personal and professional network can help you launch professionally into portrait photography, especially if you have an interest in general portraiture such as senior or engagement photography. A fair number of my university students use their own classmates and friends as subjects, and initiate a word-of-mouth campaign about their talents. This in turn may result in more work and extra income. I have had several students that paid their way through college doing primarily portrait work for other students.

Lastly, for those interested in working in the world of large-audience publications. No matter what type of publication you aspire to shoot for, many will pass your portfolio over if it is void of portraiture. Even landscape photographers need to have an image or two of a person included in their pristine shots. The editorial world is driven by human-focused stories, and when it is obvious that a photographer can indeed work with people and make quality portraits, they are more likely to be hired and/or sent on assignment (**Figure 2.3**). A wise editor told me one time after sending him my portfolio of mostly landscapes and images of Texas ranch life that although my exposures and compositions looked good, he didn't see any people in my images. I knew then that I had to embrace portraiture in order to make a living.

At their core, portrait photographers genuinely love working with people and telling their story visually. A portrait, as you'll see throughout this book, is often the most unique way of telling that story.

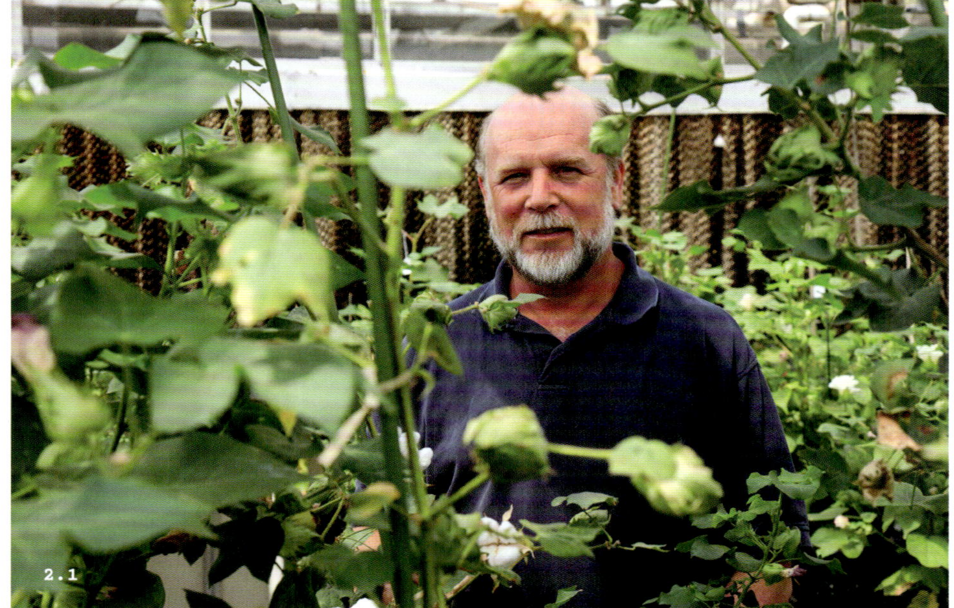

2.1

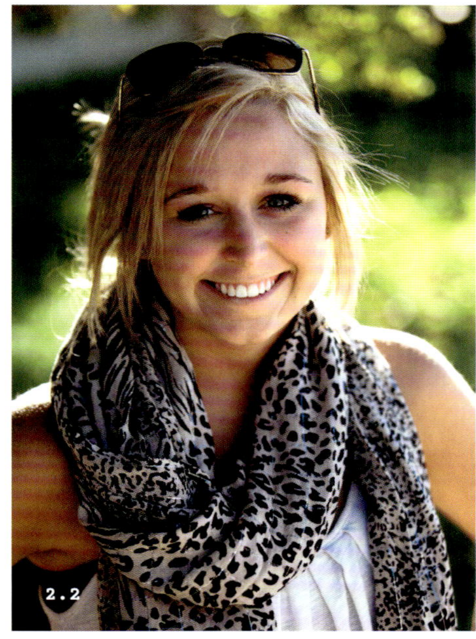

2.2

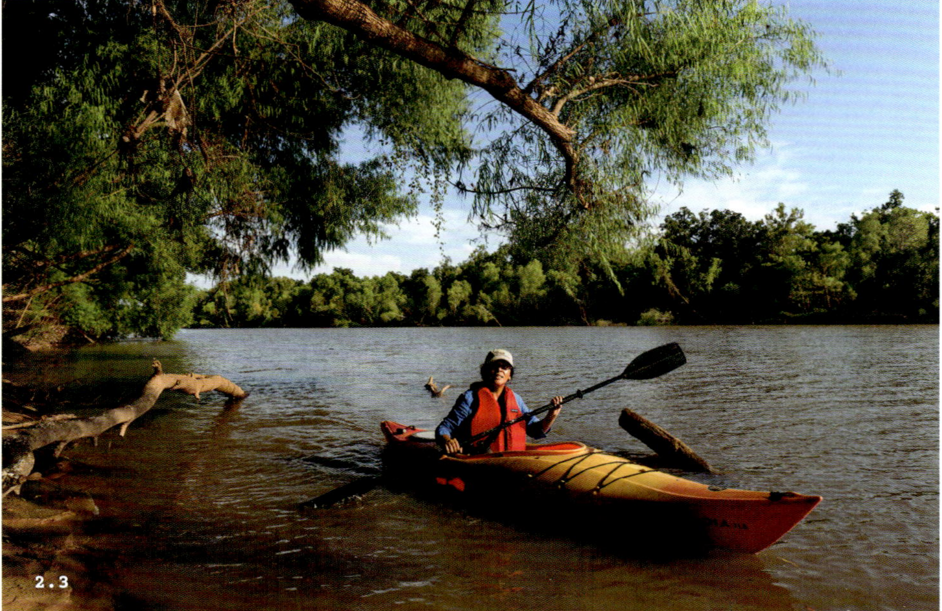

2.3

2.1 One of my first serious, on-assignment attempts at environmental portraiture was with one of the top cotton crop researchers in the world. Talk about pressure!
ISO 400; 1/200 sec.; f/8; 67mm

2.2 The versatility of an original portrait can be great! Consider the possibilities and creative utility this image serves for this subject, a recent university graduate.
ISO 100; 1/250 sec.; f/2.8; 80mm

2.3 After realizing I enjoyed shooting portraits, I started to heavily incorporate it into the work I was already doing with conservation publications and organizations, such as The Nature Conservancy. I firmly believe being able to shoot portraits in remote locations is a strong reason why I'm hired in many cases.
ISO 200; 1/500 sec.; f/7.1; 24mm

JUST ABOUT ALL types of photography incorporate portraiture somehow. Even wildlife photography employs techniques used to make great portraits in capturing stunning images of creatures the world over. While many forms or genres of photography employ portraiture to varying degrees, the portraiture field and industry itself also dictates or identifies a number of different types of portraits. To my knowledge, there is no concrete typography of the different sub-genres of portrait photography, and it's not my intention to invent one here. However, I believe it is useful to become acquainted with several popular forms of natural light portrait photography that not only help segment the genre and professional field, but also inspire their counterparts in said field.

General and Family Portraiture

Of all the sub-genres of portrait photography, this is probably the broadest. It encompasses our contemporary, yet traditional, perspectives on portraiture. Types of general and family portraiture include the traditional family portrait, children's portraiture (**Figure 3.1**), senior and graduate photography, as well as couples and engagement portraits, etc. The purpose of this type of portraiture is to concentrate attention fully on the subject(s), and the audience for such images is typically a small and intimate one, largely comprised of family and friends of the subject(s). Although narrative is inherent in this type of portraiture, the intention is about making the subject look the best they can in an image that can be presented immediately and archived for later viewing, hence the heavy amount of reminiscing and nostalgia over seeing these types of portraits made in the past. Likewise, this type of portraiture is arguably the most important type of portraiture (**Figure 3.2**). These are the types of portraits that are the first things saved when a house is burning down. They inherently mean more to a family or an individual than any portrait published in a million-plus-circulation magazine simply because they are the types of portraits we make or have made of our loved ones. As a society, we cherish these portraits and hold them dear to our memory, even long after we're gone.

Environmental Portraiture

If general and family portraiture is the broadest sub-genre of natural light portrait photography, then environmental portraiture is the most stylistically versatile. It's not uncommon to see many corporate/commercial portraits made in an environmental portraiture style because of their ability to incorporate more narrative information about the subject(s) (**Figure 3.3**). Environmental portraits have their roots in editorial photography, and they focus on portraying the subject(s) in contexts that help communicate something about their life story, or at least the parts of said story that are relevant to the editorial story for which they are made (**Figure 3.4**). If you are stuck thinking about what an environmental portrait looks like, imagine regional and state magazine features on local businesses or artists. More than likely, the portraits of the people being featured in such stories position the subjects within an environment that contributes to the article's text and overall story. Environmental portraits are stylistically repurposed in a number of different sub-genres and types of photography. They are a relatively popular form of portraiture overall because of their narrative appeal.

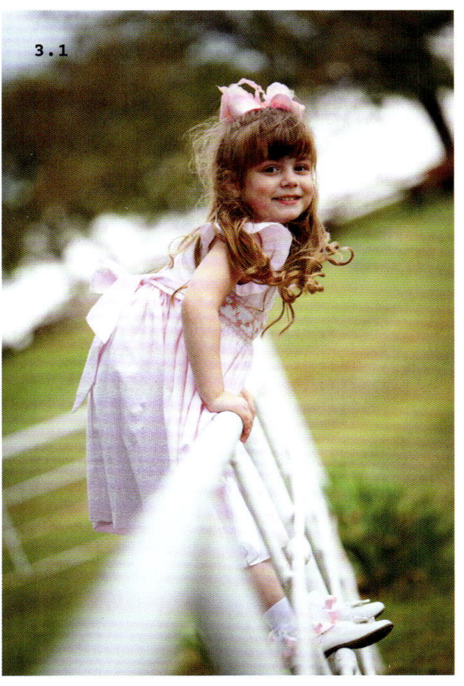

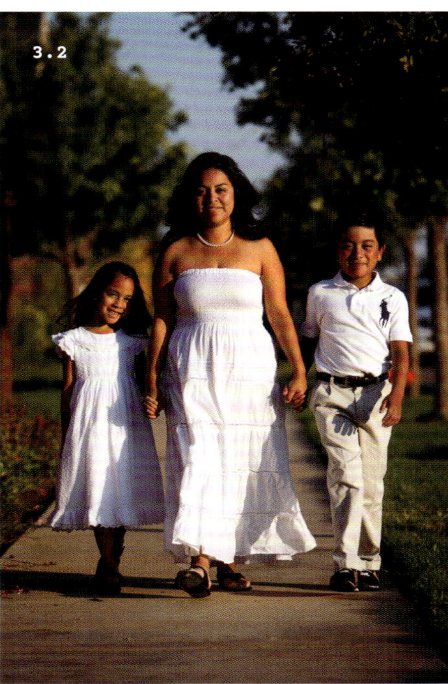

3.1 Children's portraiture is one of the most cherished and challenging forms of the discipline.
ISO 400; 1/2500 sec.; f/2.8; 155mm

3.2 Families depend on good portraiture to not only celebrate their unity but also to create a historical record (a visually creative one) that will hopefully be passed down from generation to generation.
ISO 200; 1/5000 sec.; f/2.8; 130mm

3.3 Environmental portraits are extremely effective at relating information to a general audience, which is one of the reasons many corporations, like Invenergy, choose to use them in place of traditional corporate portraits. These images do a better job of communicating their brand to consumers.
ISO 400; 1/320 sec.; f/5.6; 135mm

3.4 By the image alone, we don't know much about the human subject, but we can infer that she enjoys trail riding in the mountains. This is due not only to the environment around her, but to the smaller details of her person and horse as well, such as the type of hat she is wearing and the small packs on the back of her saddle.
ISO 200; 1/640 sec.; f/5.6; 48mm

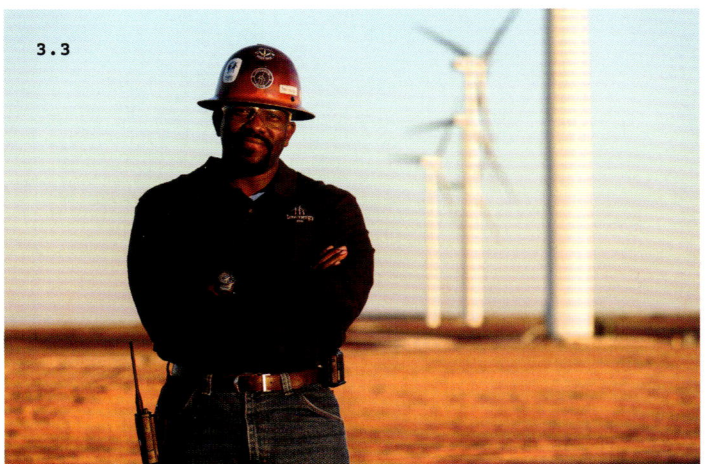

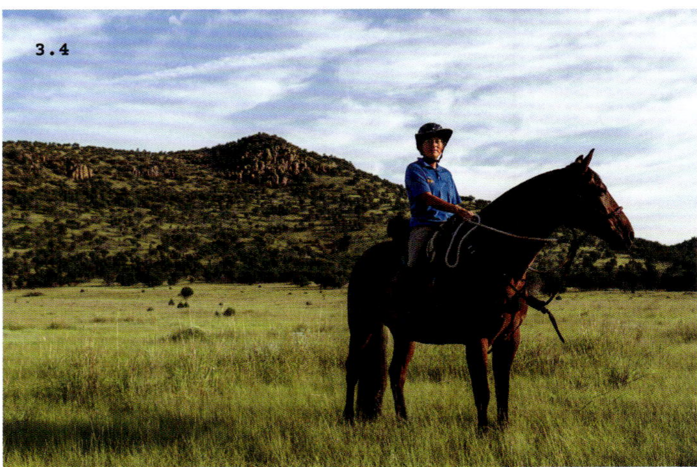

Candid and Street Portraiture

Candid portraits depart from our traditional notion of a portrait because the subject isn't necessarily looking at the camera and posed in a certain way to look their best. Instead, the photographer is concerned with "catching a moment" while still introducing technique that feels and looks more like portraiture than documentary (**Figure 3.5**). Recently, street photography has become more formalized as a genre of documentary photography and visual art, and many street portraits have a familiar feel to them—completely un-staged, sometimes captured off the cuff. Yet, they evoke a raw, possibly more authentic reaction from their viewers. I'll be the first to say that street portraiture can be relatively difficult if you do not spend much time familiarizing yourself with the urban context in which many of these portraits are made, or if you are hesitant to approach strangers for a picture (or even photographing them without their knowledge). However, these types of portraits offer great man-on-the-street, real-life moments in portraiture (**Figure 3.6**). Likewise, many of these types of portraits are constructed and presented so the image's audience can either relate to or infer abstractly information about the subject and his context. Similar to environmental portraiture, it isn't uncommon to see this style of portraiture and photography in general applied to other sub-genres of portraiture.

Headshots

Headshots are exactly what they sound like. They are portraits that concentrate on the subject's face (**Figure 3.7**). Largely used as a means of identifying the subject, these are nonetheless an essential sub-genre of photography. Professionals use them, actors and actresses use them; some of the most popular portraits of children are actually headshots. Although they seem simple, making great headshots is far from easy without great light and good technique. The industry necessitates that photographers have a hold on how to make these types of portraits, and I personally never leave a shoot, especially an editorial one, without making a few headshots of my subject(s).

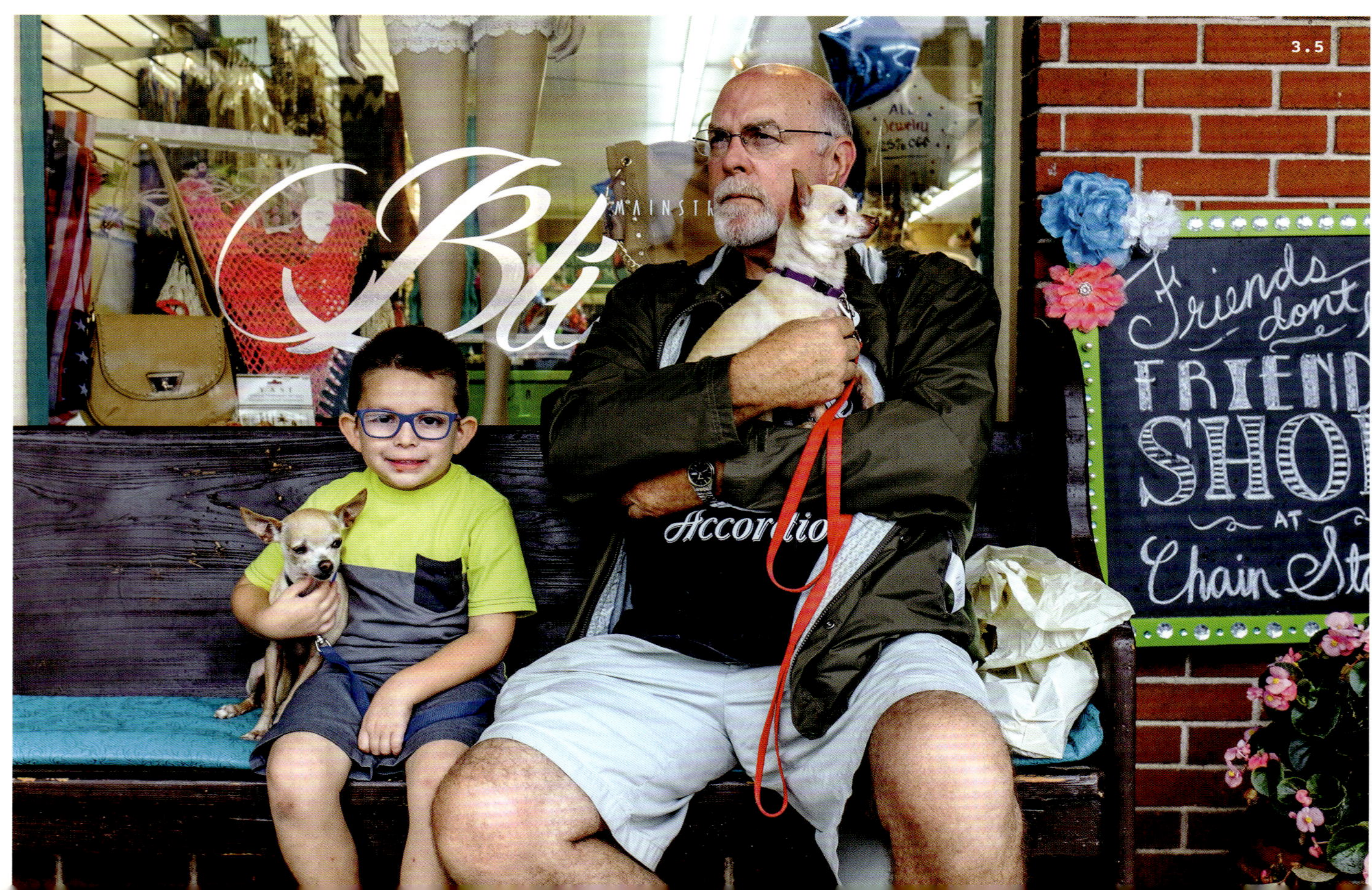

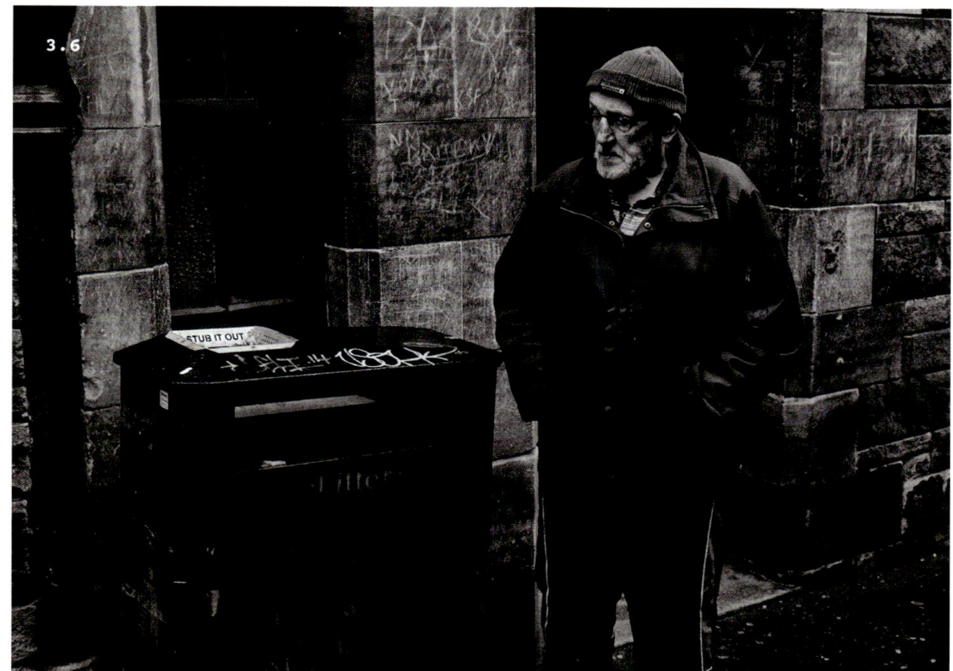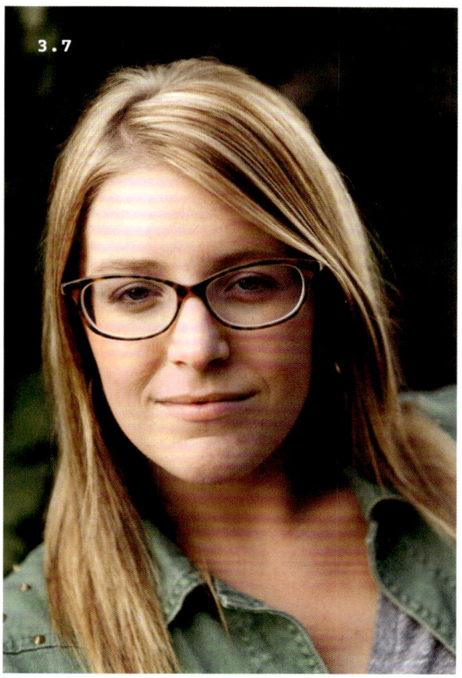

3.5 I came across this grandson and grandfather duo sitting with their Chihuahuas in hand. I asked politely if I could make a portrait of them, received approval, and made just one image.
ISO 500; 1/60 sec.; f/4; 23mm

3.6 Some street portraits simply encourage the viewer to think about the subject and environment together, to read their own narrative in the image. What does this image of a man in Edinburgh, Scotland, evoke in you?
ISO 3200; 1/500 sec.; f/5.6; 23mm

3.7 A good headshot incorporates good light, simple but dynamic composition, and a background that does not take away from the subject's face and eyes, the main focus and the primary route through which other humans connect with the subject.
ISO 200; 1/1000 sec.; f/2.8; 70mm

Share Your Best Candid or Street Photograph!

Once you've captured a great candid or street photograph, share it with the *Enthusiast's Guide* community! Follow @EnthusiastsGuides and post your image to Instagram, using the hashtag *#EGCandid* or *#EGStreet*. You can also search that hashtag to be inspired and see other photographers' shots.

4. A SHORT NOTE ON CONCEPTUALIZATION

BEFORE WE LAUNCH into the rest of the book, I want to make a quick note about pre-visualization and developing your vision as a portrait photographer. No matter what type of portrait photography you wish to dive into, it's important to bear in mind that growing as a photographer has a great deal to do with refining your vision—your ability to see images. This is particularly true for portraiture. Certainly, knowing your gear and tech is vital, as well as keeping up-to-date with current technologies and how they might positively affect your work. However, the most inspiring and successful photographers are those that are constantly thinking about the *image*, not the technology.

Previsualization is thinking about, or conceptualizing, the portrait you are going to make before you make it. This might happen right after you've been given a portrait assignment from an editor, just before a shoot with a happily engaged couple, or weeks before a shoot as you're walking through a particularly visual part of your city. Either way, the point behind previsualizing your portrait is creative preparedness.

Much like how exercise helps you build a better, healthier body, or how reading increases your ability to write and critically synthesize information, continual thought toward making images will indeed help you not only see photography, but make yours better! I encourage you to always be curious and diligently observant of changing light conditions, interesting compositions and environments, and if you are editorially minded, aware of stories around you that might add to great portraits. As a portrait photographer, all of this observation, even if it will never be put to use, is like stockpiling memories of photographic information that might be accessed later on any given shoot. A lifestyle portrait photographer might intentionally go out looking for new locations (called scouting) a week before making any portrait, or an environmental portrait photographer might notice a small space in a home or office as she walks down a hallway to meet her featured subject. In any case (and there is an infinite number of them), the ability to see before making the portrait, no matter how far or near in the future that portrait may be, will strengthen your creative vision and your work process (**Figure 4.1**).

As I'll point out later in the book as well, previsualization can sometimes pose a hindrance to your photography. Some photographers, yours truly included, can get so wrapped up in making a portrait we've previsualized that we miss another opportunity on the same shoot or in the same location. This especially rings true when completing an actual shoot. There have been a number of times upon leaving a shoot that I think to myself, "I wish I would have positioned the subject next to that fence," or, "I should have had them sit down in the tall grasses." Remember that although previsualization is a key part of your growth as a photographer, it can easily become a crutch in your process. Remain as vigilant and observant of photographic opportunities, even while you are shooting. This will, in turn, increase your openness to something new and your ability to be productive while working and creating images.

4.1 Ever since I started cycling, I wanted to combine photography with the sport. I rode this dirt road many times, always envisioning in my head an environmental portrait of a rider in its path to emphasize the adventuresome nature of dirt road riding in West Texas. Months later, I shot this portrait of my friend Will while golden hour the light was close to setting, executing the concept with the help of my previsualization.
ISO 200; 1/1000 sec.; f/2; 90mm

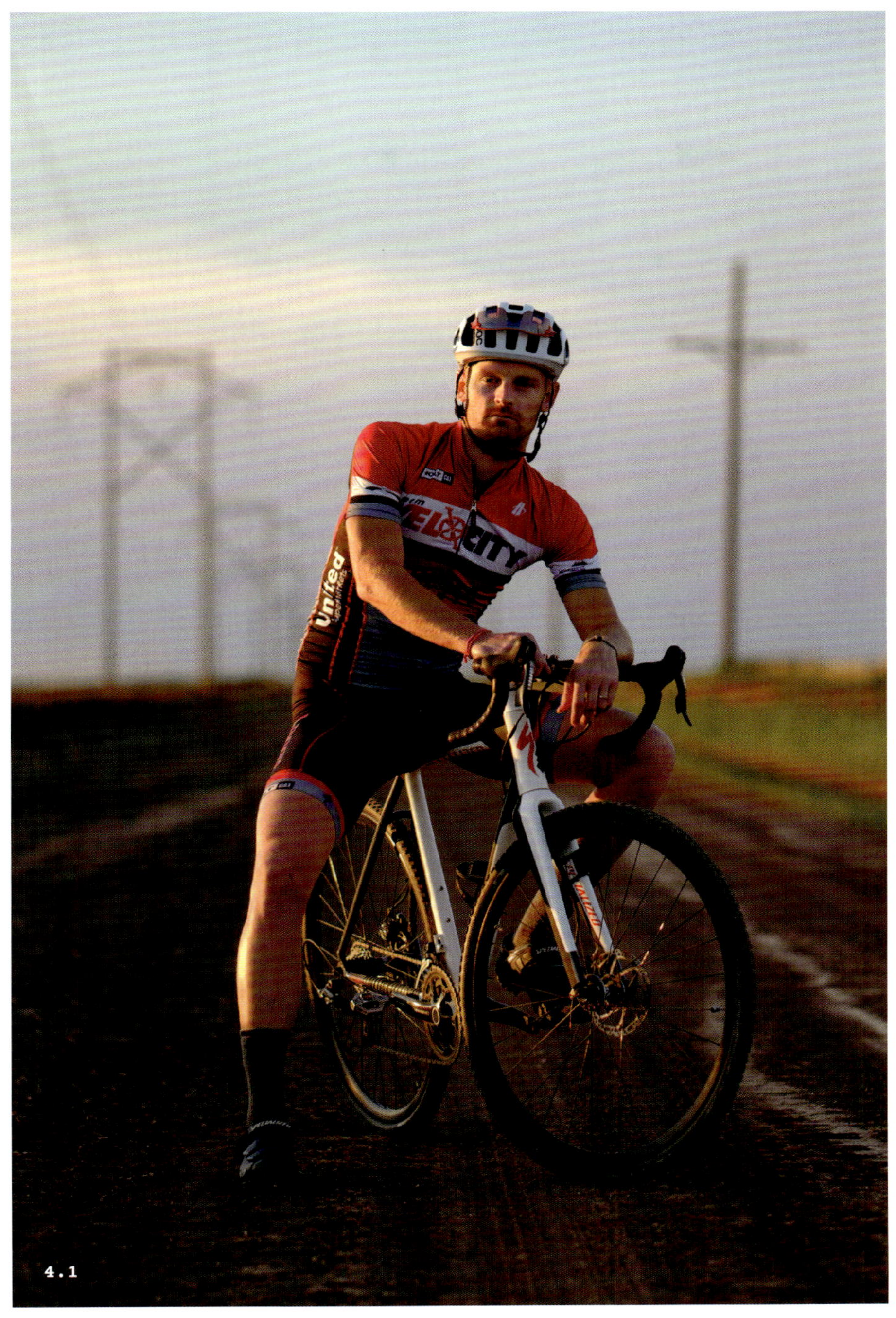

4.1

2

EQUIPMENT AND SETUP

You can't make a picture without a camera, and this chapter is all about setting your camera up in a way that affords you creative control that's efficient from the outset. The camera has many functions and capabilities, but we'll only stick to the most pertinent of them to get you up and running as a portrait photographer. This chapter also highlights a few key concepts about the lenses you use and an additional piece of equipment that comes in quite handy: a reflector. Bear in mind that equipment is only one (rather small) variable in creating great portraits. Nothing supersedes your own vision and creativity. Gear, however, is essential, and the creative potential your equipment offers makes it worth discussing.

5. THE AUTOMATIC PORTRAIT SETTING
(AND WHY YOU SHOULD AVOID IT)

WELL, WE MIGHT as well get this out of the way.

I'm a control freak when it comes to the actual camera. There are a lot of things in photography for which we have to remain flexible—some of which we'll highlight in this book. But the camera is one of the variables that I want complete control over (or as much as I can get). Unfortunately, the automatic portrait setting (**Figure 5.1**)—the little icon on the exposure mode dial of a DSLR camera that looks like a profile—does not allow for much control at all. I advise against using it.

Let's back up a bit, though, and give the automatic portrait setting its due. For what it's worth, the automatic portrait setting on any camera *is* actually programmed to set the user up as well as it can for making portraits. Much like its other automatic cousins on the exposure mode dial, it's preset to provide a typical combination of ISO, shutter speed, and aperture (the functions of the camera that mechanically make up the exposure triangle) that's fitting in both exposure and aesthetic for a specific type of photograph—in this case, a portrait.

The automatic portrait setting is geared to do two things: one, to ensure a proper exposure based on the level of light in a scene; and two, to ensure that the resulting image is made with settings generally used in portraiture. This means that the camera will automatically try to open the aperture as much as possible to achieve the smallest possible depth of field (**Figure 5.2**). We'll discuss depth of field a little later, but suffice it to say, the automatic portrait setting sets you up to make images with your portrait subject in perfect focus and a background that is sufficiently out of focus. This is a visual characteristic of many portraits, and the automatic setting does its best to get us there. The automatic setting is a great place to start for those unfamiliar with making their own exposures manually or for those looking for some visual inspiration.

Why am I so against using the automatic setting if it has our best interest in mind? It all comes down to what the camera can't do. It can't think. It can't be creative. It can only do what we tell it—nothing more, nothing less. When you choose to use the automatic portrait setting, you are relinquishing technical and aesthetic control to the camera and applying a generic preset to your photographic process. Although this may sound ideal at first, the more you become acquainted with your camera and its functions, the more you may feel that your creativity is constrained by the automatic settings. What if you didn't want the background to be completely out of focus for your portrait? What if you needed a faster shutter speed to capture an action-oriented portrait? What if you wanted to intentionally underexpose a portrait to give it just the right mood?

5.1 The automatic portrait mode on most camera models is identified by an icon that looks like a person's profile.

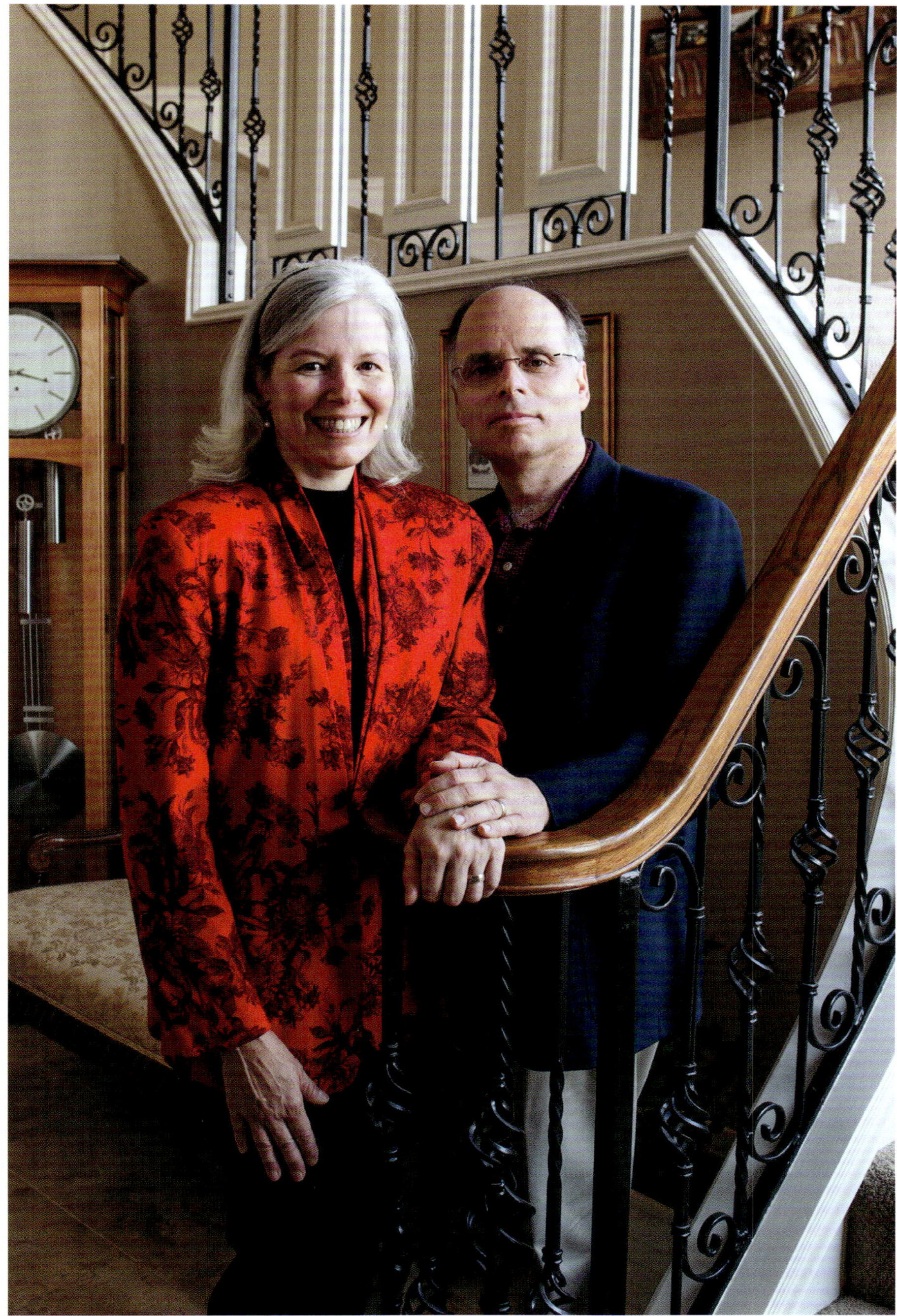

5.2 In automatic portrait mode, the camera set the aperture to f/5.6, set the white balance to automatic, adjusted the ISO automatically, and set the shutter speed. All in all, it did a great job at exposing the scene, but I prefer to be in more control of choosing my exposure preferences.
ISO 640; 1/40 sec.; f/5.6; 32mm

6. USE APERTURE PRIORITY EXPOSURE MODE

TO GAIN AS much control as possible over the design elements of your portraits, it's best to use the creative exposure modes. These include Programmed Exposure, Shutter Speed Priority, Aperture Priority, and Manual. To be even more specific, I suggest sticking to only two of these for the majority of your portrait work: Aperture Priority and Manual (**Figure 6.1**).

Although it's not in this book's purview to go over how exposure is achieved, having a working knowledge of this concept is extremely helpful in order to adequately operate the camera in Aperture Priority and Manual exposure modes. The camera settings are in your complete control in Manual exposure mode, and as a result, the image that you produce will ideally be as close as possible to what you envisioned in your mind. In Manual exposure mode, you'll be able to manipulate the camera's functions along technical and visual lines to create the overall look of the image. Although Manual exposure mode seems intimidating (and it is, at first), mastering its use is the foundation for knowing how the other creative exposure modes work. Knowing how to operate in Manual allows you a more controllable experience when working with these other modes.

That being said, I work mostly in Aperture Priority, and I advise you to do the same. This exposure mode allows you to control the aperture setting manually, and the camera automatically sets the shutter speed for you.

As we'll highlight later in this chapter, one of the first camera functions I consider when it comes to portraiture is the aperture setting, which controls the image's depth of field. Depth of field is a crucial concept and characteristic of photography. My second consideration in portraiture is how much of the image I want in focus. With a quick turn of the dial, Aperture Priority exposure mode lets me manipulate the function of the camera that controls the depth of field in my image. If I need very little depth of field, I can quickly open the aperture to f/2.8 (**Figure 6.2**), or if I'm looking to have the entire environment of the portrait more in focus, I can shoot at f/8 (**Figure 6.3**). Since the camera sets the shutter speed automatically to complete the exposure equation, the Aperture Priority mode makes it easy to compensate for under- or overexposure with another flick of a dial. Having a foundation in Manual exposure makes translating exposure compensation to other exposure modes fairly painless.

As with all functions and practical processes of the camera, the more you use a certain exposure mode, the more you learn to control it technically and creatively. It's of little wonder that many portrait photographers rely on the Manual or Aperture Priority exposure modes, and it makes sense for you to shift to one of these modes as soon as you feel comfortable with them. First, learn all you can about Manual exposure. Then negotiate those concepts over to using Aperture Priority, and you'll set yourself up well for being a versatile photographer in many portrait scenarios.

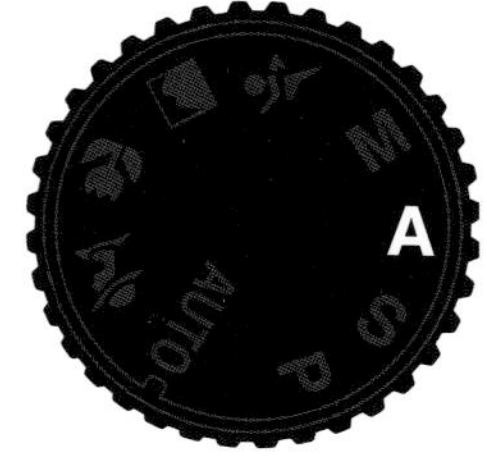

6.1 Aperture Priority mode, identified on Canon cameras as AV and on most other cameras as A, allows the photographer to manually select the aperture setting while the camera automatically sets the shutter speed—an extremely efficient mode for many portrait photographers.

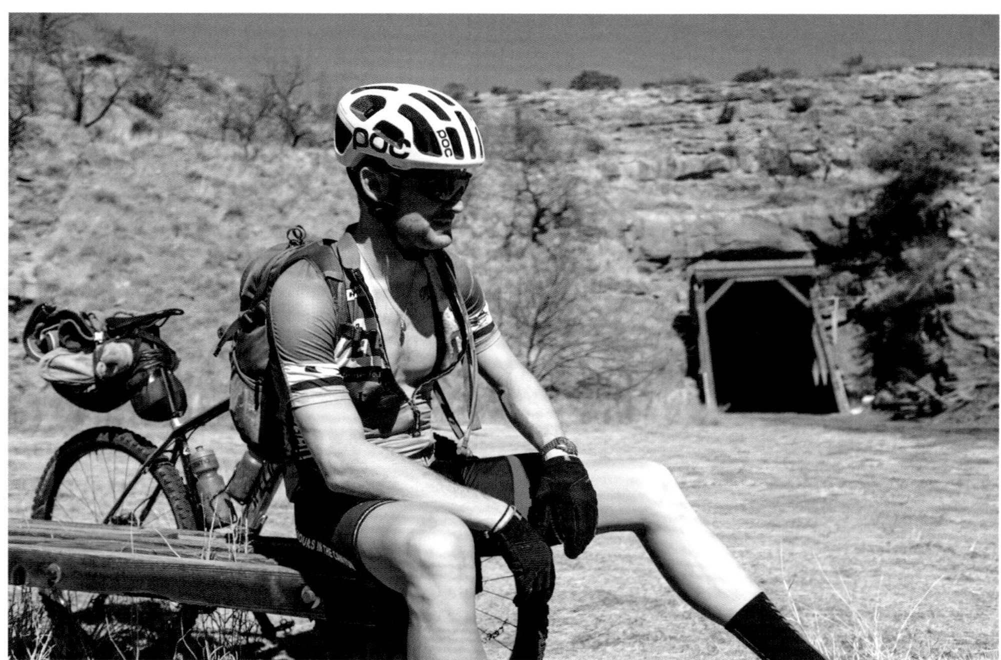

6.2 To ensure the background canyon wall did not run too much into my subject's head, I used Aperture Priority and an aperture of f/2.8 to knock it sufficiently out of focus.
ISO 200; 1/1250 sec.; f/2.8; 23mm

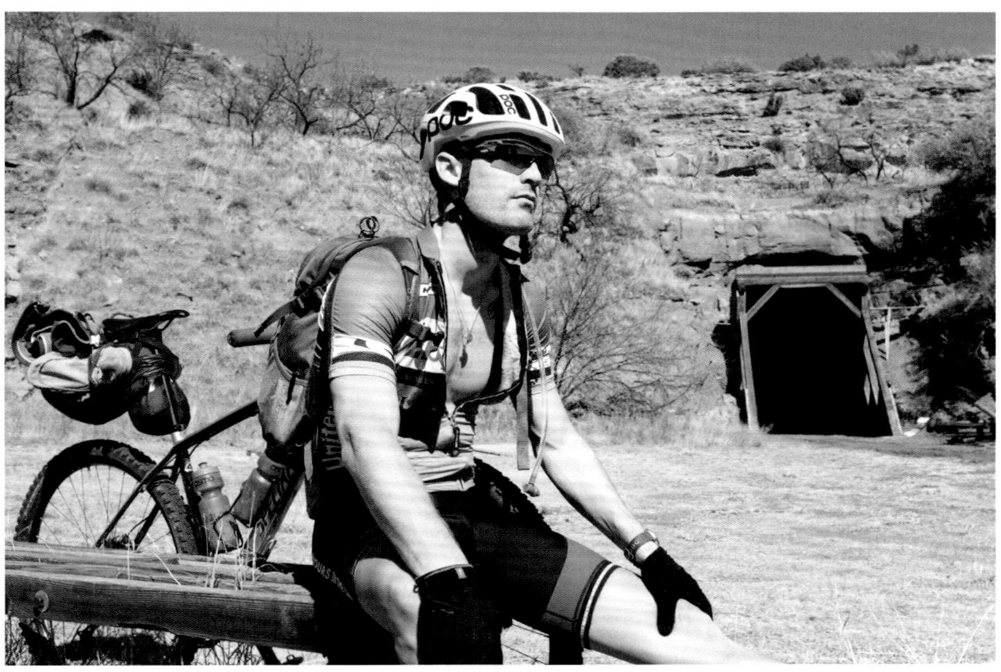

6.3 However, to provide myself some options for editing during post processing, I shot this portrait at f/8 to bring the canyon wall and old railway tunnel entrance into focus. This choice also emphasizes their narrative importance in the mountain biker's journey.
ISO 200; 1/600 sec.; f/8; 23mm

7. ISO AND NOISE LEVELS

ISO IS THE foundation for exposure. Technically, it is a numerical representation of the speed at which your camera's digital sensor accumulates light. For a good exposure, ISO typically has an impact on your choice of shutter speed. Your ISO setting also has a great impact on the level of noise in the photographic image.

Noise is a result of your sensor gaining up its ability to capture light. When you increase your ISO, the sensor struggles to fill in visual informational gaps as a result of being pushed to capture light more quickly. Out-of-place pixel coloration and blotchiness may occur, which interfere with the look of an image—namely its perceived sharpness and color saturation (**Figure 7.1**). There is a great deal of engineering language that can be used to explain the presence of noise, but suffice it to say that as you increase your ISO, you'll also increase the level of noise in your image.

So, why be concerned with noise levels? Typically, high noise levels are undesirable in portraiture. This isn't to say that noise has no aesthetic value whatsoever. In fact, noise is often equated to that oft-sought-after look of increased grain in film stock of higher ISO speeds. Yet, for the most part, increased noise levels do not treat your portrait subject very well. Noise can make a face and environment look distractingly textured (something I'm sure many portrait subjects would not appreciate), and make edges that are actually in focus look a bit soft. The effect of noise on an image is compounding, meaning that as you increase your ISO, the effects become more noticeable and less manageable.

As you can see, it's often a good approach in portraiture to shoot with as low an ISO speed as possible. Doing so ensures you are starting the photography process with the least amount of noise possible. Of course, this all depends on the amount of ambient light you have at your disposal. Although it would be nice to espouse that ISO 100 or 200 are the ideal ISOs for all portraiture, the fact is that not all lighting levels were created equal. A clear day with a great amount of light is a nice scenario in which to shoot with relatively low, almost noise-free ISOs ranging from ISO 100 to 400 (**Figure 7.2**). However, stepping indoors, no matter how well lit an interior appears to our

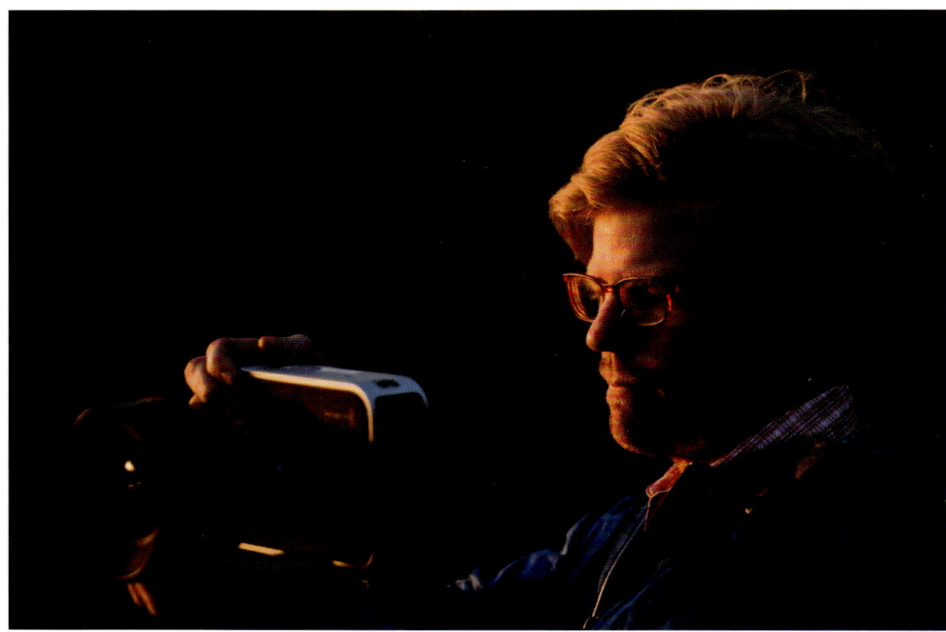

7.1 In this portrait of photographer Jacob Copple, I had to turn the ISO up to 1600 to shoot with a fast enough shutter speed to maintain focus. As a result, I introduced visible noise, particularly in the shadows and background.
ISO 1600; 1/100 sec.; f/2.8; 78mm

eyes, might necessitate increasing your ISO to over 1,000 to obtain a shutter speed fast enough to capture a sharp image while hand-holding the camera and lens.

To some degree, noise is something photographers have to tolerate. However, we should keep it at bay. Remember, shooting with as low an ISO speed as possible is the best approach to mitigating the negative effects of noise. This will always be the case. Fortunately for photographers, camera manufacturers are continually wrestling with this issue and keep pumping out equipment that allows you to shoot at increasingly higher ISOs with lower and lower noise levels. Who knows—maybe one day we can stop concerning ourselves with ISO and noise levels altogether!

7.2 ISO 100 is a very clean, noise-free ISO that is ideal for most types of natural light portraiture, especially headshots.
ISO 100; 1/2500 sec.; f/1.8; 85mm

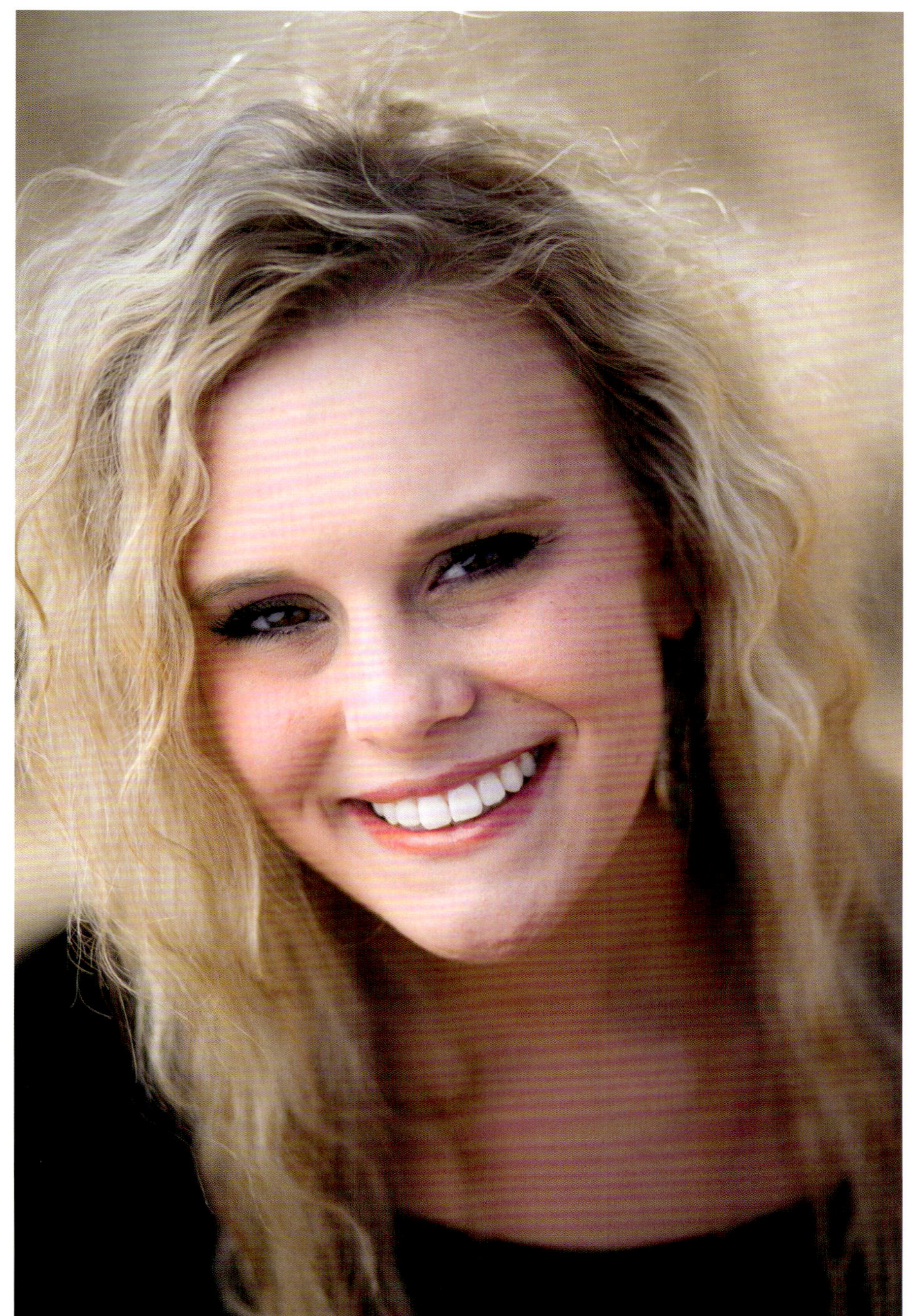

IF THERE'S ONE mechanism I favor over the others on the camera, it's the aperture. Actually, the aperture is located in the lens, not the camera body, and is comprised of a ring of overlapping metal leaves that open or close based on the user's preference. Like ISO and the shutter, the aperture has a technical function: it's the mechanism that completes the exposure triangle. It's also a mechanism that can provide great aesthetic value for portraits.

The aperture controls an image's depth of field—the amount of an image that appears in focus while looking *into* the frame. Depth of field is determined by the point at which the image is focused, or the *plane of critical focus*. Depth of field expands toward and away from the camera based on the aperture setting. This makes the aperture one of the most effective tools at the photographer's disposal because changing its size effects the perceived depth of field in an image. Aperture values, which are often referred to as f-stops, are denoted as fractions related to the size of the opening in the lens (**Figure 8.1**). The more open the aperture, the smaller the identifying denominators will be; e.g., f/2.8, f/4, and f/5.6. The more closed the aperture, the larger the identifying denominators will be; e.g., f/11, f/16, and f/22. Essentially, the smaller the denominator, the more open the aperture, and vice versa.

Now, all of these numbers *do* translate into visual results. The more open an aperture is, the shallower the depth of field, i.e., the more out of focus the background behind your subject and

the foreground in front of them will be. Conversely, the more closed the aperture is, the wider the depth of field will be. For example, a portrait made with an aperture set to f/1.8 (**Figure 8.2**) will have considerably less depth of field and a more out-of-focus background than the same portrait made with an aperture set to f/8 (**Figure 8.3**).

The depth of field in an image says quite a bit about the important visual and narrative elements of the photo. Visually, a completely out of focus background can be attractive, but the image may lack visual depth. Of course, this all depends on how you compose a portrait. Narratively, an out of focus background drives the viewer's eye directly to the most important subject or area in the frame. The significance of other indiscernible subject matter is reduced (**Figure 8.4**). To make a cinematic analogy, what is left in focus—your portrait subject—is the lead actor of the image, while everything else is the supporting cast. Likewise, a background that is in focus can be busy and distracting, but if composed purposefully, it might also let the environment in which the subject is photographed play a stronger supporting role (**Figure 8.5**). As you'll see later in this book, much of how depth of field (or the lack thereof) affects the image is also reliant upon how the portrait is composed.

Typically, though, photographers control the aperture in order to direct the majority of attention to the main subject or subjects of the portrait. This means we tend to think about

portraits as having a relatively shallow depth of field in order to command the viewer's eye to our subject. I recommend starting out with an aperture setting of f/4 or f/5.6 to obtain a shallow depth of field, and working your way to a smaller aperture if you desire more area in the frame to be in focus.

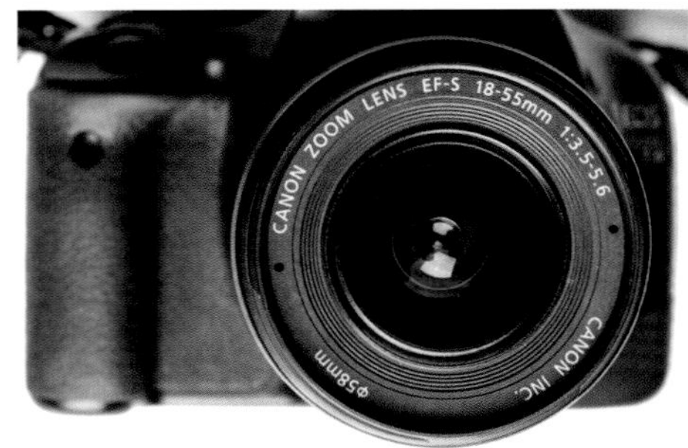

8.1 The maximum aperture of any lens is typically labeled on the front of the barrel. In this case, the maximum aperture is 1:3.5-5.6. This means that at the widest focal length of this zoom lens, the maximum aperture is f/3.5. At the longest focal length, it is f/5.6. This is referred to as a variable aperture lens.

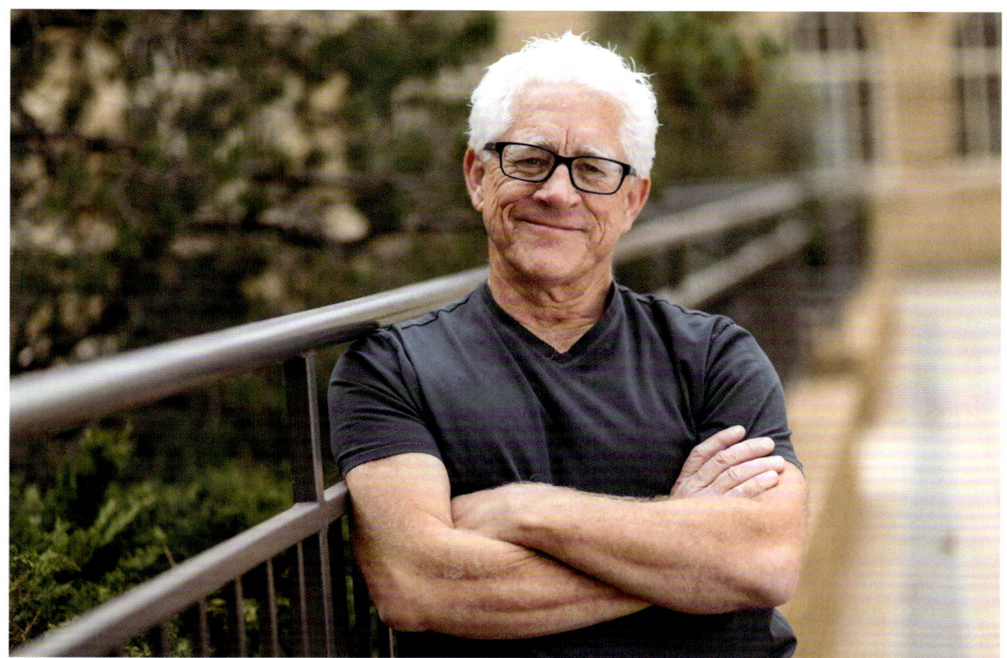

8.2 At f/1.8, a very open aperture for any focal length, the depth of field is minimal. This concept is conveyed here by the large amount of out-of-focus area in the image.
ISO 100; 1/1600 sec.; f/1.8; 85mm

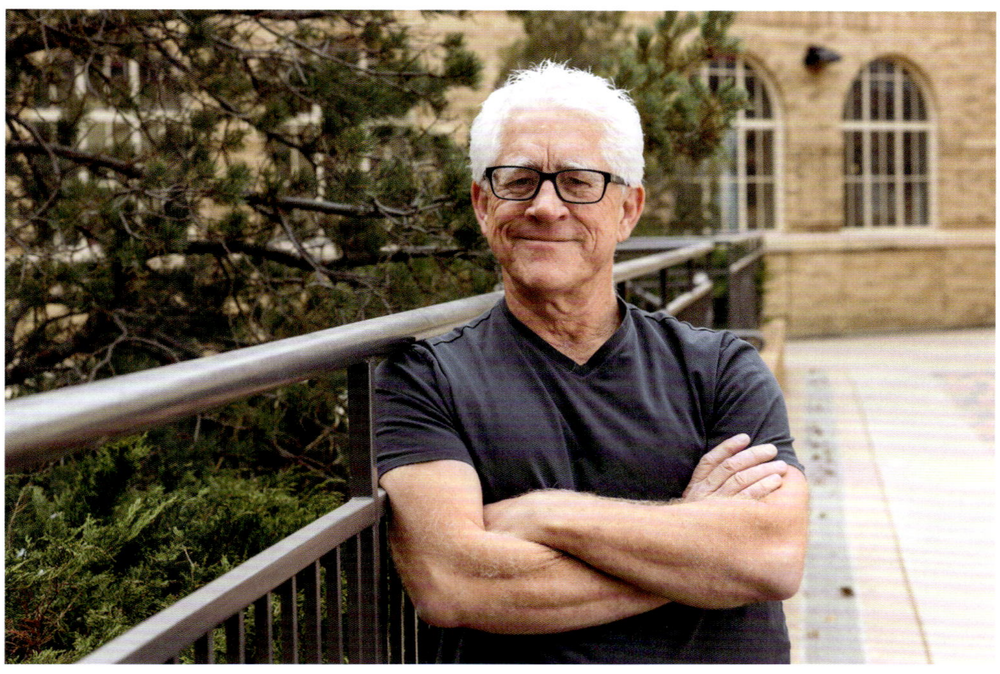

8.3 When the aperture is stopped down to f/8, the depth of field increases. This means more of the portrait in front of and beyond the subject will be in focus. In this image, this change in depth of field makes the background busy and distracting.
ISO 100; 1/80 sec.; f/8; 85mm

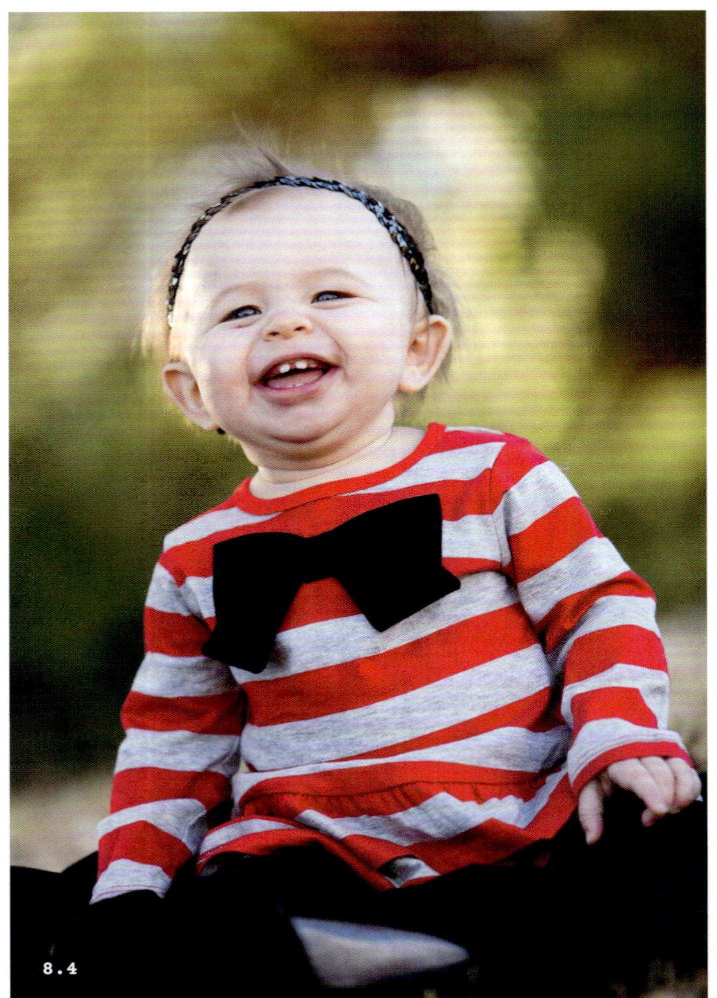

8.4

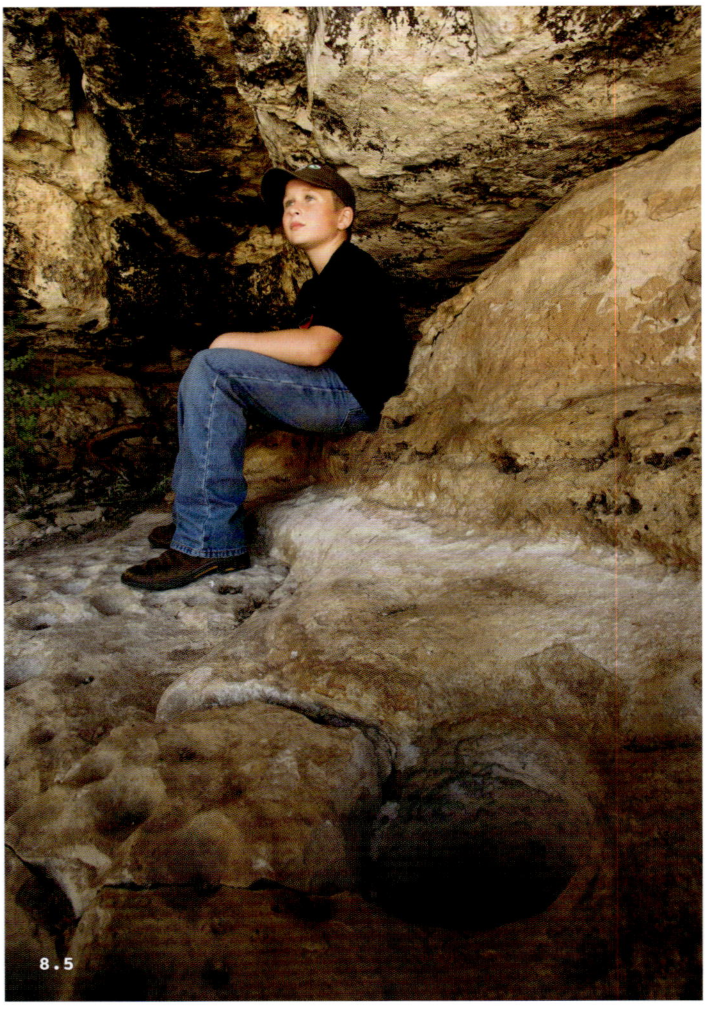

8.5

8.4 I set the aperture to f/2.8 for this portrait so the trees in the background wouldn't take away from the portrait subject.
ISO 200; 1/800 sec.; f/2.8; 150mm

8.5 I used an aperture of f/16 for this environmental portrait of Logan to ensure the ancient, man-made hole appeared in focus in the foreground. In this case, the environment shows the portrait subject's passion for history and archaeology.
ISO 400; 1/50 sec.; f/16; 17mm

8.6 Using a 50mm lens set to f/4 dropped the background out of focus enough to not be a distraction.
ISO 100; 1/60 sec.; f/4; 50mm

8.7 Although still not necessarily a distraction, using the same lens and aperture combination at a distance farther from the subjects brings the background more into focus, essentially increasing the image's depth of field.
ISO 100; 1/60 sec.; f/4; 50mm

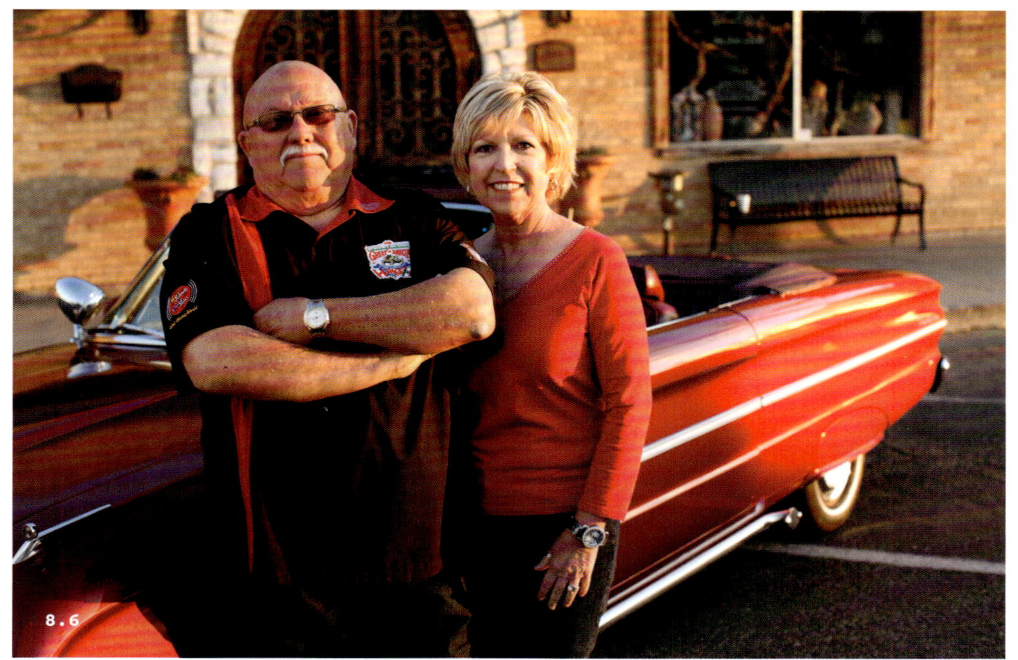

8.6

Distance and Visual Depth of Field

The aperture is not the only thing that affects the depth of field. Regardless of lens and aperture, the visual effect of the aperture setting will change based on your distance from your subject. The closer you move to your subject and maintain focus on it, the more out of focus the background will appear (**Figure 8.6**). The more distance between your camera and the subject, the larger the depth of field will seem (**Figure 8.7**). Technically, the depth of field is not changing; it only appears so because you are bringing the plane of critical focus either closer to the camera or farther away from it. Depth of field expands from the plane of critical focus and is limited by the optical possibilities of your lens, so these effects may come in handy either creatively or strategically during your shoot.

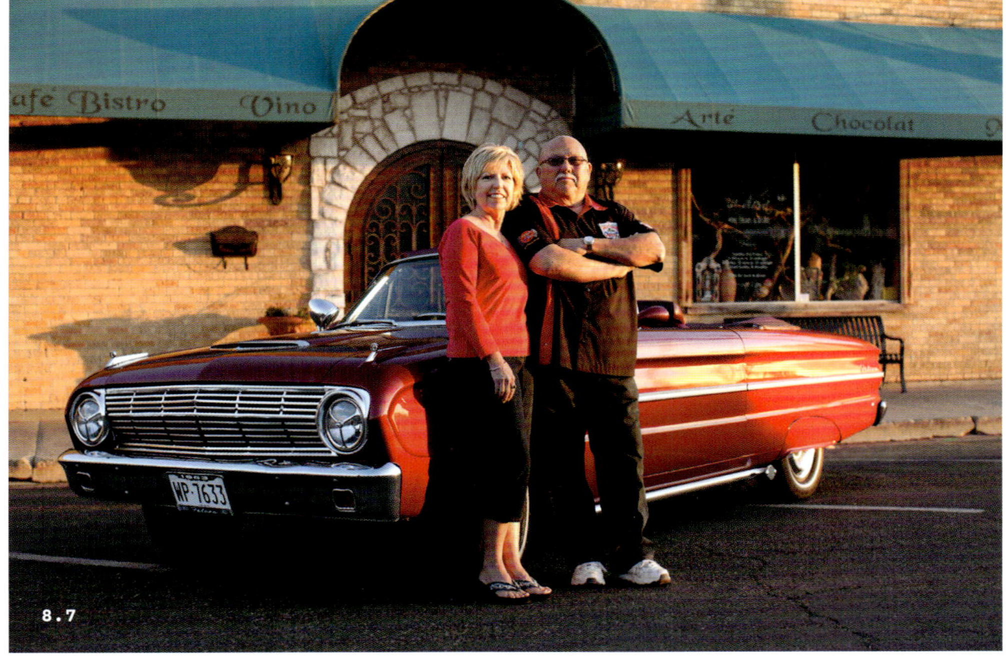

8.7

9. SETTING YOUR WHITE BALANCE

WHITE BALANCING (WB) simply refers to setting the camera's white balance controls to ensure accurate coloration in an image. In essence, you are fixing the camera so that what is truly white in your frame appears truly white in the image.

Each light source, even the sun, has a color temperature. This is a fancy, scientific way of saying that each light source casts a color. If you study any light source, you'll notice it. For example, incandescent, or tungsten, light bulbs cast a yellow-orange color, and fluorescent lights, depending on their generation, cast a green- or magenta-tinted color. The sun, which is the standard by which light coloration is practically measured, casts a light more white than the other source. Although our eyes have no problem adjusting to see white under any lighting coloration, the camera is not so capable. It's up to the user to help it out by setting the white balance.

At this point you may be asking: what does all this talk about color temperature mean for portraiture, and why not just use the automatic white balance setting?

Much like the automatic portrait exposure mode, the automatic white balance setting takes a great deal of control away from the photographer in terms of making accurate or meaningful white balance choices. Automatic white balance works well, but it is not foolproof when it comes to accurately measuring the color temperature of the light source used in your portraits (**Figure 9.1**). Automatic white balance is *always* striving to interpret an accurate coloration of the light sources, which takes creative freedom from the photographer. Perhaps the photographer wants the image to be tinted in a strong blue, such as what an incandescent white balance setting offers. By moving away from the automatic setting and into the preset white balance settings, or even into fully custom white balance settings, the photographer gains both consistency in coloration and creative control.

Even though white balancing a photographic scenario technically refers to ensuring that anything white in your shot will appear white in the image, it ultimately means that any coloration from the light sources is neutralized. Whites appear truly white, and skin tones are absent

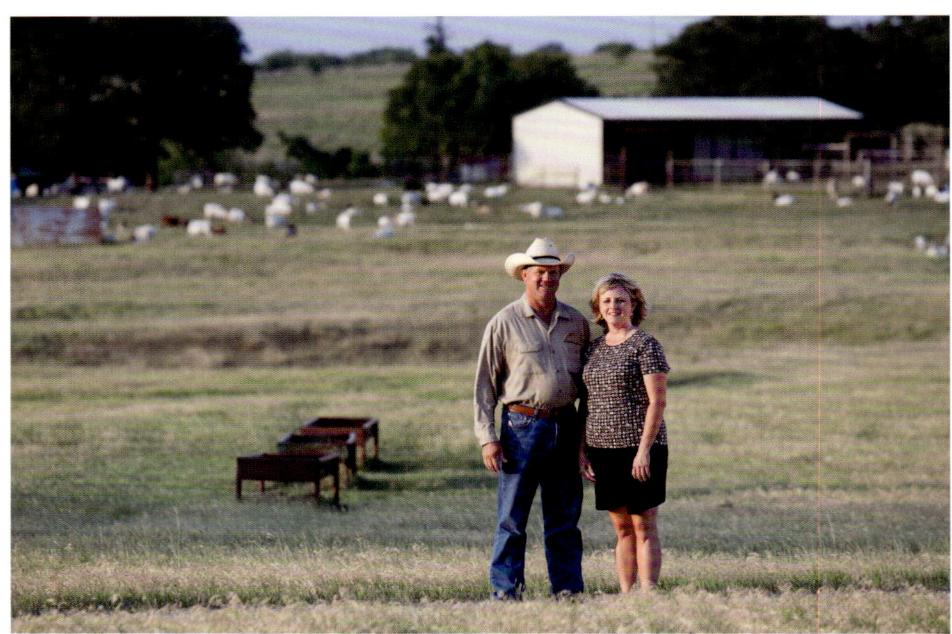

9.1 Although the color is not that inaccurate, I feel the automatic white balance setting cooled the late evening light too much in this portrait of a ranching couple. I would have preferred the image to be warmer to reflect the golden hour light at the beginning and end of the day.
ISO 100; 1/250 sec.; f/4.5; 200mm

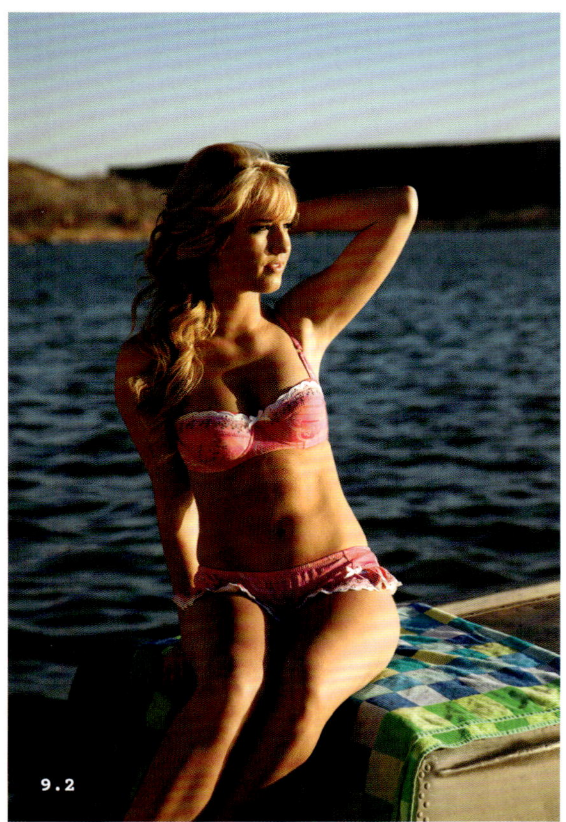

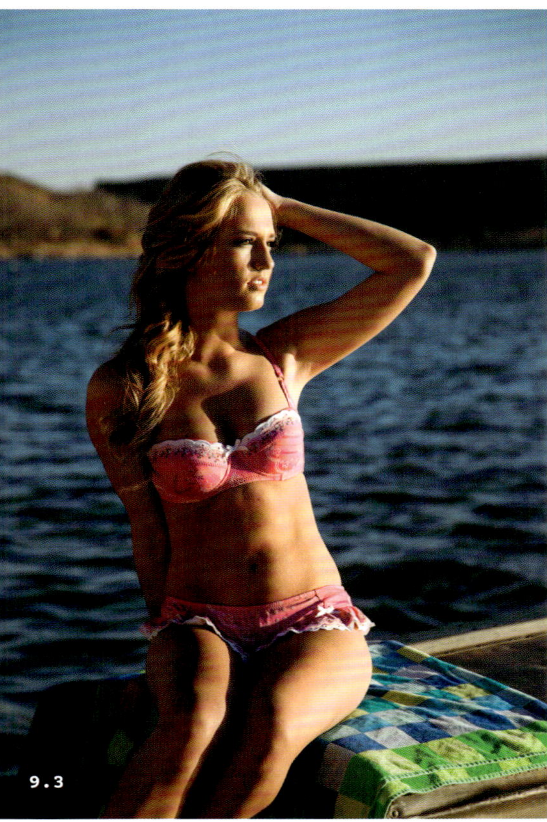

9.2 The automatic white balance setting used for this portrait warmed the tones too much. Although the subject doesn't look all that bad, the blue of the water and the sky are reduced, making those elements look less natural and inviting. **ISO 50; 1/250 sec.; f/4.5; 88mm**

9.3 Moving the white balance setting from automatic to daylight reduced some of the warmth in subsequent images. The golden hour light was still warm enough for the subject, but the reduction in white balance helped the water and sky maintain their natural blue coloration. **ISO 50; 1/250 sec.; f/4.5; 105mm**

of any inaccurate color tinting. For a large population of portrait photographers, being able to replicate accurate skin tones and colors in an image is paramount (**Figure 9.2** and **Figure 9.3**). Nothing is more distracting than a slight green colorcast that makes the subject look sickly, or an overly warm colorcast that suggests the subject is jaundiced. Such examples are extreme, but they nevertheless highlight why setting the white balance on your camera prior to shooting is a key consideration.

When working with natural light portraits, setting the white balance can sometimes be tricky. Typically, natural light portraiture assumes that direct or indirect sunlight is the light source. Most, if not all, digital cameras capable of varying white balance settings have a preset for such light (often referred to as Daylight white balance). This setting, which is usually identified by an icon of a sun (**Figure 9.4**) is preconfigured to white balance the color temperature of direct sunlight, which is somewhere around 5200 degrees Kelvin, or 5200K. For the most part, this preset works well to accurately re-create skin tones and colors photographed in such light. If the sun's rays are impeded by cloud coverage, the light's color temperature will be cooler. Moving the white balance setting to the Cloudy preset will counteract this by warming up the scene in your image. It essentially adds a warm, yellow-orange filter on top of the shot to mitigate the cooling blues conveyed in cloudy scenarios. As long as you know the type of light source you are working with, you can most likely find a preset for it in the camera's white balance menu.

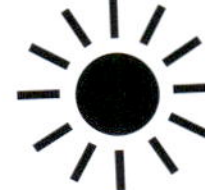

9.4 Most camera manufacturers use an icon of a sun to denote Daylight white balance. For natural light photographers, this is an ideal white balance to maintain fairly accurate skin tones, especially in outdoor settings.

Of course, each photographer uses the camera's white balance settings to his or her liking. Many natural light photographers use a warmer white balance setting because an intentionally warmer, slightly more orange coloration in an image can be flattering to the subject (**Figure 9.5**) by making it look like they were photographed in the golden hours of the day. Also, viewers tend to react positively to coloration that is more warm than cool, particularly when working to show off a portrait subject's face and skin tones. This is simply a creative, stylistic choice made on the photographer's part. I often favor setting my white balance to Cloudy for portraits, even if the lighting conditions technically call for Daylight.

To that end, anyone wishing to convey a certain message or mood about their portrait subject might choose to intentionally and drastically shift their white balance settings. For example, you might switch your white balance setting to Tungsten if you want everything else in the frame to appear more blue (**Figure 9.6**). The Tungsten preset is technically intended to counteract the intense warmth of incandescent bulbs, so it essentially layers a blue filter over the image. In this case, though, the setting is used as a creative effect rather than a tool to achieve accurate color.

Set your white balance to help you achieve the objective of your portrait. If your intention is to replicate accurate skin tones, I suggest setting your white balance to either a custom setting (each camera has a specific way of setting custom white balance values) or a preset that most closely matches the light source (direct or indirect sunlight, in the case of most natural light portraiture). If your intention is to create a more flattering coloration for skin tone or to stylistically imply meaning by making drastic shifts in white balance, then do so at the beginning of your shoot. It's better to start with settings that are as close to what you want with your end result. If you are shooting in the RAW file format (and why wouldn't you?), you can easily adjust the white balance later with post-processing software, such as Adobe Lightroom or Photoshop.

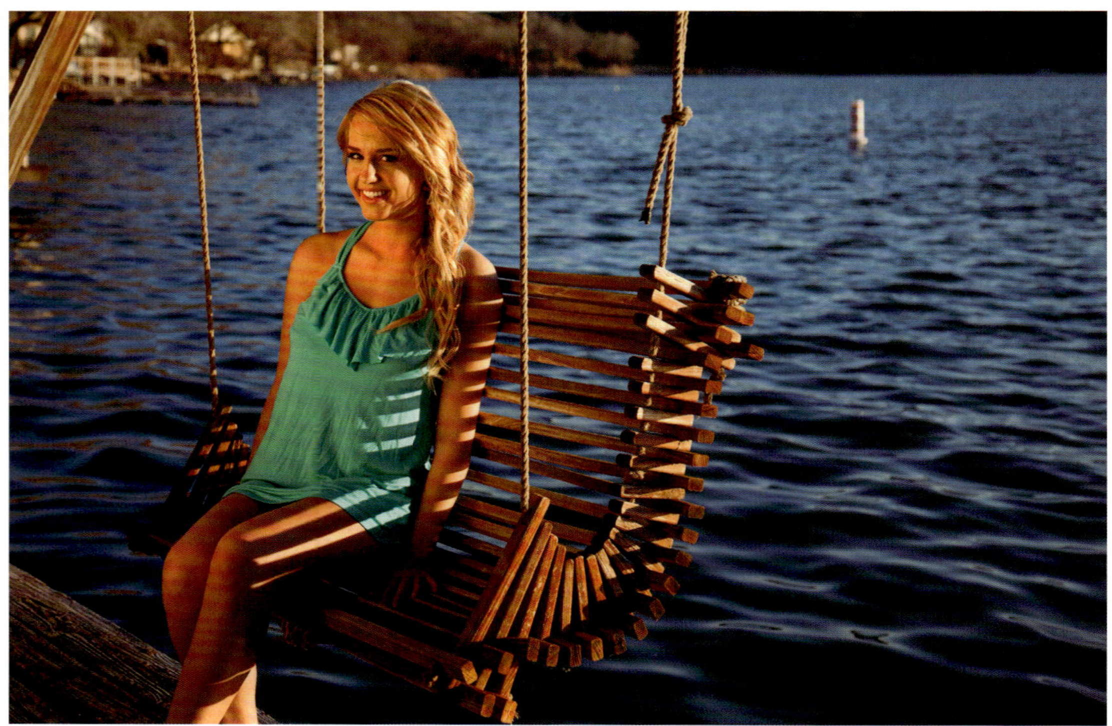

9.5 For this image, I used a custom white balance slightly higher than daylight white balance to add a hint of warmth, further conveying the mood set by the golden hour light. Additionally, I used a warmer reflector to bounce back sunlight into the model from camera left. **ISO 50; 1/125 sec.; f/4.5; 58mm**

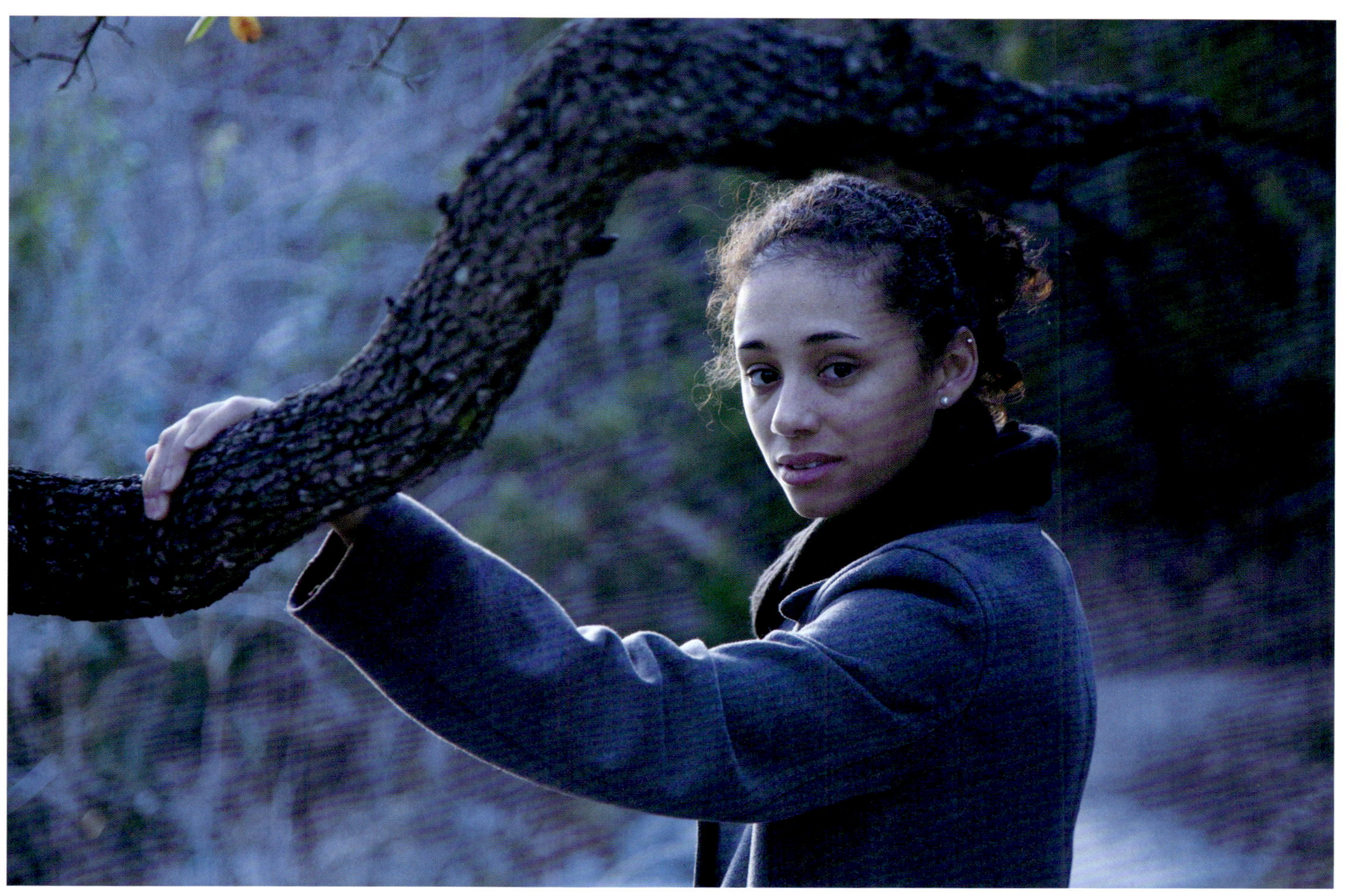

9.6 Using tungsten or incandescent white balance for natural light portraits is often done to create an image with more blue tones. Trying to convey sadness or loneliness? Cool off your white balance.
ISO 200; 1/25 sec.; f/4; 105mm

THE KIT LENS that came with your camera or a standard zoom lens is really all you need for great portraiture. I know plenty of professionals that shoot portraits with a kit zoom lens, and I'm quick to grab my 24-70mm for the same reason. However, the search for the perfect portrait lens and focal length is a highly subjective journey. Some folks enjoy using lenses with only one focal length (called a *prime* lens), and some folks want nothing more than a very fast lens (a lens capable of opening its aperture as much as possible).

To find the portrait lens that works best for you, it helps to know a few key characteristics of lenses and focal lengths. These characteristics include a lens's maximum aperture opening, the quality grade of the glass, and its build quality. The most important characteristic to consider, however, is lens *perspective*.

Perspective refers to the size of the subject as it appears in the frame and the spatial relationship objects have to each other. All lenses are identified by the focal lengths they provide. Wide-angle focal lengths range from 8mm to somewhere around 35mm; standard zoom focal lengths range from 24mm to 70mm; and telephoto focal lengths go beyond 70mm. Lens focal lengths exist on a limited range, from ultra-wide to super-telephoto. However, it's most important for us to correlate focal lengths to the perspective they visually convey. The shorter the focal length (the more wide-angle the lens), the more *expansive* the image's perspective will be. This means that subject matter in the foreground will appear much larger compared to all other subject matter, and the distance

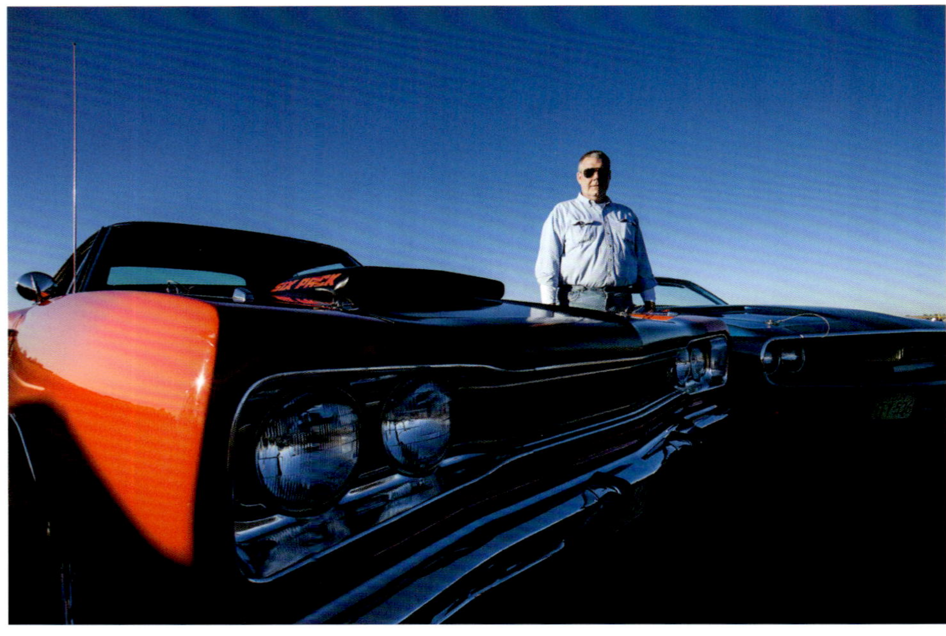

10.1 Using a super-wide-angle focal length expands the distance between the car headlights closest to camera left and the actual portrait subject. The size of the headlights compared to everything else in the frame is overly exaggerated as well.
ISO 200; 1/160 sec.; f/16; 17mm

between the foreground and background will appear more extensive (**Figure 10.1**). Inversely, as the focal length increases (telephoto lens), the perspective changes to reveal a more compressed image. This *compression perspective* closes the distance between the foreground and background, which makes the background seem more spacious (**Figure 10.2**). *Normal perspective* falls in between expansive and compressed perspectives. Normal perspective visually conveys the same perspective of our own eyes, displaying subject matter in proportionate relationship to each other as we see them outside the viewfinder. Normal perspective is typically associated with 50mm (thus explaining the popularity of such prime lenses) (**Figure 10.3**). Although the numbers next to the abbreviation for millimeters might be an impressive talking point at the local camera club, it is the correlation between those numbers and perspective that will inform your creative decisions regarding making great portraits.

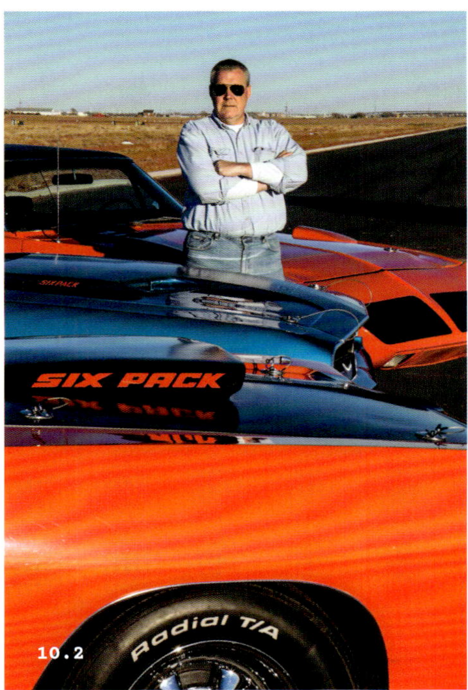

10.2

10.2 A longer focal length was helpful in pulling all of the vehicles together, or compressing the visual distance between them, creating a layered portrait of the car owner.
ISO 200; 1/80 sec.; f/22; 105mm

10.3 A 50mm perspective most accurately conveys the way our eyes see the world around us, and it is an extremely useful lens when you want to avoid distorting anything in the frame.
ISO 100; 1/1600 sec.; f/2; 50mm

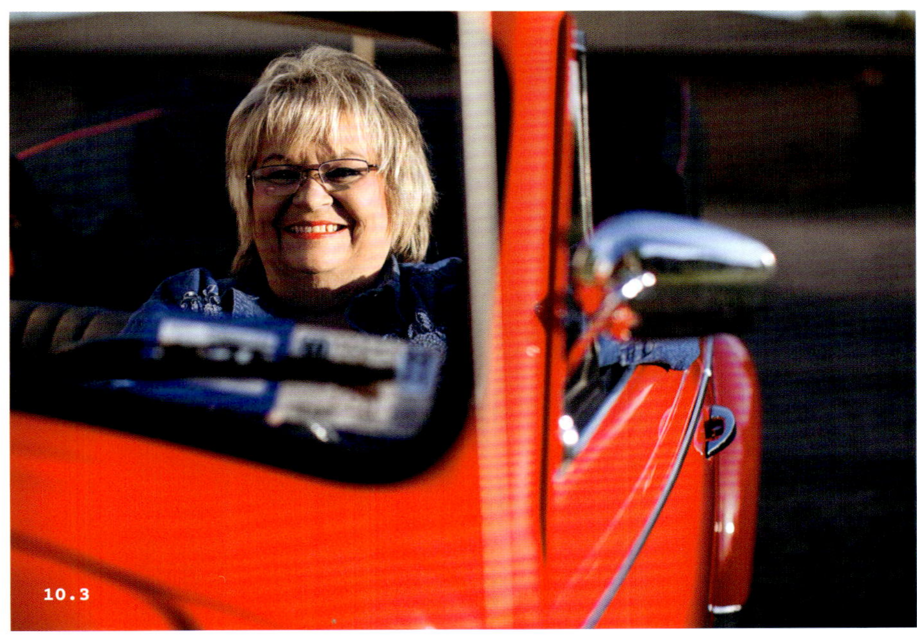

10.3

Secondary to perspective, it's also worth noting that the shorter the focal length is, the more depth of field the image frame gains. The longer the focal length is, the smaller the depth of field will be. For example, a 32mm lens set to f/4 will yield more depth of field (**Figure 10.4**) than a 105mm lens set to f/4, which will yield little depth of field (**Figure 10.5**). Some argue that there is no difference, but you can't argue with how the images look. This information may come in handy when you are looking to either include more environment in your portrait, or if you want to isolate the subject against a soft, out-of-focus background.

10.4 Expansive perspectives often make an image look as though there is more depth of field than the aperture (f/4 in this case) could provide.
ISO 100; 1/50 sec.; f/4; 32mm

10.5 The more you zoom in on an image, the more the visible depth of field decreases, as long as you maintain the focal point on the subject.
ISO 100; 1/50 sec.; f/4; 105mm

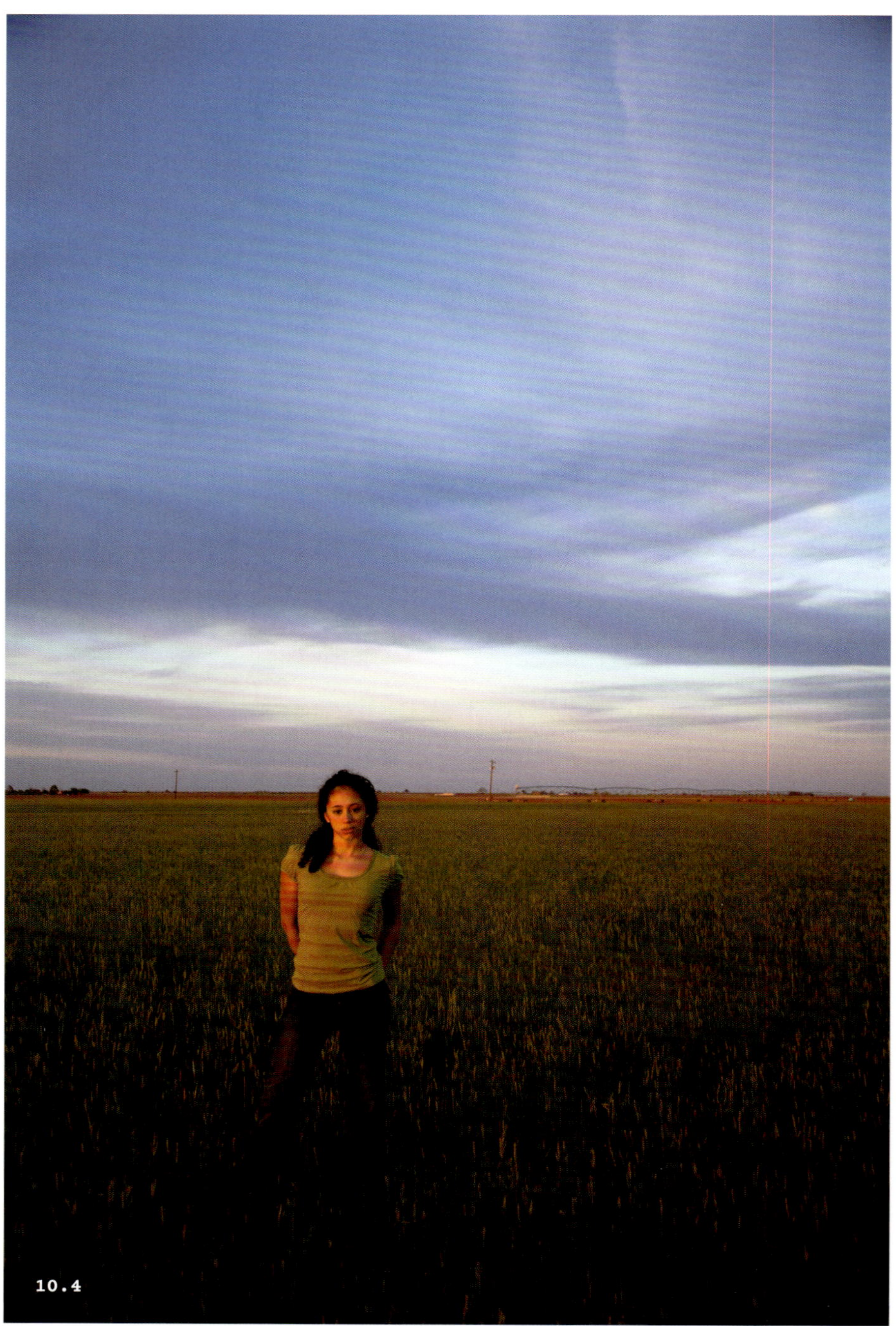

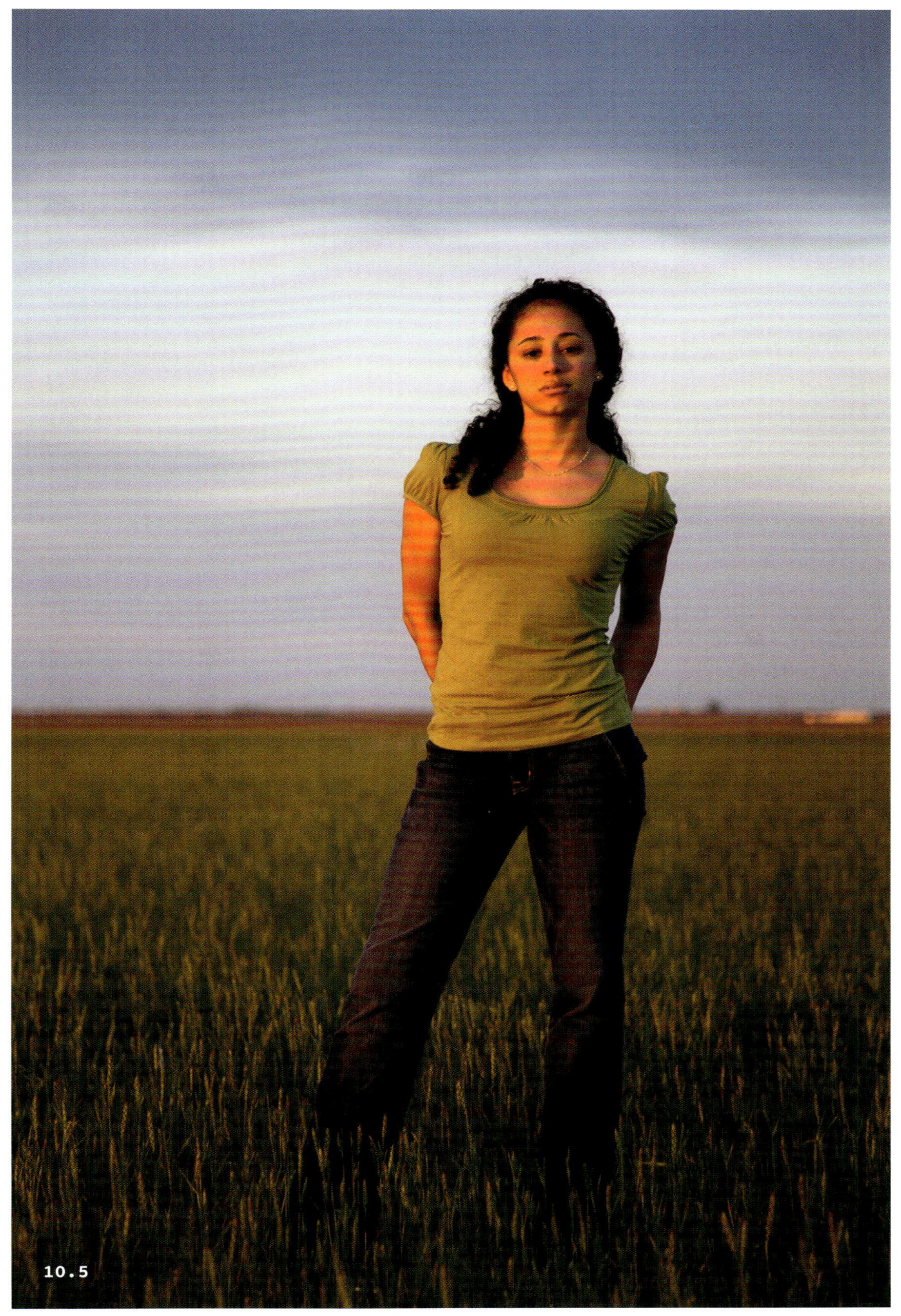

10.5

Although great portraits are made at all focal lengths, it's good to start out using a standard to medium-telephoto focal length that offers a slightly compressed perspective. A great favorite amongst portrait photographers is the 85mm focal length. It is longer than 50mm and compresses the portrait subject a bit with the background; yet, it does not distort features like a wide-angle focal length would. The 85mm prime lens is practically made for portraiture.

No matter the manufacturer, 85mm primes are fast lenses (the maximum aperture is very large) that open up to f/1.8 (some even open up to f/1.2). This translates into an increased ability to knock the background out of focus, directing full attention to the subject in your portrait (**Figure 10.6**).

If you don't want to purchase an 85mm lens, or you need the flexibility of a zoom lens, a standard zoom lens that ranges from 24-70mm will work nicely when zoomed all the way out (or at least past 50mm). Zoom lenses do not have such large maximum apertures, but they provide slight perspective compression and don't distort the image, so they are great alternatives to the 85mm. Personally, I find myself using a 24-70mm lens that opens to f/2.8 much more than the 85mm f/1.8 I also carry in my bag (**Figure 10.7**).

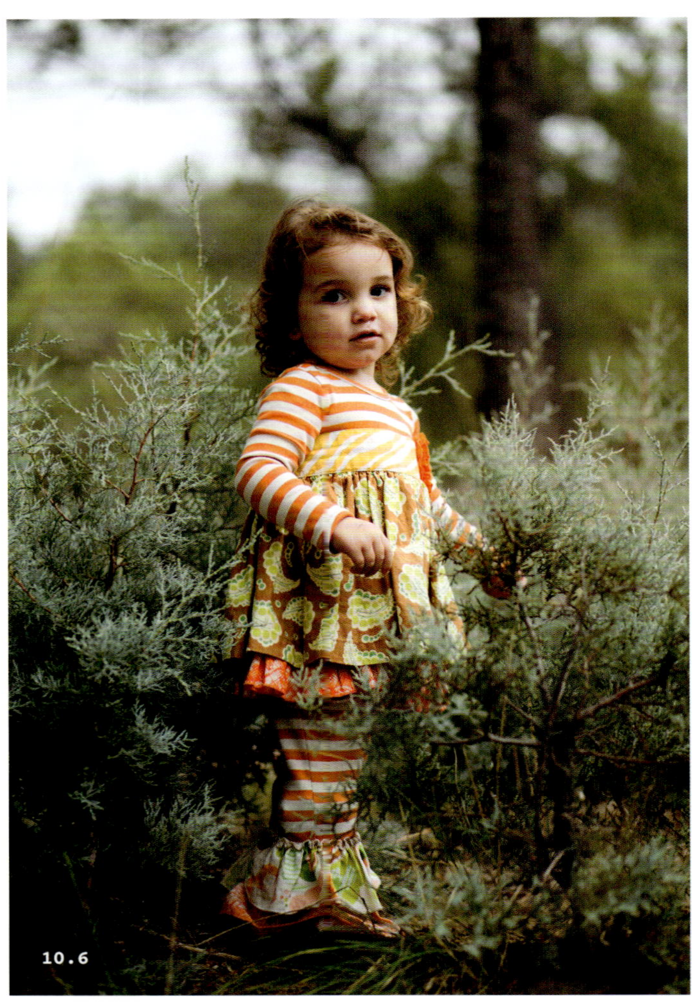

10.6

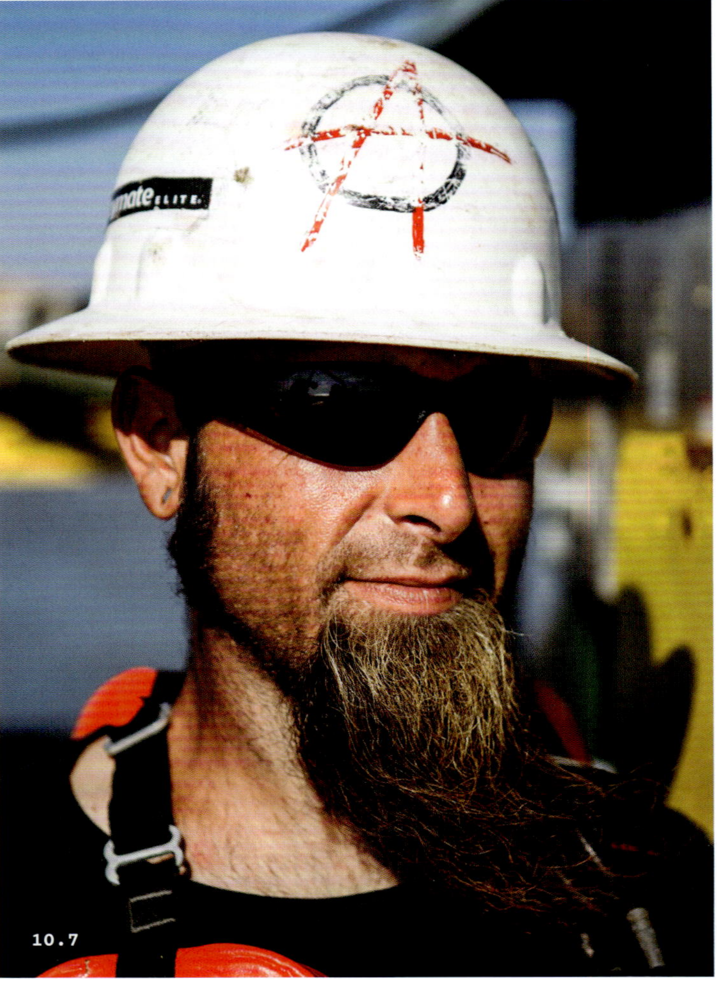

10.7

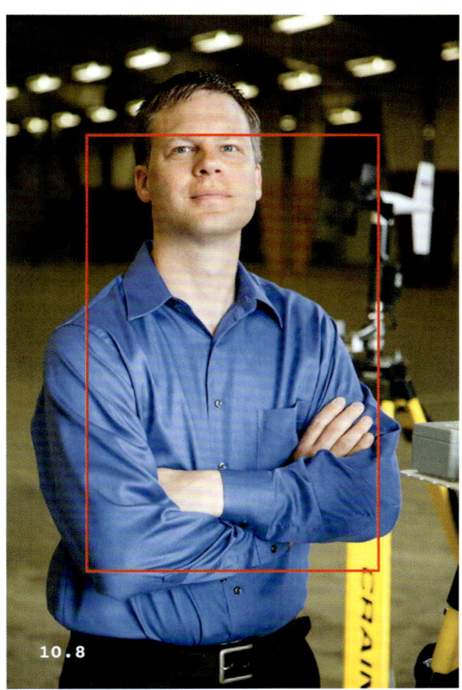

Sensor Size's Effect on Focal Length and Perspective

One of the most confusing things about digital photography is identifying the difference in DSLR sensor sizes and how they affect your image. Although all DSLR sensors and many mirrorless camera sensors share the same 2:3 length-to-width dimensional ratio, not all of them are the exact same size. Most entry-level cameras have a slightly smaller sensor than their higher-end family members. We refer to these as cropped sensors, while calling their larger brethren full-frame sensors. A full-frame sensor is the same size as a frame of 35mm film. Cropped sensors (referred to as APS-C sensors) are smaller, and their size is associated with their crop factor. For example, a Nikon APS-C sensor has a crop factor of 1.5x. A Canon APS-C sensor, on the other hand, has a crop factor of 1.6x. The larger the crop factor (Canon's, in this case, is slightly larger), the smaller the sensor (**Figure 10.8**).

So, what does this mean for your portrait making? Full-frame sensors treat the focal length you are using as just that—the focal length you are using. When shooting with a 50mm lens on a full-frame camera, you will be shooting at a true 50mm perspective. That same 50mm lens on an APS-C camera body will visually display a different perspective. Although many folks like to say that an APS-C sensor's crop factor multiplies the focal length you are using, I like to think about its effect on the perspective with which I'm shooting. You see, if you are using that 50mm lens on an APS-C sensor with a 1.5x crop factor, you are actually seeing (and shooting) with the perspective of a 75mm lens on a full-frame sensor. Many folks purchase 18-55mm kit lenses with their APS-C camera bodies. In full-frame numbers, this lens translates into a 27-82.5mm lens. If you are using a camera with a cropped sensor in it, simply find out the crop factor and multiply it by the focal length you are shooting with in order to determine the actual perspective you are producing in your images.

Remember that 85mm lens I made out to be the best thing since sliced bread? On a cropped sensor with a 1.5x crop factor, its perspective equates to that of a 127.5mm focal length on a full-frame sensor. This isn't necessarily a problem; it's simply something to be aware of. Just so you know, if you do want to achieve something close to an 85mm perspective using an APS-C sensor, you'll want to use a focal length slightly over 56mm.

11. NAILING FOCUS

IN PHOTOGRAPHY, THE viewer's eye naturally goes to the focus point in an image. For making portraits, this is a very important concept to bear in mind. Missing your focus may mean the viewer's eye is distracted by a busy background, or that some unintentional visual element is gnawing at the viewer's field of vision.

Typically, it is best to focus on your portrait subject's eyes (**Figure 11.1**). Although there may be stylistic, creative, or narrative reasons to do otherwise, focusing on the eyes allows your viewer to immediately connect with your portrait subject. There is something special about eyes—something sentient and telling. When we talk to other people in everyday life, we look them in the eye to feel an engaging connection to them. Why not try to replicate that in your portraits?

Focus is one of those things that you're going to really nail; but, believe it or not, sometimes you'll also really miss the mark. Focus is a determinant of two things: where the plane of critical focus is placed, and the amount of depth of field you achieve based on your aperture setting. The plane of critical focus is an invisible geometric plane that represents the exact distance from the camera to the point where the lens is focused. Depth of field emerges in front of and behind the plane of critical focus. You can assume that the depth of field available with an aperture setting of f/3.5 will be much smaller than the depth of field available with an aperture of f/16. Per this logic, placing the plane of critical focus on a portrait subject's eyes with an aperture of f/4, for example, will provide sufficient depth

of field for both of the subject's eyes to be in focus (**Figure 11.2**) while also knocking the background out of focus. However, an aperture setting of f/1.8, achieved with some prime lenses, does not offer nearly the depth of field as f/4 (**Figure 11.3**). With a very shallow depth of field, micro movements made by the photographer could easily shift the plane of critical focus away from the eye. I have missed the mark on my fair share of portraits shooting at such low aperture settings. Although we enjoy shallow depth of field, we must remain vigilant of where our focus is placed.

So, how do you set yourself up to ensure more in-focus shots than out-of-focus shots? First, I suggest using auto-focus. It's efficient, accurate, and most importantly, controllable if you spend the time learning to use it. After ensuring auto-focus is turned on (it's usually a switch on the lens), press the shutter button halfway down to activate it. If equipped, you can also press your camera's back button focus.

Second, also set your camera to a one-shot auto-focus mode that allows you to set your focus and recompose without shifting focus forward or backward as long as you keep the shutter button depressed halfway. While using these tools, you can feel confident your plane of critical focus will remain where you placed it as long as you don't physically move toward or away from your subject, and limit your movements to only recomposing the frame. When it comes to auto-focus, this is how the majority of portrait photographers are set up.

Third, I suggest using just one of the several auto-focus points that are available in your camera. Most cameras come with all auto-focus points enabled, meaning that the camera makes the decision on the most important subject in the frame, and focuses there. Using just one auto-focus point allows you to make this decision, instead. It also allows you to place focus in specific areas around the frame—wherever an auto-focus point exists. In addition to using auto-focus and a one-shot auto-focus mode, I also suggest using the center auto-focus point (**Figure 11.4**). Not all auto-focus points are created equal; certain points are more accurate than others (the center auto-focus point is usually the most reliable). With these three functions established, you are able to use the strongest auto-focus point to nail focus on your subject's eye(s) and recompose if necessary without shifting your focus forward or backward. Using these three functions will help you control focus for your portraits.

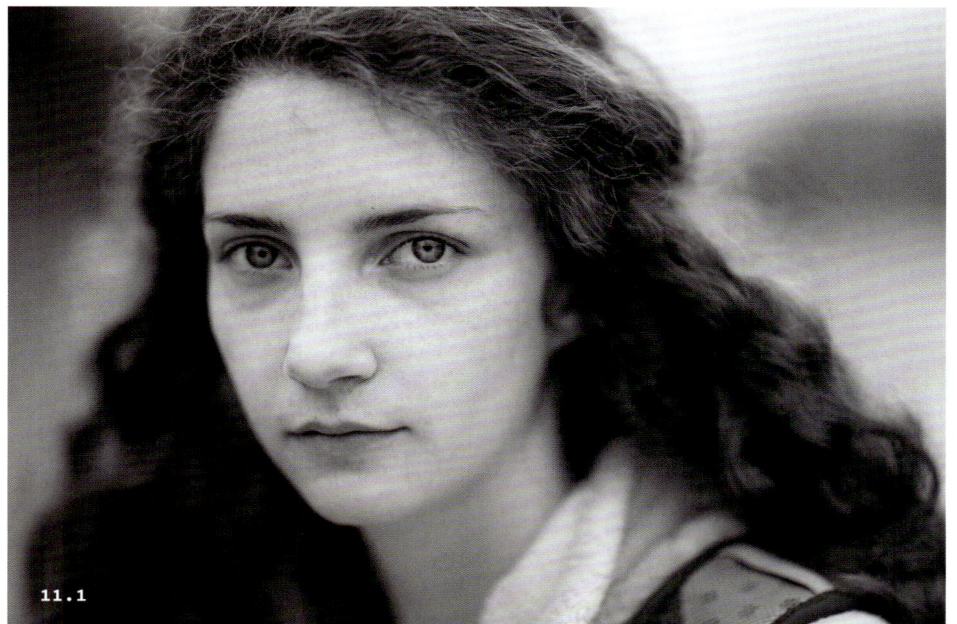

11.1

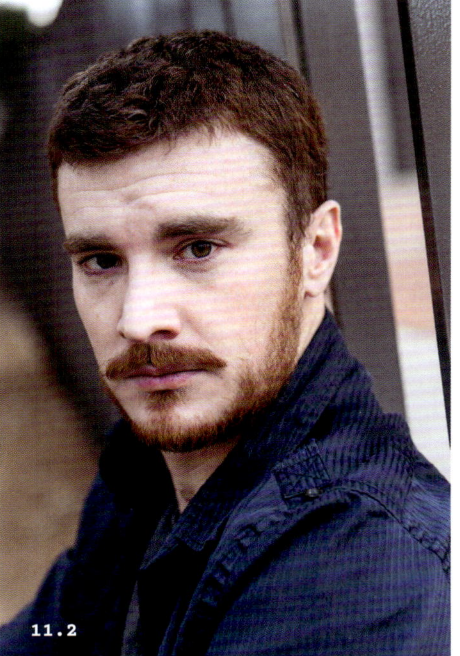

11.2

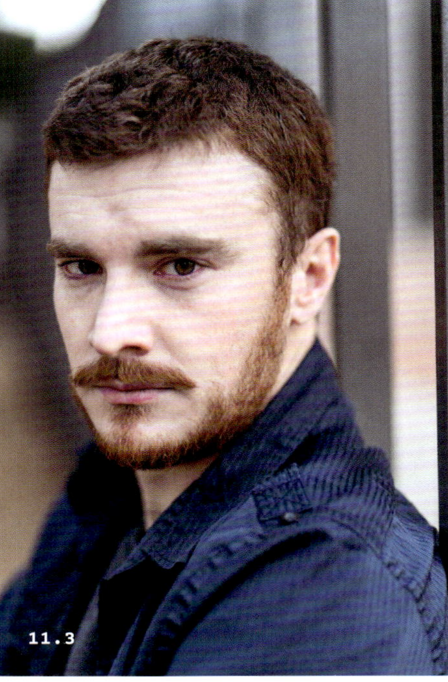

11.3

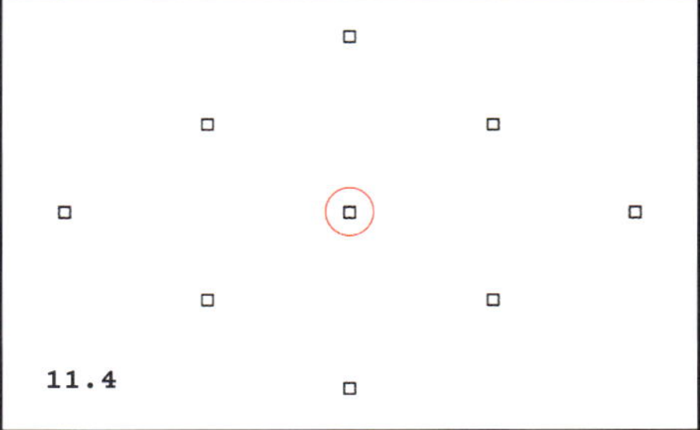

11.4

11.1 Nailing the focus on the eyes, or in this case, the eye closest to the camera, is technically appropriate for portraits, and a great way to directly engage your viewing audience!
ISO 200; 1/800 sec.; f/1.2; 85mm

11.2 At f/4, the aperture provided enough depth of field to keep the plane of critical focus on the eye closest to the camera. Both eyes are in focus, but the background is sufficiently out of focus.
ISO 100; 1/60 sec.; f/4; 85mm

11.3 Although f/1.8 is an attractive aperture value, it offers such shallow depth of field that when I recomposed the image after focusing on the eye closest to the camera, the plane of critical focus shifted and forced the eye out of focus.
ISO 100; 1/250 sec.; f/1.8; 85mm

11.4 This illustration highlights the nine auto-focus points you can choose to use individually or together. However, the middle auto-focus point is typically the strongest at grabbing focus.

12. MINIMUM SUSTAINING SHUTTER SPEED

HAVE YOU EVER finished a shoot in which the light was perfect, your compositions were engaging, and your rapport with your subject was great—only to find later during review that a good deal of your images were out of focus? As you recall, you did everything you could to ensure your focus was placed appropriately. What happened? This can be one of the most frustrating experiences for photographers.

If this has happened to you (and it happens to everyone), you exceeded what is called your minimum sustaining shutter speed. This mouthful of a term refers to the slowest shutter speed with which you can successfully hand-hold camera and lens without your own body's movement throwing your shot out of focus. Although we are often not aware of it, our body is constantly in motion. Despite our greatest efforts to properly hold a camera with complete stillness, our bodies are not the most stable of platforms. When shooting with a shutter speed below your minimum sustaining shutter speed, the camera moves too much during exposure, resulting in a blurry shot.

Luckily, it's easy to determine a minimum sustaining shutter speed. As a rule of thumb, the minimum sustaining shutter speed is relative to the focal length you are using for any given shot. The idea is to match the denominator of the shutter speed to your focal length. For example, if you are shooting with a 200mm focal length, the corresponding minimum sustaining shutter speed would be 1/200 of a second. If you are shooting at 85mm, the minimum sustaining shutter speed would be 1/80 of a second (**Figure 12.1** and **Figure 12.2**). Shooting at or faster than the minimum sustaining shutter speed associated with any focal length will more than likely result in avoiding your body movement forcing a shift in the focus of your image.

Bear in mind that the information above is a general rule, and won't necessarily be appropriate for every situation. In fact, the more you shoot and work with a particular lens, the better acquainted you'll be with its form factor. Once your muscle memory adjusts to its weight and shape, your minimum sustaining shutter speed for a particular focal length may drop considerably. As with anything, the more time you spend practicing, the more capable you will be. Stylistically, I prefer to shoot with a fairly wide-angle perspective. I frequently use a focal length of 24mm or wider, and my minimum sustaining shutter speeds for such focal lengths have slowed down substantially since I started shooting. At times, I feel confident I can create a sharp handheld shot at 1/8 of a second with a 24mm lens. That's pretty slow (slower than what's needed for the vast majority of my portrait work).

This is a great rule to keep in mind during your shoots. Although image stabilization was created to mitigate our body movement's effect on image sharpness, it's not foolproof. I enjoy technology that greatly improves our capabilities with the camera, but I'm always cognizant of my minimum sustaining shutter speed— particularly for portraits.

12.1 Looking closely, you can see that the image shifted during exposure. This result is due to using a shutter speed slower than the minimum sustaining shutter speed for an 85mm lens.
ISO 100; 1/40 sec.; f/5.6; 85mm

12.2 To ensure I was shooting faster than my minimum sustaining shutter speed at 85mm, I opened up the aperture a bit more than one full stop. The image, especially the eyes, is tack sharp because I was able to handhold the camera and lens without incurring any micro-movements during the shorter exposure.
ISO 100; 1/100 sec.; f/3.5; 85mm

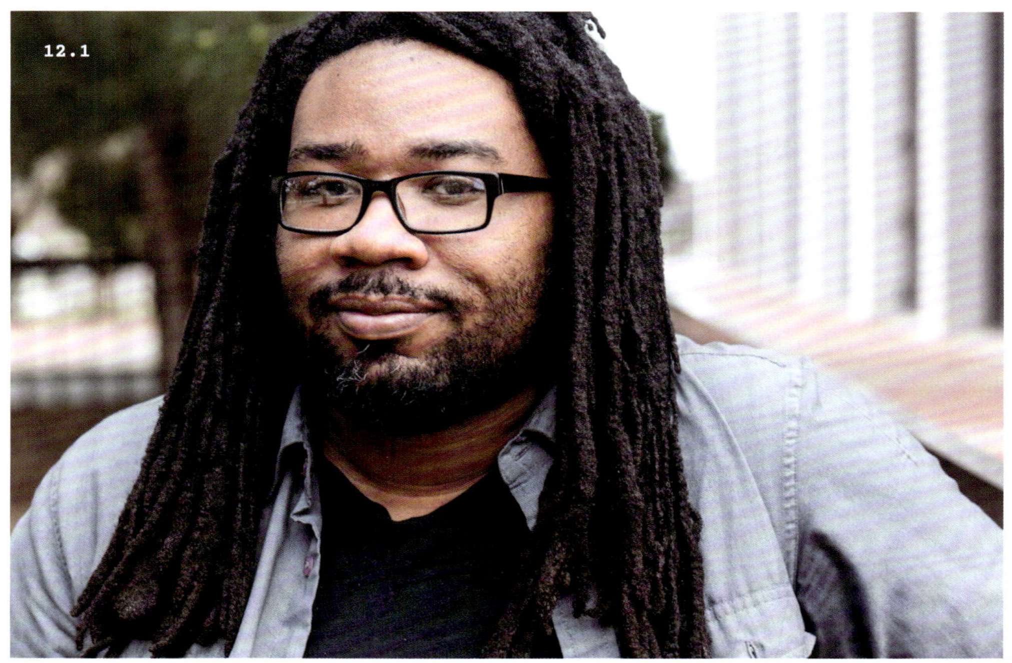

12.1

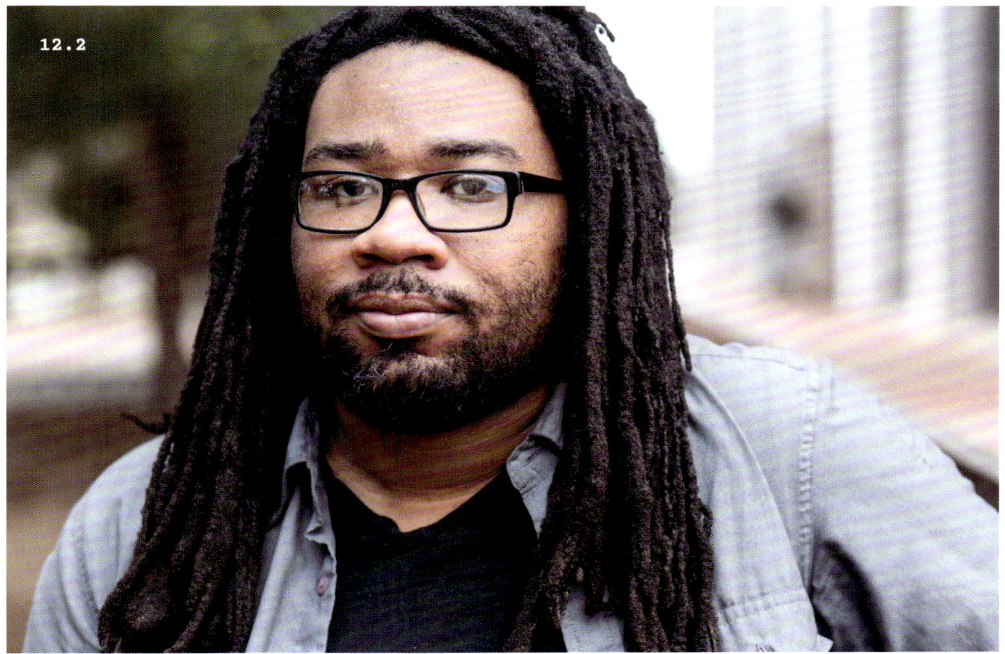

12.2

13. GET A GRIP

ONE OF THE most popular accessories for portrait photographers is a vertical grip, and for good reason: it helps eliminate the potential for camera shake from hand-held shots that adversely affect your image sharpness. A vertical grip allows the photographer to keep his right hand in the same position regardless of the orientation of the image (**Figure 13.1**). Without a vertical grip, most photographers hold the camera with their right hand on top, and rest the weight of the camera in their left, more stabilized hand (**Figure 13.2**). A vertical grip allows the right hand to stay in the same "home" position with both horizontal and vertical frames, which can increase the photographer's confidence when taking hand-held, vertically oriented shots.

Of course, there are other benefits to using a vertical grip. One is extended battery life. Since grips usually attach and communicate with the camera through the camera's battery compartment, all power sources then are moved to the grip itself. Vertical grips usually have enough room for two batteries, which gives the camera twice the battery life. Of course, adding a vertical grip and an additional battery to your camera makes it heavier, but there is a trade-off for just about every gain.

A second benefit, and one that might not be as well known, is that a vertical grip has shock absorbency. OK, so maybe a hard piece of plastic is not all that shock absorbent, but it does make for a great excess piece of material between the ground and your camera should you ever drop it. Speaking from experience, it's better to drop a camera on its vertical grip than directly on the body. I once yanked a camera out of the seat of a semi-truck only to watch it fall to the concrete below. To this day, I believe the vertical grip and lens hood, two accessories between the ground and the camera, saved not only the shoot, but also the camera (and my bank account).

It's also worth noting that there is an aesthetic to a vertical grip that conveys a certain mentality about the photographer. It has a professional connotation that you may or may not prefer. A vertical grip alone does not make anyone a professional photographer, but a professionally minded portrait photographer wants to instill as much confidence as possible in her subject. It's superficial, but if the presence of a vertical grip makes the subject more confident that you can handle the shoot and provide pro-quality material, a greater level of trust will be formed between subject and photographer. With that trust, the photographer can tap into a wider range of portrait possibilities with the subject.

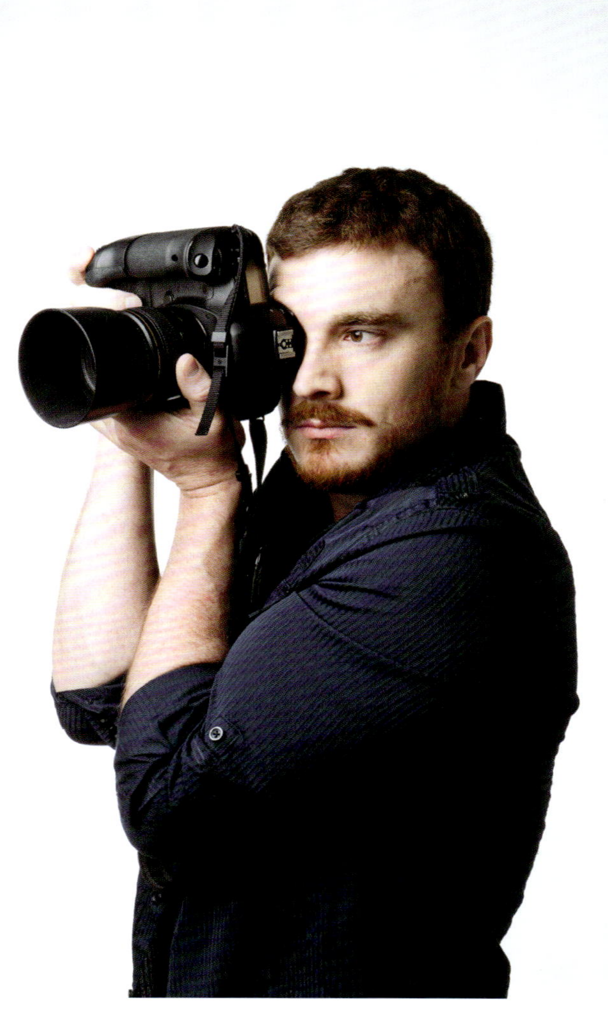

13.1 With a vertical grip attached to the camera, the photographer can maintain a similar position shooting vertically as he does shooting horizontally. This allows for the right elbow to be pushed up against the body, further stabilizing the shooting posture.

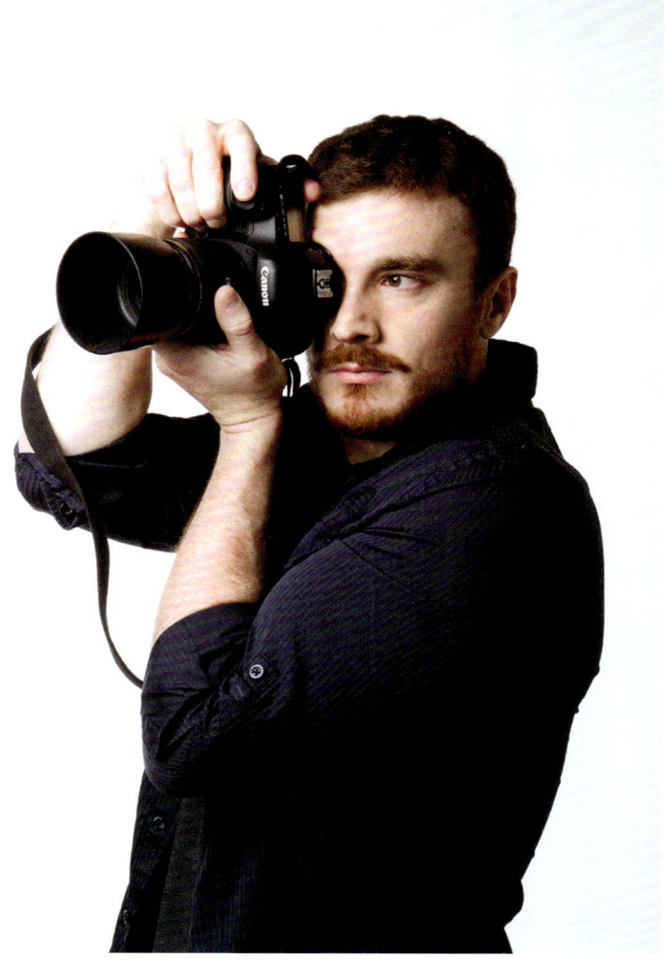

13.2 Although some photographers prefer to not use a vertical grip, properly holding a vertically oriented shot without one forces the right elbow up and away from the body, diminishing its stabilizing force.

MORE SPECIFICALLY, BUY a five-in-one reflector that offers you flexibility and creative options. A reflector kit is extremely valuable for natural light portrait photographers as well as photographers who use artificial light. Reflectors come in all shapes and sizes, but I recommend getting one that is small enough for an assistant to hold. I favor a 42-inch reflector (**Figure 14.1**). A five-in-one (they make seven-in-one reflector kits, too) doubles not only as a reflector, but also as a diffuser and an anti-fill due to its modular design. Personally, I use the diffuser more than the actual reflector. In the same vein, I generally also use the diffuser as a reflector (more on this in the next chapter).

A reflector is one of the most value-laden pieces of equipment a photographer can purchase. Reflectors can be relatively inexpensive, but some cost hundreds of dollars. The costs are usually driven by their material's sturdiness and durability over long periods of time. As long as you treat your reflector right, you'll save money toward equipment in the long run; a $100 reflector kit can last a very long time.

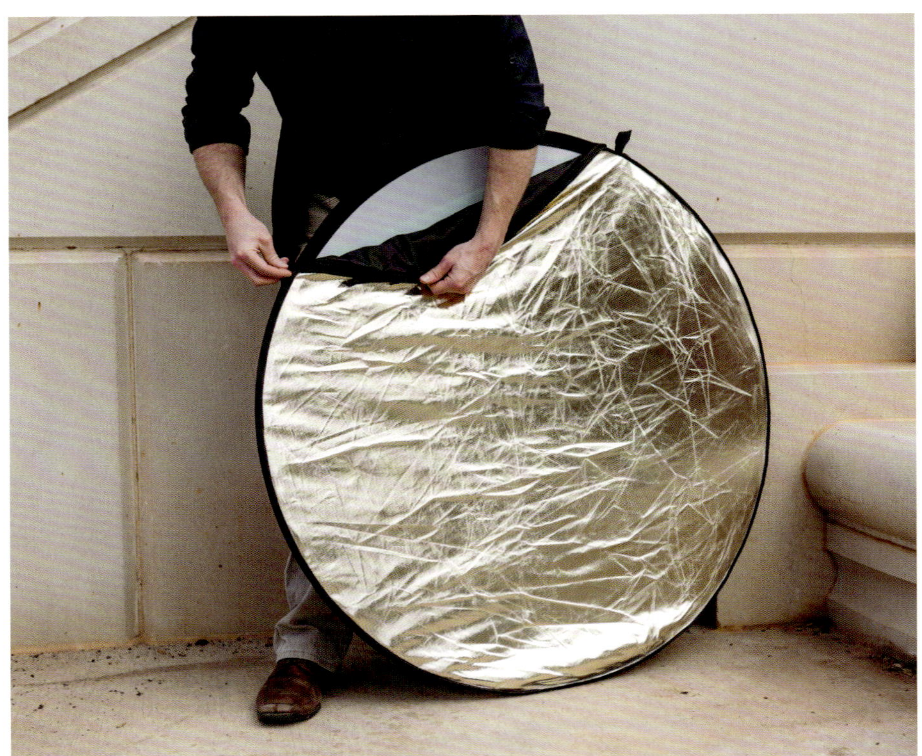

14.1 A five-in-one reflector can be a natural light portrait photographer's greatest tool. Most include a gold or sunlight reflector, a silver reflector, a black (anti-fill) reflector, and at least one diffuser, which serves as the reflector's rigid structure.

A Note on Buying Equipment

All this talk about acquiring and using equipment leads me to a very important point. The equipment we use for photography is comprised of simple tools. That's it. No one piece of equipment makes us better photographers. It's our ability to partner vision with the skilled use of those tools that allows us to express creativity through great photographs. With that in mind, I encourage you to have a healthy perspective on making equipment purchases—a perspective that strikes a balance between quality, durability and equipment life, and cost-effectiveness.

Frankly, the most affordable gear is often constructed with the lowest quality materials and craftsmanship, making for a cheap product. The most expensive equipment is built with the best materials and manufacturing. My advice is to be deliberate in your gear acquisition: do your research and resisting impulse purchases.

Let's take lenses for example, one of the most varied categories of equipment in terms of quality, durability, and cost-effectiveness. Different lenses come in at different price points, and for good reason. As the price goes up, *typically* so does the quality of the glass inside it. The build materials go from plastic to metal, and weather sealing is integrated (durability). The lens speed (maximum aperture opening) usually increases the higher the price of the lens is, as well. *Usually*, the sharpest, fastest (in terms of aperture opening and actual speed of operation), and most durable lenses come at a premium.

Again, the key is to be deliberate about your purchases. For example, I primarily shoot with Canon equipment, and I've always used L-series lenses during my professional career. The L-series comprises Canon's top-of-the-line lenses, and although they are extremely sharp and perform at very high levels, they are expensive. The lenses have to outlast multiple camera bodies (I have one ultra-wide lens that is now 20 years old), and I have to see myself consistently using it to justify the expense. A couple of years ago, I was in the market for a standard portrait lens: an 85mm prime. I looked at the L-series 85mm f/1.2 lens and assumed I would get it since I knew the build quality of that line would ensure it was a well-constructed lens. The $2,000+ price tag, though, was a bit

steep for how much I thought I would use it, so I rented one for a trial period. As cool as that piece of glass looked on the end of my camera, I found it to be a slow focuser and too heavy to have sitting in my bag. I did some further research and learned that many folks I trust were more satisfied with the non-L-series 85mm f/1.8 because it incorporated a faster autofocus system and was still seemingly just as sharp. I looked at it, took a few test shots, saw the $400 price tag, and made the purchase. Many of the portraits you see in this book shot at 85mm were made with that lens.

This purchase was deliberate and completely appropriate for my circumstances. I don't use 85mm as much as I use shorter focal lengths, so I didn't need the heavier build quality of the L-series lens (since the cheaper one will see more of my bag than it will action), *and* it focused faster, making it a better performer without shirking image quality. I go through this thought process for every purchase I make. I use the standard zoom focal length range over half the time, so I will make the extra investment for the L-series 24-70mm f/2.8. The same goes for the L-series 70-200mm f/2.8 (but I don't go in for the image stabilized version, which saves me some more money).

The point is to justify every purchase you make, whether it's camera bodies, lenses, lighting equipment, or computers. Professionally, one of the ways folks get into serious debt is through over-investment in equipment that they either don't use or don't know how to use well. The same also goes for non-professionals. I am a big believer in investing in high-quality gear, mostly because it will last longer than the cheaper equipment if well maintained. I also believe in doing your research, which often requires renting the equipment to see how it works with your style and process before committing to the purchase. If spending a hundred dollars to test a lens for a week saves you over a thousand on an ill-made purchase, I'd say you came out on top (especially given that you probably made a few good images during that trial period).

Don't create undue financial stress over equipment. Doing your research and testing is a good way to feel rationally and creatively confident in your acquisitions.

3

WORKING WITH NATURAL LIGHT

Light makes photography possible. We've been studying it for centuries. Portrait photographers finesse our use of light, natural or artificial, and we've learned to use it in specific ways for a variety of scenarios. This chapter highlights several of the most important things all portrait photographers should know about how to use light. The first three tips are about studying and becoming aware of the light we use for portraits. The remaining four tips highlight useful technique considerations that can be employed in your shoots depending on how you want to use the light in your work. You'll see many tight shots of faces and busts, as well as some black and white images. This is all in an effort to place the emphasis on light singularly, as well as on light as it hits parts of the body.

Ultimately, this chapter is about encouraging you to be diligently alert and receptive to the value of the light around you. Being passionate about light is part of what makes us photographers. Learning how to use light to your best advantage edifies that role.

PORTRAIT LIGHTING, ESPECIALLY when we think of it as a natural source that simply exists around us, can be somewhat intimidating. Not only do we have to consider the technical function of the camera, we also have to take into account the technical characteristics of light, such as color and intensity, its quality and placement, and how it affects the message of your photograph. That's quite a few balls to juggle before snapping a single image. Many folks think that the studio environment is overly complicated, but finding good natural portrait light can also be a difficult task. That's why it helps to train your eye to identify great portrait light all around you.

I advise seeking out and studying dimensional light. This means the light should have the ability to create visual depth. For example, I enjoy shooting portraits with light coming into a room from a large window (**Figure 15.1**). When the portrait subject is placed near the window, one side of the face features a soft light that transitions into shadow on the other side. The presence of shadow alongside light creates dimension. It gives us a sense of how the face is shaped, as well as how it fits into the rest of the environment. Light and shadow are extremely important visual elements that create depth and give your image visual nuance.

Of course, not all light is soft window light, but all light can be dimensional. Harsh, late-afternoon light can create a starkness that is fitting for portraits made in the desert (**Figure 15.2**). Extremely soft, diffused light can be very useful to highlight the smoothness of a baby's head (**Figure 15.3**). The key is to always be looking for good light and knowing how to recognize it.

So, how do you go about identifying the best light for your subjects? By using your eyes, that's how!

OK, that may sound a bit overly simple and sarcastic, but it's amazing what the untrained eye misses when it comes to photographic light. My family thinks I'm crazy, but every time we go to a restaurant, I'll select a table next to a window, just to see how the light pours across the faces of those sitting with me. I love finding new areas for great natural light, and I encourage you to be alert to the possibility of finding them as well. Analyze the characteristics of that light. Would you define it as a soft light? A harsh light? How about the source of the light itself: is it the sun alone? Or, is the sunlight indirectly pouring through a window? Is the light bright and are the shadows very dark? Is there anything reflecting light into the shadows? Is there an interesting or troublesome color cast to the light, and if so, where is it coming from? Asking yourself why the light that you are seeing is conducive—or not—for portraiture is one of the most important ways to continue growing as a photographer. Light is, after all, the basis for photography!

The remainder of this chapter will focus on concepts that reinforce this notion of being diligently alert to identifying possible ways to use natural portrait light. The following pages will introduce several ways of working with and manipulating light per our technical (camera) limitations and our aesthetic (creative) desires. The chapter also provides a great foundation for working with artificial light sources, which are modeled on existing natural light conditions.

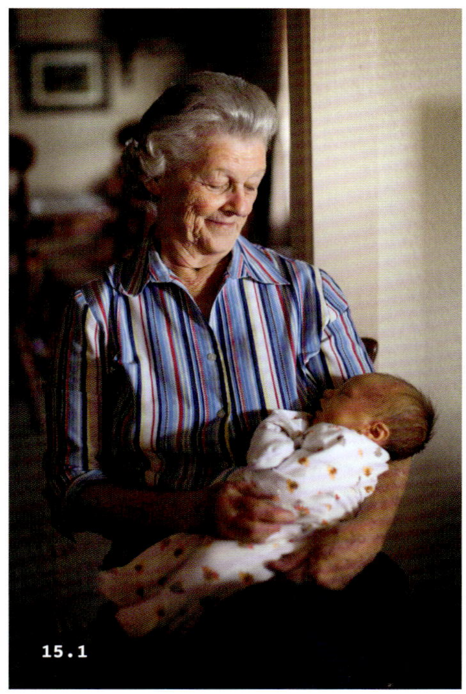

15.1

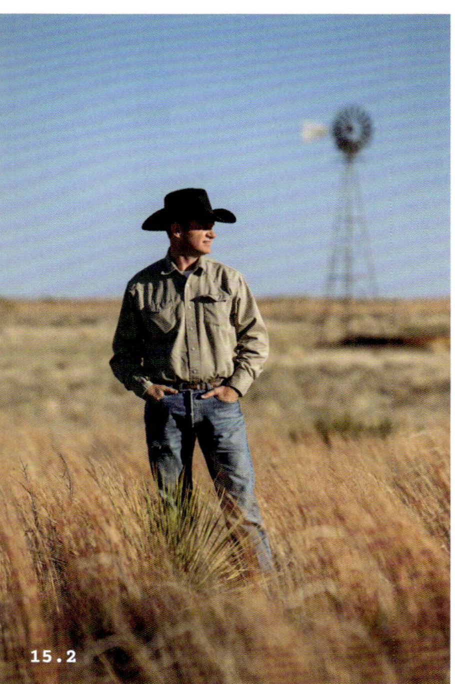

15.2

15.1 I love environments that are lit by great window light. This type of light is diffused, and creates ambiance and visual depth. I couldn't pass up this sweet portrait of my grandmother holding my nephew as they both sat in the light of a farmhouse window.
ISO 400; 1/125 sec.; f/1.6; 50mm

15.2 Direct sunlight in the afternoon or early evening might be the most appropriate light to convey the story of an environment, such as this dramatic light on the Texas high plains, a place mostly void of trees and water.
ISO 100; 1/1000 sec.; f/4.5; 200mm

15.3 Soft window light is lovely when gently wrapped around a baby's or young child's head and face. The light shows off depth, and its qualities match the peaceful, innocent characteristics of such a subject.
ISO 400; 1/400 sec.; f/1.2; 50mm

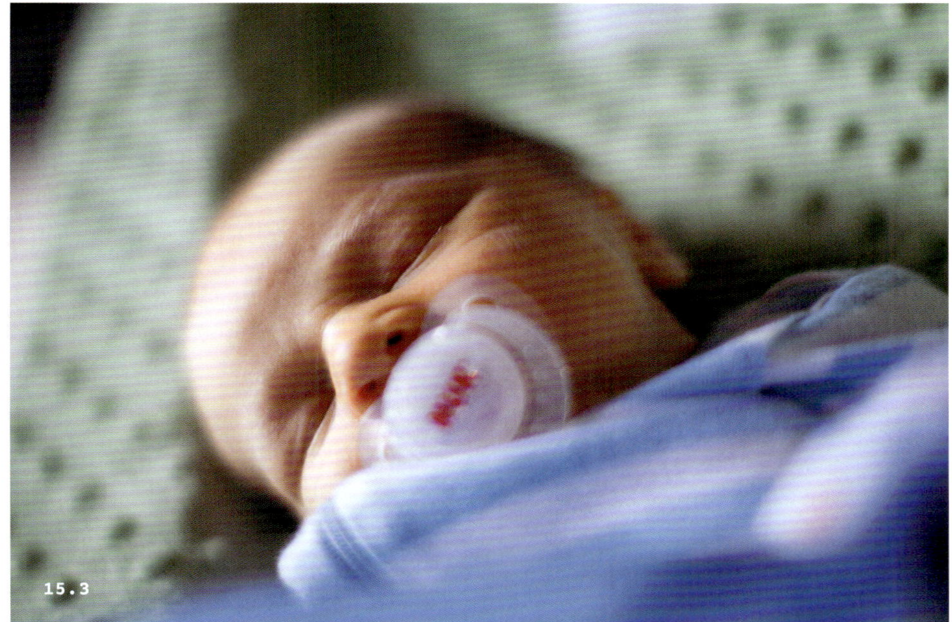

15.3

ONE THING THAT differs between natural light photography and the artificially lit studio environment is your ability to manipulate the position of your light source(s). It's quite easy to move an artificial light, but impossible to move the sun.

With natural light portraiture, two considerations are the direction from which the light source is hitting your subject and your position relative to the light source. When you started out in photography, you probably thought that as long as the light was behind you, you'd make a decent image. However, the direction from which the light source hits the portrait subject is one of the primary determinants of the light's dimensionality. When the light is over your shoulder, you are essentially using what is called on-axis lighting. All of the shadows will be thrown behind the subject, nowhere to be seen in the image. This effect flattens the depth of the subject, and it can be quite unappealing and undynamic (**Figure 16.1** and **Figure 16.2**).

One of the most interesting aspects of using light specifically is the ability to create and utilize shadows. Therefore, be sure to consider the direction of the light source as it hits your subject. Right before a shoot starts, when the subject is on location, imagine what the light will look like as if it were moving around him. Better yet, make the subject spin around slowly as you visually study the way the light hits him. No matter your position, making the subject turn to or away from the light source will reveal different shadow detail (**Figure 16.3** and

Figure 16.4). Do the shadows become more noticeable? When do they tend to recede or disappear? Take note of how the shadows fall. Shadows pull the viewer's eye into the image, and aid your photograph in telling its narrative.

Remember your spinning subject? What if you spun around, too, always facing your subject? Not only would you see a change in shadow characteristic, you would also see dramatic change in the amount of shadow and background in the image (**Figure 16.5**, **Figure 16.6**, and **Figure 16.7**). For example, when you turn to a point where the light is hitting your subject at a 45-degree angle from behind and to the side, the shadows will become evident on the face. Depending on how high the sun is in the sky, the light might create a classic loop or Rembrandt style for your portrait. At 90 degrees to the side, you will notice the light covers half of the face, leaving the other half in shadow. This hatchet lighting is popular when conveying naturally dramatic, sometimes aggressive characteristics.

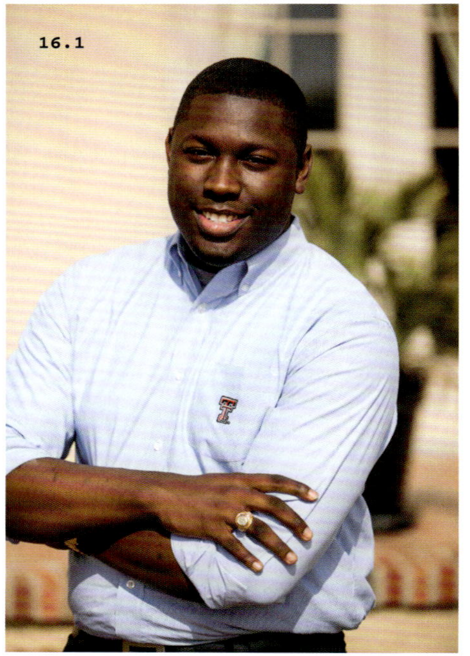

16.1

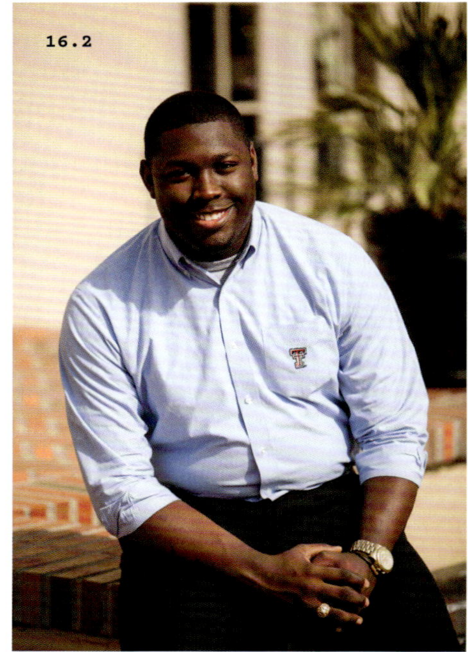

16.2

16.1 On-axis lighting throws shadows back from the subject, eliminating depth and dimension. This shot was made with direct sunlight that, although behind me, was at a high angle in the sky, providing shadow underneath features such as the nose, chin, and arms.
ISO 100; 1/3200 sec.; f/2.8; 125mm

16.2 Turning the subject and myself nearly 90 degrees off-axis (away from the sun) created dimensional shadows on the subject's face.
ISO 100; 1/3200 sec.; f/2.8; 140mm

16.3 Positioning your subject relative to the light source will determine where shadows fall. In this portrait, the light source is hitting Preston nearly straight on, so his shadow is straight back and a bit toward the camera.
ISO 100; 1/800 sec.; f/4; 64mm

16.4 Simply rotating Preston's head toward the camera changes how the light hits his face. Now, it's hitting him from the left, and a new arrangement of shadows adds different dimensionality to the face.

16.5 Visualize the light by looking at your subject as you rotate with them, changing your own position relative to the light source. On-axis, over-the-shoulder light lacks defini-tion, but is useful when the entire front of the face needs to be lit.
ISO 100; 1/1600 sec.; f/4; 64mm

16.6 Positioning your subject with the light behind them makes for soft light on the front of them and great backlight behind them. However, depending on your background, you may have issues with exposure.
ISO 100; 1/400 sec.; f/4; 64mm

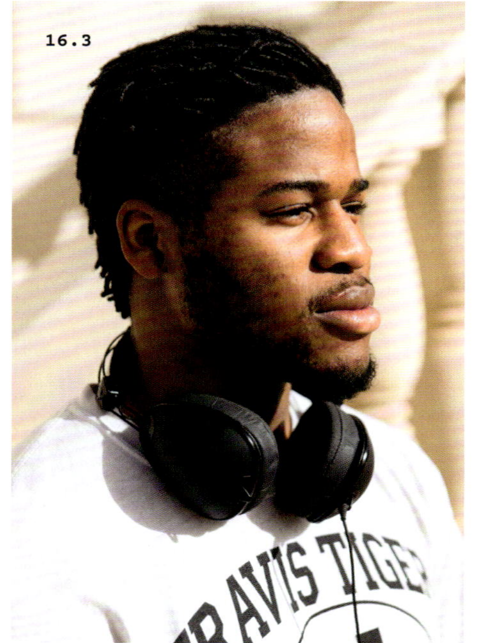

16.3

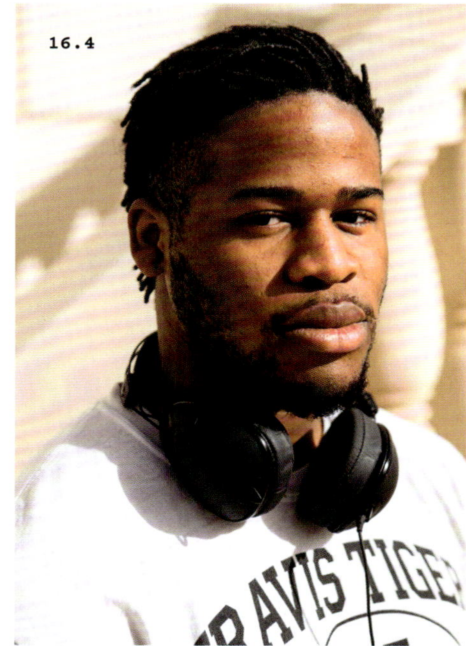

16.4

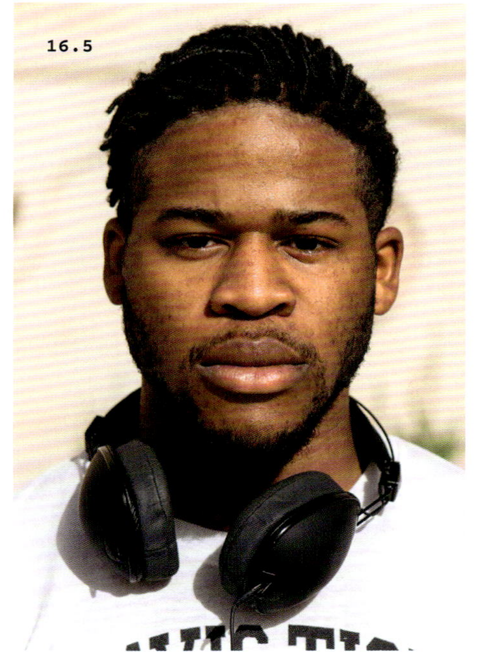

16.5

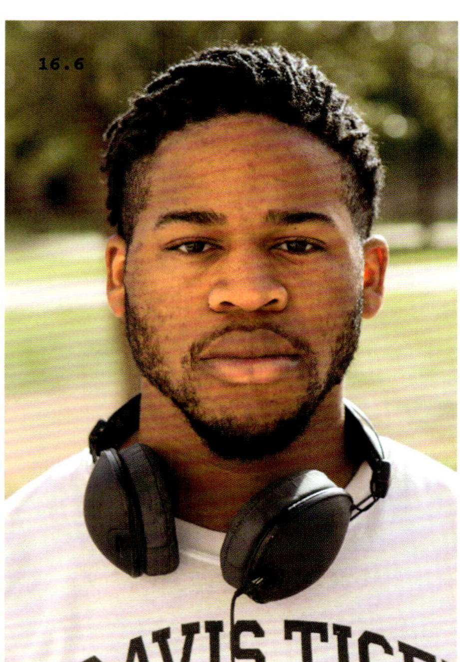

16.6

At 180 degrees, the light is simply behind the subject, and in front of you. When the camera is positioned appropriately, this is useful lighting for a silhouette.

The point is to be extremely cognizant of the direction from which the light source hits your subject and your relative position to it. Pay attention to how the shadows appear and what they are saying about your image. To create dimension in your portraits, position your subject and yourself so you're using off-axis light. Off-axis light does *not* come from straight over your shoulder to hit your subject square in the face. Off-axis light creates visible shadow, and as a result, creates contrast and emotion in your imagery.

On-axis light has its appeal, but for the most part, you are probably better off using some form of off-axis light, in which a lit side *and* a shadowed side of the face are evident. You can turn a portrait subject's face away from the light source, letting the shadows fall toward the camera (we call this short lighting), or use light that is just off-axis from center, where the shadows fall away from the camera (we call this broad lighting). There are varying degrees to how short or broad the lighting for a portrait might be, but ultimately, it's about creative appeal and storytelling.

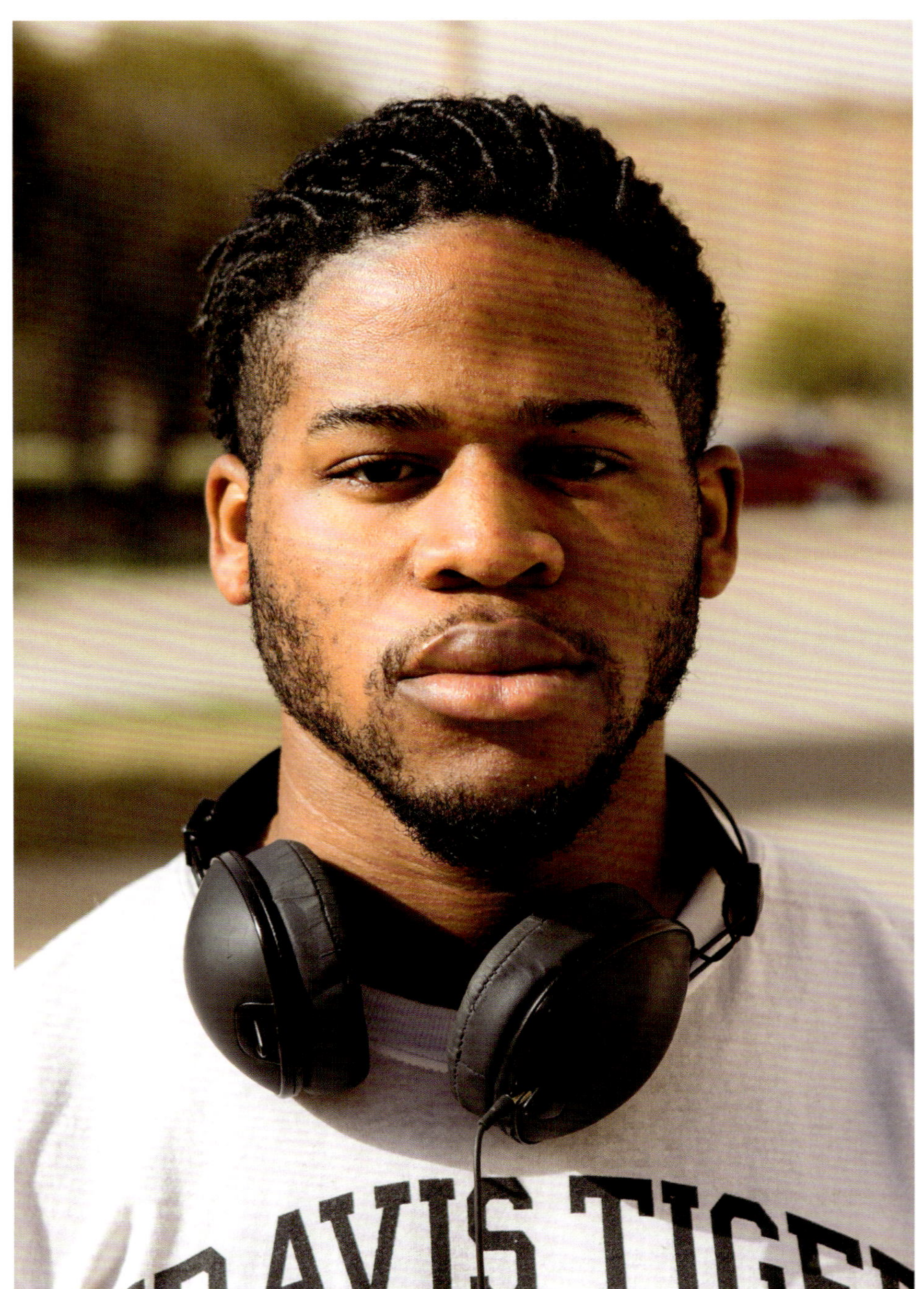

16.7 As your position changes relative to the light, as well as to your subject's position, the shadows in the portrait will convey a great deal of meaning. This hatchet (side) lighting, created by placing your subject at a 90-degree angle to the light, is considered a dramatic way to use the light to convey intrigue, attitude, or undefined edginess about your subject.
ISO 100; 1/640 sec.; f/4; 64mm

Use Golden Hour Light

The golden hours—the hour after the sun rises and the hour before it sets—is often *the* light photographers want to work with. This light is naturally warmer and somewhat softer than midday light since it's diffused by atmospheric debris (dust, smog, moisture) that exists closer to the earth. Daytime light between the golden hours shines at a different angle and cuts through less of this debris, and is often more intense than the camera's sensor can handle, making over- or underexposure more likely (**Figure 16.8**).

Golden hour light is also the most dimensional light. Take a look at the shadows the next time you are shooting during the last hour of the day. Since the angle of the sun is lower in the sky, the shadows it creates are elongated, and thus have more depth. Light from this angle also helps us avoid distracting shadows on the eyes created by the subject's eyebrows. For that matter, any shadow created by the protrusions of the human face look more natural and less problematic during the golden hours than any other time of the day.

I like to describe golden hour light as tangible. It helps provide the appearance of a third dimension in the image while using a two-dimensional medium, and its warmth is extremely attractive. It doesn't hurt to scout a location before a shoot to see the potential such warm light will have for your portrait subject. Although you only have approximately one hour of really great direct light to work with, a bit of preparation and vision can make that golden hour a productive one!

`16.8` The warmth of the light hitting the children is a result of the sun's rays passing through the densest parts of the atmosphere near the earth's horizon. This golden hour shot was made 10 minutes before sunset, when the sunlight was near its warmest and softest.
`ISO 100; 1/1000 sec.; f/2; 50mm`

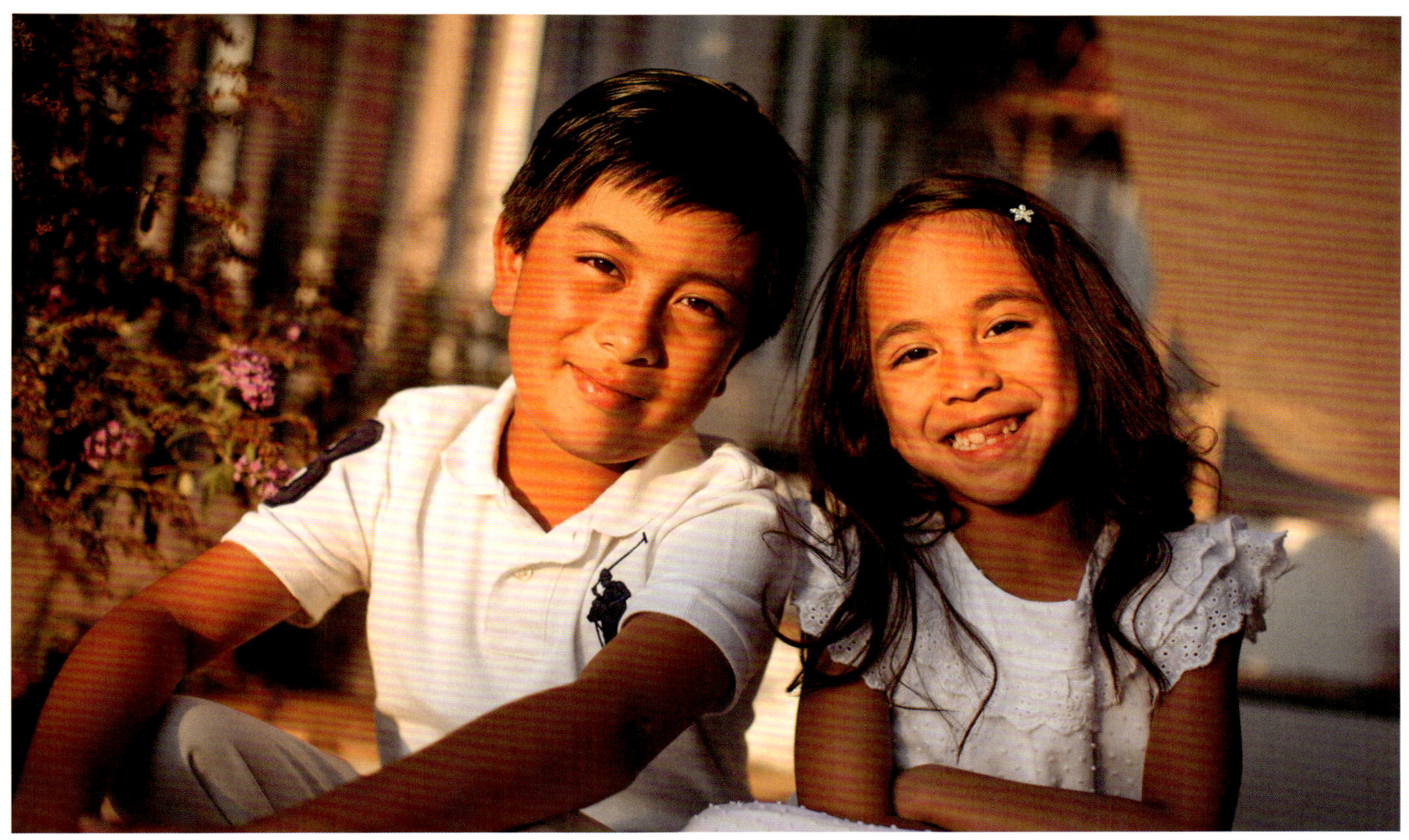

LIGHT QUALITY DESCRIBES the hardness or softness of the light. Most practically, the quality of the light refers to how hard the transition from light to shadow is on your portrait subject. Like many things in photography, the quality of light exists on a ranging continuum from very hard, where the shadows are blocky and sharp, to so soft that the shadows do not appear at all. Luckily, we have three general terms that describe points of light quality. We refer to these as the three degrees of diffusion.

Direct light, the first degree of light quality, is unimpeded light from the sun. This type of light is usually very intense, and its shadows are very hard-edged. Essentially, you could take a marker and draw the line that separates the shadowed side of the subject from the lit side. This type of light is very natural, and can be used to convey rawness and attitude (**Figure 17.1**). It can, however, be somewhat unattractive for certain types of portraiture, such as headshots and beauty shots, since the shadows create structures on the subject's face and form.

Diffused light, the second degree of diffusion, is the exact opposite of direct light. Shadows become increasingly non-existent the more diffused the light is. Diffused light bounces off of all surfaces from many angles, mitigating any strong directional characteristic of the light. Light essentially fills everything, so shadows are not apparent as a result. An overcast day, in which light from the sun travels through thick layers of moisture in the air, is a perfect scenario for using diffused light. This type of light is ideal for simple portraiture of just about anyone, and is especially great for children, females, and families (**Figure 17.2**). Since shadows are filled in by diffused light from every direction, this kind of light is great for blemished or heavily wrinkled faces. Although diffused light is the type of light that can be useful for just about any portraiture, it does lack a degree of dimension and emotional appeal for a great deal of editorial or story-driven portraiture.

The third degree of light quality, and the most often used, is *directionally diffused* light. Directionally diffused light sits between direct and diffused (hence the name). Directionally diffused light *is* the continuum on which the other two qualities of light anchor. Characteristically, directionally diffused light offers a lit side and a shadowed side to the portrait subject, but the transition from one to the other is soft and less delineated (**Figure 17.3**) than that of direct light. It offers the best of both worlds: dimension-creating light and shadow; and soft enough light to relieve those not-so-great attributes on face and form. We are most often exposed to portraits shot with directionally diffused light, from family-style portraits to editorial, on-location environmental portraits. Directionally diffused light comes in a variety of forms, and was used in many of the portraits you see in this book. It's little wonder a great deal of research and development in the artificial, studio lighting industry is geared toward creating a range of light modifiers that help us replicate this type of light.

So, what is the real difference between these three degrees of diffusion? Directionally diffused light is found in all sorts of places naturally (as we'll discuss in the next tip), but it's created by increasing the size of the light source relative to your subject until the light is completely diffused. Simply put, the smaller a light source is relative to your subject, the harder the light, meaning the more defined the shadow becomes. As the light source increases in size, the softer the light, or shadows, become. For example, direct light is very hard and the source (in natural light portraiture) is often the sun. We all know the sun to be this large glob of fire some 93 million miles away; however, to the eye (and relative to your subject's head), it is extremely small. The surface space of the sun is not large enough for light to have any wrap-around if, say, the sun was at a 70-degree angle to your subject. Although very powerful, the sun is a relatively small light source. Diffused light, created naturally by overcast conditions, is essentially free of shadows because the clouds act as one large light modifier, increasing the size of the light source to be as big as the sky!

Keep in mind that even though the three degrees of diffusion simply specify *light quality*, one is not better than the other. Light quality simply refers to a characteristic of the light. All qualities of light work well in some situation. Direct light may be great for creating a portrait in a desert to connote the starkness and heat of the environment, but it might not be great to showcase the innocence of a young child. To each their own, they say, when it comes to style and approach, but it helps to be aware of where and when to find great light.

I advise seeking out and using directionally diffused light when appropriate for two reasons. First, it's simply a great type of light for just about anything, from fashion and family photography to editorial and corporate portraiture. It's dimensional, emotional, and easy to visually consume. Second, directionally diffused light is all around us. Seeking it out and finding varying levels of it is great visual practice for a portrait photographer. Check out the next tip for more on finding and using this extraordinary type of portrait light!

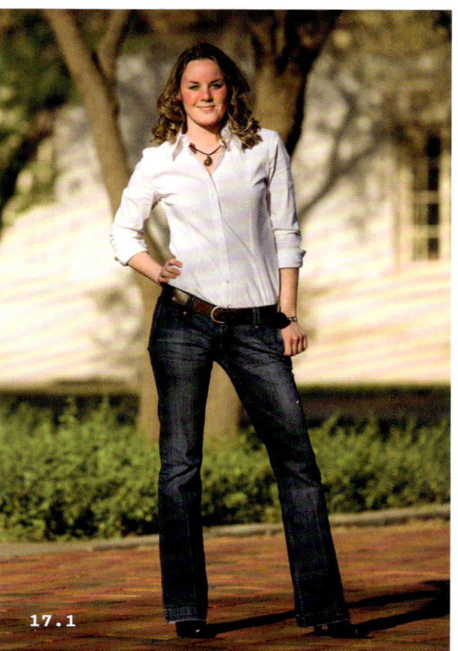

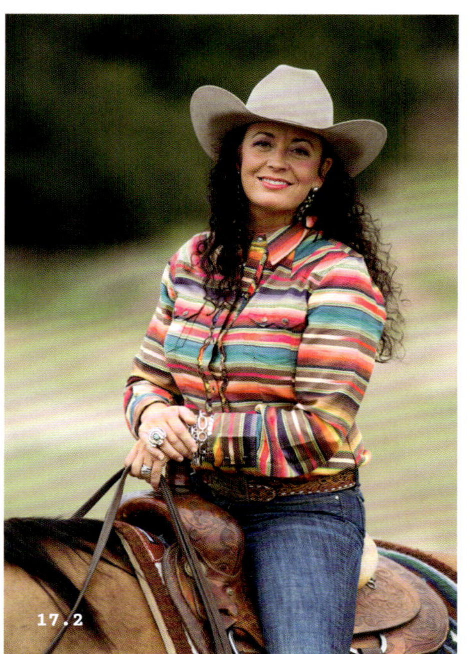

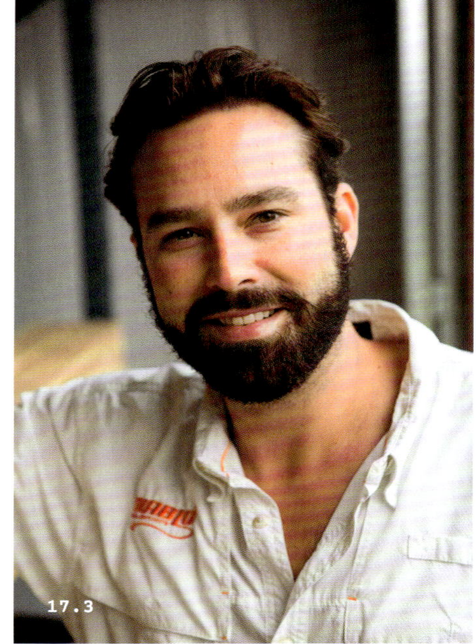

17.1 Direct light is visually defined by dark, hard-edged shadows (e.g., the shadow on the subject's nose). In natural light portraiture, these shadows are most often created by the sun.
ISO 100; 1/1250 sec.; f/4; 200mm

17.2 Cloud cover creates diffused light, and it naturally dissipates shadows. This type of light is especially useful for fashion, young children, and females.
ISO 400; 1/250 sec.; f/4; 300mm

17.3 Diffused light still has direction, but the transition between light and shadow on your subject is much softer than hard, direct light. You can see the gradual change of light intensity crossing the subject's forehead, nose, and form.
ISO 100; 1/200 sec.; f/3.2; 70mm

18. USE WINDOW LIGHT

I IMAGINE SOME of your favorite natural light portraits are made with window light. Portrait photographers just can't get enough of it! Window light is a form of directionally diffused light that not only allows a photographer to use great light while working indoors, but it also refers to directionally diffused light found in external environments. Call it a poor man's studio lighting, but goodness is it nice (**Figure 18.1**).

Window light creates beautiful directionally diffused light *only* if the light coming in through the window is *indirect*. This means the sun cannot actually be shining through the window onto your subject. That would be direct light. Indirect sunlight coming through an opening such as a window bathes your subject in less intense light, which can help control exposure of other non-sunlit areas in the frame. And, because the window is almost always larger than the sun relative to the size of your subject, the light will have a soft quality.

Just as the previous section states, the quality of light changes based on the size of the light. This holds true for window light, as well. Window light is a bit easier to previsualize and work with in this case. A small window will offer a harder directionally diffused light than a large window (**Figure 18.2** and **Figure 18.3**). Likewise, moving a subject farther away from a window of any size will make that window a smaller, harder light source. If you want that extremely smooth directionally diffused light, find a relatively large window (a four-by-six-foot window) and move your subject closer to it until you are happy with the quality of light (**Figure 18.4** and **Figure 18.5**). As you do, the surface space of the light source will shine on areas of the face otherwise covered in shadow by facial features (the nose, eyebrows, cheeks, etc.) and fill them in with light.

Natural window light is relatively controllable, as long as the sun is up, since you can change the subject's distance and position to the light source. Place your subject with the window parallel to their line of sight, and have them face you. This gives you soft hatchet (or side) lighting (**Figure 18.6**). Turn your subject toward the window and the lighting more closely resembles a classic loop lighting scenario (**Figure 18.7**). Place your subject below the center of the window, and you'll achieve an artistic Rembrandt style.

The term "window light" doesn't just apply to light coming through windows. The same *type* of light—that nice, directionally diffused portrait light—exists as long as indirect light is serving as the primary, or key, light source for your portrait. Outside, the first place I look to recreate this type of light is open shade (**Figure 18.8**). The shadowed side of a building is a great place to start. Even on overcast days, being close to the side of a large structure can be enough to create light and shadow across your subject's face and body. I look for doorways, archways, caves, and just about anything that opens up into indirect light. The idea here is to have a more intense, but indirect, primary source of light hitting your subject from one side and some sort of structure that essentially blocks that same light from hitting the other side.

In review, window (indirect, open shade) lighting is good. A word of caution: for the most part, it is distracting to include the actual light source in the image (**Figure 18.9**). Unless you have a really good compositional or narrative reason for including the actual window in the portrait, it's best to leave it out. More than likely, the window will be overexposed, and it might not fit the portrait very well. I encourage you to avoid this visual distraction if possible and conceptually appropriate.

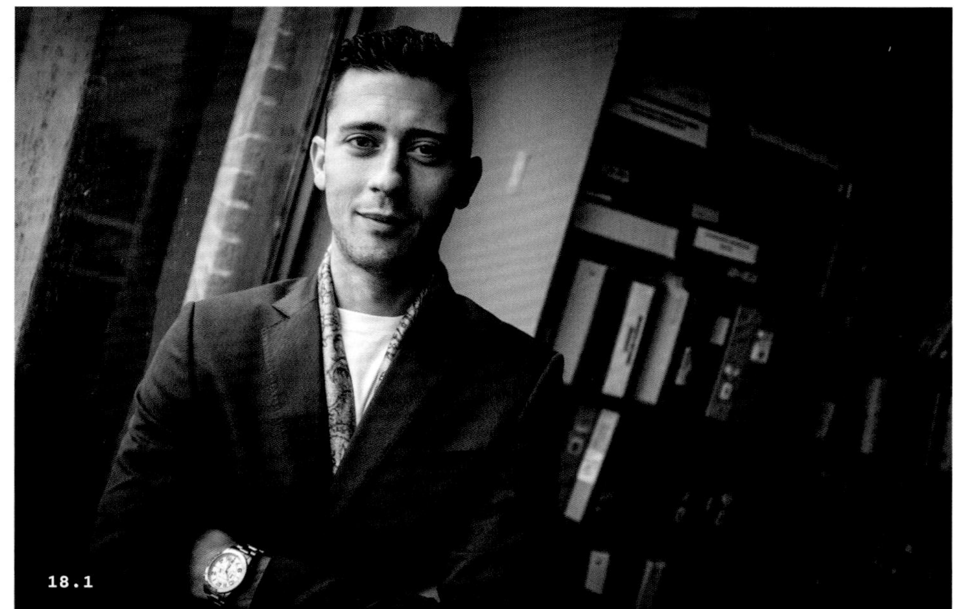

18.1

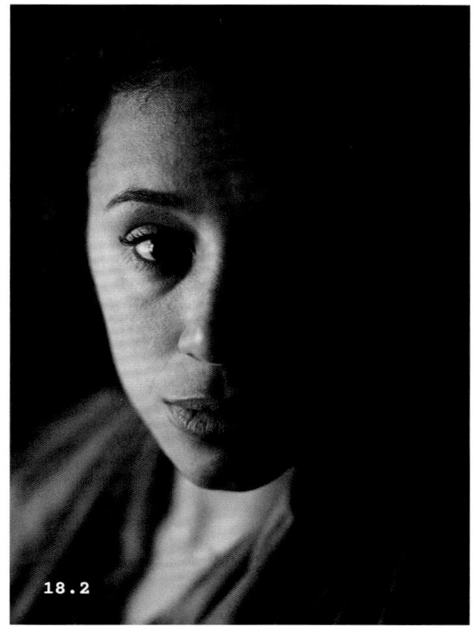

18.2

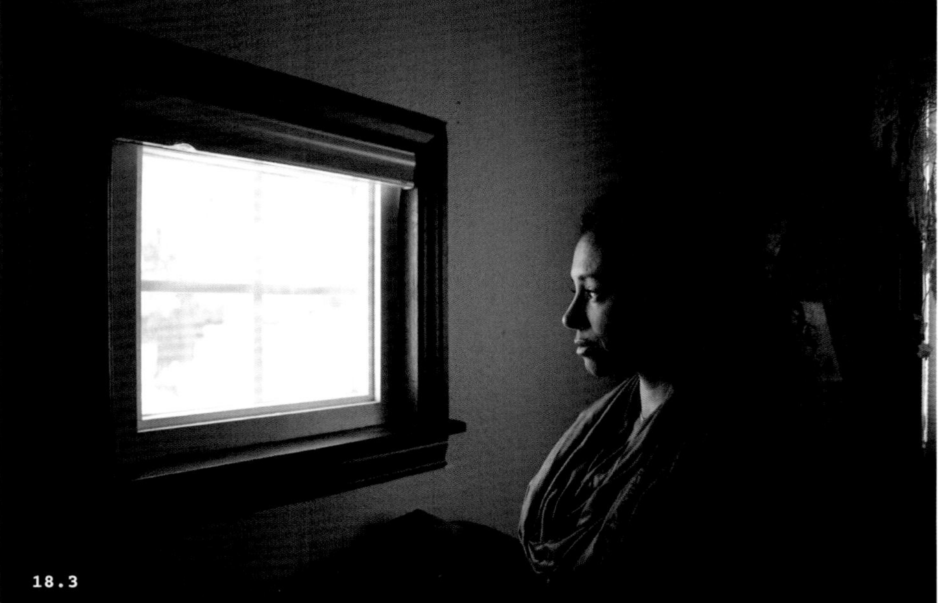

18.3

18.1 Floor-to-ceiling windows are great directionally diffused light sources. I couldn't help but make a portrait of my friend Anthony as he stood in front of a wall of these windows.
ISO 400; 1/150 sec.; f/2; 23mm

18.2 Although directionally diffused, the light hitting the subject is hard, and high in contrast since the window is relatively small compared to the subject (see **Figure 18.3**).
ISO 200; 1/160 sec.; f/1.8; 85mm

18.3 Compared to an adult subject's body, an 18-inch square window is a rather small light source.

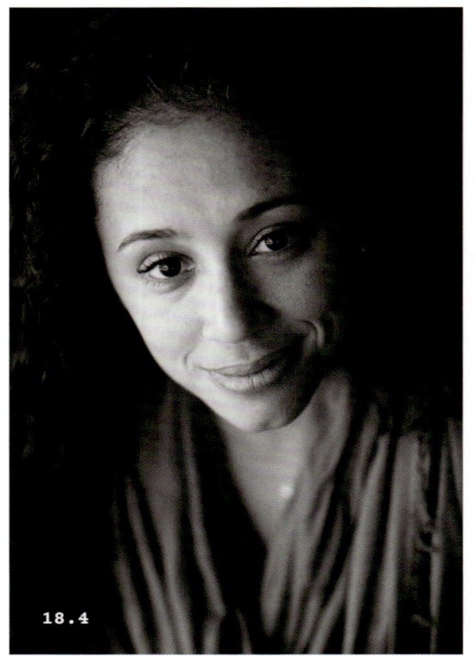

18.4

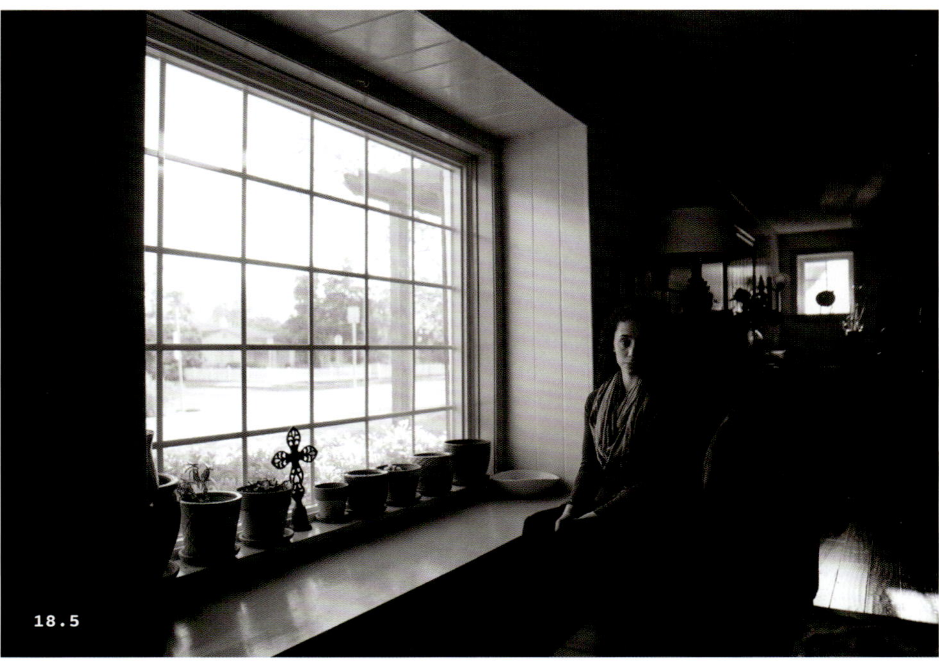

18.5

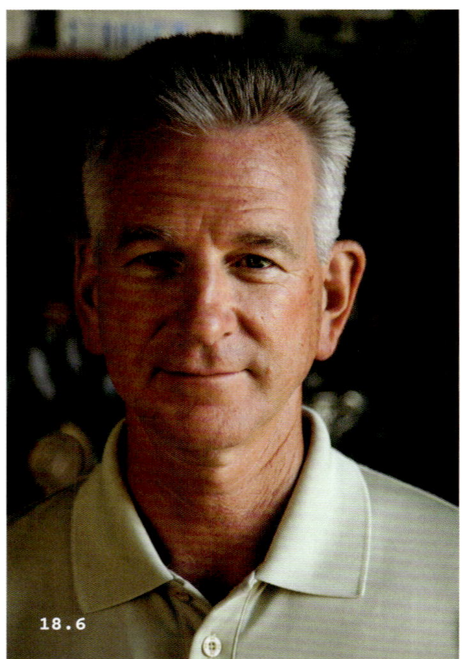

18.6

18.4 Increasing the size of the window increases the amount of coverage on your subject (see **Figure 18.5**). It also softens shadows, an effect that can be very appealing for general portraiture.
ISO 200; 1/160 sec.; f/1.8; 85mm

18.5 The closer your subject is to a light source (such as a window), the softer the light will be. I'm attracted to photographing my subject at one end of large windows so they can be turned in to the expanse of light.

18.6 To provide NCAA football coach Tommy Tuberville a masculine look based on light alone, I turned him parallel to the large window in his office. This created a soft light that transitioned into darker shadow straight down the middle of his face.
ISO 800; 1/100 sec.; f/4; 105mm

18.7 Turning the bride away from the camera and toward the large window allowed more light to hit the shadowed side of her form to close the shadow of her nose neatly under her right nostril. This shadow is the indicator of the classic Loop lighting style.
ISO 400; 1/50 sec.; f/2.8; 200mm

18.8 In this portrait, I placed professional speaker Gary Schwantz against a wall that blocked direct sunlight from hitting him, leaving open, indirect light from the sky as the primary, directionally diffused light source.
ISO 100; 1/1250 sec.; f/2; 85mm

18.9 A window can often be overexposed to the point that it detracts from the image more than it contributes. It's often best to leave window light sources out of the frame and let the light do the talking.
ISO 400; 1/50 sec.; f/5.6; 45mm

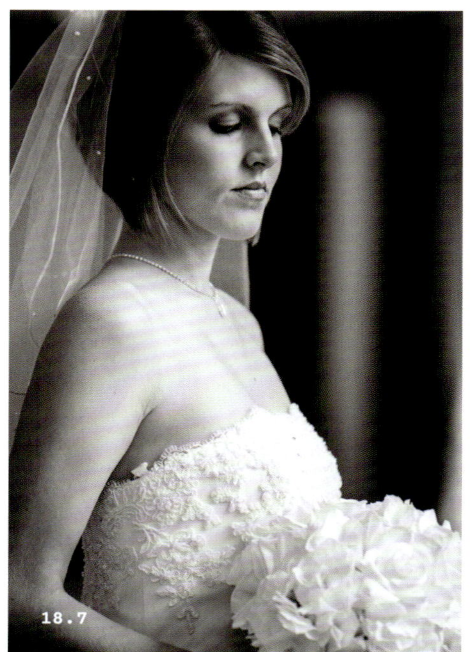

18.7

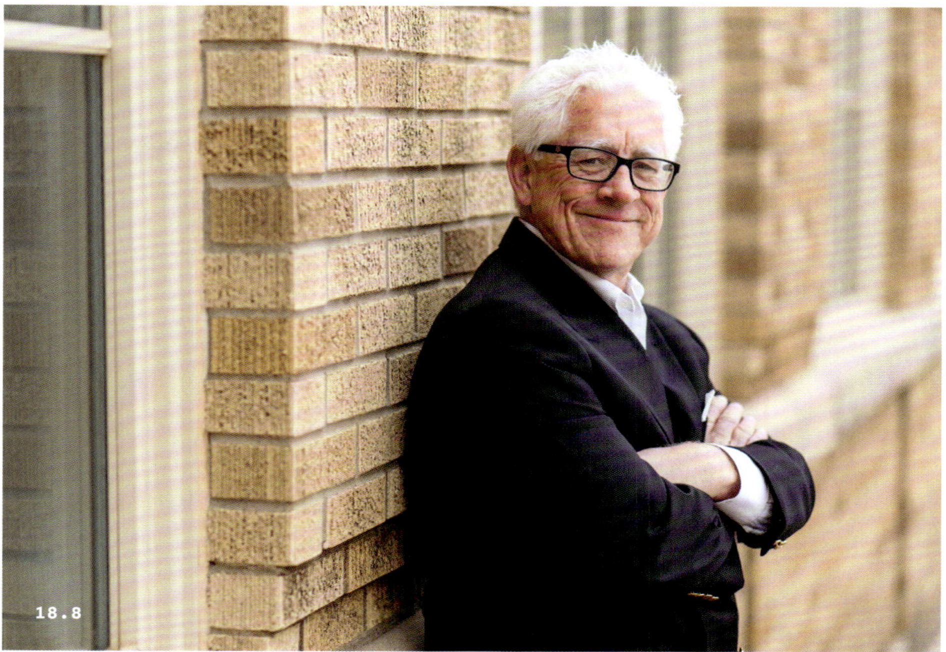

18.8

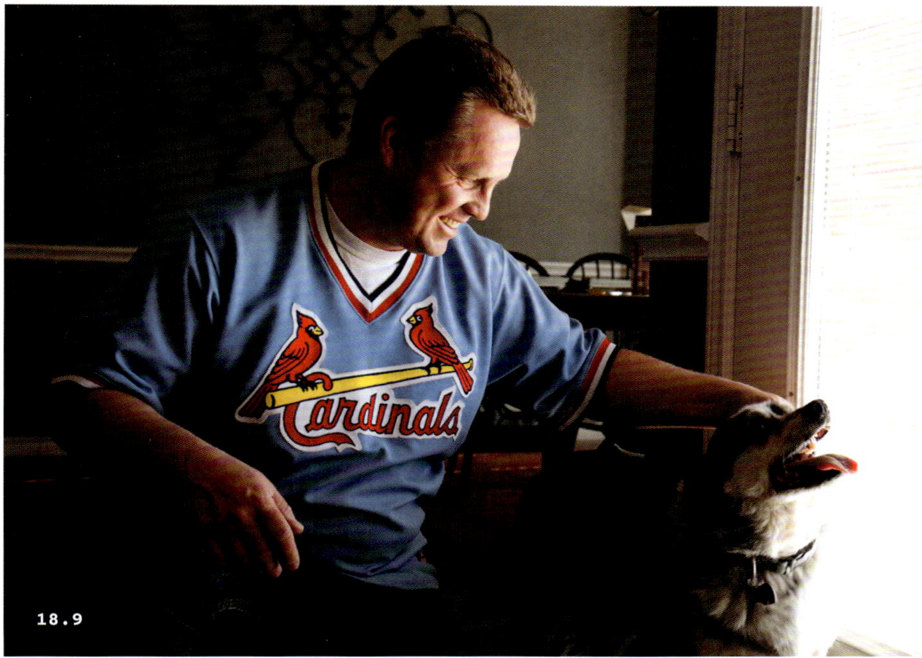

18.9

Share Your Best Window-Light Shot!

Once you've captured a shot with great window light, share it with the *Enthusiast's Guide* community! Follow @EnthusiastsGuides and post your image to Instagram, using the hashtag *#EGWindowLight.* Search that hashtag to be inspired and see other photographers' shots, as well.

19. ADD BACKLIGHT FOR SEPARATION AND AFFECT

WHEN IT COMES to creating dimension with light, nothing stands out like good use of backlight. Otherwise called kicker light, backlight helps separate the subject from an abstract or busy background, creates depth to the face and body of a subject (even if what is backlit is actually out of focus), and looks cool (**Figure 19.1**). Backlight, depending on how intense it is and how much of it shows up on the subject, can be an aggressive, dramatic light that provides a certain type of edge to the portrait.

Technically, backlight is comprised of a light source hitting your portrait subject in the back with a certain amount of light that wraps around onto her face and body. Typically backlighting is brighter than the primary light, which helps stop the eye from wandering into the background (**Figure 19.2**). Backlight is also often used on the shadowed side of your subject if she is lit from the front, mostly to keep the shadow from merging too much with the background (**Figure 19.3**). Backlight can appear on one or both sides of the subject, and it can even appear from above, although we usually refer to this as hair light (**Figure 19.4**).

Speaking of hair, backlight is great for it! Hair has a great reflective quality that allows it to shine when hit slightly from behind, above, or to the side (**Figure 19.5**). If your subject is blessed with voluminous locks, the effect is further exaggerated. Not only are you backlighting for dimension and separation, you

are gaining a bit of "glow" for the portrait. Likewise, backlight is nice for defining jawlines (**Figure 19.6**). I tend to favor subtler backlighting that pronounces the outline of a face or body, but it can still be quite effective when the light is fairly harsh.

Finding backlight can sometimes be frustrating, so it helps to have an idea of how we identify it or generate it in natural light portraiture. In the studio, all you need to do is set up another artificial light, but you have to hunt for it when you're shooting elsewhere. One sure way to incorporate backlight is to turn your subject away from the primary light source (usually the sun) (**Figure 19.7**). You'll have to watch your exposure levels since backlighting will provide more contrast. You can employ this same strategy in open shade, but instead of using the sun as a backlight, you'll use the indirect light source: the sky (**Figure 19.8**). Finally, any reflective surface can serve as a backlight source. Water, windows, or, of course, a formal reflector, are all great sources for creating backlight. We'll discuss using reflectors at the end of this chapter, so keep the principles of using and identifying the direction of the light source in mind.

Before I start sounding prescriptive, let me say that *not all portraits have or need backlight*. However, it can add the technical and effective emphasis to a portrait. It provides you another way to create depth *and* emotional appeal. If it's available and appropriate, why not use it?

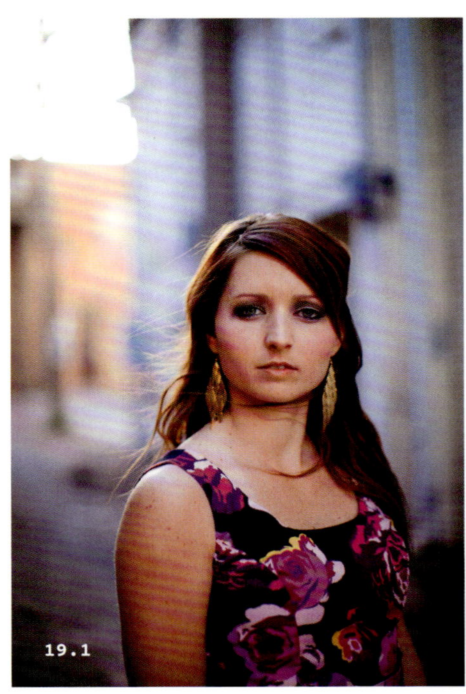

19.1 Even though the background is adequately knocked out of focus, the backlight highlighting the subject's hair and arm help further separate her from it and increase dimension in the image.
ISO 100; 1/400 sec.; f/1.4; 50mm

19.2 The backlight on this field biologist stops the viewer's gaze on the subject rather than letting it wander too far past him into the woods.
ISO 200; 1/400 sec.; f/2.8; 160mm

19.3 I reflected just enough back-light on this subject to lighten the camera-left side of her dark hair to keep it from blending into a similarly dark background.
ISO 400; 1/125 sec.; f/2.8; 175mm

19.4 While the sun was high in the sky, I pulled Roy Seiders, co-owner of Yeti Coolers, out from the shade of the building enough that the light hit the top of his head. I used a reflector to bounce sunlight back onto one side of his face to create the rest of the lighting scenario.
ISO 50; 1/200 sec.; f/2.8; 54mm

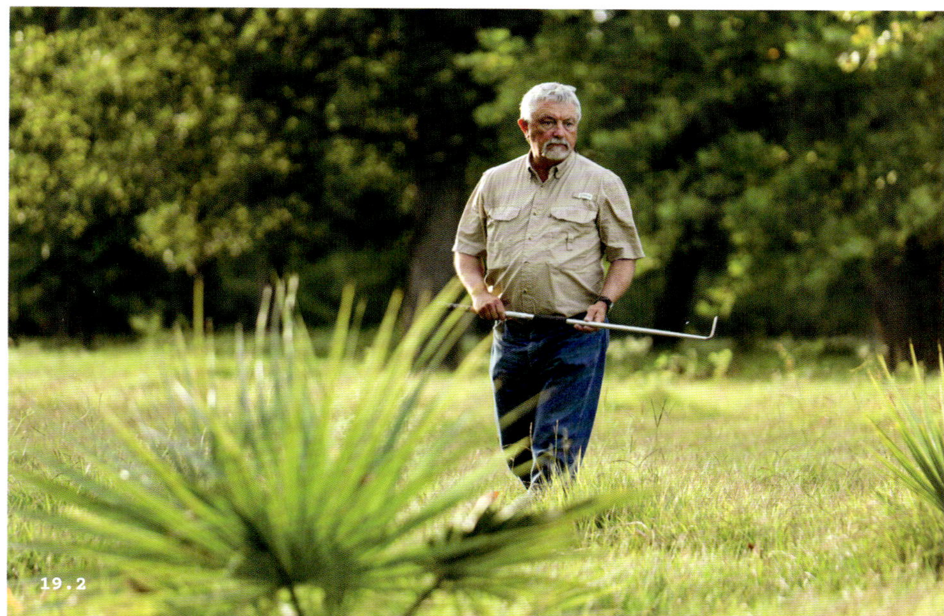

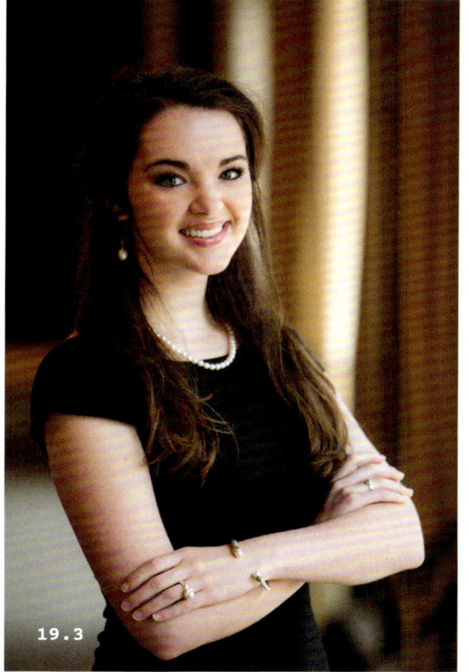

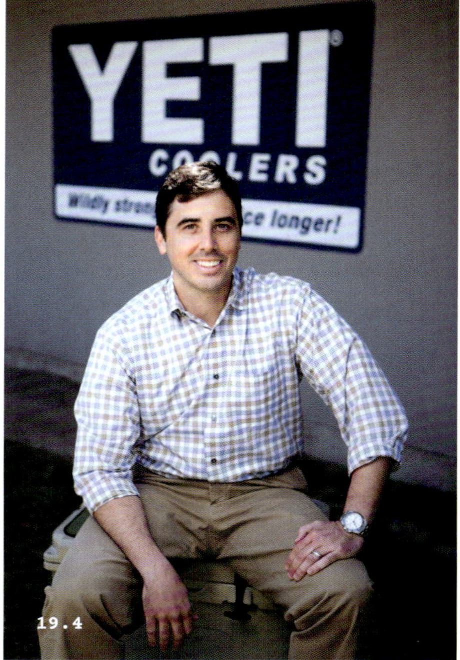

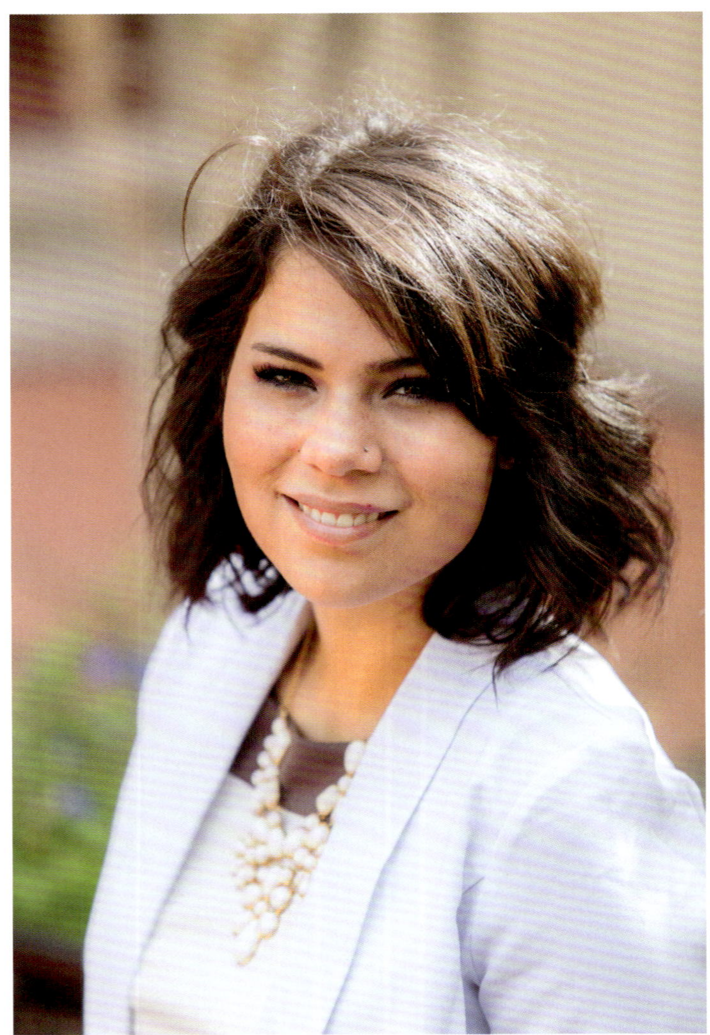

19.5 To take advantage of the subject's voluminous hair, I situated her so the sun peeked over a tall wall and backlit her without affecting the light and/or shadows on her face.
ISO 100; 1/320 sec.; f/3.2; 200mm

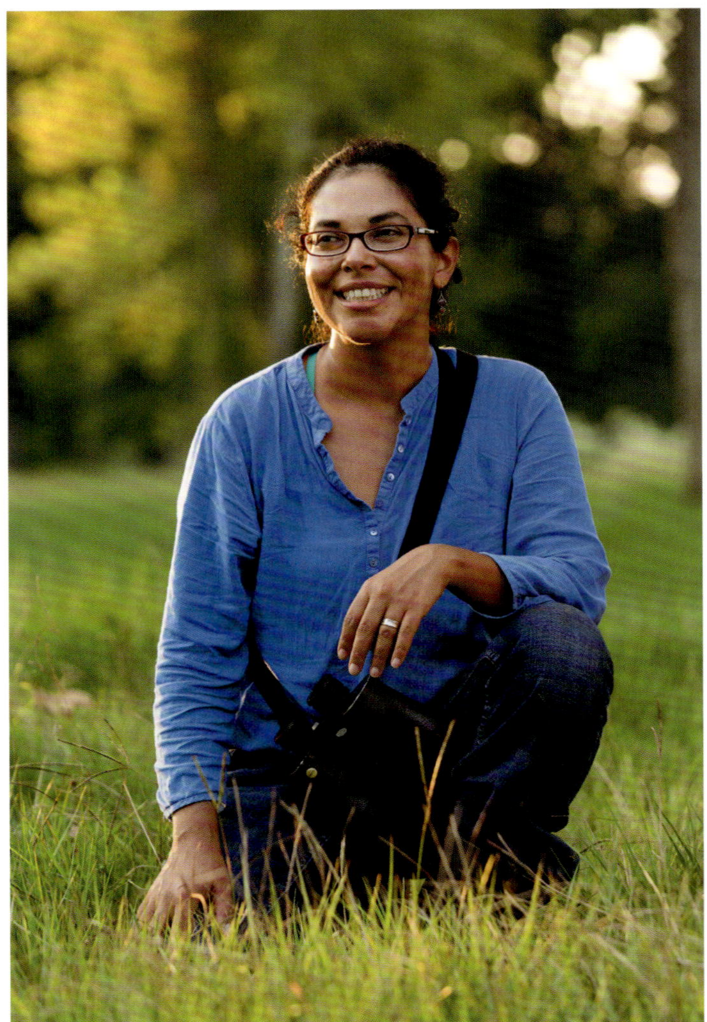

19.6 Late evening light is a great backlight because it sits low enough on the horizon to backlight facial features, like it did for this Nature Conservancy biologist's jaw line and cheeks.
ISO 400; 1/160 sec.; f/4.5; 145mm

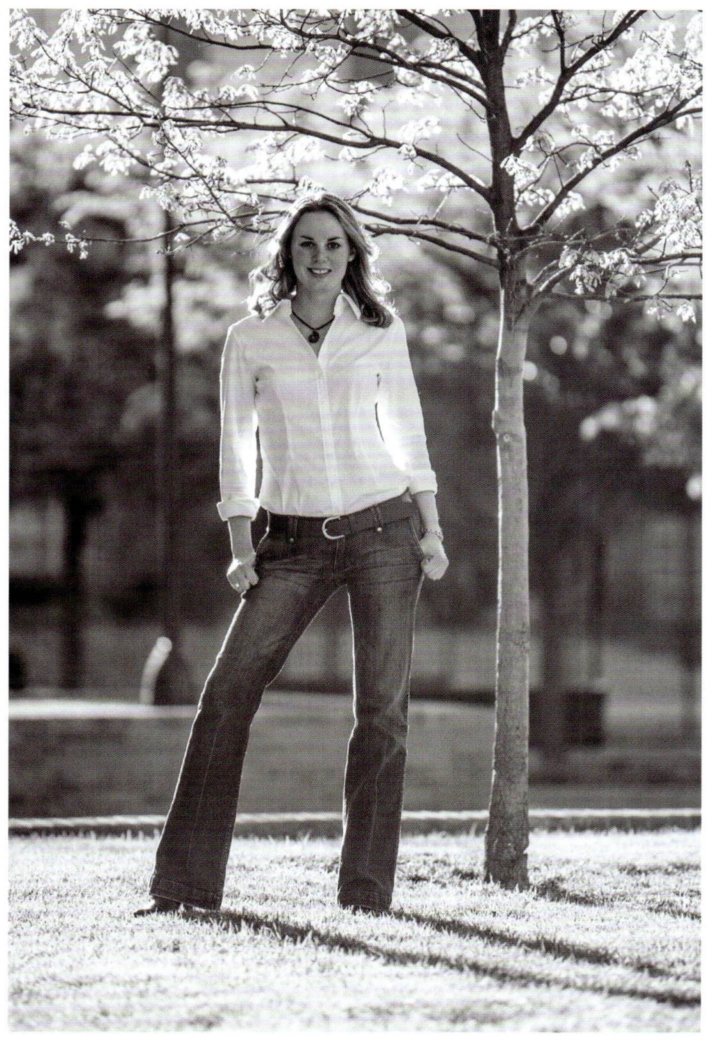

19.7 By turning the model against the early evening direct sunlight, I was able to use slightly directionally diffused lighting on her face and body, simply by shooting in her shadow. **ISO 100; 1/640 sec.; f/2.8; 200mm**

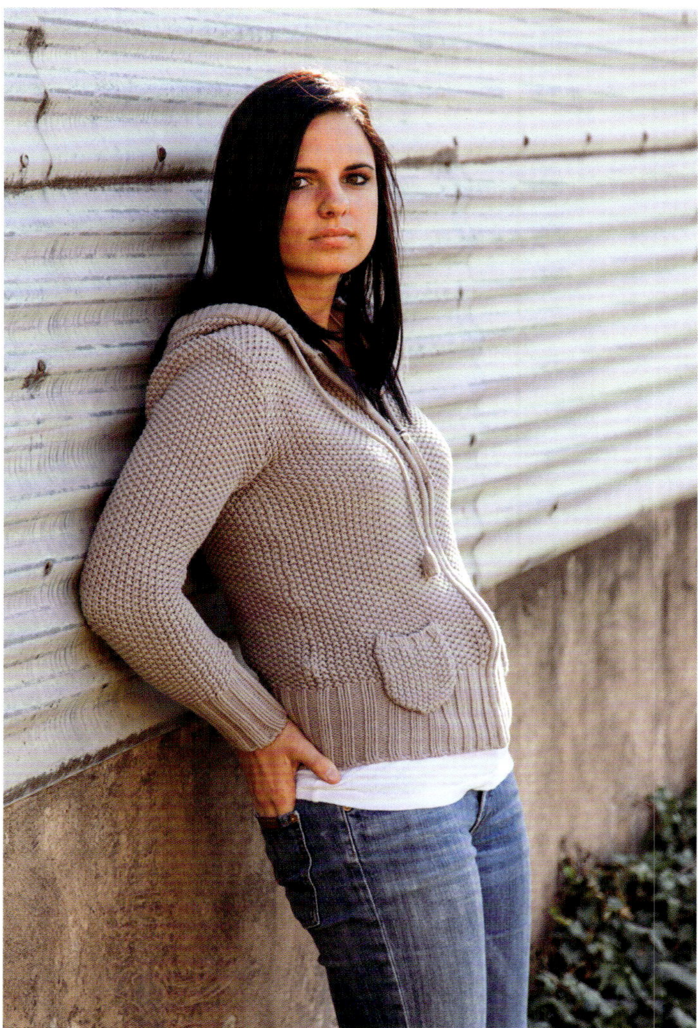

19.8 Although the top of the model's head is lit by direct light from above the structure, the subtle backlight running down her body is from the open, indirect light of the sky to camera right. **ISO 200; 1/200 sec.; f/4; 105mm**

20. CREATE FILL LIGHT

REMEMBER THAT REFLECTOR I encouraged you to buy in the previous chapter? It's one of the natural light photographer's best friends. It's certainly one of mine, and it always comes with me on my shoots. In fact, I usually have two reflectors in different sizes.

The reflector's main purpose is to reflect light in a variety of ways. Three ways that come to mind are using the reflector to create fill light, using it to create primary (key) light, and using it as a backlight.

I imagine a reflector is used most frequently as a fill-light source. A fill light is simply a source of light that helps *fill* in the shadowed side of your portrait subject (**Figure 20.1**). With a reflector, this is accomplished by placing the shiny or white surface in a way that catches a bright source of light, such as the sun, and reflects it onto the subject. If you are using the sun as a primary light at a 45-degree angle to the right of your subject, a reflector can be used to fill in light when it is placed to the left of your subject at a 45-degree angle or more. Since a reflector is typically manageable by one person or placed on a stand, it can be easily moved on axis to reflect more or less light. A reflector placed at a more drastic angle to your subject, say, at 90 degrees, will reflect more light than one placed at 45 or 30 degrees.

Using a reflector as a fill light is a great way to reduce the dramatic effect of dark shadows on the unlit portions of your subject. Keep in mind that even though the reflector is being used as a fill, it is still considered a light source, albeit a less intense one. That means that all of the characteristics of light come with it. As you move a reflector closer to your subject's shadowed side, the reflected light becomes more intense, creating less contrast between light and shadow. The opposite applies if you move it further away from your subject.

Of course, a reflector can be used in other ways. I often employ a reflector as a main or key light (**Figure 20.2**). This requires turning the subject more into the shade and reflecting the brighter light into one or both sides of her face. An example of this scenario has already been highlighted in the previous section, in which you turn your subject away from the sun, using it as a backlight. A reflector placed opposite the direction of the sun will reflect light back onto the face (**Figure 20.3** and **Figure 20.4**).

Likewise, reversing your subject's position and using the sun as your main light allows you to use the reflector to create a backlight (**Figure 20.5** and **Figure 20.6**). Since most traditional reflectors are easily bent and physically contorted, the backlight can be manipulated quite a bit to hit your subject with varying amounts of intensity and coverage.

As you can see, reflectors are very valuable to the natural light portrait photographer due to their stylistic (and physical) flexibility. Although they have been around for a long time and come in many shapes and sizes, I'm always amazed at the innovative and creative ways some photographers use them. Reflectors are one of the first things I encourage photographers to have in their "toolbox."

A stylistic word of caution: when using a reflector as a fill or key light source, don't reflect from low angles unless you are going for a ghoulish look. It's often our tendency to angle the reflector up when reflecting natural light because the sun is above us in many cases. However, this forces shadows upward, which can be quite distracting and unappealing, especially when creating a key light with the reflector (**Figure 20.7**). Certainly, there are times when reflecting from below helps, especially when we are not reflecting direct light. However, always be cognizant of the direction of the light source and the shadows it creates. Unless the image calls for under lighting, I suggest holding the reflector more perpendicular to the ground (parallel to your subject) (**Figure 20.8** and **Figure 20.9**). This provides a more natural reflection and mitigates those pesky shadows that drift upward from the nose, eye-sockets, and other facial features.

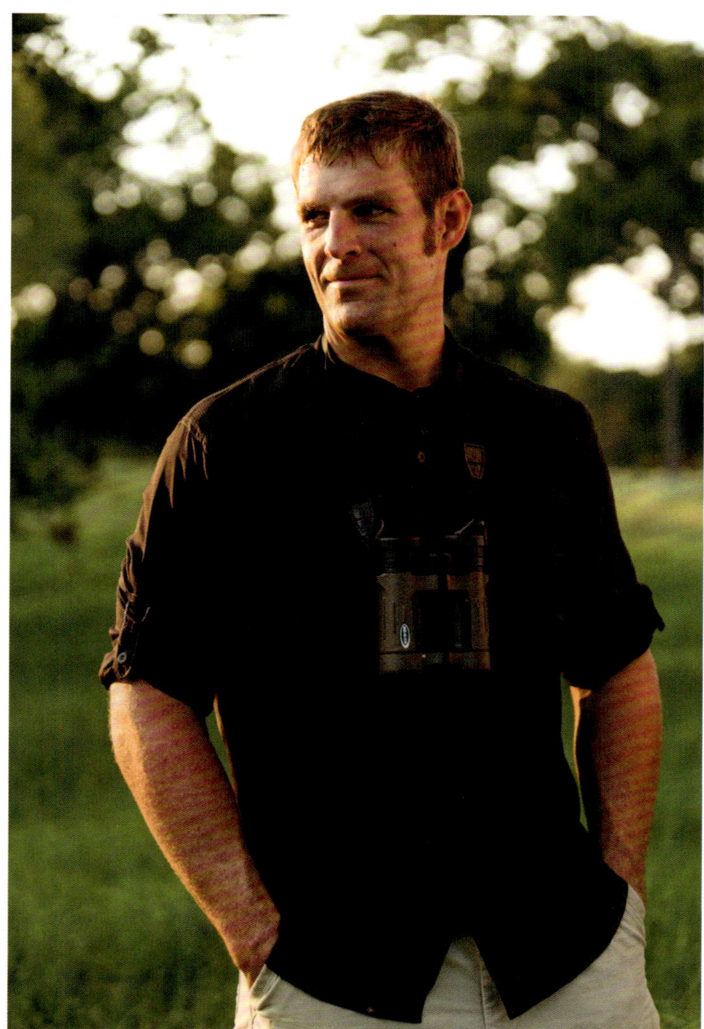 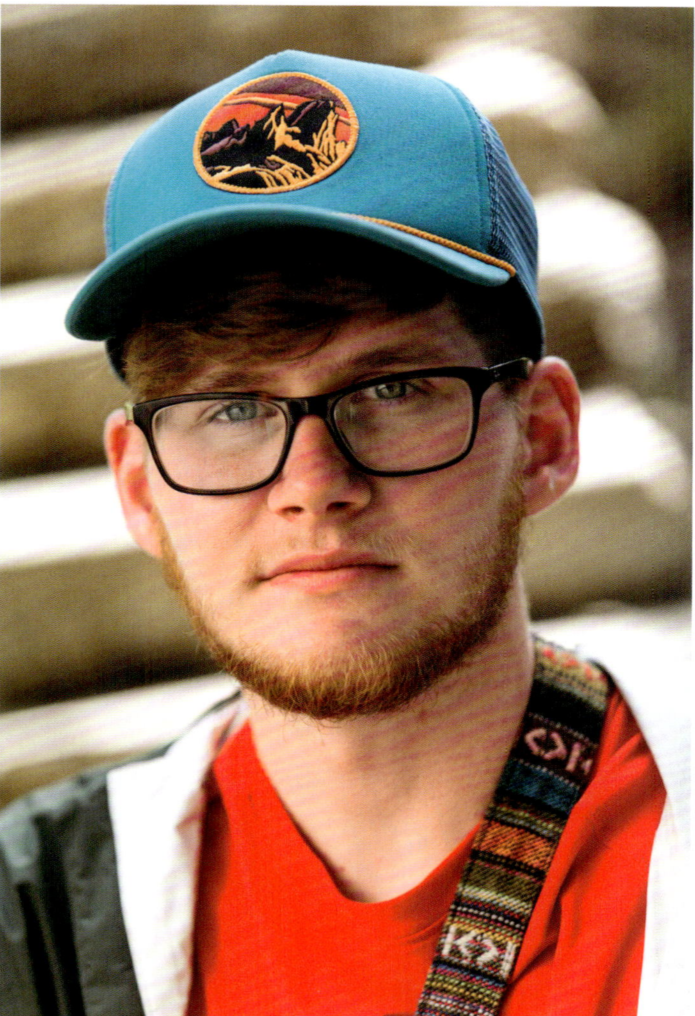

20.1 Since the subject was wearing a black shirt, and I was using the direct sunlight as a backlight, I used a white reflector to capture detail on the shadowed side of the subject's face to ensure it was well lit and the binoculars were noticeable.
ISO 400; 1/640 sec.; f/2.8; 70mm

20.2 Although I could have used fairly diffused light on this subject, reflecting light onto the camera-left side of his face gives the image visual depth.
ISO 200; 1/800 sec.; f/2.8; 140mm

20.3 Turning the subject away from direct sunlight provides great backlight. However, the exposure on his face is fairly low due to the intensity of said backlight.
ISO 200; 1/1600 sec.; f/2.8; 70mm

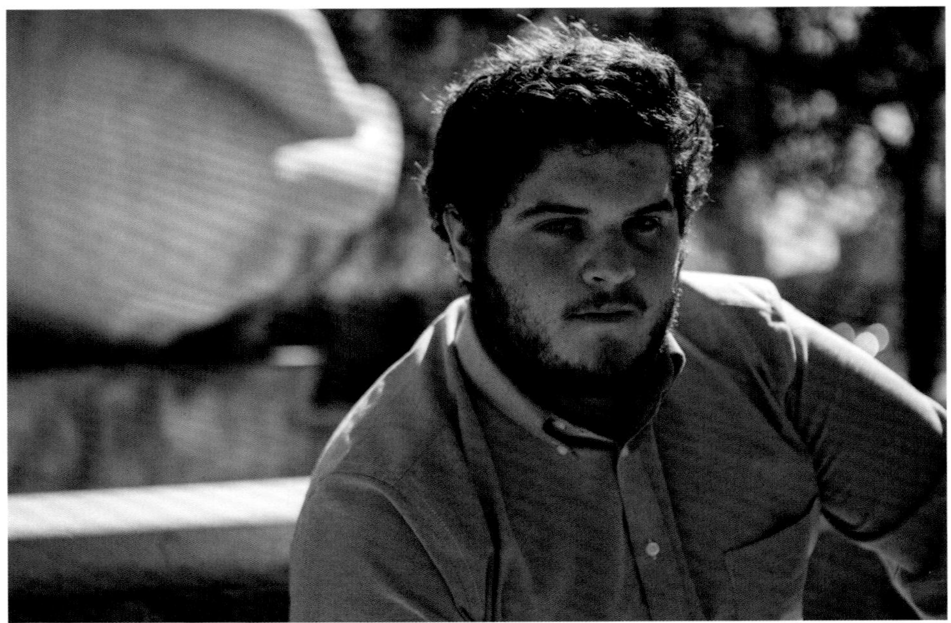

20.4 I used a reflector from camera left to increase the exposure and add contrast between light and shadow across the subject's face. This adds a dynamic value to the portrait.
ISO 200; 1/4000 sec.; f/2.8; 70mm

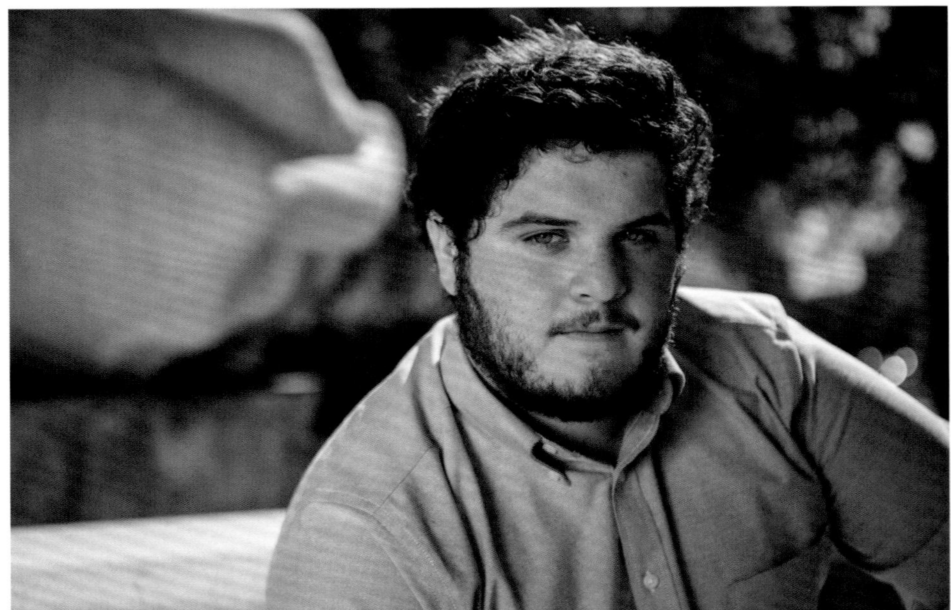

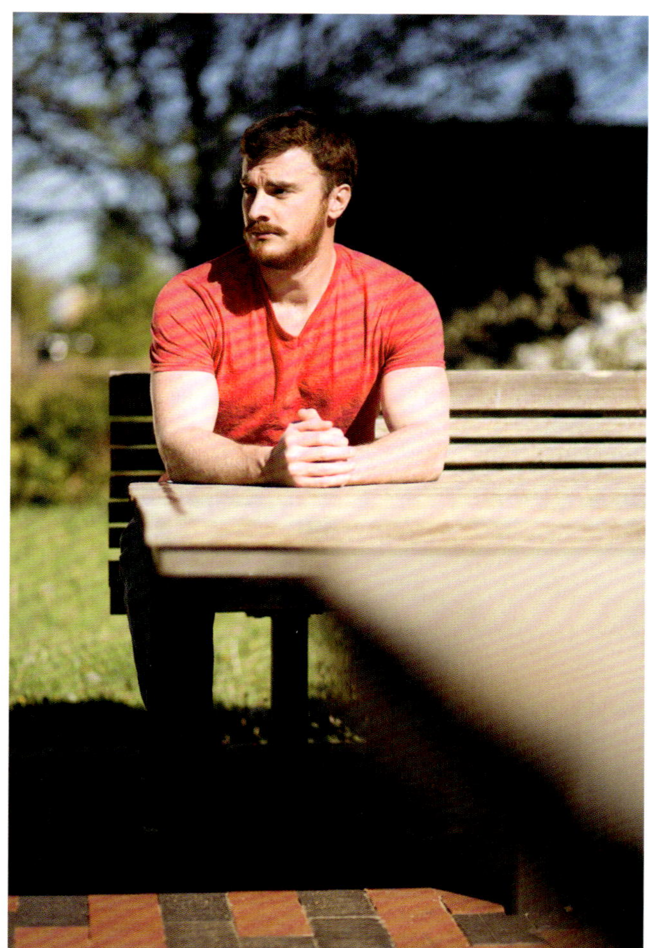

20.5 When using harsh, direct light is appealing, a reflector is a great way to create backlight to separate the subject from the background (see **Figure 20.6**).
ISO 100; 1/5000 sec.; f/1.8; 85mm

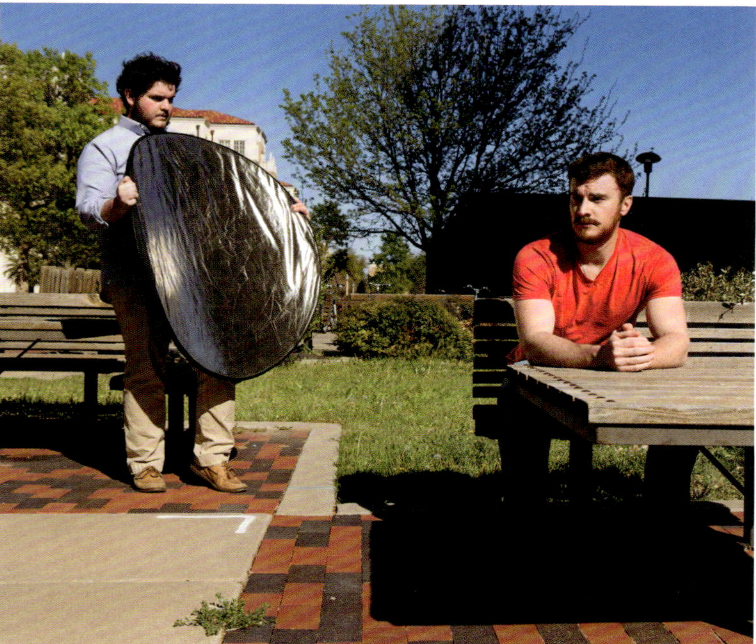

20.6 To create the backlight for this portrait, my assistant held a silver and gold reflector nearly opposite of the sun and bounced the majority of the reflected light onto the back of the subject.

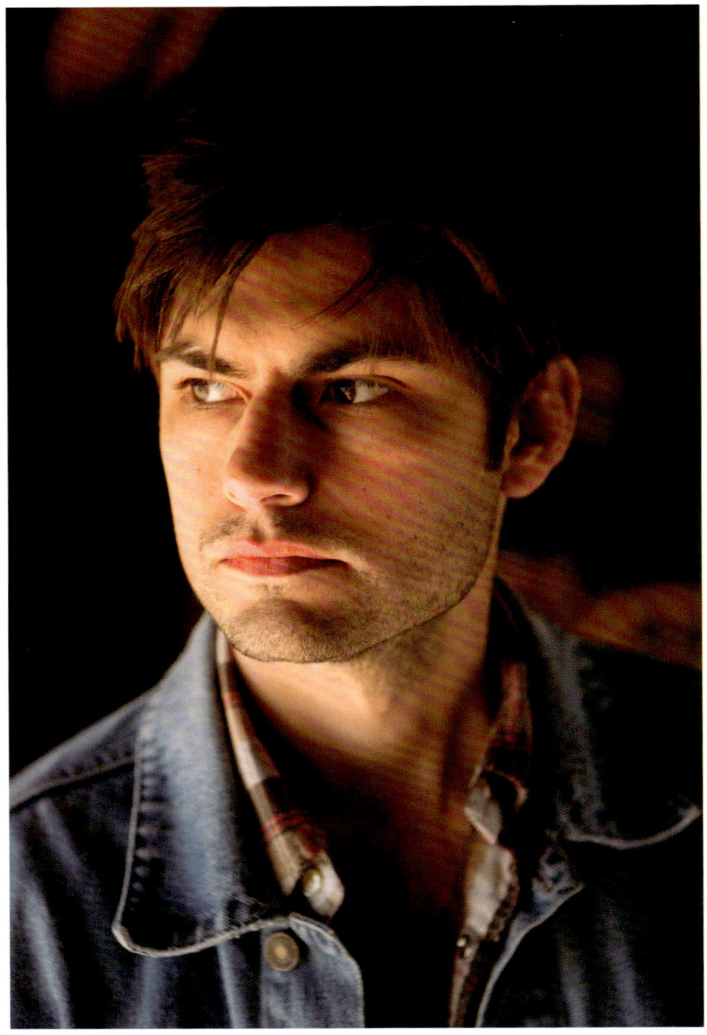

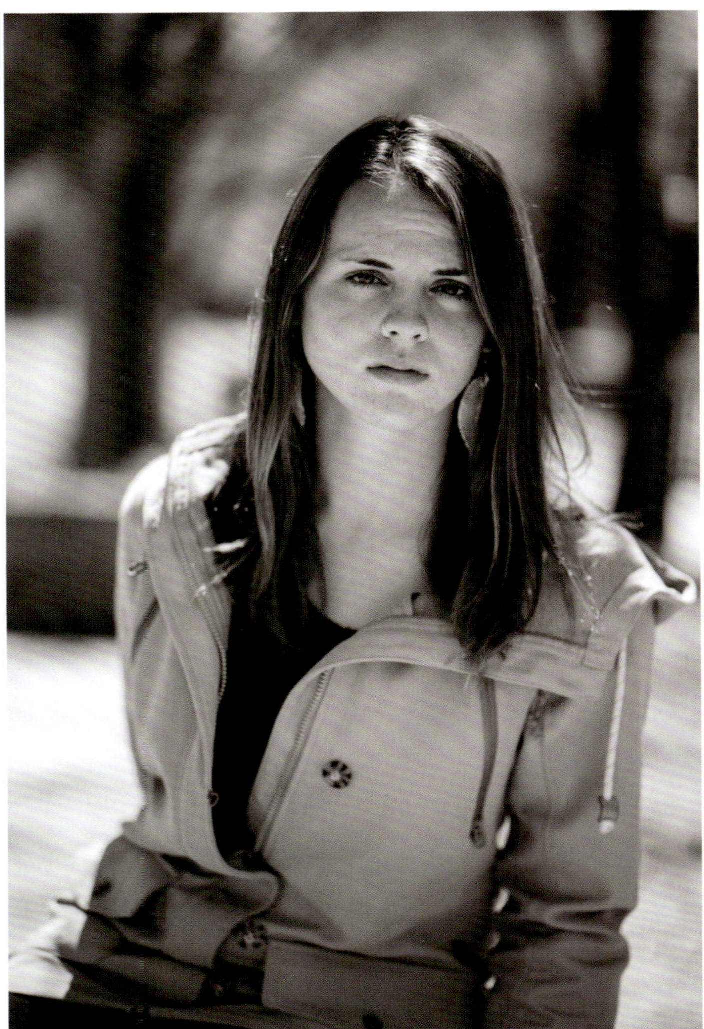

20.7 Reflecting light from upward onto the subject can be distracting or unappealing when the reflected light is more intense than the rest of the light hitting the face, creating unnaturally dark shadows.
ISO 200; 1/125 sec.; f/2.8; 62mm

20.8 Although lit from below, the reflector was moved to a more parallel angle to the subject to reduce the light's intensity, taking with it the distracting shadows under the eyes.
ISO 200; 1/4000 sec.; f/1.8; 85mm

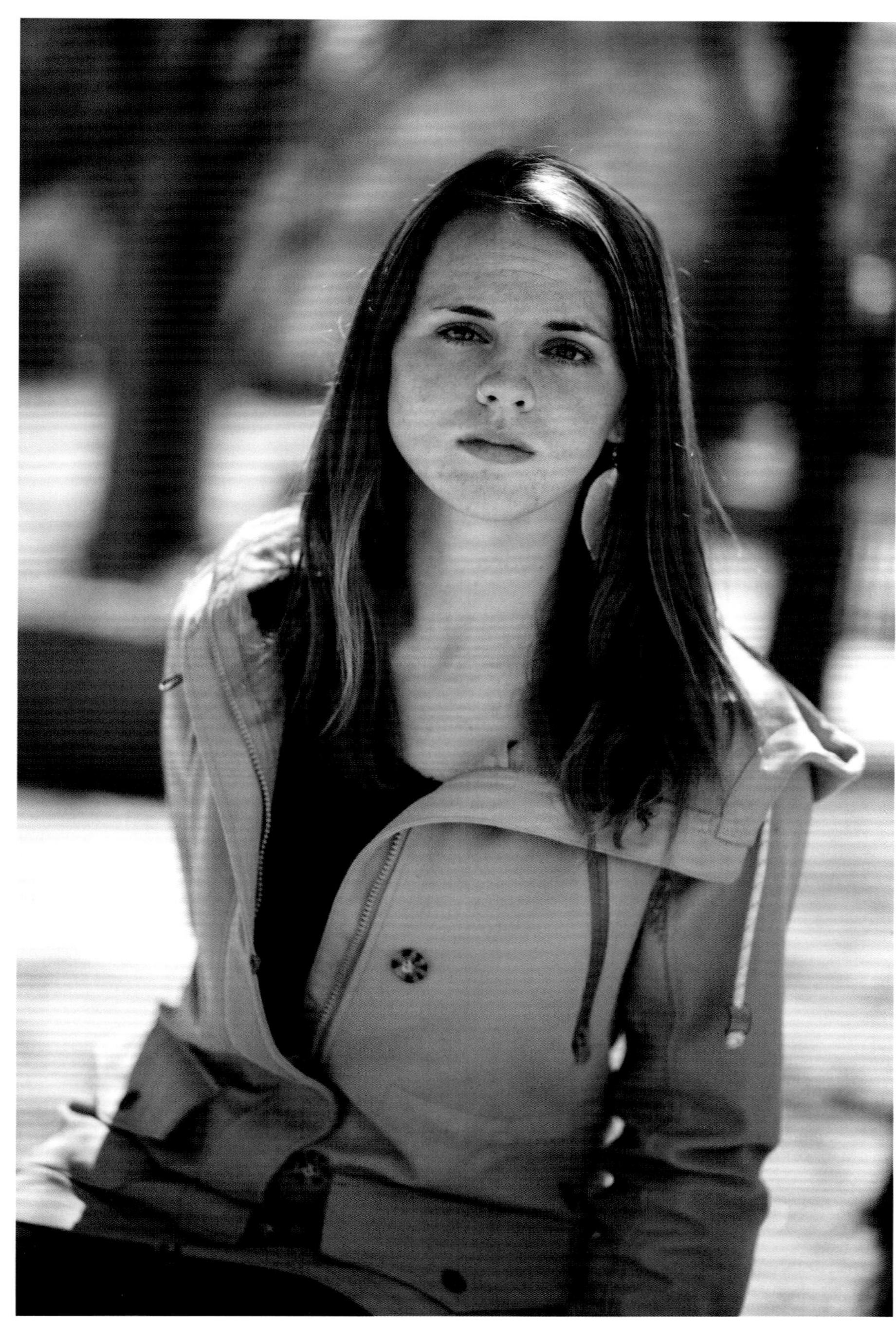

20.9 To ensure the background canyon wall did not run into my subject's head, I used aperture priority and an aperture of f/2.8 to knock it sufficiently out of focus.
ISO 200; 1/5000 sec.; f/1.8; 85mm

Which Reflector Do You Use?

Most reflector kits come with reflectors of several types of reflective surfaces. Typically, these include a gold and silver surface, a surface with a mixture of gold *and* silver, a white diffuser that can be used as a white surface, and a black surface (also known as an anti-fill, which we'll talk about in the next section). With all of these options, it sometimes may be difficult to decide which one to use.

A gold surface will create a very warm reflection (**Figure 20.10**). It takes whatever light is hitting it and warms it up even more. So, if you are shooting with early morning or late evening golden hour light, a gold reflector will intensify that warmth in reflection. Although this might be desirable, it can also make your subject look a bit jaundiced. A silver reflector, on the other hand, provides a punchy reflection that is often the same color temperature as the light reflected in it (**Figure 20.11**). Some photographers don't like the visual coolness of a silver reflector and decide to use the mixture of silver and gold. This mixed reflector is often referred to as a Daylight reflector.

Personally, I like the Daylight reflector more than either the gold or silver, especially as a background or kicker light. However, I most often use one of the diffusion panels as a white reflector for fill and main-light situations (**Figure 20.12**). It provides a more muted, less intense reflection since it is somewhat transparent. It cuts down on the "pop" of a reflector's shiny surface, offering a softer, more natural reflection that doesn't augment the color of the reflecting light source much.

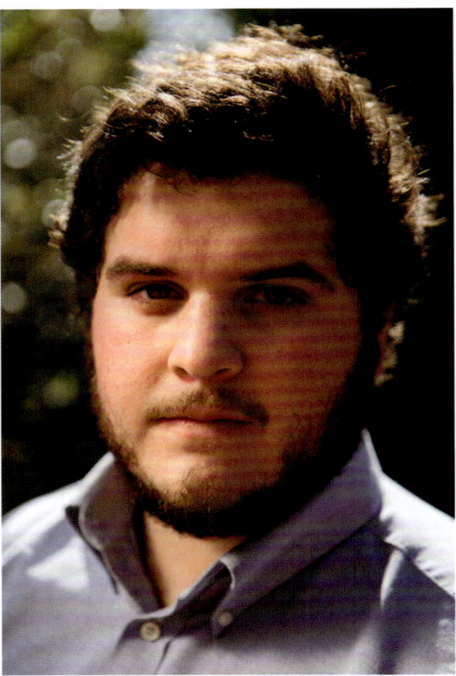

20.10 The gold reflector in many kits is useful for warming up the light hitting your subject, but it can often be too warm (read: orange) when using late afternoon and golden hour light.
ISO 100; 1/1000 sec.; f/2.8; 67mm

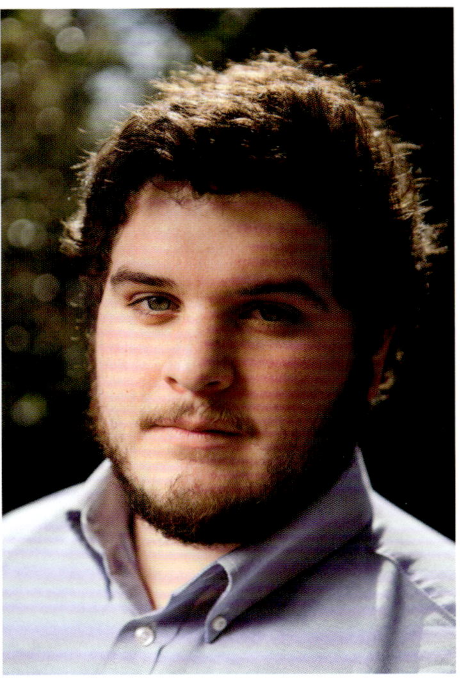

20.11 Silver reflectors seem to reflect a more intense light compared to gold and daylight reflectors. They are great for retaining the color of the light source, and providing a more brisk light source if one is needed.
ISO 100; 1/1250 sec.; f/2.8; 70mm

20.12 My go-to reflector is actually the white diffuser that comes in many reflector kits. White provides a less intense reflection, and I use it for primary light rather than more reflective surfaces.
ISO 100; 1/1000 sec.; f/2.8; 70mm

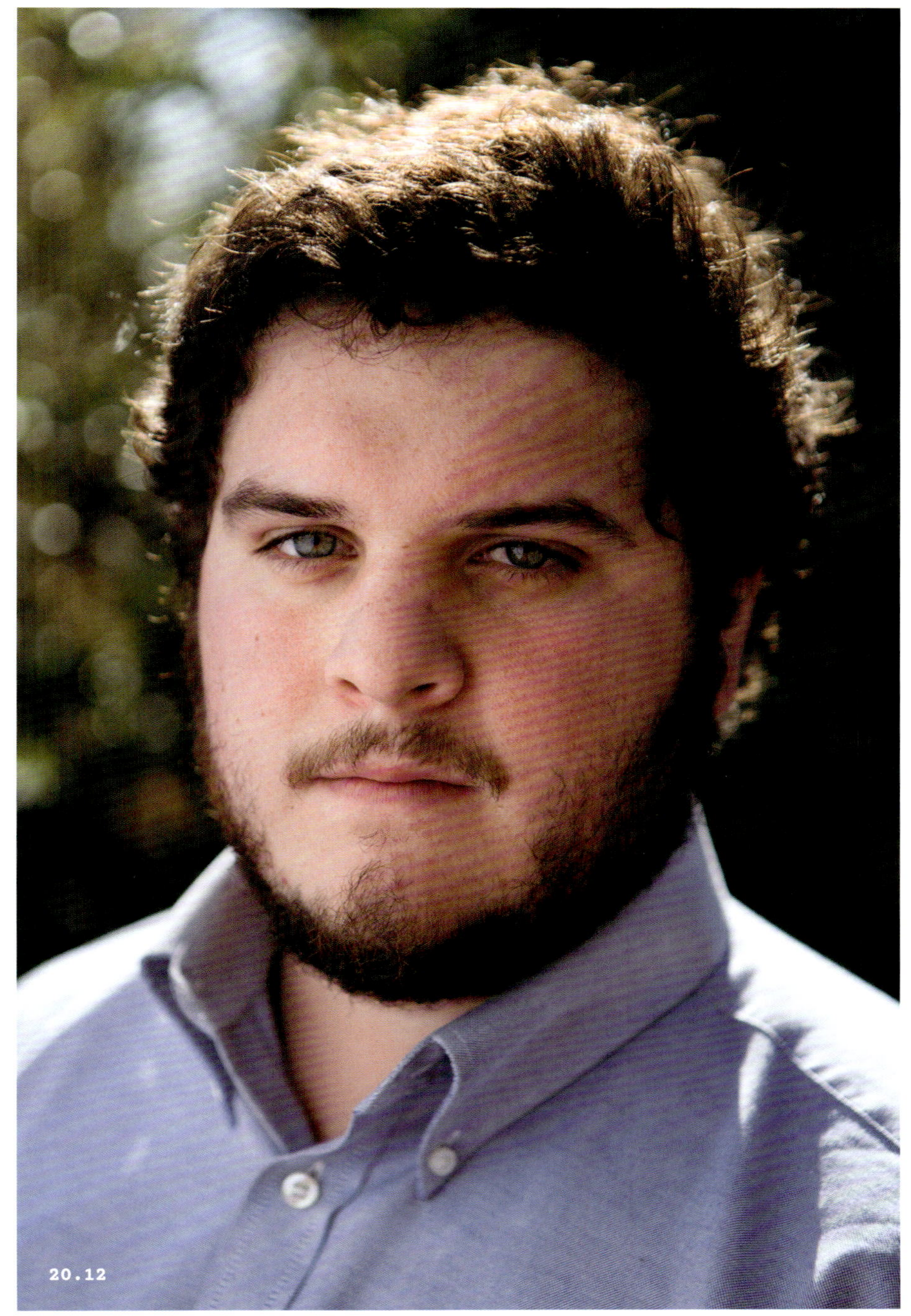
20.12

21. MODIFY THE LIGHT

REFLECTION, AS POINTED out in the previous section, *is* a form of light modification. Many beginner photographers stop there; however, assuming it is the only option we have for manipulating natural light other than bringing in artificial sources such as strobes and flashes. In reality, there are options that can be used in combination with reflection.

If reflection is one way to modify the light, diffusing it is another. Diffusing light is a way of making any source of light softer and less intense. Typically, we diffuse a very hard source of light, like the sun. Diffusion is a sure way to get those nice, soft shadows that gradually fade into light; it allows you to customize the light, making it work for you even in cases where the sun is shining directly on your subject (**Figure 21.1** and **Figure 21.2**).

The reflector kit mentioned in the previous chapter typically comes with a diffusion panel with reflective surfaces zipped to it. Removing the reflectors leaves a semi-transparent material for diffusing light (**Figure 21.3**). The denser the diffuser panel, the softer the light will be. Likewise, the closer you move the panel to your subject (think extremely close if you are shooting headshots), the softer the light will be.

Don't have a formal diffuser panel? No problem. I've successfully used white bed sheets or blankets, semi-frosted plexiglass, sheer curtains, greenhouse walls, and a host of other semi-transparent materials for diffusers. The idea is to simply to place something that will diffuse light between your subject and the light

source. Using a diffuser also opens up opportunity for shooting in the middle of the day. Direct daylight between the golden hours lacks color and dimensionality. Placing a diffusion panel between the sunlight and your subject transforms that light, and the direction of the light can be altered a bit based on the angle of the panel relative to your subject.

I often use a diffusion panel to soften primary (key) light sources. When the panel is placed close to the subject, it is usually large enough to also fill in the shadow side of the face with some light. I also use a reflector to create a backlight in this type of situation (**Figure 21.4** and **Figure 21.5**). This is a great setup for creating headshots at any time of the day (you just may need a few hands to help hold the diffuser and reflector).

Another way to modify light is to use a black reflector, called an anti-fill. A black reflector has nothing to do with softening or lightening shadows; instead, it deepens them. Want your shadows darker? Use a black reflector. Many reflector kits come with a black surface, and the closer you move that surface to the shadowed side of your subject, the deeper the shadows become (**Figure 21.6**, **Figure 21.7**, and **Figure 21.8**). I've found that black felt is also a great anti-fill material, particularly since it has no sheen to it.

Why would you need to use a black reflector to deepen the shadows in the first place? In many natural light portraiture situations, there is some remnant of reflection in the shadowed

side of your subject. Even if you are shooting with direct sunlight, that light is probably reflecting off of something else and then back onto your subject. A black reflector doesn't reflect light; it simply blocks it from hitting the subject. Increasing the shadows creates more contrast between light and shadow, which can make your subject appear more dramatic.

Black reflectors are also great for creating shadows where there are none. Many location-based fashion photographers will forgo using artificial lights when it is overcast outside, opting to use a large black panel, instead. When light is evenly reflected from all around your subject (such as in overcast conditions), a black reflector pressed close to your subject blocks reflection and darkens the side of the face or body the reflector is facing to create instant shadows. They will be soft, but at least they will be there.

Like reflectors, the tools that allow us to modify light are all around us and can be employed creatively. To reiterate, working successfully with light means recognizing good portrait light, knowing how to position your subject in it, and being able to manipulate or modify it to meet your needs. Using these tips will certainly have you on the right path to always seeing and using great portraiture light.

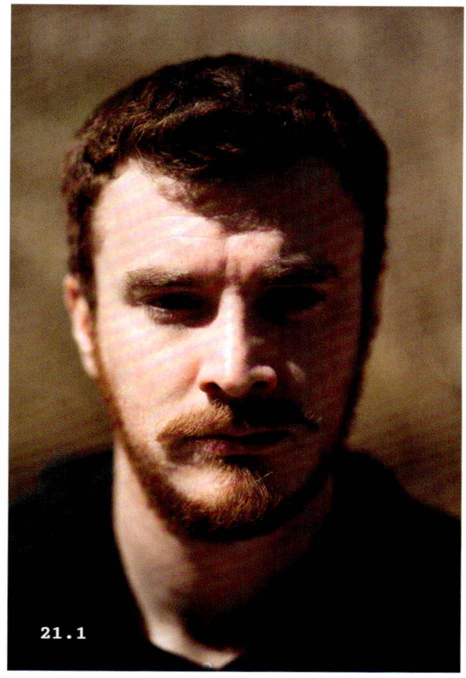

21.1

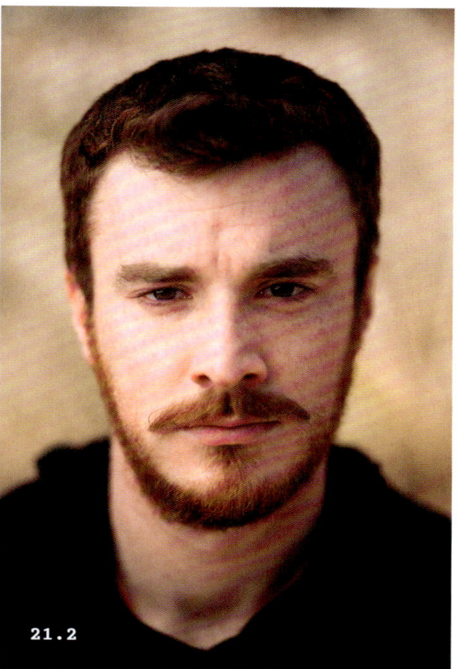

21.2

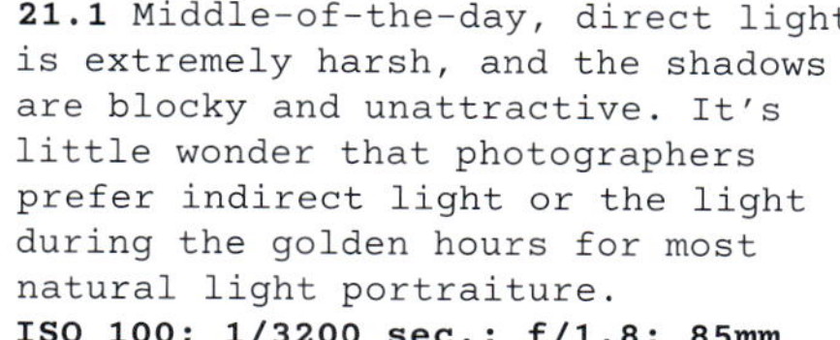

21.1 Middle-of-the-day, direct light is extremely harsh, and the shadows are blocky and unattractive. It's little wonder that photographers prefer indirect light or the light during the golden hours for most natural light portraiture.
ISO 100; 1/3200 sec.; f/1.8; 85mm

21.2 Placing a formal diffuser or semi-transparent material between an otherwise hard light source and your subject allows the light to disperse, filling in those dark shadows and easing the transition from light to shadow across the face.
ISO 100; 1/2000 sec.; f/1.8; 85mm

21.3 Diffusion panels range in size and shape, but they all accomplish the same task—to spread light around and knock its intensity down. For portraits of individuals or small groups, I recommend using a 42-inch diffuser panel (these often come with a reflector kit).

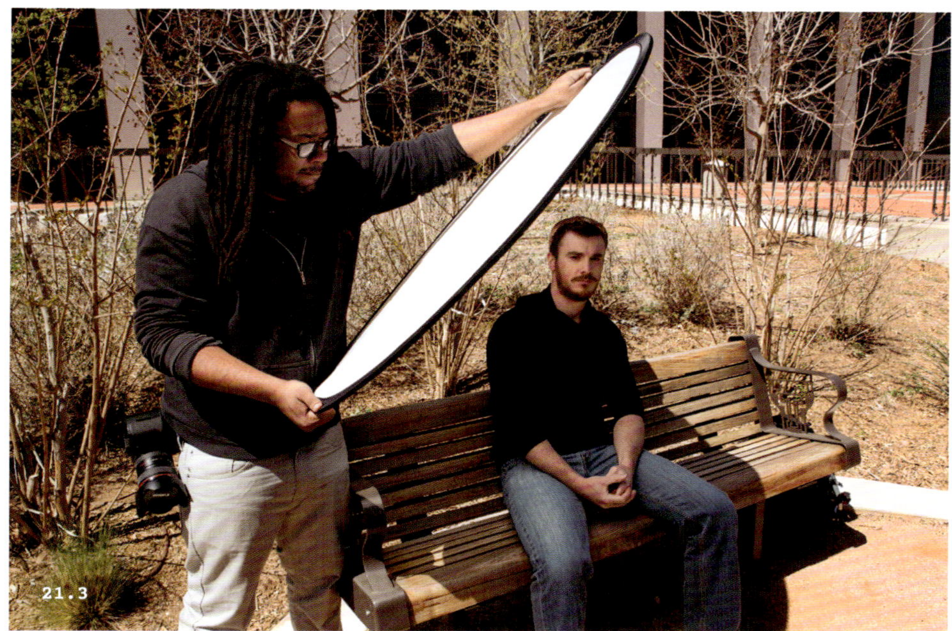

21.3

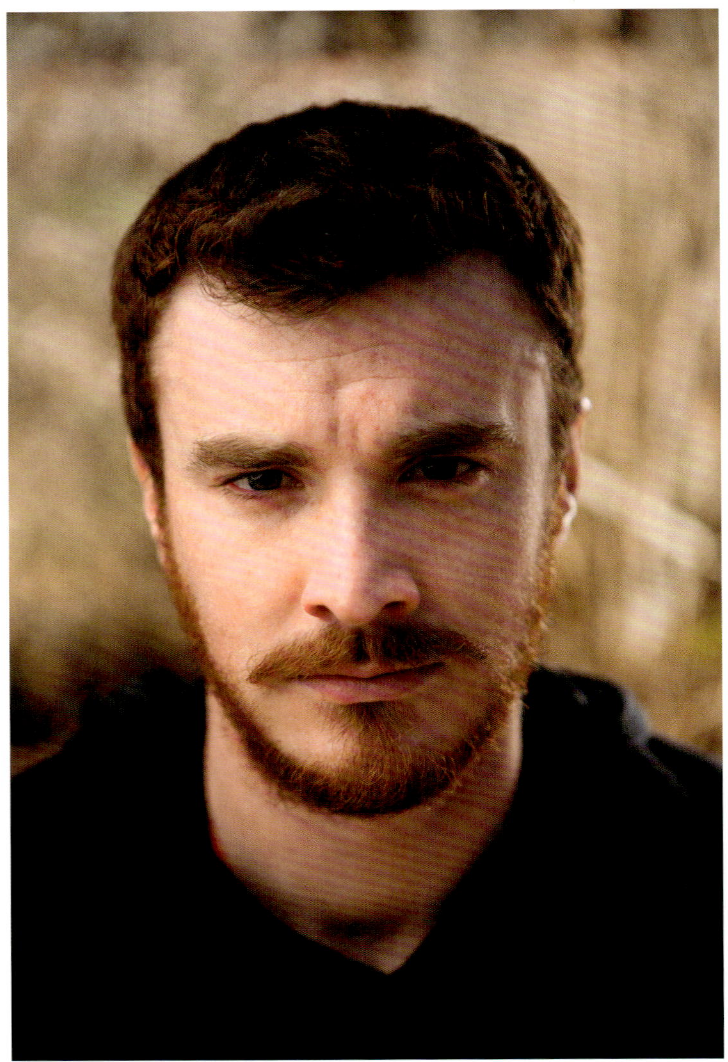

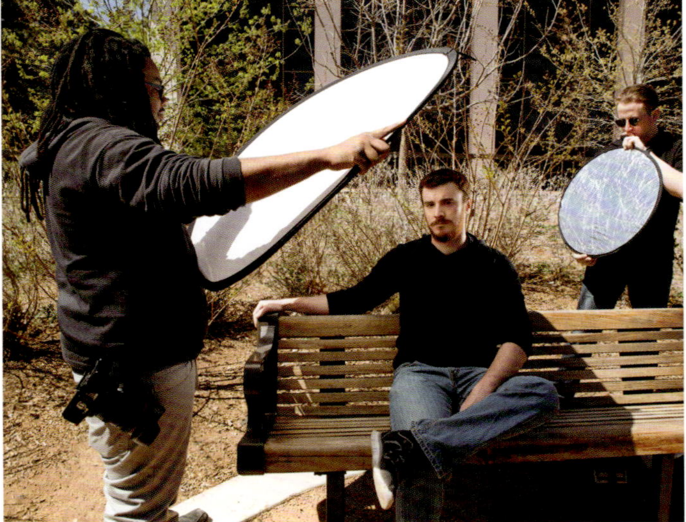

21.4 Other than diffusion, which makes
the harsh, midday lighting more appealing,
a subtle backlight adds dimension to
the shadow side of the subject.
ISO 100; 1/1000 sec.; f/2.8; 70mm

21.5 While the diffuser spreads out the
intensity of direct sunlight, the small
silver reflector placed back right from
the camera pushes the sunlight back at
him to separate him from the abstract
background.

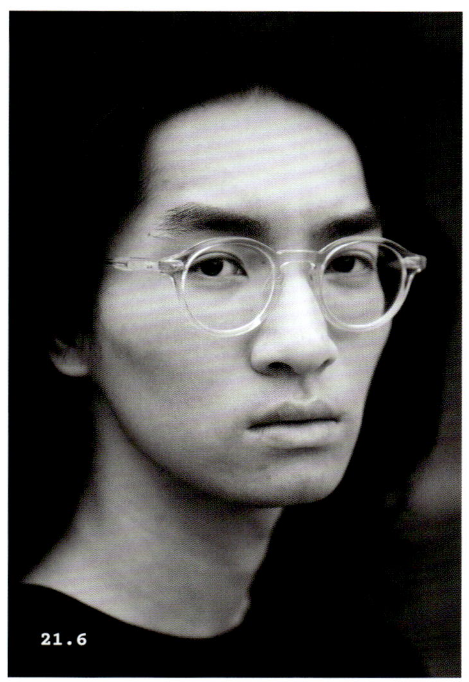

21.6

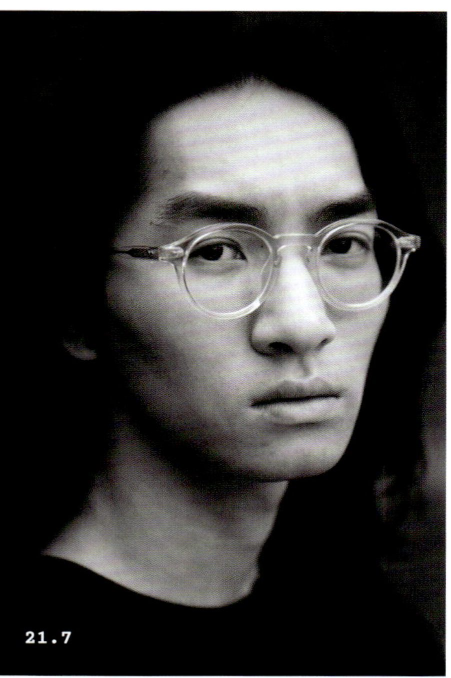

21.7

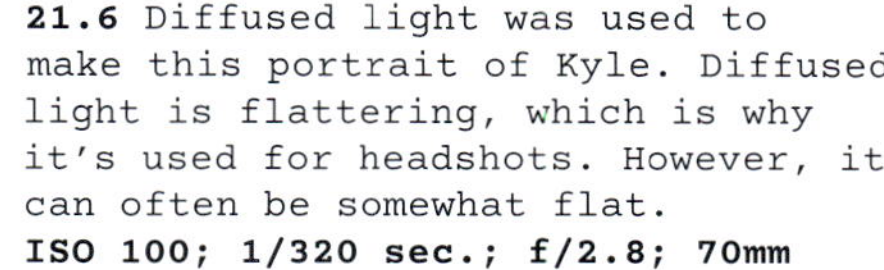

21.6 Diffused light was used to make this portrait of Kyle. Diffused light is flattering, which is why it's used for headshots. However, it can often be somewhat flat.
ISO 100; 1/320 sec.; f/2.8; 70mm

21.7 By adding a black, anti-fill reflector just off camera (see **Figure 21.8**), the right side of Kyle's face becomes darker, which highlights the structure of his facial features and adds dimension and mood.
ISO 100; 1/320 sec.; f/2.8; 70mm

21.8 Under diffuse lighting conditions, the silver reflector doesn't do much for backlight, but the black reflector placed camera left darkens the shadows on Kyle's face. The closer the panel is moved to the subject, the darker the shadows become, and vice versa.

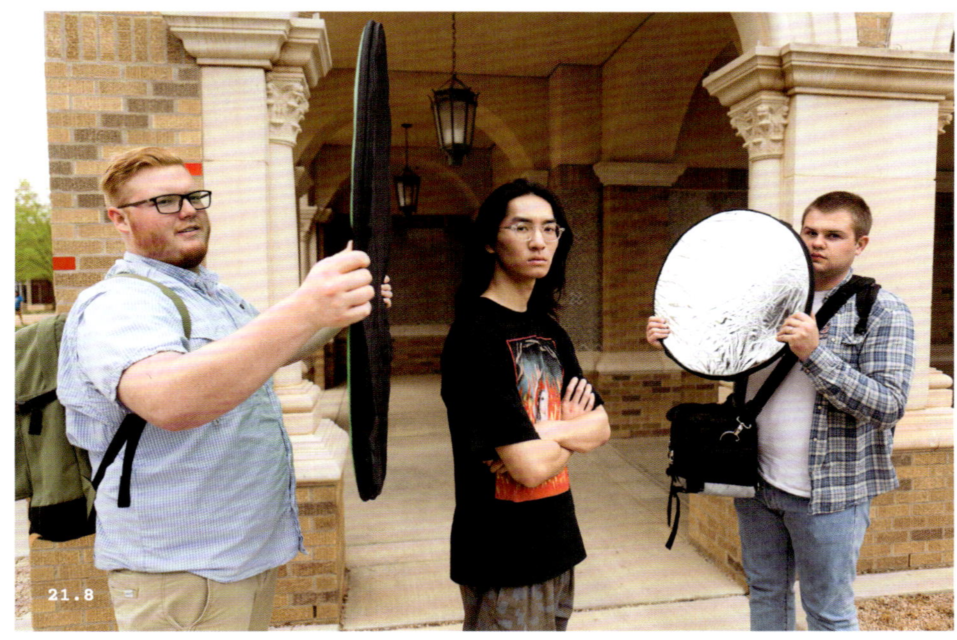

21.8

4

COMPOSITION

Composing portraits isn't necessarily different than composing other types of photographs. Photographic composition is all about directing the eye. For portraits, our specific goal (the majority of the time) is to direct the viewer's eye to the eye of the subject.

This chapter points out useful considerations to take while composing portraits. As you'll notice, many of the compositional techniques for making great portraits are used to create dimension in an image, even if your intent is simply to use shallow depth of field to isolate your subject.

Lastly, I want to point out that images are rarely made employing just one compositional approach. In many cases, multiple techniques are used to achieve the desired image. Appreciate each compositional technique for what it accomplishes, but know that some of the greatest portraits are made using several of these techniques in order to introduce not only the subject, but also a bit of the environment and story.

COMPOSITION IS ALL about how the space within the photographic frame is used. Although being contained by this barrier might feel constricting, limitations breed creativity. There's a lot of potential for using that space, but it helps to know how to approach the frame with essential foundational compositional principles.

When it comes to portraits, no one has written a definitive rulebook, particularly when it comes to how much of our subjects we include in our frame. However, we have a general understanding of how to frame our subjects in terms of the viewer's distance from them. Portrait photographers generally have three ways to frame their subjects: full-length portraits, medium portraits, and headshots.

Full-length portraits are exactly what they sound like (**Figure 22.1**). Their purpose is to give the viewer an idea of how the entire subject looks. This is an important type of framing because it's generally how we see everyone we encounter socially. It also showcases how portrait subjects relate to their surroundings, which is more important for some types of portraiture than for others.

Medium-framed portraits are tighter than full-length portraits, but provide more of your subject in the frame than traditional headshots. Typically, the bottom of medium portraits can start just above the knees, but can also capture the belly button up to the head (**Figure 22.2**). Popular among individual, family, and senior portraits, medium framings are great for bringing the subject closer to the viewer without being so intimate that we don't gather much contextual information about them.

Headshots, both as a genre and a way to frame up a portrait subject, are shots that are composed tightly on the subject, typically above the breast line and sometimes close enough to cut the top of the head out of the frame (**Figure 22.3**). As pointed out in chapter one, headshots and closely framed portraits are all about the subject's face and expression. It's a great way to frame for an intimate engagement with the subject. I consider it a necessity to shoot one on each outing with my subjects.

Although this chapter is full of information on how to approach composing your portraits, this is a good place to mention creating images that are dynamic. It's one thing knowing how to frame up different types of portraits based on the viewer's distance from the subject, but it's also important to know those small things that can make a portrait interesting, creative, and engaging.

And with that, I'll leave this discussion on portrait-framing lengths with one of the strongest and simplest tips for composing: weight one side of the image more than the other with your subject. It's one of many compositional tips and techniques that direct the eye to your subject. Placing your subject off to the left in a full-length framing is a way to drag the eye to the subject (**Figure 22.4**). As the eye scans across the image (in a fraction of a second), it takes in background information that is contributing to the subject; this extra information, even if aesthetically abstract, can strongly emphasize the subject.

You don't have to use this approach for every shot. In fact, portraiture—and photography as a whole—would be boring if such a directive existed. Composition is a well-explored topic, one that embraces different techniques being used together to make stronger images. It makes sense that creating visual symmetry can be an effective way of composing your portrait. However, consider why that symmetry is necessary in your image. Is it because the leading lines converge somewhere in the distance behind your subject (often referred to as a vanishing point) in a way that enhances the portrait? Or, is it that you are so close to your subject that centering their face in the frame is the most compelling composition (**Figure 22.5**)? Either way, this is your opportunity to explore the potential of your photos and discover other ways of making them compositionally dynamic.

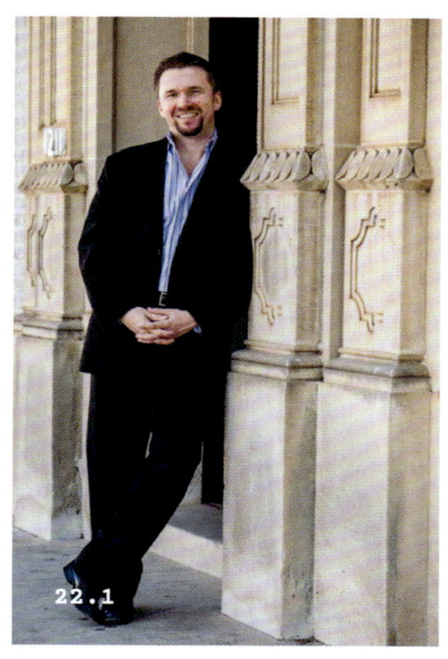

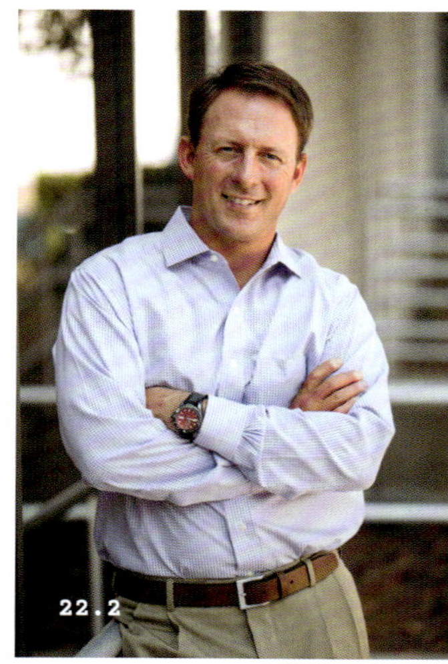

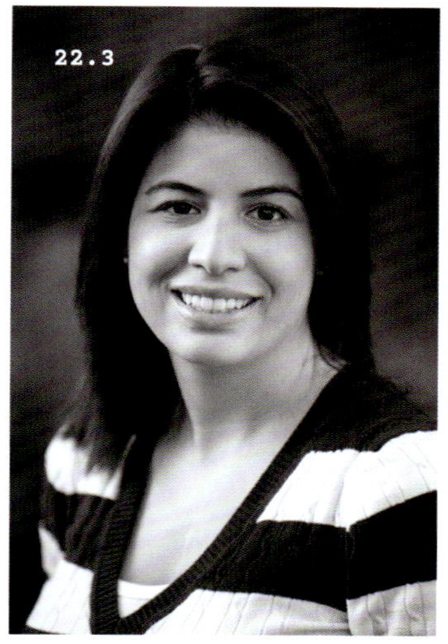

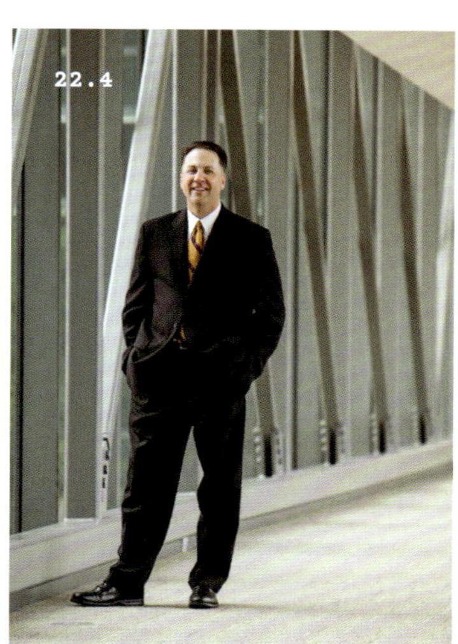

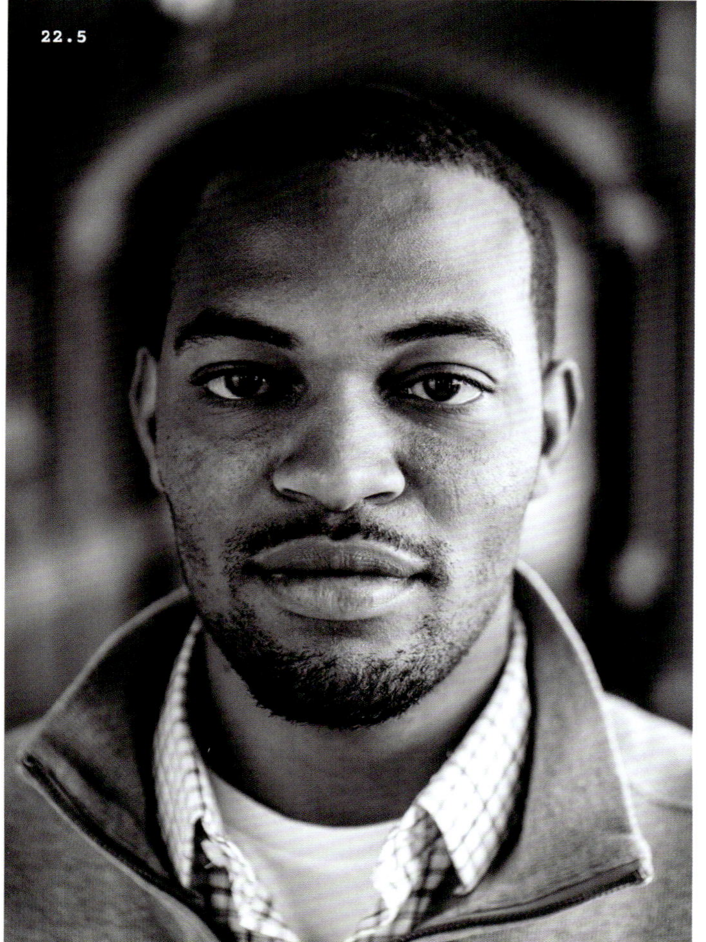

22.1 This full-length portrait of composer and conductor Tomasz Golka gives you a more complete idea of what he looks like and how he relates to structure and other subject matter around him.
ISO 200; 1/200 sec.; f/4; 115mm

22.2 A medium shot is nice for creating a bit more intimacy with your subject, focusing more on bringing the viewer's and subject's faces closer together without sacrificing too much environment or your subject's form.
ISO 50; 1/200 sec.; f/2.8; 120mm

22.3 Headshots are fairly tight shots that focus primarily on the face for a multitude of reasons: identification, emotion, artistic form, and the like.
ISO 200; 1/250 sec.; f/2.8; 125mm

22.4 In this corporate full-length portrait, I placed the subject in the left side of the frame to allow the eye to move to and/or from him in the image's composition. This allows for a nice background to play a stylistic and directive role in the frame.
ISO 400; 1/250 sec.; f/4; 200mm

22.5 My optical distance from the subject, as well as the nice framing structure in the out-of-focus background lend an appropriateness to centering the subject's head in the shot.
ISO 400; 1/160 sec.; f/2.8; 70mm

23. RULES ARE RULES

THE CONCEPTS OF composition have been passed down for centuries through art, architecture, and just about anything else that has visually captivated society—there are certainly a few thoughts about what works and what doesn't. Photography has been heavily influenced by these rules because they often pave the path to successful images.

The rule of thirds is one of the most popular compositional rules for photography. Inspired by older rules, such as the golden mean, the rule of thirds divides the photographic frame into horizontal and vertical thirds (**Figure 23.1**). The rule assumes that photographers place important subject matter and horizon lines on or near these "third lines." The image is then partitioned off in a way that can draw the eye into the frame and then offer meaningful, narrative content.

Practically speaking, the rule of thirds is a guide for photographers to use the visual real estate of the frame. I encourage everyone to remember the rule of thirds each time they make an image. Ultimately, it suggests weighting one side or area of the frame more with subject matter than others. Placing a portrait subject in the middle of the frame can be halting for the eye, and a horizon line placed in the middle of the frame creates competing areas of visual interest (**Figure 23.2**). Using the rule of thirds creates composition that is balanced, visually appealing, and offers narrative insight. If composition in some part is about controlling the eye, the rule of thirds is the foundational aid in doing so.

It would be easy for me to pontificate on the rule of thirds and other compositional "rules" that have great value to us as visual creators. However, keep in mind that sometimes, rules are meant to be broken (**Figure 23.3**). Placing your subject in the middle of the frame for the sake of halting the eye can be exactly what the image needs. Certain environments lend themselves to symmetrical composition, so it makes sense to place your subject in the middle of the frame. Breaking the rule of thirds might not be your go-to compositional method, but doing so can be very powerful in the right situation. When breaking the rule of thirds, do so with intent. It should be clear that placing your subject and/or horizon in the middle of the frame (or perhaps mostly out of the frame) is done strategically.

Again, the rule of thirds and its compositional ancestors exist for a reason. They are the foundation for centuries of visual design. It's important to consider their value while designing portraits, so the subject is complemented by other structures, backgrounds, and horizon lines in the image. However, it's equally important to recognize when the rule defeats the purpose you've devised for your shoot.

23.1 Visualizing the rule of thirds is often like visualizing a tic-tac-toe board placed over your frame, except your goal in this "game" is to place your subject matter on or very near a horizontal or vertical line that segments the image frame into thirds.
ISO 100; 1/640 sec.; f/4; 130mm

23.2 As much as I love the expression on the subject's face, I'm a bit troubled by how she is centered in the frame with so much empty real estate existing to her left and right. Both sides create visual tension for the eye, confusing it on where to move beyond the girl.
ISO 200; 1/320 sec.; f/1.8; 85mm

23.3 Centering the cyclist in the shot is a broken rule attenuated by the composition of the road, it's vanishing point, and its use as a visual frame around most of the subject. It doesn't hurt that the subject is prominent in the foreground, either.
ISO 200; 1/400 sec.; f/2.8; 130mm

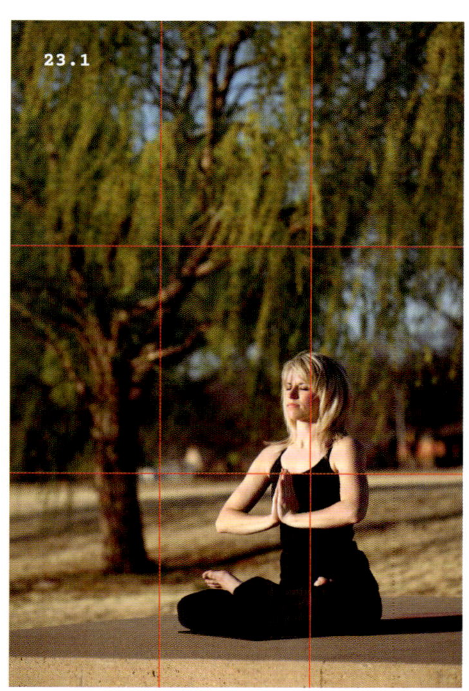

23.1

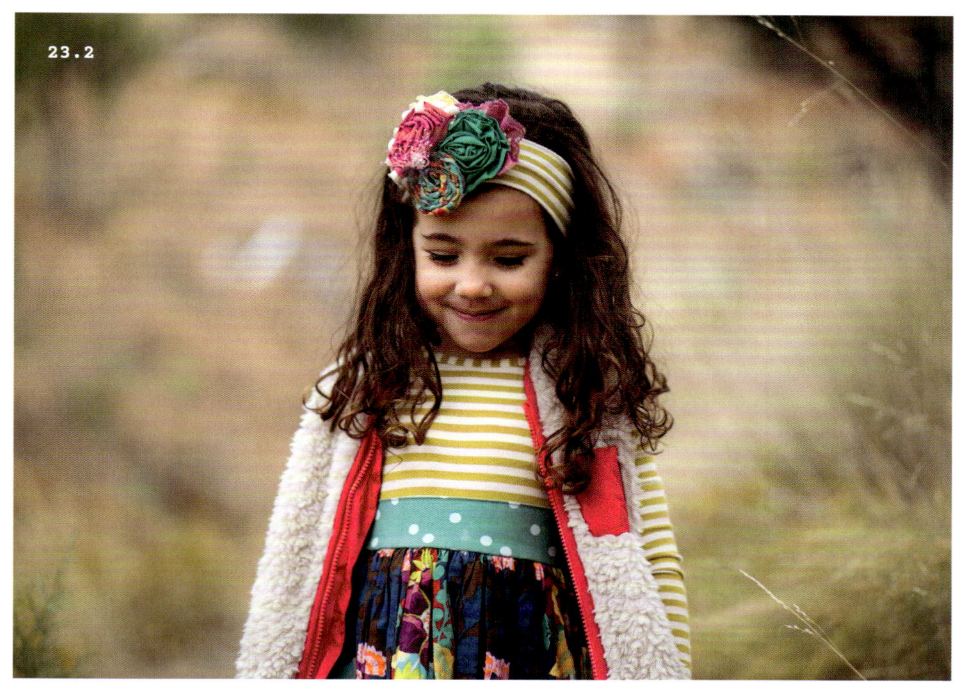

23.2

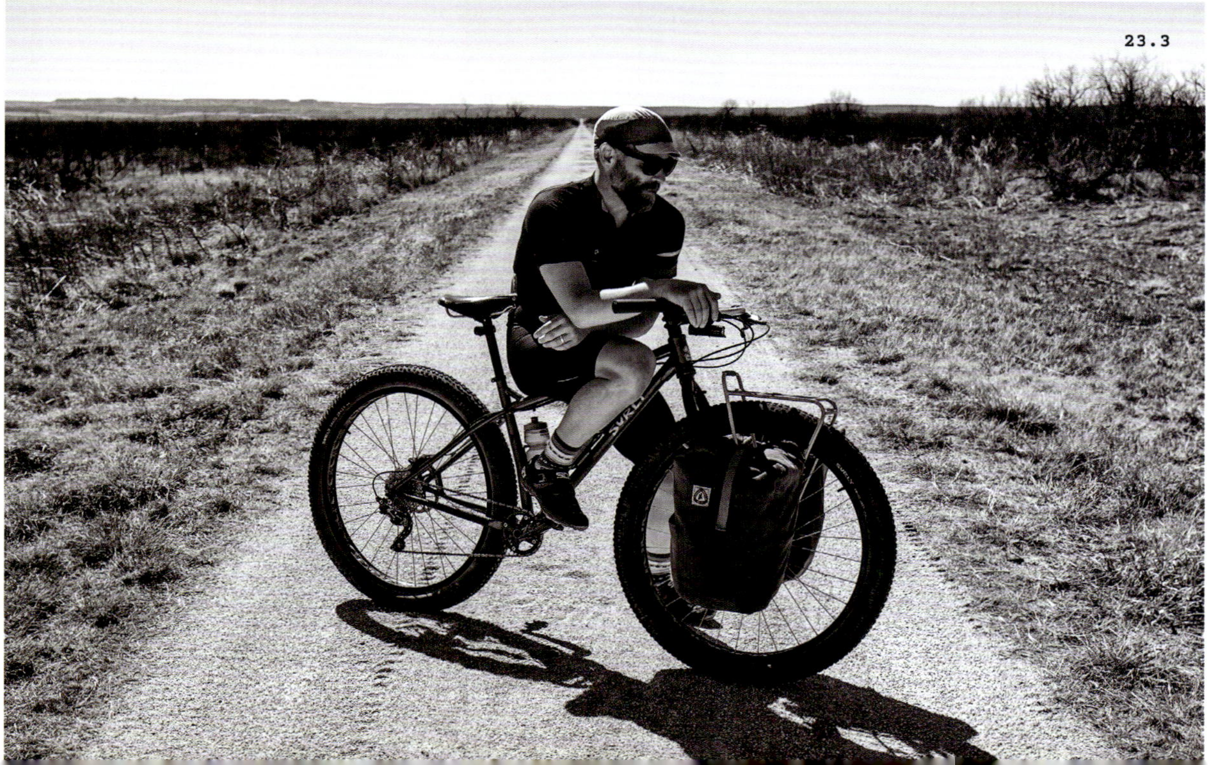

23.3

IF YOU WANT to strongly direct the viewer's eye in your frame, leading lines are your best compositional friends. Whether you start with your subject as a foreground anchor for a set of leading lines that stretch across the frame, or you place your portrait subject farther down, leading lines are attractive elements in any frame.

When it comes down to it, there are two types of lines: real and implied. Photographers work with both, and each has its benefits. Real lines are, well, real. They are comprised of actual structure in your image that appears to have linear qualities, whether they are straight or curved. For example, a fence can be used as a set of leading lines when you shoot down it toward your subject (**Figure 24.1**). The fence is a real structure that can be exploited for its linear characteristic.

An implied line is not made up of a singular structure in the frame, nor is it comprised of any combination of structures that were meant to work together to form a line. Instead, an implied line is one that we see amongst compositional structure. As photographers, we position ourselves to create the perception of a line in the frame that leads the viewer to or away from the subject (**Figure 24.2**).

Lines can appear in our frames a number of different ways. We can shoot straight *into* them, so they appear as horizontal or vertical structures across the frame (**Figure 24.3**). Or, we can shoot straight *down* them, conveying depth into the frame in front of and beyond our subject (**Figure 24.4**). Although both ways of approaching shooting with leading lines is appropriate and creatively effective, I think the latter is more engaging. When photographing down a set of real or implied leading lines, you are more strongly pulling the eye into *and* across the image, especially if you compose the lines to move from one side of the frame to the opposite side. In essence, when you are shooting down leading lines, you are creating a diagonal vector on which the viewing eye travels in the image.

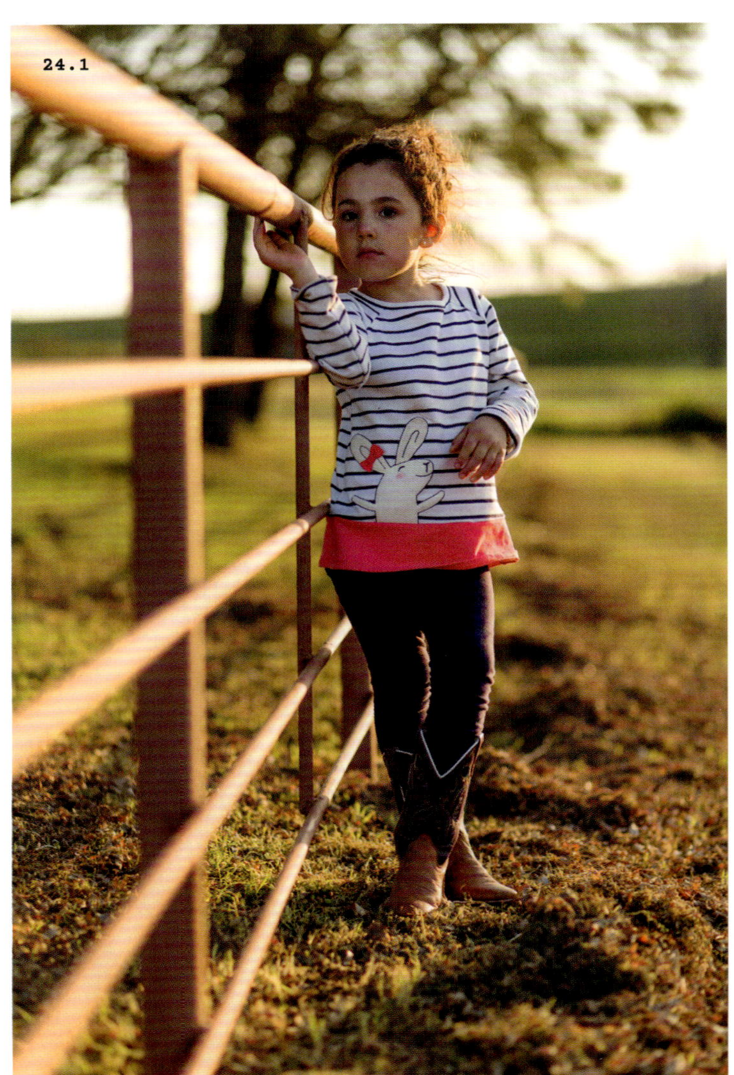

24.1 The glowing lines of the pipe fence serve well as a real line that leads the eye to the subject.
ISO 100; 1/640 sec.; f/2; 85mm

24.2 Although the subject is in the foreground, the trees serve as a nice implied line that moves you across (to the subject) and into the frame.
ISO 100; 1/640 sec.; f/2.8; 145mm

24.3 Photographing almost straight into the staircase creates visual layers out of the tops of the steps, which serve as a nice, directly lit pattern to place behind the subject.
ISO 200; 1/1000 sec.; f/2.8; 160mm

24.4 The row of chairs and the reflection in the conference room made for a great line down which to shoot this corporate environmental portrait.
ISO 200; 1/60 sec.; f/4; 60mm

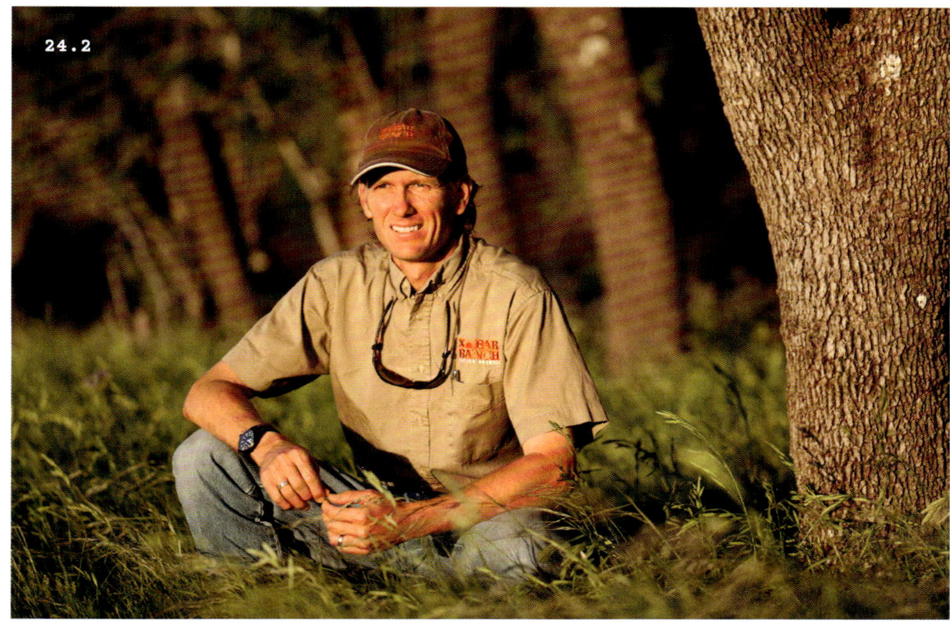

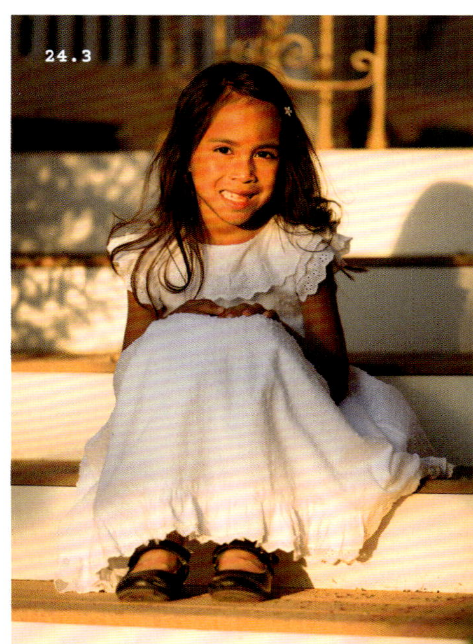

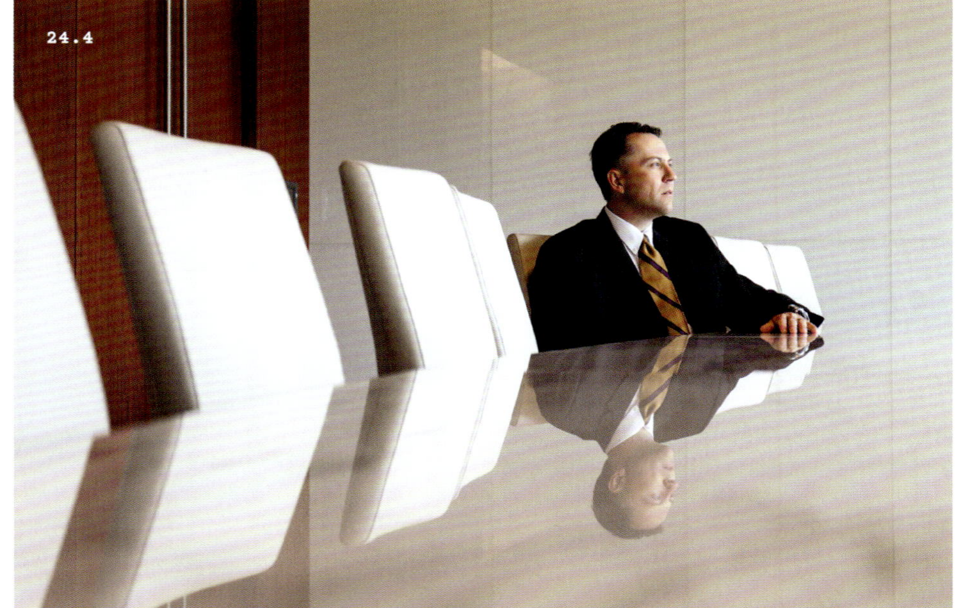

Diagonal lines always appear more dramatic. Of course, there's no need to always be shooting down a leading line to create the appeal of a diagonal line. Simply placing a diagonal line or compositing in a way that the real or implied lines in the shot appear more diagonal is a great way of introducing this eye-catching structure.

Finally, it's worth mentioning that some lines are incredibly obvious while others seem to elude us. Like light, it's our job as photographers to be diligent of the things around us that make for great photography, and it's useful to train your eye to see elements like leading lines. Real lines are fairly recognizable as compositional structure, while implied lines take a bit of training to see. Start noticing how structures can line up for you even when you're not photographing. Exercise your eye and mind to see implied lines and pre-visualize how you can stress that line in a portrait (**Figure 24.5**).

Furthermore, lines often present themselves when we orient the camera in different ways. Perhaps the real *or* implied line(s) are missed when we look through a horizontally oriented camera, but when we turn the camera to a vertical orientation, the image falls into place. In some cases, using what's referred to in cinematic terms as a Dutch angle, where the horizon line is leaning, opens up the image's composition to a new set of leading lines (**Figure 24.6**). Doing so may also create an extra level of quirkiness, drama or uneasiness to a portrait, depending on what you want to say with it. The point is to always be discovering lines. Don't forget to explore your options when the camera is at your eye. Re-orient your camera to see the potential for another perspective on lines for your image's composition.

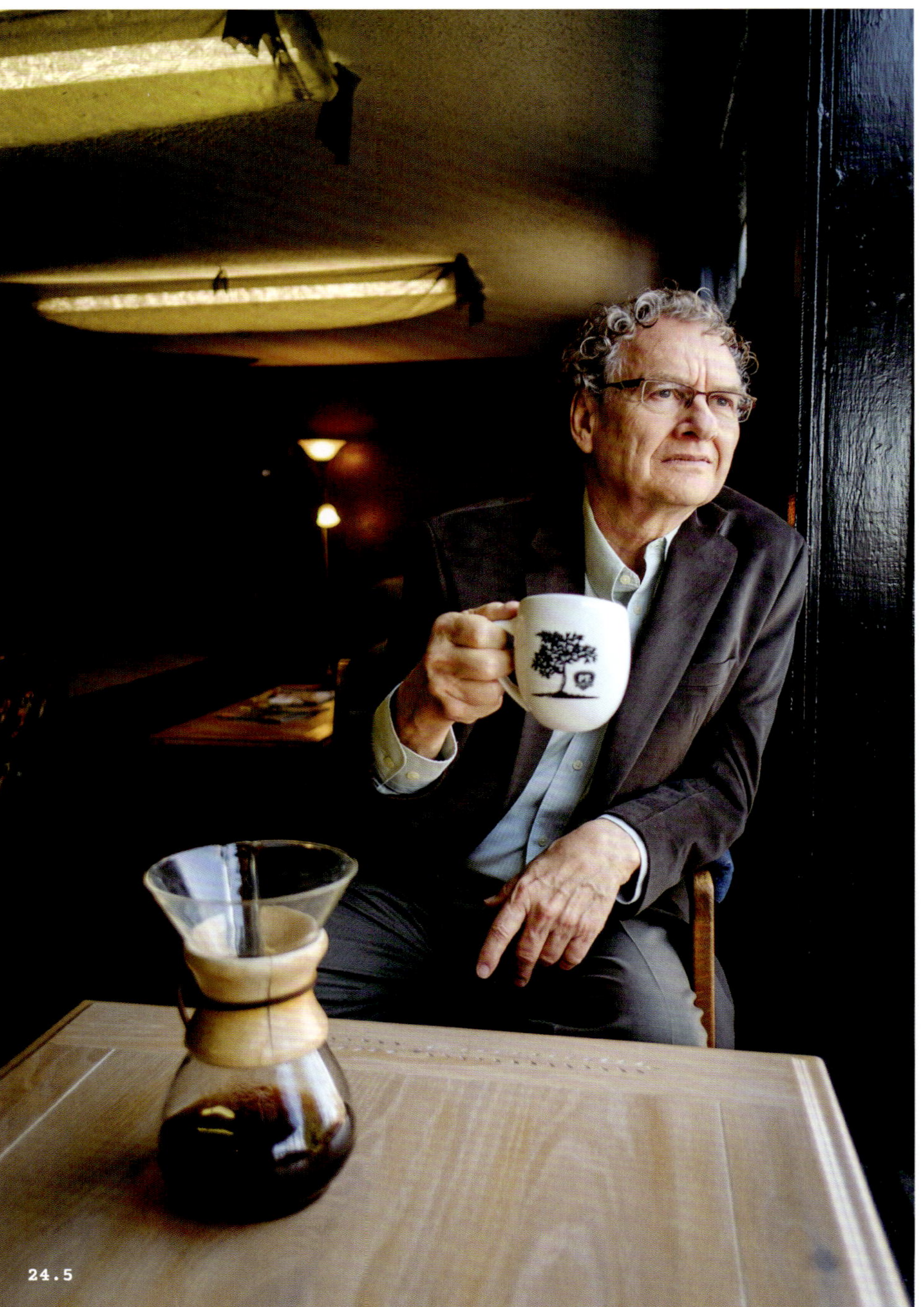

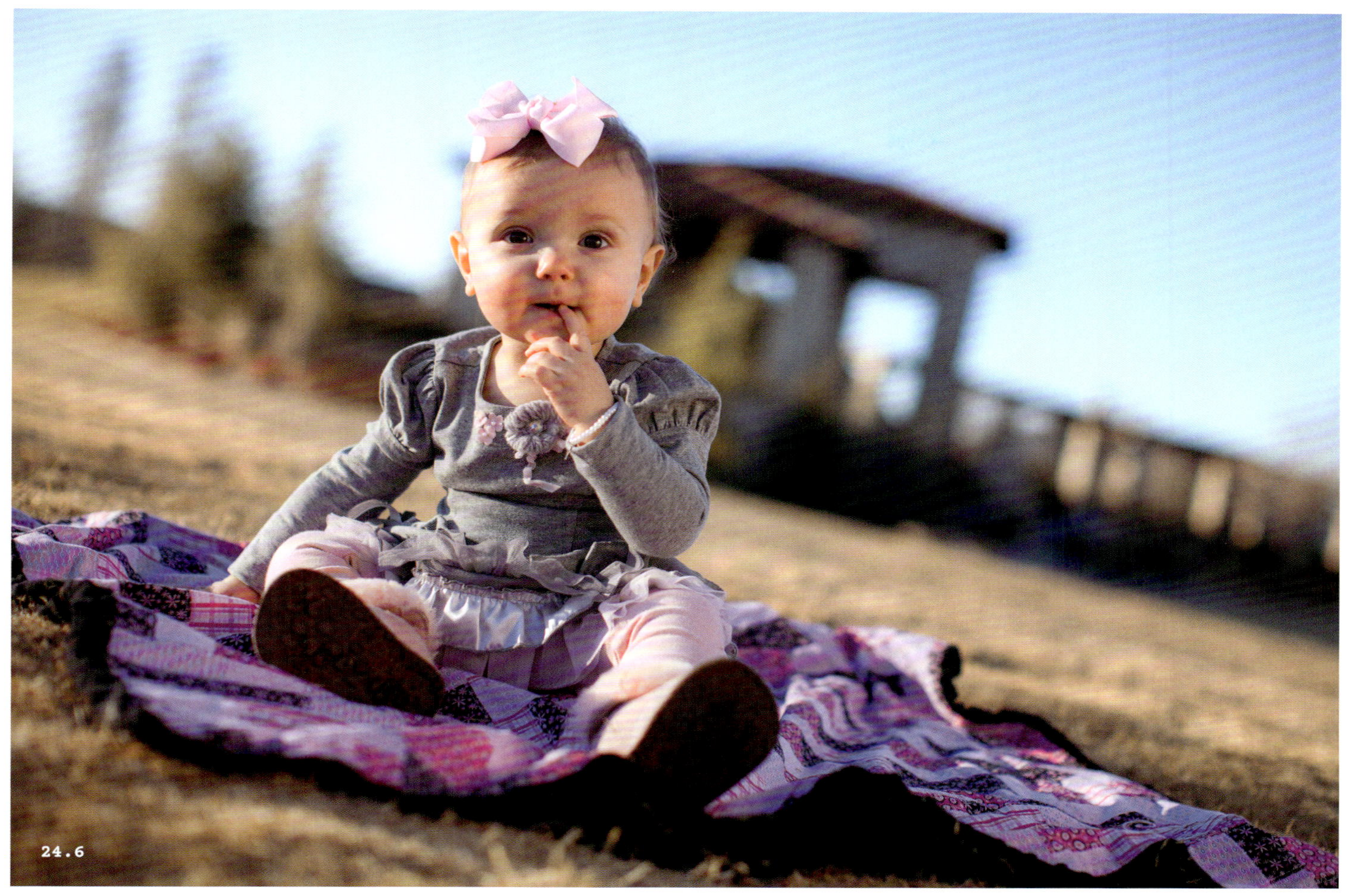

24.6

24.5 This portrait gained quite a bit of depth once I noticed the implied line the overhead lights were creating when I moved to a wider focal length.
ISO 200; 1/125 sec.; f/2; 18mm

24.6 Tilting the camera over provides an inherently attractive (although not always in a positive way) means of finding yourself to the subject. In this portrait, the leaning horizon also visually relates well to the quirkiness of the toddler's expression.
ISO 200; 1/5000 sec.; f/2; 50mm

25. FRAME YOUR SUBJECT

POSSIBLY ONE OF the most exciting compositional techniques is using visual structure to surround your portrait subject in a way that directs the viewer's eye to her. Referred to as framing, this technique is akin to using an actual frame, like a doorframe, to creatively pinpoint the exact spot you want your viewers to look. This is an extremely effective way of composing your portrait subject, and it can have great storytelling appeal.

A frame, like leading lines, can be made up of real frames, such as windows, archways, and doorframes. In many environments, these are readily available frames, and since the human eye is conditioned to seeing them as such, they work perfectly for drawing quick attention to your subject. Frames like this can be large or small, and they're usually fairly evident to the image viewer (**Figure 25.1**). They are, after all, literal frames.

Frames can also be constructed within the image based on how it is composed. In other words, frames are often created with just about anything that will surround the subject and push the eye toward him. For example, a tree branch arching over your subject can push the eye directly to her (**Figure 25.2**). A framing device does not need to be a complete frame, wrapping the subject with some sort of structure. Rather, it can be something that strongly forces the eye to the most important part of the image.

One of my favorite frames to use is not a physical structure at all. Shadow, a sometimes-overlooked frame, forces you to look at the light (**Figure 25.3**). If you surround your subject with shadow, or place them next to a large amount of it, it makes for a great framing device. Based on exposure values, shadow can drop to deep black and be an effective frame, or it can retain some environmental detail that complements your subject. Either way, you can always look for a way to incorporate shadows in framing your subject.

Framing, like all techniques, is most beneficial when used in conjunction with other compositional elements. For portraits that need some environment, look for leading lines that draw the eye to the device that frames your subject (**Figure 25.4**). As we'll discuss a bit later in the chapter, foreground subject matter can also play a role in framing your subject with narrative and environmental information. When considering using multiple compositional techniques together for an image (and you almost always will), the limitations for arranging your image in order to creatively move the viewer's eye to your subject are reduced.

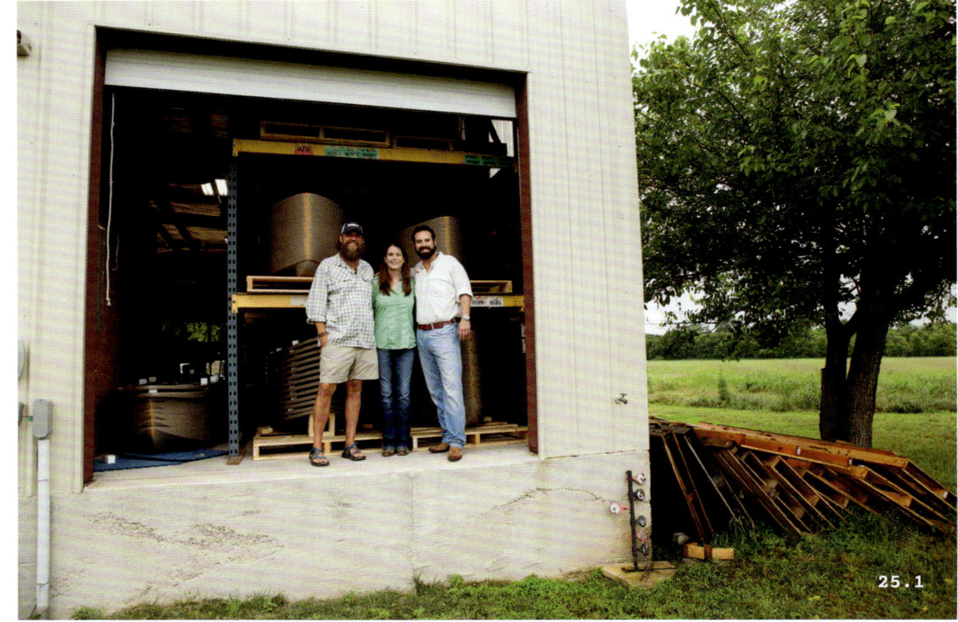

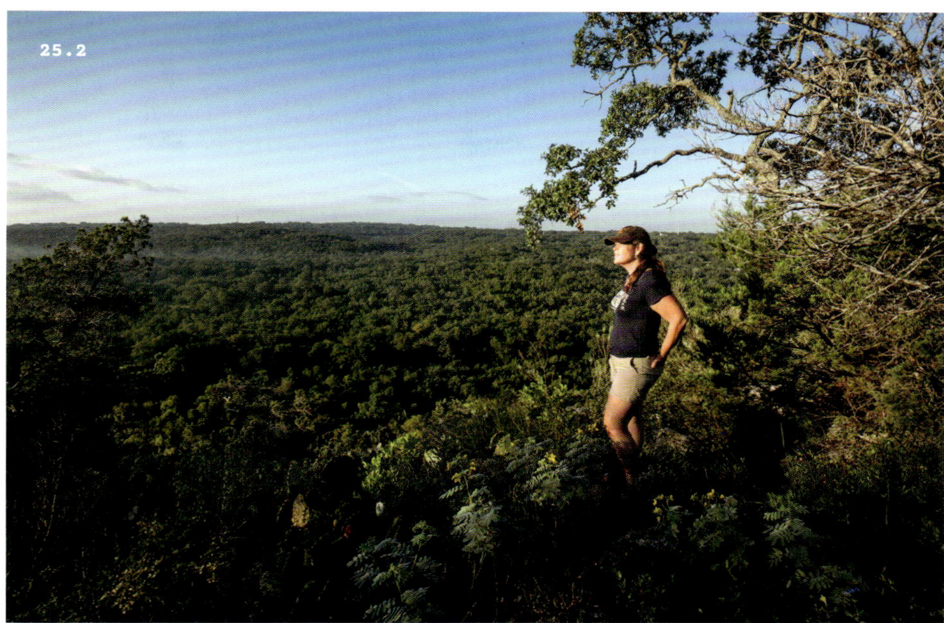

25.1 When photographing this small kayaking company, I found a nice frame for an environmental portrait in their loading bay door.
ISO 100; 1/100 sec.; f/5.6; 24mm

25.2 The live oak's overhanging branch served as a nice visual frame for this Nature Conservancy preserve manager.
ISO 200; 1/60 sec.; f/16; 17mm

25.3 When the shadow and light contrasts enough, explore your opportunity to use the darkness as a frame around your lit subject.
ISO 100; 1/100 sec.; f/4; 175mm

25.4 The out-of-focus line in the bottom right of the frame is a great way to move the eye back into the shot, moving you toward the doors framing the subject's head.
ISO 200; 1/400 sec.; f/2.8; 130mm

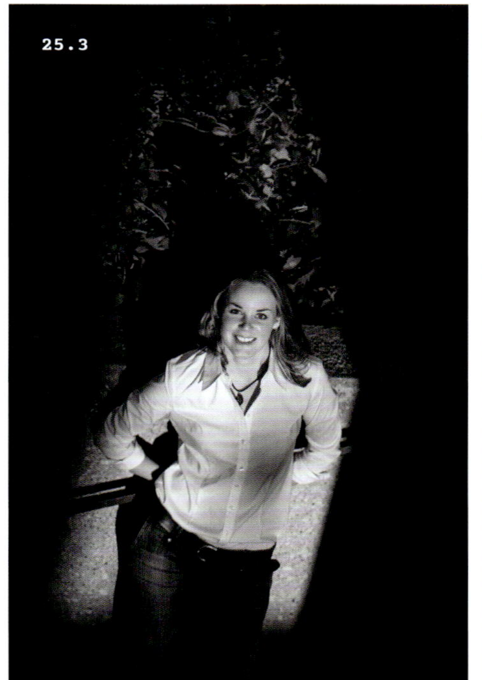

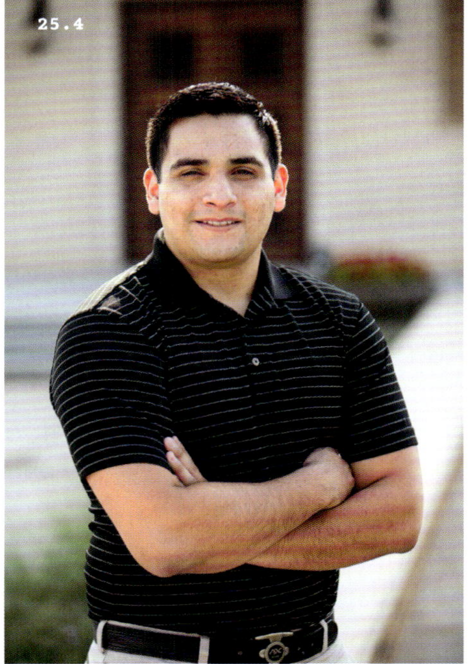

26. PAY ATTENTION TO THE BACKGROUND

IF THERE'S ONE thing I see new photographers failing to consider, it's the background. We get so wrapped up in focusing, setting depth of field, and finding correct exposure that we forget to actually see if the background is worthy of the portrait we just worked hard to devise. The background could be so bright that it draws the eye away from your subject. Or, it could be in focus just enough that the structure behind your subject distracts the viewer. A pole could be growing out of your subject's head! Before you snap the photo, it's worth giving more than a quick glance at the background.

The background does not have to say much, or anything at all, but it can break an image. Although there are no official rules regarding the background, there are a few things I like to keep in mind when it comes to the area beyond your subject in certain types of portrait photography.

For tighter portraits, such as headshots, find a background that lacks linear structures (such as tree limbs, fence stakes, and the like). Also, choose one that will go out of focus when using a shallow depth of field, and essentially becomes an abstract environment that won't distract from the subject (**Figure 26.1**). I especially do not want the background in these types of shots to overexpose, unless it is stylistically necessary. I tend to find subdued lighting for this type of portraiture, therefore reducing the risk of a brighter background.

For family and general portraiture—much of which is shot from just above the knee or tighter—I tend to follow the same guidelines. Again, this is the type of portraiture that relies heavily upon shallow depth of field and backgrounds that don't distract too much. However, the background is an important part of the portrait subject's narrative. For example, a college senior might be photographed leaning against recognizable campus architecture (**Figure 26.2**). When the background is a more essential part of the portrait, it might be a great idea to introduce a bit more compositional appeal to it. Out of focus layers, for example, work well; as do backgrounds of backlit foliage and colorful flowers (**Figure 26.3**). When it comes to out of focus backgrounds, explore the many possibilities. The idea is to use a background that isn't too busy and distracting.

The background is an even more essential part of many editorial style portraits, such as environmental portraits. In this case, the background is the environment and an important element in communicating a story or message about the portrait subject (**Figure 26.4**). These portraits are often made at wider focal lengths or with more depth of field, bringing the background (and foreground) more into focus. For these instances, I suggest placing your subject (especially his head) in the part of the background that is void of structure. Environmental portraits can certainly be made at shallow depths of field, but since the background always plays a larger part in the shot, compose it so that your subject stands out. If you are concerned that the background may be a bit distracting, it's a good idea to use your camera's Depth of Field Preview button to get a quick look at how in-focus the background becomes after placing your focus on the subject.

Ultimately, paying attention to the background is all about either reducing its potential for distraction or ensuring that it complements the narrative of your subject without becoming an eye-sore or attention hog. Remember, the next time you are making any type of portrait, look beyond the subject.

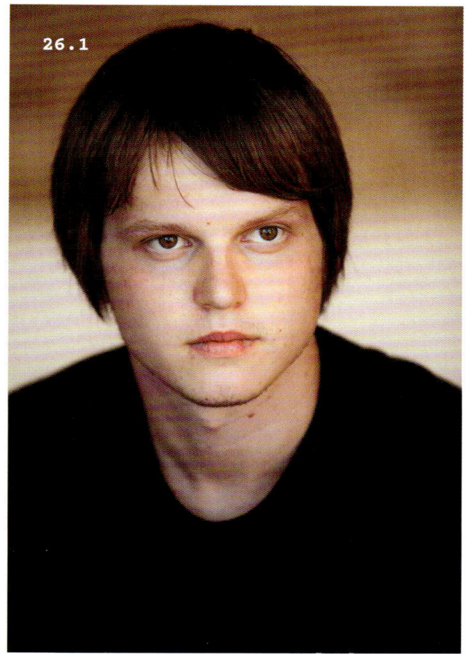

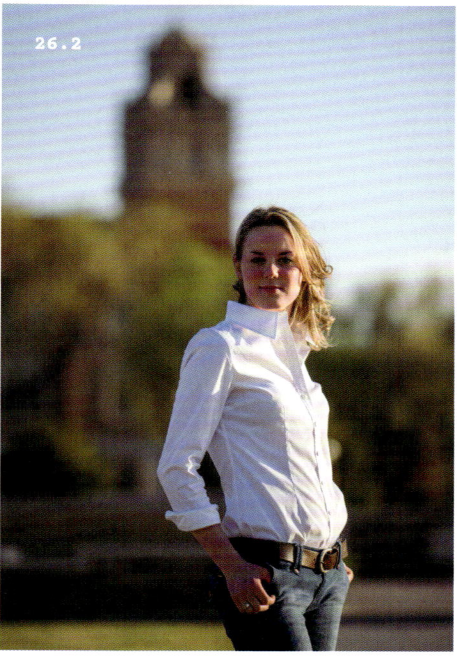

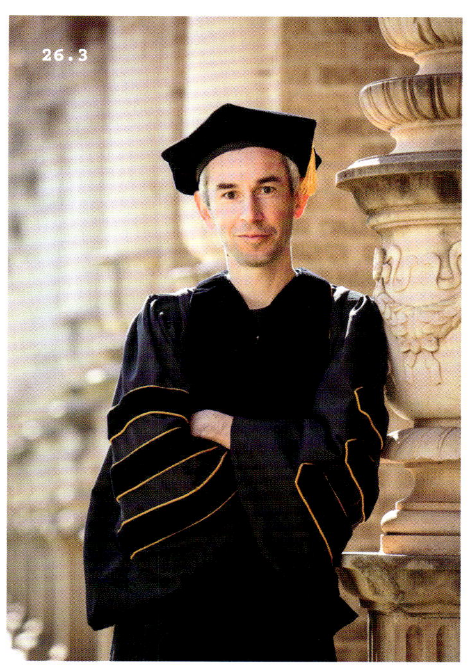

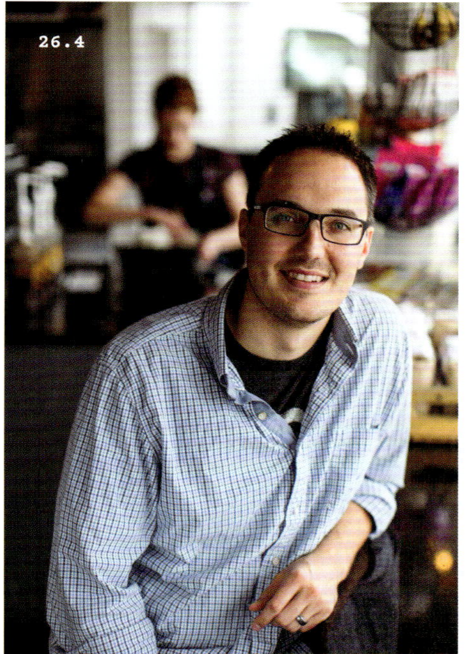

26.1 The background in this headshot is completely abstract and undistracting thanks to extremely shallow depth of field and muted, properly exposed light values and color tones.
ISO 400; 1/160 sec.; f/2.8; 180mm

26.2 Although out of focus, the still-recognizable iconic Texas Tech University bell tower serves as a nice background for this graduating senior's portrait.
ISO 100; 1/1600 sec.; f/2.8; 160mm

26.3 The layers in the background, although out of focus, serve as a nice, abstract pattern for the eye. They also provide a nice bit of academic context for the portrait.
ISO 200; 1/200 sec.; f/4.5; 160mm

26.4 I made several images of this coffee shop owner before the employee moved into the background behind the counter. Her presence provides a nice narrative element for the entrepreneur's environmental portrait.
ISO 200; 1/1250 sec.; f/1.8; 50mm

27. MOVE CLOSER

IT'S BEEN SAID many times over that in order to create more interesting images, move closer to the subject or action. The same applies to portrait photography. We're pretty comfortable staying at a respectable distance (physically or optically) from our subject; however, zooming in or physically moving closer to your subject also moves the viewer closer to them, capitalizing on the relationship you create between subject and audience, be it a portrait of a daughter for her mother or a Wall Street executive for the readers of an economic periodical.

Getting closer to your subject creates greater intimacy with them (**Figure 27.1**). Humans, as social creatures, heavily read into non-verbal communication, such as body language, gesture, and facial characteristics. Reducing the perceived distance between subject and camera pushes the viewer into a distance in which non-verbal cues are easily read. As a result, the viewer becomes more interested in the image *and* the subject since they are given a greater opportunity to learn more about him without the use of words or audio.

Not all portraits need to be made at very close distances for them to be engaging. I don't mean to argue away from full and medium shots (especially since I tend to gravitate toward them as an environmental portrait shooter). I will argue, though, that we can do a better job of moving the viewer closer to the subject occasionally to exploit their tendency to really focus on the subject. Some of the most powerful portraits throughout history (think about Steve McCurry's portrait of Sharbat Gula, better known to Western audiences as The Afghan Girl, who appeared on a 1985 *National Geographic* magazine cover) are those that move the viewer so close to the subject that everything else around the subject becomes void.

The question, then, becomes: how close is too close? The answer depends on the purpose of the portrait. I think it's best to answer this question with a few things that you might want to avoid regarding the top and bottom of a person's head.

First, avoid cutting through the subject's chin with the bottom of the frame (**Figure 27.2**). It's best to always give the indication that the subject does indeed have a neck, so composing the bottom of the frame (especially for headshots) so the neck is visible is a good idea (**Figure 27.3**).

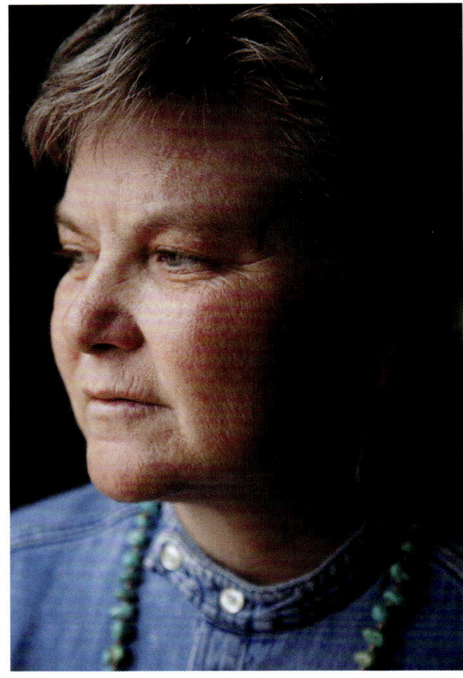

27.1 Getting closer allows you to frame your portraits tighter and convey a great deal of intimacy with the subject, like I did with a portrait of writer and artist Kippra Hopper.
ISO 400; 1/40 sec.; f/4; 75mm

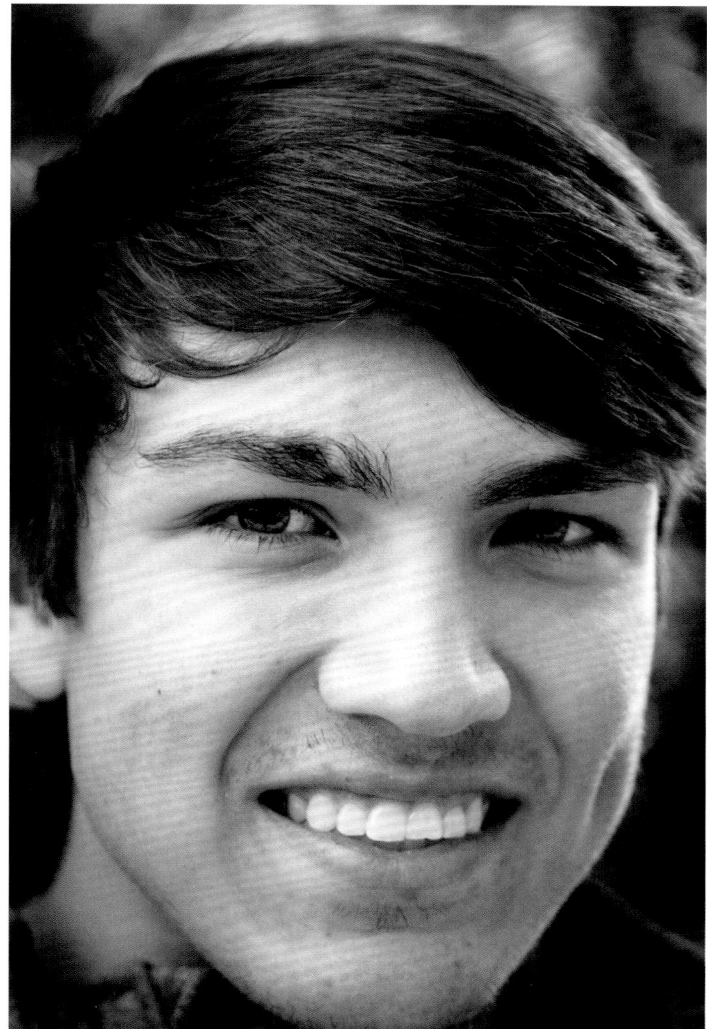

27.2 Although this image feels too tight to begin with, one of the more irksome characteristics is the chin being cut off.

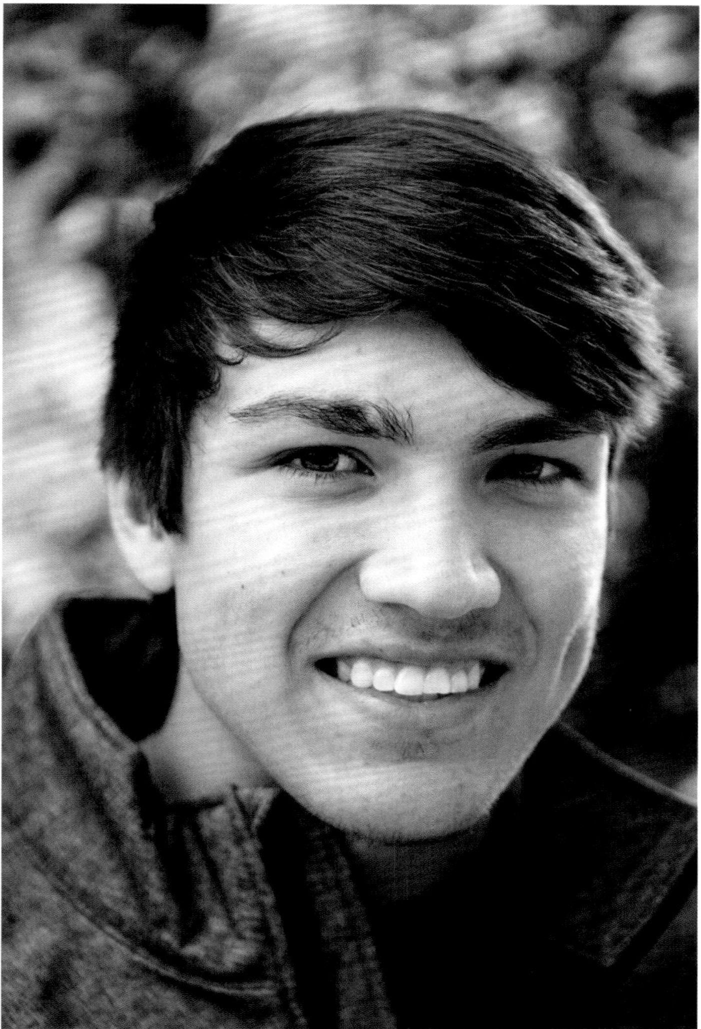

27.3 A more backed out framing of the portrait allows the chin "room to breathe" and the next is exposed, creating a more complete, natural visualization of the person being photographed.
ISO 100; 1/640 sec.; f/2.8; 70mm

Second, if you're tight enough to be cutting off the chin, consider how much of the top of the head is being cut. It has become trendy over the years to create portraits and headshots so close to the subject that the top of the head is cut off. I like this proximity, and it certainly forces the eye to engage the subject. However, there's a fine line between cutting too far into the forehead and cutting too little into the top of the head. If your subject has a full head of hair, I suggest cutting no lower than the hairline, and instead, leaning toward leaving a good bit of that hair showing underneath the edge of the frame (**Figure 27.4**). However, don't cut just a few millimeters of hair out of the frame for risk of making the image look incomplete (**Figure 27.5**). This is a rather subjective call. Finding a middle ground between intimacy and awkward composition is the ideal solution here.

Finally, a warning: when moving in close to your subject with a wide focal length (shorter than 50mm), beware of how distorted your subject becomes. Wider focal lengths increase the level of optical distortion present in the image (**Figure 27.6**). Place a human subject amidst that distortion, and our perception of reality becomes, well, distorted. The closer you move a wide focal length to your subject, the more likely his nose will elongate, his chin will become larger, and his face will bulge toward the camera. The closer you compose his face to the side of the frame, the more it will stretch toward that side. The effect increases as the focal lengths get wider. All lenses distort to some degree, but wider focal lengths do so more obviously. It's a good idea to avoid moving a wide focal length so close to your subject that all you can see in the frame is his head. It won't come across as the subject would like.

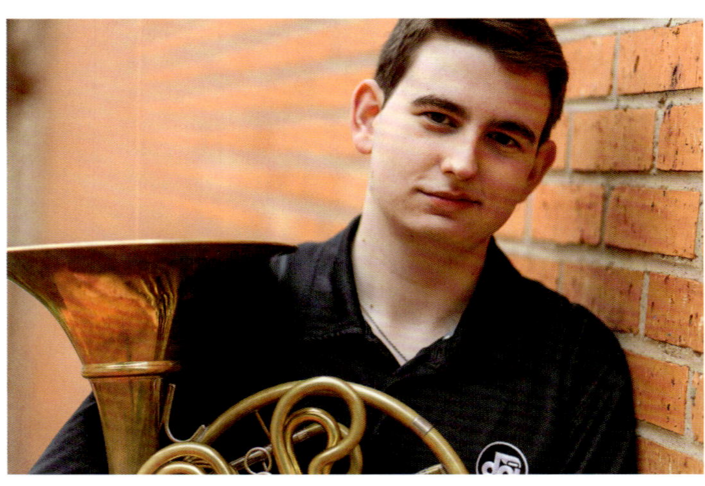

27.4 Cutting into the top of the head to create a framed intimacy with the subject is stylistically popular, as long as there's still enough hair underneath the top edge of the frame to give the viewer context to the subject's head and form.
ISO 200; 1/320 sec.; f/1.8; 85mm

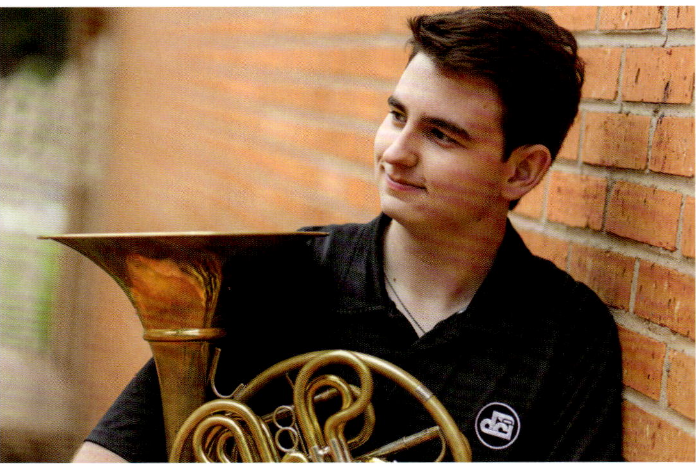

27.5 Consequently, cutting off too little of the top of the head simply results in a poorly composed image that leaves the viewer wondering about the top of the subject's head. This is visual tension best reduced as much as possible.

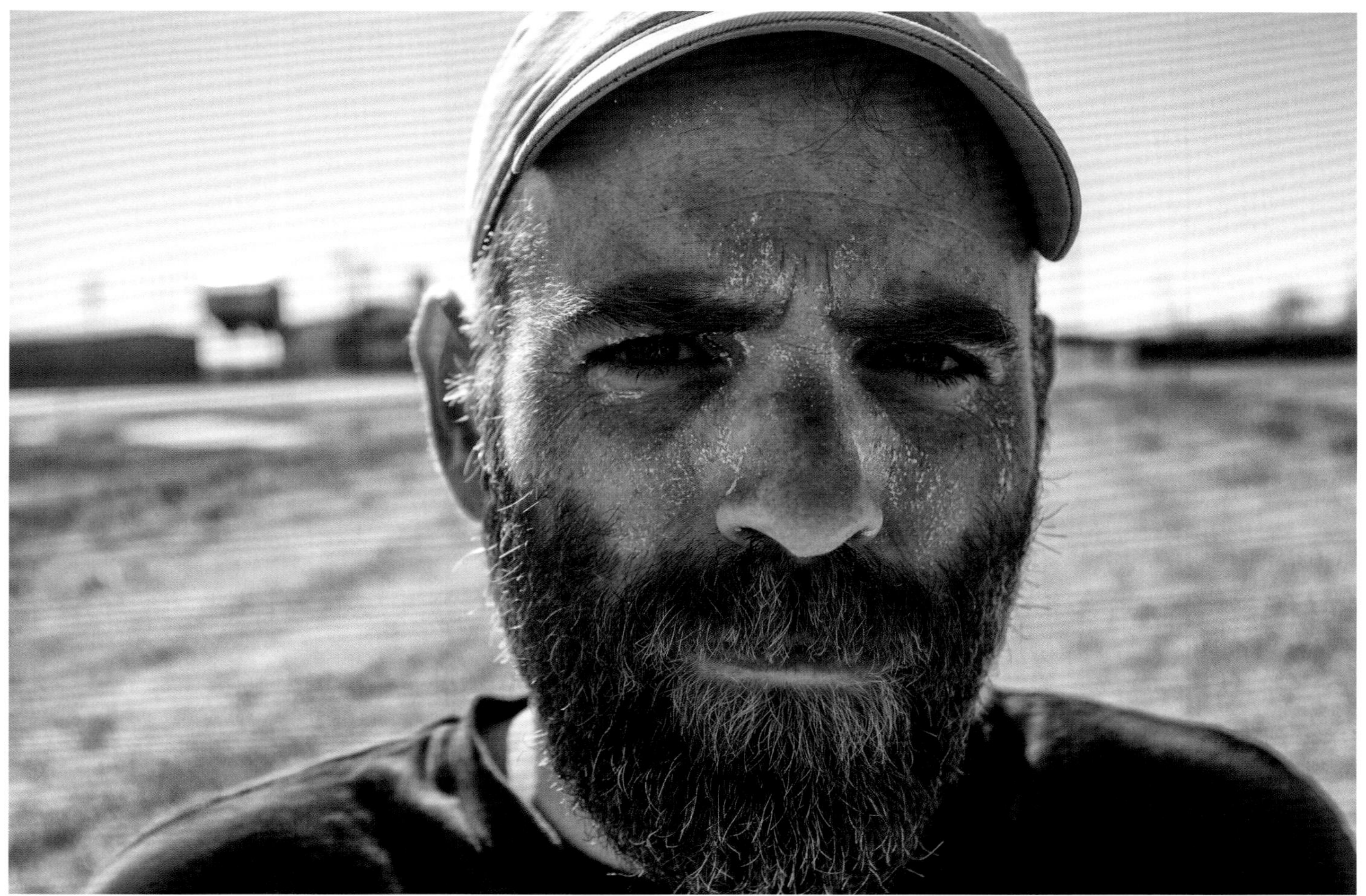

27.6 In trying to create a portrait of a weary bikepacker after a couple days in the desert, I pushed a wider focal length close to his face, making it bulge toward the camera. Personally, I don't care for how much it does push toward the camera while also composing the bottom of his beard out of the frame.
ISO 200; 1/400 sec.; f/2.8; 130mm

28. GET SOME PERSPECTIVE

THIS HAS MORE to do with optics than anything else, but your lens perspective will often determine your portrait composition. Perspective refers to how everything in your shot appears in spatial relationship to each other. For example, normal perspective describes how we perceive everything with our own eyes. Photographically, this is achieved with a 50mm lens on a full-frame sensor—hence the popularity of that focal length for just about any type of photography outside wildlife and sports (**Figure 28.1**). You'll start to introduce differences in perspective with anything wider or more telephoto than 50mm, and it's important to know how such differences might work for or against your portrait photography.

Aside from normal perspective, the two other perspective types photographers consider are expansive and compression. Optically, the wider your focal length is, the more expansive its provided perspective. Subsequently, the longer your focal length is, the more compressed its perspective becomes. Both have increasingly dramatic visual effects.

When a perspective is expanded, the foreground becomes relatively larger than the background and the visual distance between the two grows. Ultra-wide focal lengths like 14mm and 16mm are champions of creating this expansive look, and it's little wonder why landscape photographers pine over lenses that offer these characteristics. However, wider focal lengths can certainly be useful for the portrait photographer, particularly when creating environmental portraits (**Figure 28.2**). Expansive perspective can also convey a sense of importance about your subject, particularly when framing her from the waist up. This perspective pushes her toward the camera and somewhat farther away from her environment, making her the largest subject in the frame (**Figure 28.3**).

Expansive perspective does have its disadvantages for portraits, though, and they are very apparent. Ultra-wide focal lengths (anything wider than 24mm on a full-frame sensor) can severely distort a subject's face or body. Believe me, your subject will not appreciate being made to look like Pinocchio. I try not to shoot any wider than 24mm when composing the subject from just a few feet away (**Figure 28.4**); I lean more toward 35mm for such shots. I certainly suggest avoiding shooting headshots at anything wider than 50mm.

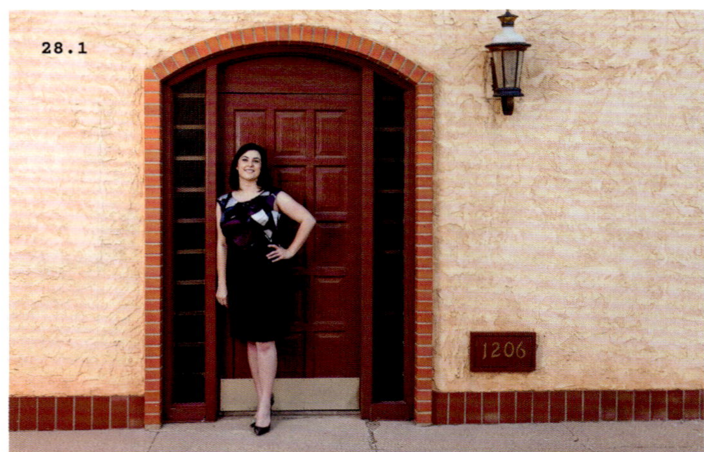

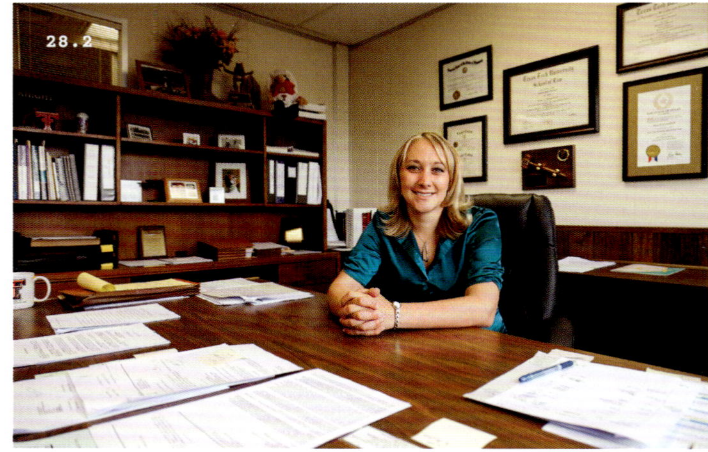

28.1 50mm is a great focal length for full-length portraits, especially when composed against architecture that you do not want to distort. **ISO 100; 1/125 sec.; f/2.8; 50mm**

28.2 I used a wide-angle, expansive perspective to not only showcase the attorney's office, but to also force the desk to surround the subject with her work. **ISO 200; 1/50 sec.; f/4; 24mm**

28.3 Pushing a wide angle focal length toward the subject allows her to jump from the background, which visually looks farther away from her than it is in reality. This is a great way to create depth in your environmental portraits. **ISO 400; 1/250 sec.; f/2.8; 17mm**

28.4 Still, at 24mm, the expansive perspective distorts the body. In this shot, my wife's head is slightly larger in relation to the rest of her body, a result of it being composed toward the left and top edges of the frame and angled slightly down on her. **ISO 100; 1/500 sec.; f/5.6; 24mm**

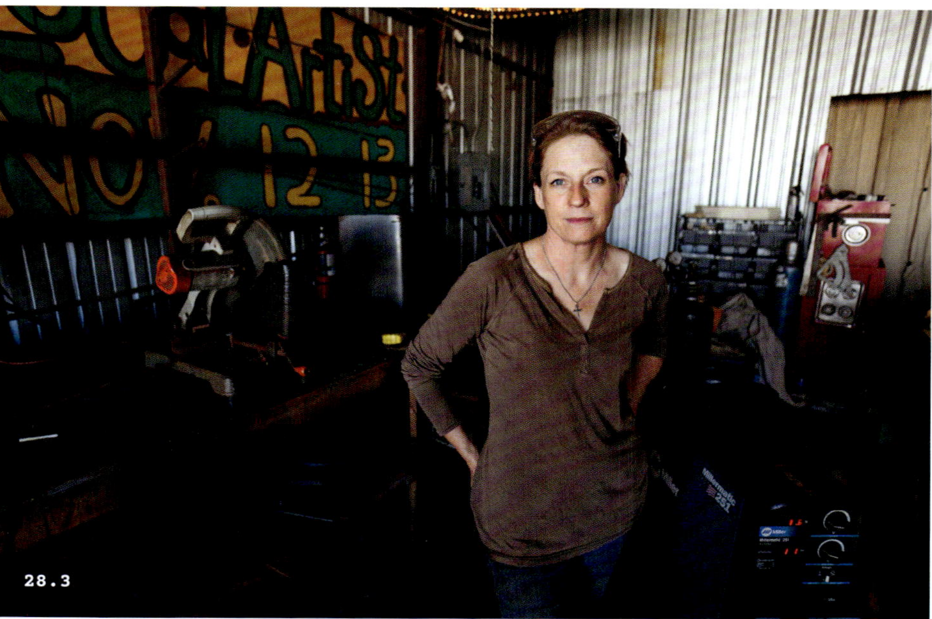
28.3

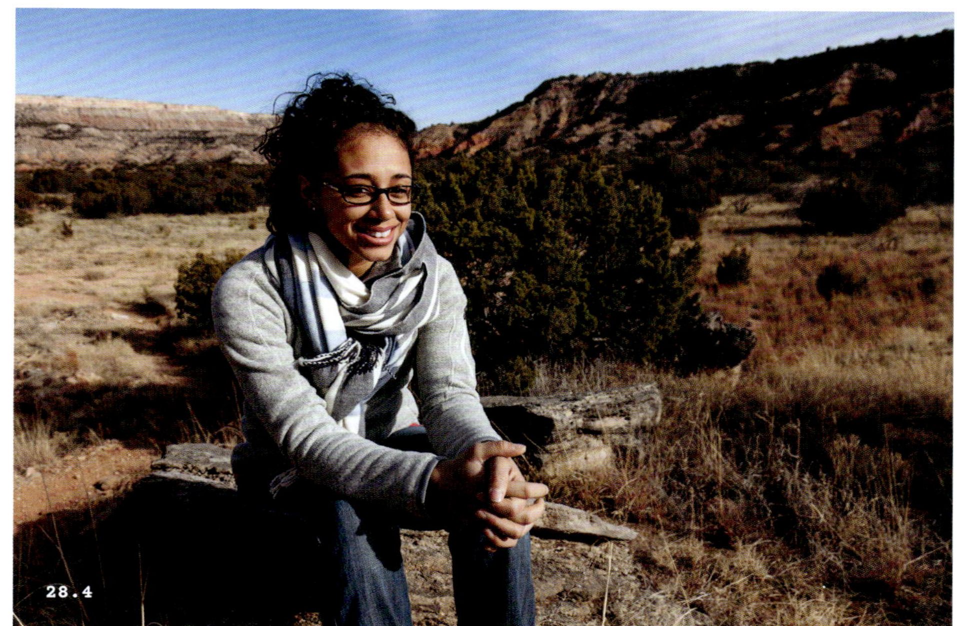
28.4

As the focal length gets longer, the image becomes more compressed. This means the foreground and background become visually closer together, flattening the optical expansion inherent in wider focal lengths. As it turns out, this is great for most portraiture (**Figure 28.5**). My favorite longer focal length is around 200mm. When combined with a shallow depth of field, using a more compressed perspective isolates your subject well, especially when the background is relatively uncomplicated. It's also a great way to pull a background of narrative significance closer to the subject, and it illustrates (even elaborates), scale (**Figure 28.6**).

The downside to compressed perspectives is that they are sometimes low on environmental information (**Figure 28.7**). It's not an insufficient perspective for environmental portraits; it just may not be the best choice when the subject and the background are within close proximity to each other. However, other than the stability needed to shoot with longer focal lengths, they are a great go-to for technically achieving a non-distorting, compressed perspective for your portraits.

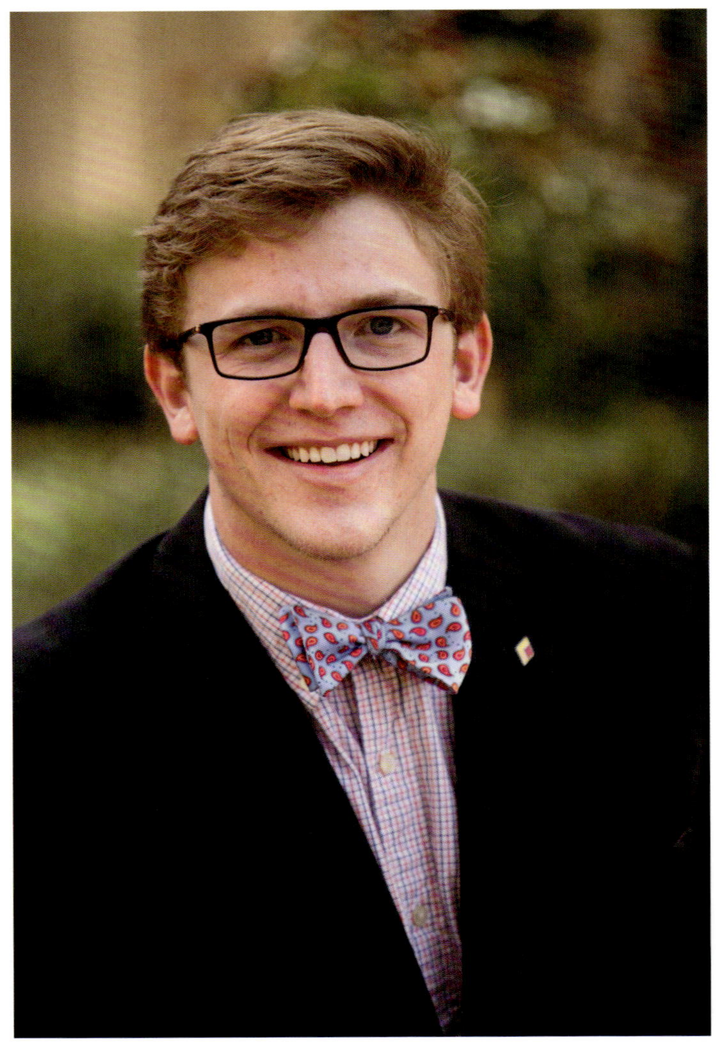

28.5 Compressed perspectives created by longer focal lengths do not distort the subject (especially their face). ISO 100; 1/250 sec.; f/2.8; 195mm

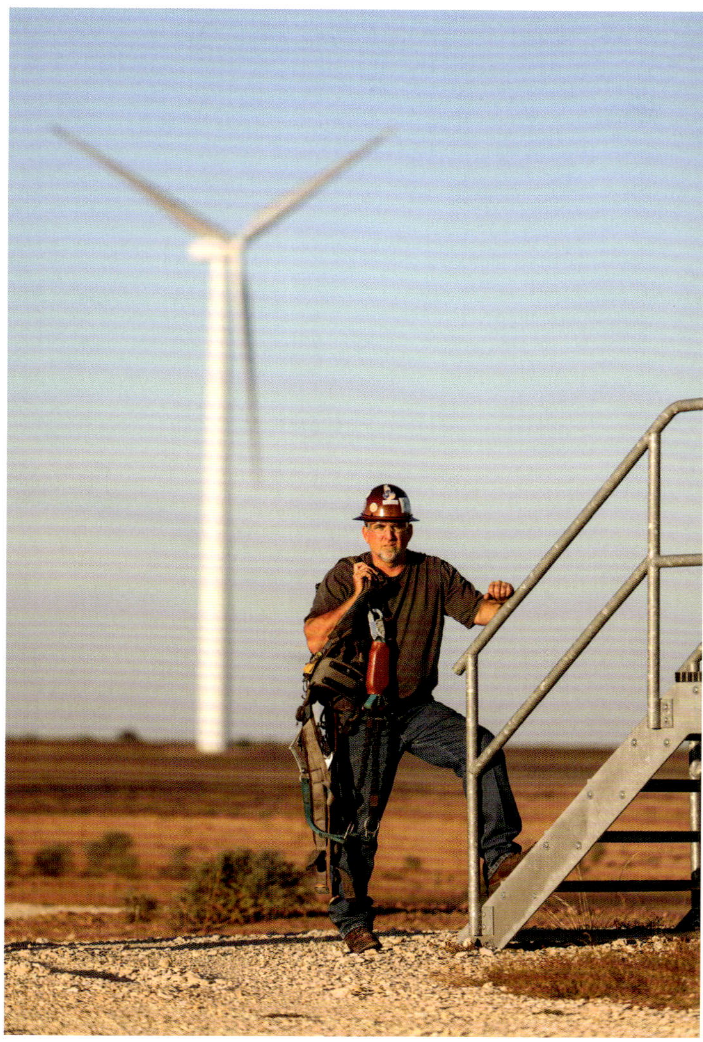

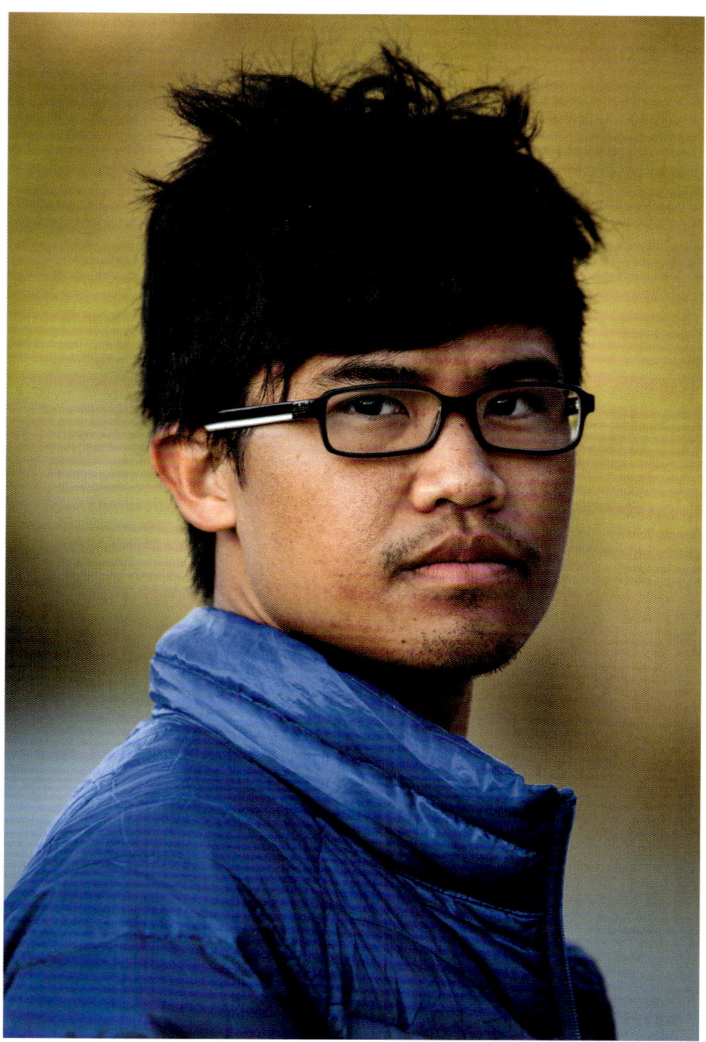

28.6 I used a longer focal length to compress the foreground and background together, bringing that lone wind turbine closer to the turbine technician than in reality for narrative purposes.
ISO 50; 1/640 sec.; f/2.8; 170mm

28.7 In many cases, the longer the focal length you use, the less environmental information will be included in the frame with your subject, especially when you also use a shallow depth of field.
ISO 200; 1/200 sec.; f/4; 300mm

THERE'S QUITE A bit about photography that has interpretive value. The height, or angle, from which you photograph your portrait subject can often convey subjective characteristics about him. Subjective as it may be, the angle of a portrait does typically imply certain meanings that should be well considered when photographing people.

Shooting from a lower angle than your subject has several effects (**Figure 29.1**). First, it visually makes your subject appear taller and generally larger. The second you dip below your subject's eyeline, you position the image viewer under her. This effect is heightened as your focal length becomes wider. And, as discussed in the previous tip, going too wide will extremely distort your subject. Shooting with an extremely wide-angle focal length from well below your subject is a quick way to make them look like a giant with legs a mile long. Let this be a warning that not everyone enjoys that look.

Subjectively, shooting from below also implies the subject has power (**Figure 29.2**). Looking up toward the subject can capitalize on his respectful authority in the workplace and convey an intimidating characteristic about him. Again, the lower the angle, the more powerful the subject will seem.

Consequently, shooting from a high angle forces the viewer to look down on the subject (**Figure 29.3**). Although this does not necessarily make the subject look shorter, it does reduce the ability to see much of her form. Having someone look up into the camera can help slim the size of a subject's face and neck (**Figure 29.4**). Of course, the more you have the subject look up, the potential for a cricked neck and an awkwardly angled image increases.

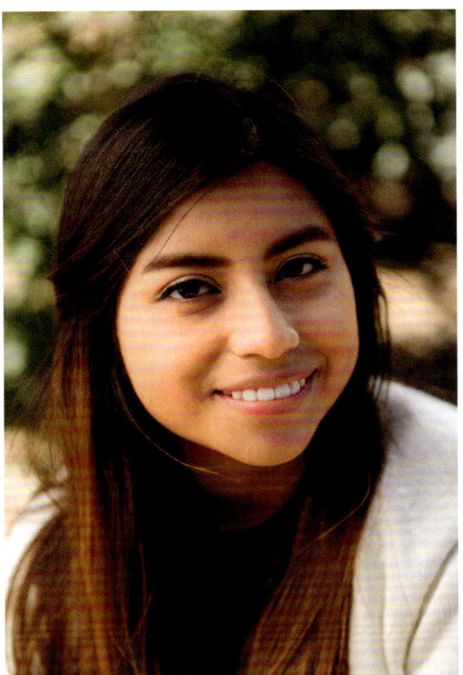

29.1 The low angle and wide focal length combines to create a larger-than-life visualization of the subject.
ISO 200; 1/2900 sec.; f/2; 18mm

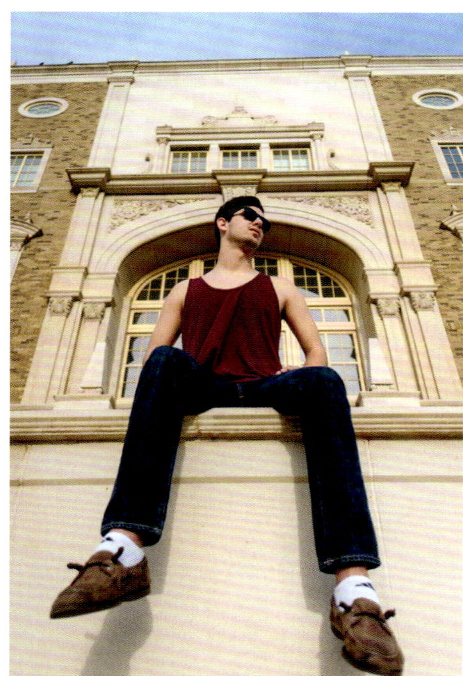 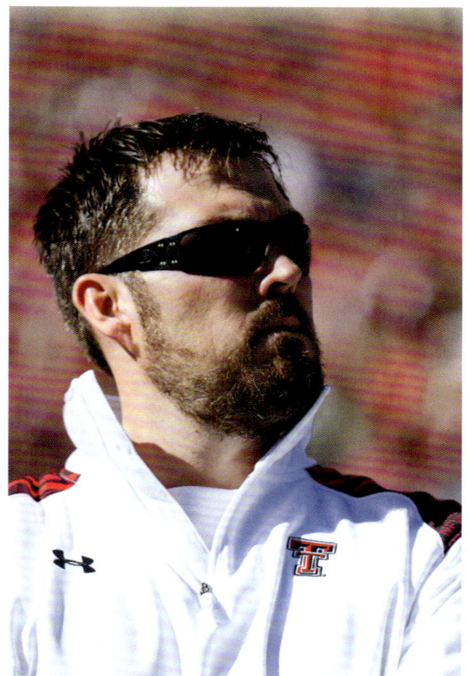 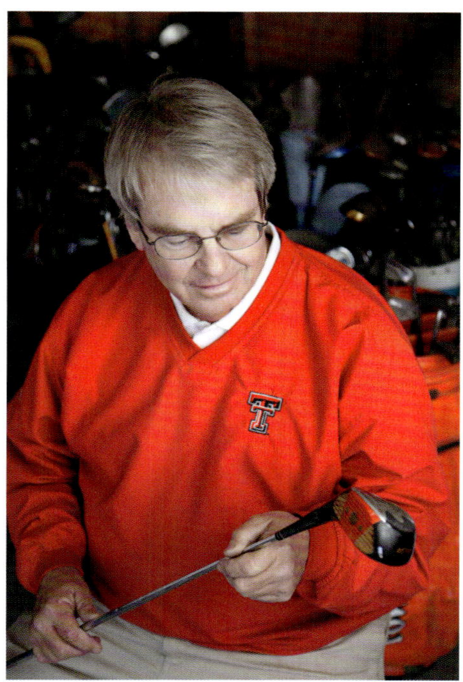

29.2 When on assignment photographing Marcus Luttrell, known for his service as a Navy SEAL and author of *Lone Survivor,* I created several portraits of him from slightly below, conveying the amount of power, and slight intimidation, he exhibits. It didn't hurt that he was a bit taller than I am, either.
ISO 100; 1/2500 sec.; f/2.8; 175mm

29.3 Photographing down on a subject is a good way to show off context when the subject is sitting, as well as to reduce any aggressive characteristics conveyed by shooting under the subject.
ISO 200; 1/40 sec.; f/4; 58mm

29.4 Photographing your subject from a slightly higher angle is a good way to use the head and chin to reduce the view of any blemishes or unflattering features in the subject's neckline.
ISO 100; 1/500 sec.; f/2.8; 70mm

However, shooting from a higher angle on the subject can meaningfully imply that she is somewhat inferior. When the viewer is looking down on the subject, he can sometimes be *looking down* on the subject (**Figure 29.5**). The subject can be made to look as if they lack the benevolent power the viewer maintains (think about some third world country charity images), or weak in the eyes of a captor or judge. Either way, shooting from a high angle can often imply a negative characteristic about your subject, one that may be unfair or disadvantageous to their reality. Personally, I'm not a fan of shooting from higher angles outside headshots and environmental portraits that must showcase an expanse of environment.

A common angle sometimes overlooked in discussion is the eyeline. Shooting from an angle that matches the viewer's eye with those of the subject is effective because we immediately engage with a subject whose eyes are at a natural level related to our own viewpoint. It also gives us a greater sense of their space and how they occupy it. For example, a child photographed from above is simply a child photographed from above, leaving the ground to become the background to the subject. However, the moment you photograph the child on her level—which often necessitates getting on the ground with her—you are now in her world (**Figure 29.6**). This is a world that we often don't contemplate because we're conditioned to look down on the child. Especially when working with subjects that are either taller or shorter (for whatever reason) than you, work to shoot portraits of them at their eye level, and the interest factor of your images will increase.

Finally, bear in mind that the subjective nature of the angle from which you shoot your portrait is largely a result of who your subject is and how he otherwise appears in the shot. Image viewers are incredibly discerning and they can tell the difference between a shot of a corporate manager photographed from slightly below and a staged shot of a mob boss. However, it's worth assessing your angle before you make portraits to insure the appropriate message.

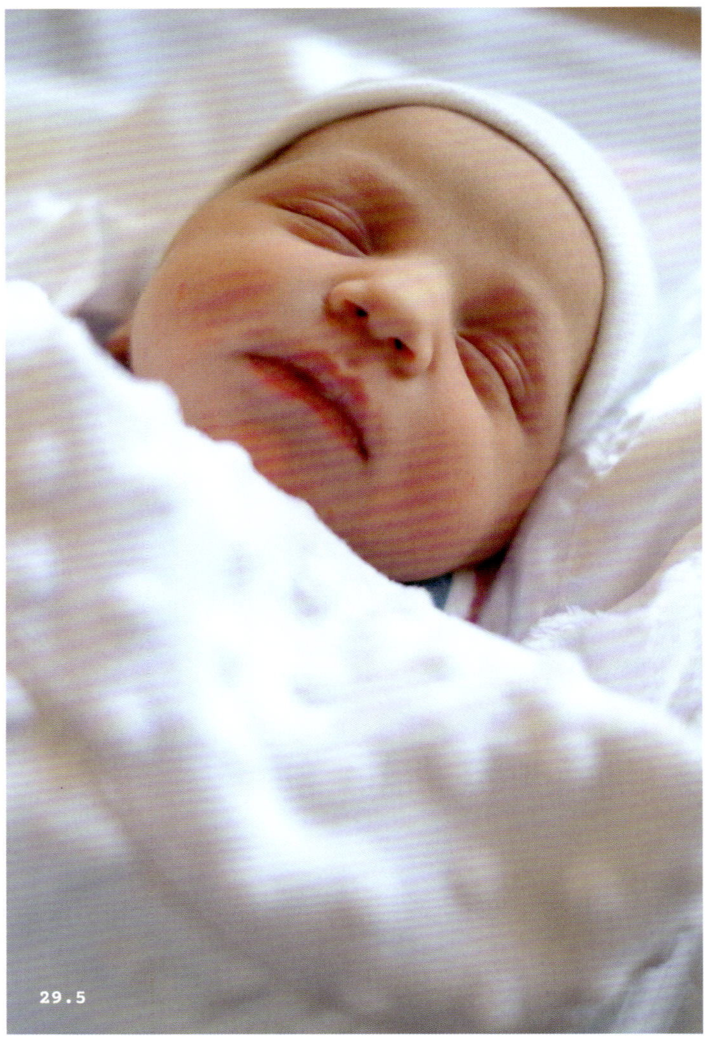

29.5 One way to show the innocence and powerlessness of a newborn is to photograph down on her.
ISO 400; 1/280 sec.; f/1.4; 35mm

29.6 Getting on my daughter's level made for a much more engaging action portrait than if I was shooting the same thing from above at the same focal length. This angle puts you in her world.
ISO 400; 1/320 sec.; f/2.8; 145mm

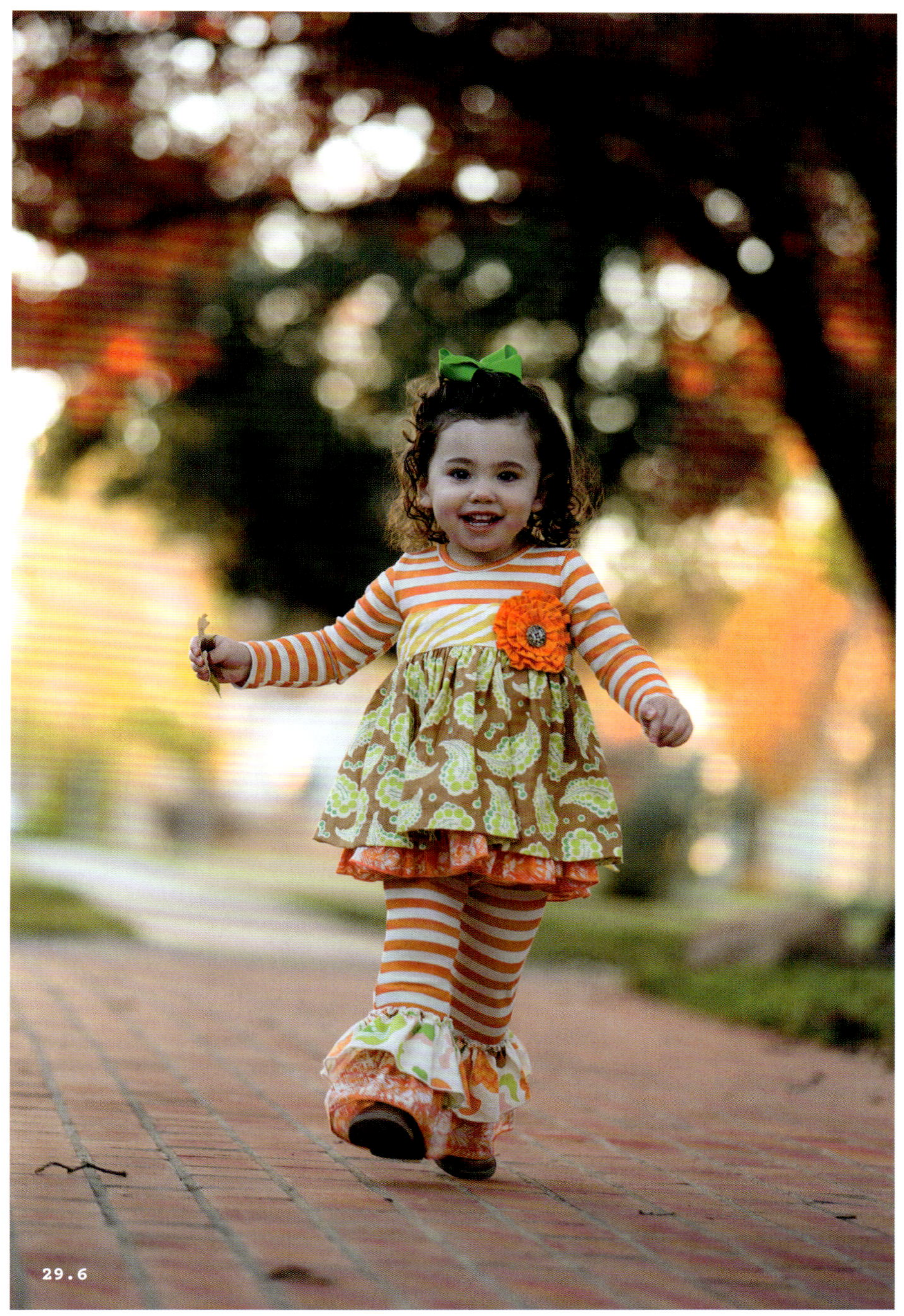
29.6

30. PUT SOMETHING IN THE FOREGROUND

AS AN EDITORIAL shooter, I'm always looking for ways to let the environment say something about my portrait subjects. However, when photographers attempt to let the environment contribute to the subject's narrative, we're prone to use the subject as our foreground interest and let the environment speak from the back. This, however, negates the significance of the environment in front of the subject. More than likely, the environment in front of the subject is also contributing to this narrative, and it's worth using. Foreground elements can be effective visual frames for your portrait subject (**Figure 30.1**). Whether the foreground structure forms a visual arch or simply a block of shadow or color, this technique lets you introduce elements that potentially contribute to the subject's story (or the story you want to imply). They can also push the viewer's eye toward the subject.

Placing something in the foreground keeps a portrait from looking flat, dimensionally and stylistically (**Figure 30.2**). Composing a portrait with relevant subject matter in the foreground includes new elements of the environment into the shot while also introducing a new way for the eye to move *into* the shot. In doing so, you are forcing the eye to see environmental foreground, mid-ground, and background. Mostly likely, your subject will be the mid-ground, and the foreground and background visually sandwich her into the frame. Although you can compose the foreground, mid-ground, and background subject matter to lead the eye across an image (say, from left to right), you're also making the eye look inward, into that elusive third dimension (**Figure 30.3**).

When composing foreground structure in your portraits, consider using shallow depth of field. This will make both the background and foreground go out of focus (**Figure 30.4**). This reduces the potential for the foreground to dominate the viewer's attention, while also surrounding your subject with that soft bokeh that so many folks enjoy about portraits.

Not all portraits demand foreground. Many types of portraits are actually damaged by it, such as some formal portraiture, headshots, and anything that might be considered traditional portraiture. However, in an era where editorial and documentary photographic styles are also appreciated in wedding and family portraiture, seeking out great foreground material for your subject might be fruitful.

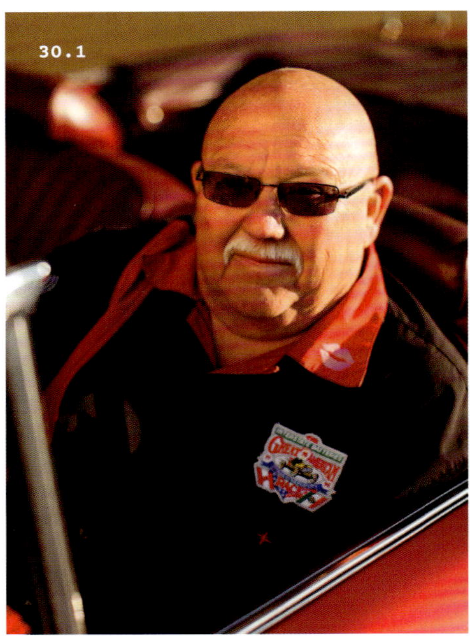

30.1 Although it only takes up a small amount of the image's real estate, the car door and the side of the windshield are great foreground pieces to project you toward the car owner. They work as great compositional frames as well.
ISO 100; 1/1250 sec.; f/2; 50mm

30.2 Placing the front of the tractor in front of the museum director created depth in the shot, something past which the viewer has to look to get to the subject and then the background.
ISO 200; 1/250 sec.; f/4; 200mm

30.3 I took advantage of the large curtain in the foreground to provide some scale and depth for the portrait of the toddler.
ISO 200; 1/400 sec.; f/2.8; 130mm

30.4 Although the foreground is out of focus, the lines leading you to the subject and beyond are still evident, serving as a great way to provide compositional depth without the need for stopping down the aperture.
ISO 50; 1/800 sec.; f/2; 50mm

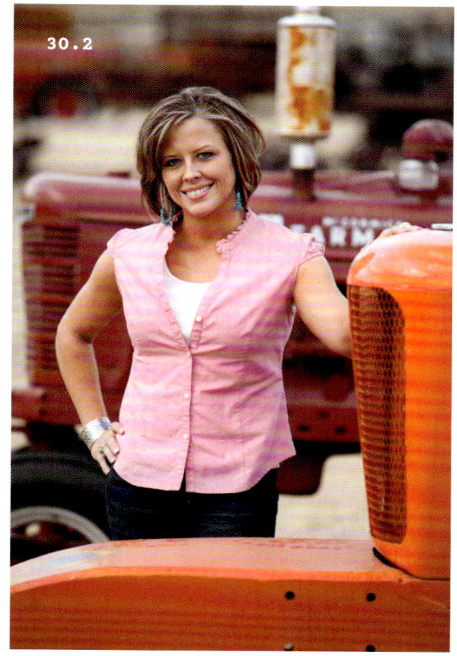

30.2

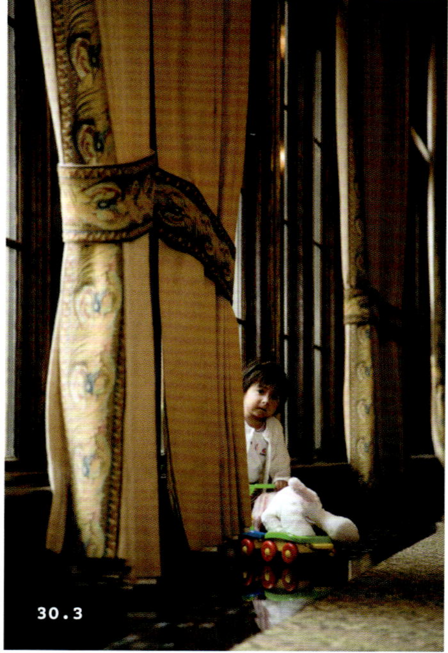

30.3

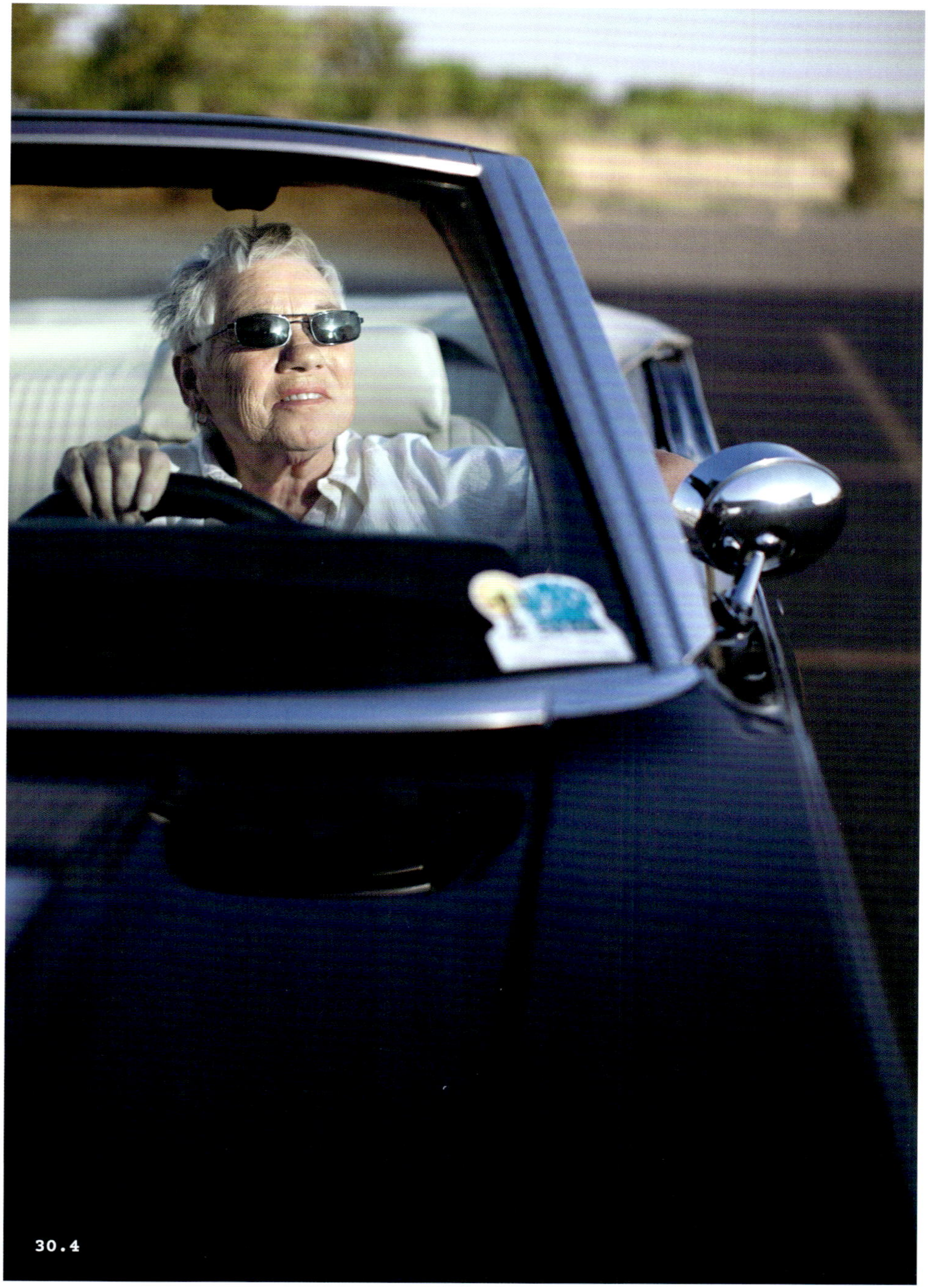

30.4

31. SHOOT THROUGH EVERYTHING

SPEAKING OF COMPOSING a portrait with foreground structure, one way to break away from the norm is to literally shoot through the structure. Before we dive too much into this, I'll mention that shooting through a foreground structure will not necessarily make for a great portrait. The structure must have a level of transparency or actual gaps to ensure the portrait subject is visible. However, when you can include structures that allow the subject to be seen, it can provide a creative compositional boost to your images.

I like to shoot through foreground structure to provide a sense of place (**Figure 31.1**). Similar to including relevant information in the foreground, when the structure through which you are shooting relates to your subject, it gives the viewer an idea about the environment in which the image is made. This environment can be abstract or it can be necessary for the subject's story. Either way, the viewer gains a bit more information when being forced to look past environmental detail to see the subject.

And, like so many other compositional techniques, this one gives you an added sense of depth (**Figure 31.2**). Relating to this notion of foreground/mid-ground/background composition, the structure through which you're shooting becomes the foreground element. Typically, it's appropriate to fill the frame with this structure in order to make the most of this technique and effect.

The question that remains is: what actually constitutes great structure through which to shoot? The answer is uncomplicated: everything that has a degree of transparency. Sheer material (such as a curtain or a bride's veil) work very well for portraits. Likewise, backlit leaves are a popular choice for senior portraits, especially when the foliage is colorful. Fences, flowers (**Figure 31.3**), and just about anything else that can be used as a creative change-up can make for nice structure. Even shooting through sun flare can be effective—this technique has become very popular in the past several years (**Figure 31.4**).

I'll close the tip with best practices for employing this technique. First, it's a good idea to vertically or horizontally fill the frame with the structure through which you are shooting as opposed to placing foreground elements in a portion of the frame. Shooting through something is just that: shooting completely through it. This makes the viewer feel like they are a part of the scene or getting to peer in on it from the outside. Second, and this is fairly important, use shallow depth of field. Even though your objective is to put structure in front of your subject, it can't be so prominent that the subject is indiscernible. If the structure is too in focus because the aperture is stopped down too much, it can make the image too busy, block the subject, or (at the very least), get in the way. Using as low an aperture as possible is ideal. Prime lenses at 50mm or 85mm focal lengths that feature extremely fast maximum apertures (which can open as wide as f/1.2 for some models) are great lenses to use for this technique.

Composing your portrait by placing structure completely in front of your subject is a great way to creatively change up composition and visual appeal. It's probably not something you want to use all of the time, but it can be something you seek out for most portrait shoots. Keep this technique in your toolbox, and you won't be disappointed when the opportunity to use it arises.

31.1 Shooting through the grass not only provides a sense of place for the subject, it also creates an entirely new, somewhat whimsical environment in which she can play.
ISO 200; 1/400 sec.; f/2; 85mm

31.2 Shooting through the plexiglass wall toward the newborn gives a sense of depth to the shot, providing a definite foreground (wall), mid-ground (subject), and background (out-of-focus context).
ISO 800; 1/250 sec.; f/2.8; 70mm

31.3 Combined with an angle on the subject's level, shooting through the corn stalks in the corn maze heightens the sense of wonder visually exhibited by the subject.
ISO 800; 1/400 sec.; f/2.8; 130mm

31.4 Even sun flare can be worth shooting through, especially to create light and airy lifestyle portraits!
ISO 200; 1/500 sec.; f/1.4; 35mm

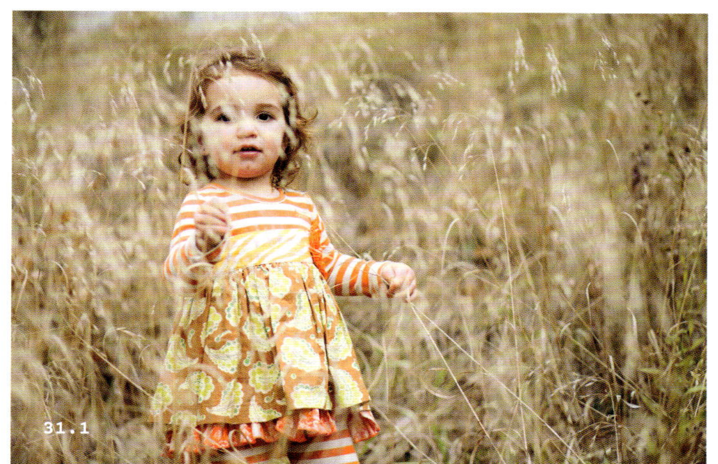

31.1

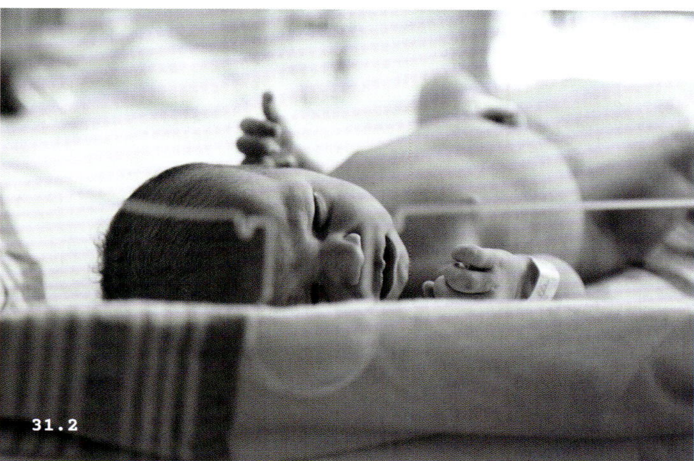

31.2

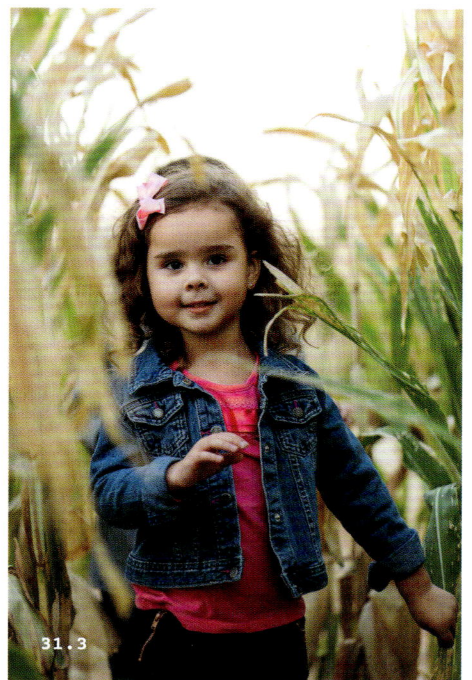

31.3

31.4

GETTING A FEEL for how you frame your subject and how much of the subject to cut out of the frame is just as much about strategic composition as it is making the subject look like they *feel* comfortable to the viewer. Sometimes the frame—the four lines making up the visual space of the portrait—can be a distracting factor based on where they are placed in relation to your subject.

There's no arguing that we use the frame to cut out small or large portions of our subject based on the type of shot we want to achieve. However, one of the most common mistakes I see students and new photographers make is cutting off too little of the subject for the framing to *feel* comfortable. Although this sounds fairly picky, many portraits cut such small portions of the subject off that the viewer might be distracted by where the placement of the frame is rather than spending time looking at the subject. It's something to keep in mind when framing up your subject.

A common example of this is seen in portraits where the sides of the subject's arms are cut off by the sides of the frame. Cutting off just the slightest amount of her arms creates an uneasy visual tension at the edge of the frame that may detract from the subject. The viewer's eye can't help being pulled to this point where the body leaves the frame. The same thing happens when cutting off even the slightest amount of the top of the head, fingers, feet, and the like.

So, how do we solve this visual stressor? The solution is simpler than you might think:

back out or zoom out from your subject, adding space between the subject and the frame (**Figure 32.1** and **Figure 32.2**). Many times, portraits are framed in a way that has an arm just barely touching the edge of the frame. Relieve this visual stressor by simply giving the subject more room to breathe, which simply means adding some space. Again, don't give the viewer an easy, distracting reason to look at a much less important part of the frame than the subject. Likewise, framing your subject too tightly against the edges of the frame places

a part of them in the "bleed" of an image if it were to ever run in a magazine or other publication. The bleed is an area of tolerance we give the printer when physically cutting the paper. Sometimes the cut is exactly where it needs to be, but sometimes it chops off more than you'd want as a photographer and you lose the arm (or top of head, or bottom of feet, etc.).

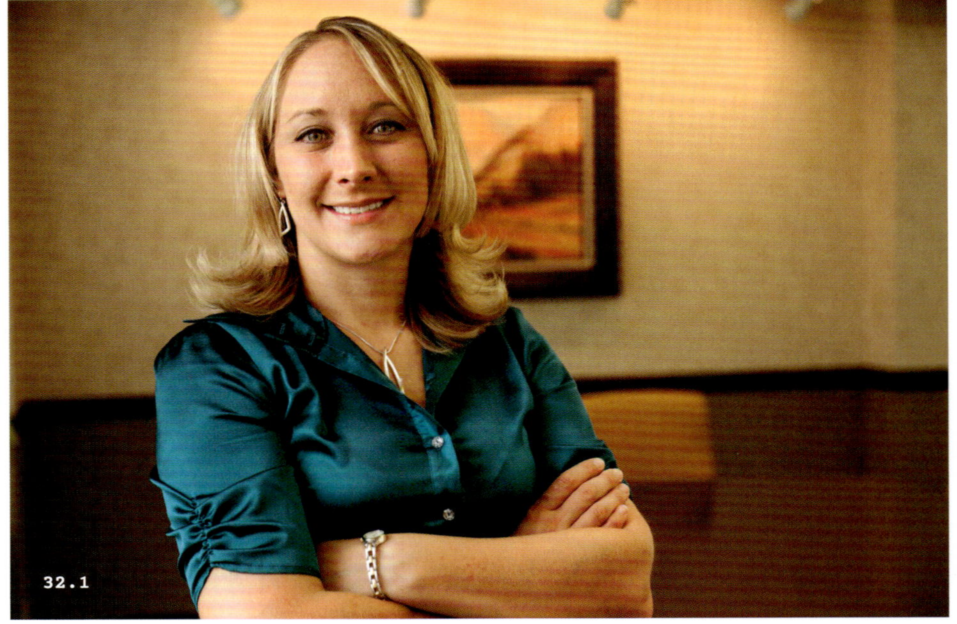

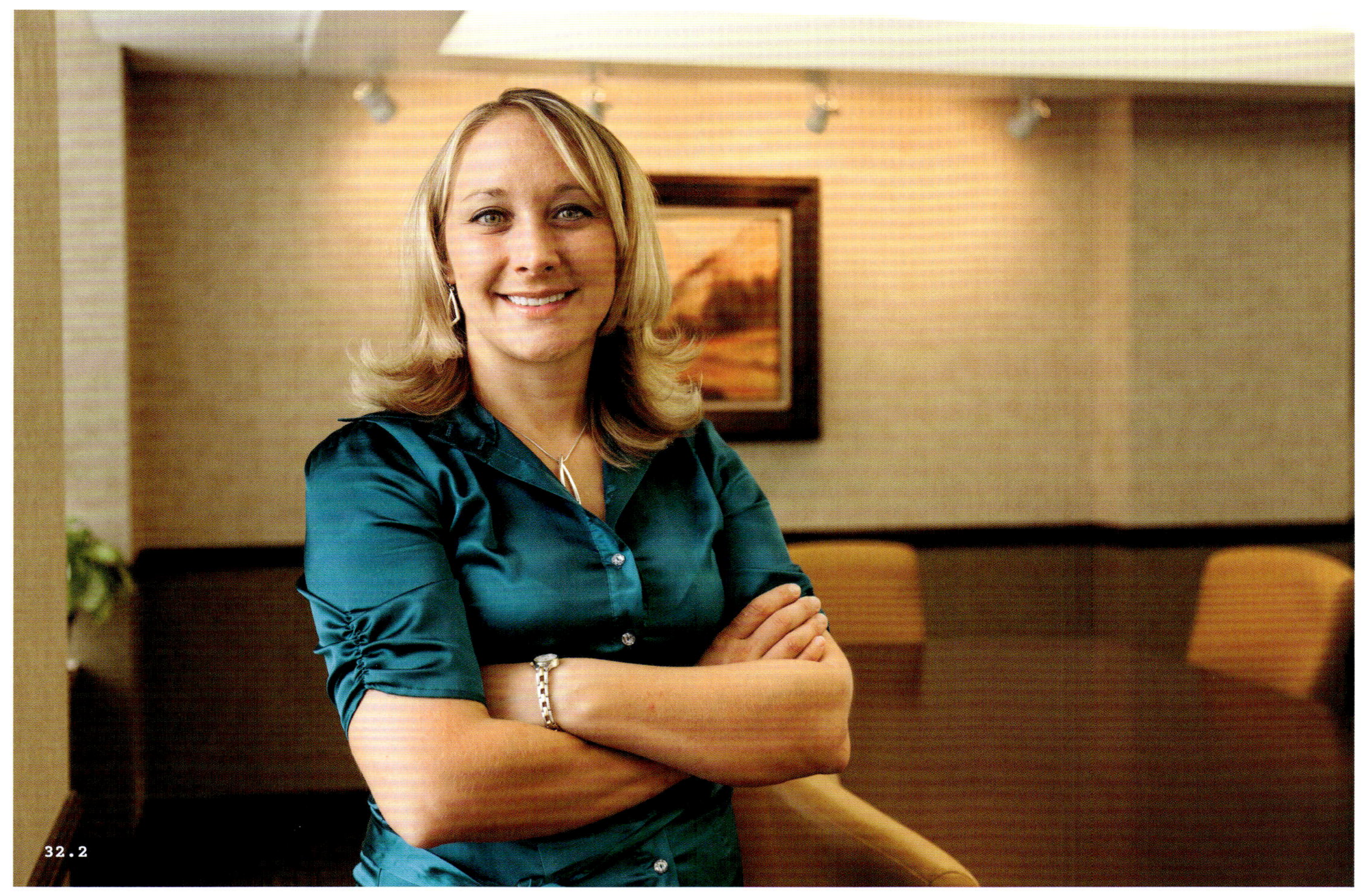

32.1 The bottom frame cutting just a slight bit of the subject's arms out of the frame creates unnecessary visual tension on the viewer, especially given that her head is completely in the frame opposite her arms.
ISO 250; 1/50 sec.; f/4; 65mm

32.2 Zooming out 15mm allowed the arms completely into the frame, mitigating the visual tension they created previously, and the environmental portrait's context did not change.
ISO 250; 1/50 sec.; f/4; 50mm

Lastly, it's useful to know what portrait photography has deemed avoidable when using the edges of the frame to minimize the amount of your subject shown in an image. The rule is fairly easy to remember: don't cut the subject off at joints. This means that using the frame to cut the subject off at the neck, elbows, waist, knees, and ankles isn't a great idea. Instead, reframe the subject to where the edges cut him off across the upper part of the chest, above the waist but below the elbows, just above or below the knees, or well below the feet (**Figure 32.3** and **Figure 32.4**). Again, we are conditioned to see the subject as an entire person, and although we need to cut portions of the subject out of the frame to create a particular look or type of portrait, we don't want to place any undue stress on the viewer in visualizing the subject. Additionally, cutting parts of fingers off can also be distracting, especially in those medium shots of your subject crossing their arms.

I'll be the first to say that it's sometimes difficult to keep from violating these rules. At the same time, though, I'm always conscious of what my framing of the subject does, both technically and as part of the overall image. Always check the edges of your frame. Take a break from looking through the viewfinder and review your images every so often during a shoot. Do your best to mitigate cutting too little of the subject out of the frame before you get to the editing process.

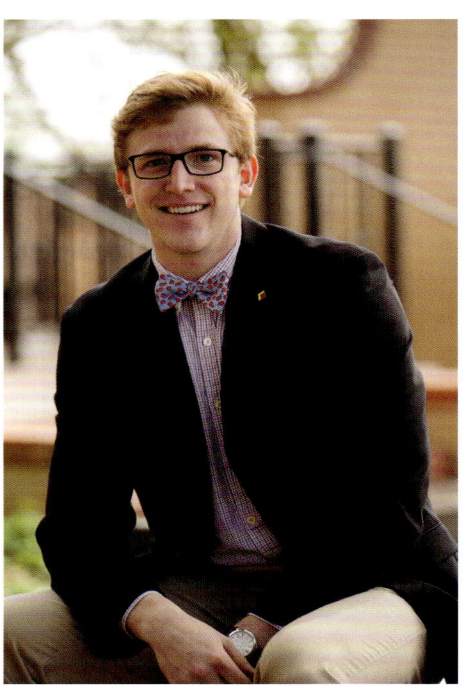

32.3 Visual tension is created where the image's frame cuts through the subject's knuckles.
ISO 100; 1/500 sec.; f/2.8; 120mm

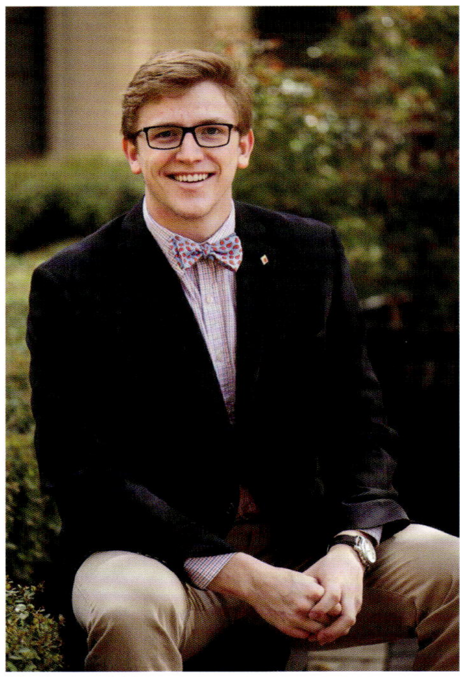

32.4 Bringing the hands completely into the frame reduces any minor visual tension their being cut off created. Although hard to notice initially, this fix quietly makes the image more effective and balanced.
ISO 100; 1/250 sec.; f/2.8; 155mm

Compose to Make Your Subject Look Their Best

My good friend and colleague R.J. Hinkle suggests that you never use the frame to cut the subject off wherever his form gets wider. This mostly refers to the top of and midway down the waist, where everyone, no matter his or her overall size, is a bit wider based on human anatomy. Doing so offers the perception that the subject is larger than they appear, and for a good majority of portraiture, this is typically unwanted.

Instead, R.J. recommends moving the edge of the frame below or above the wider parts of the subject's form (**Figure 32.5** and **Figure 32.6**). This very well might change the overall framing of the subject, but it is necessary to avoid an unflattering look and possibly a few complaints upon image delivery.

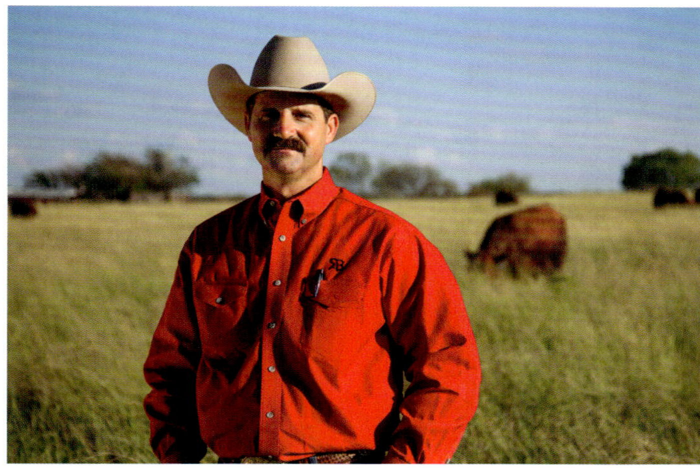

32.5 Cutting the subject out of the frame just above his midsection leaves him looking potentially larger than in reality.
ISO 100; 1/800 sec.; f/4; 73mm

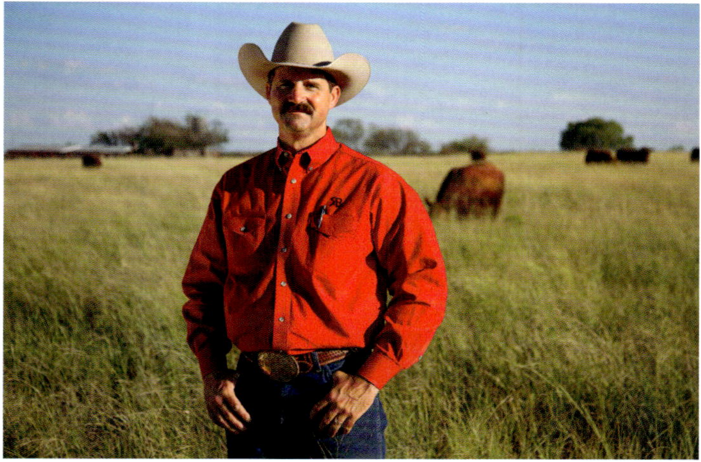

32.6 Zooming out to where the bottom of the frame is below the belt line provides the viewer a better understanding of how the subject looks, and it mitigates any troublesome issues with his overall size.
ISO 100; 1/1000 sec.; f/4; 60mm

I HAD A photography professor in college who joked about the placement of the horizon in images. In quintessential West Texan style, he'd say things like, "Make sure you're not losing any water," when referring to tilted horizons. His jokes were comical ways of explaining something important about the way an image looks. Although we often emphasize the placement of the horizon and its angle more strongly when discussing landscape photography, it still plays a part in portraits.

As mentioned earlier in the chapter, it's best to avoid placing the horizon in the middle of the frame because it can unintentionally create equal areas of visual interest that compete for your viewer's attention. This can result in visual discomfort that detracts from the subject of your portrait. We want to avoid this, and the earlier tip referencing the rule of thirds suggests such.

Let's focus on the angle at which you compose the horizon by thinking about how you naturally view the world around you. Go ahead, look around. Turn a complete 360 degrees. Unless you are in outer space, the horizon and the line it creates is naturally level. For those of you in or near the mountains, the horizon may not be *flat*, but it will still be level. We are naturally disposed to *feeling* that the horizon is level. I'm sure there's anatomical and psychophysiological research that can explain this concept, but suffice it to say that we understand our world as being "level" in association with our physical equilibrium. Otherwise, we would constantly struggle with standing.

With this in mind, consider the value in keeping the horizon level in your portraits. It feels natural. It's great for environmental portraits in which a distinct horizon line is implied or supplied in the frame (**Figure 33.1**). In many cases, especially senior or bridal portraits where the image is all about the subject, a level horizon line is less noticeable than a tilted one, and this "invisibility" is ideal.

However, unlike in other types of photography, a tilted horizon line is more acceptable in portraiture based on style and intention (**Figure 33.2**). A horizon that is "losing water" due to being tilted can often be used to imply a certain degree of drama and edginess, especially for wider portraits. Although it's best to keep the horizon level in most traditional environmental portraits, a slightly tilted horizon for fashion or individual portraits might imply some subliminal characteristics about your subject. I especially appreciate a tilted horizon in a medium portrait with a horizontal orientation (**Figure 33.3**).

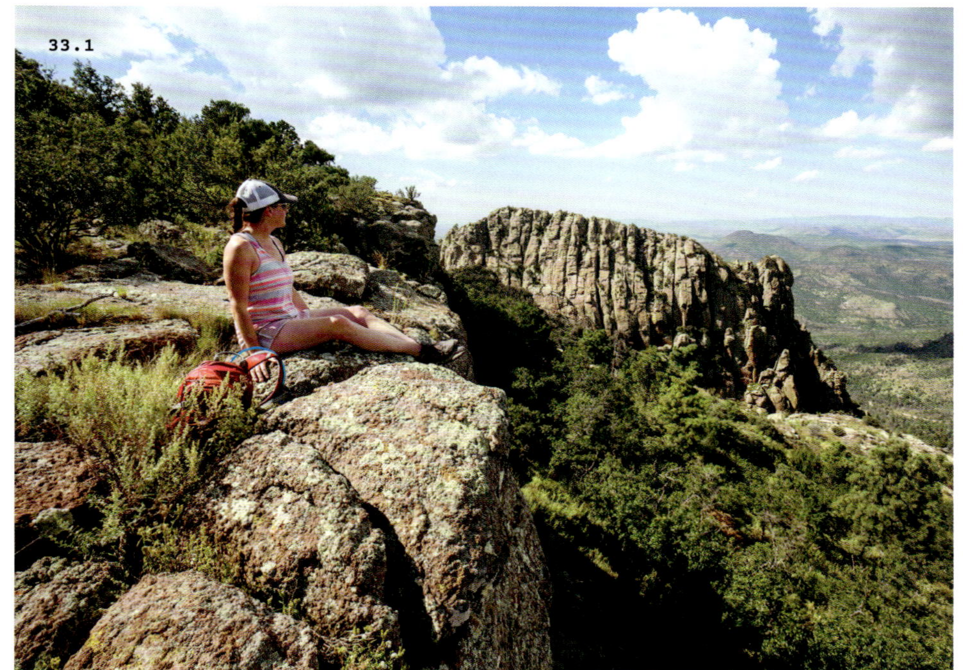

33.1

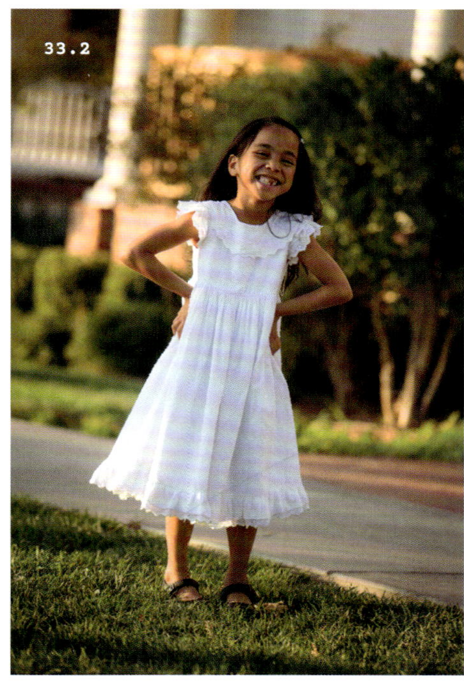

33.2

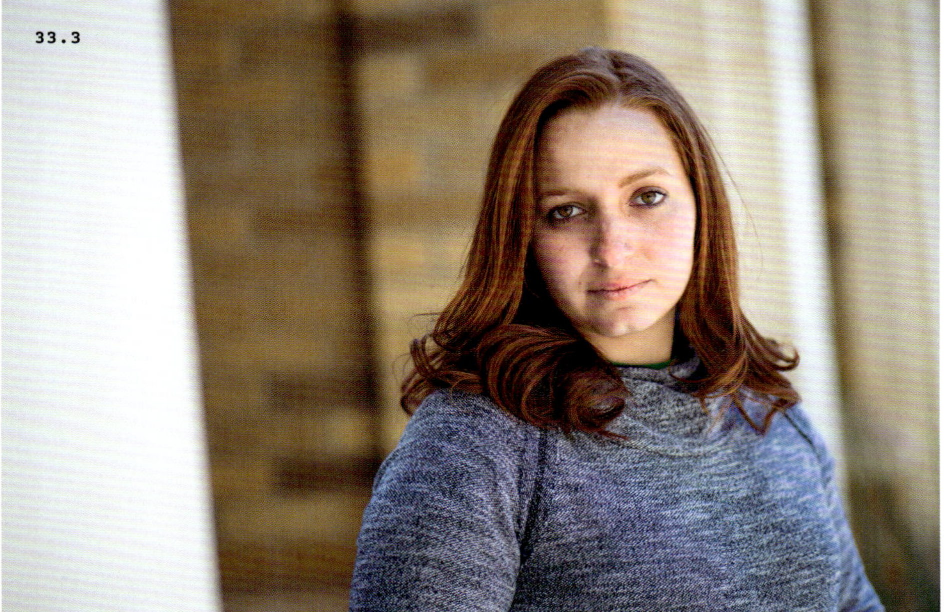

33.3

33.1 The level horizon in this wide environmental portrait leaves the viewer without any visual attention and better able to take in the entire landscape.
ISO 200; 1/100 sec.; f/22; 17mm

33.2 Moderately tilting horizons can often complement the portrait subject's personality.
ISO 200; 1/1000 sec.; f/2.8; 145mm

33.3 Slightly angling the horizon down and to the left also dynamically angles the subject toward the open portion of the frame, often referred to as the image's white space.
ISO 200; 1/1600 sec.; f/1.8; 85mm

Portraits that don't necessarily include the actual horizon line, such as headshots, can also benefit from tilting the viewer's natural perspective (**Figure 33.4**). Remember that a diagonal line in a frame creates dynamic value and interest. Bear in mind, though, that a tilted horizon can get out of hand. Remember, we're used to seeing the horizon as level, so when the horizon is dramatically tilted, it's extremely noticeable and sometimes disturbingly distracting. An extremely titled horizon suggests a level of chaos not normally desired in most portraiture. It's currently trendy to tilt the horizon, and although I don't want to discourage exploring this option, it's always worth assessing why you are doing it and considering its effect in your portraiture.

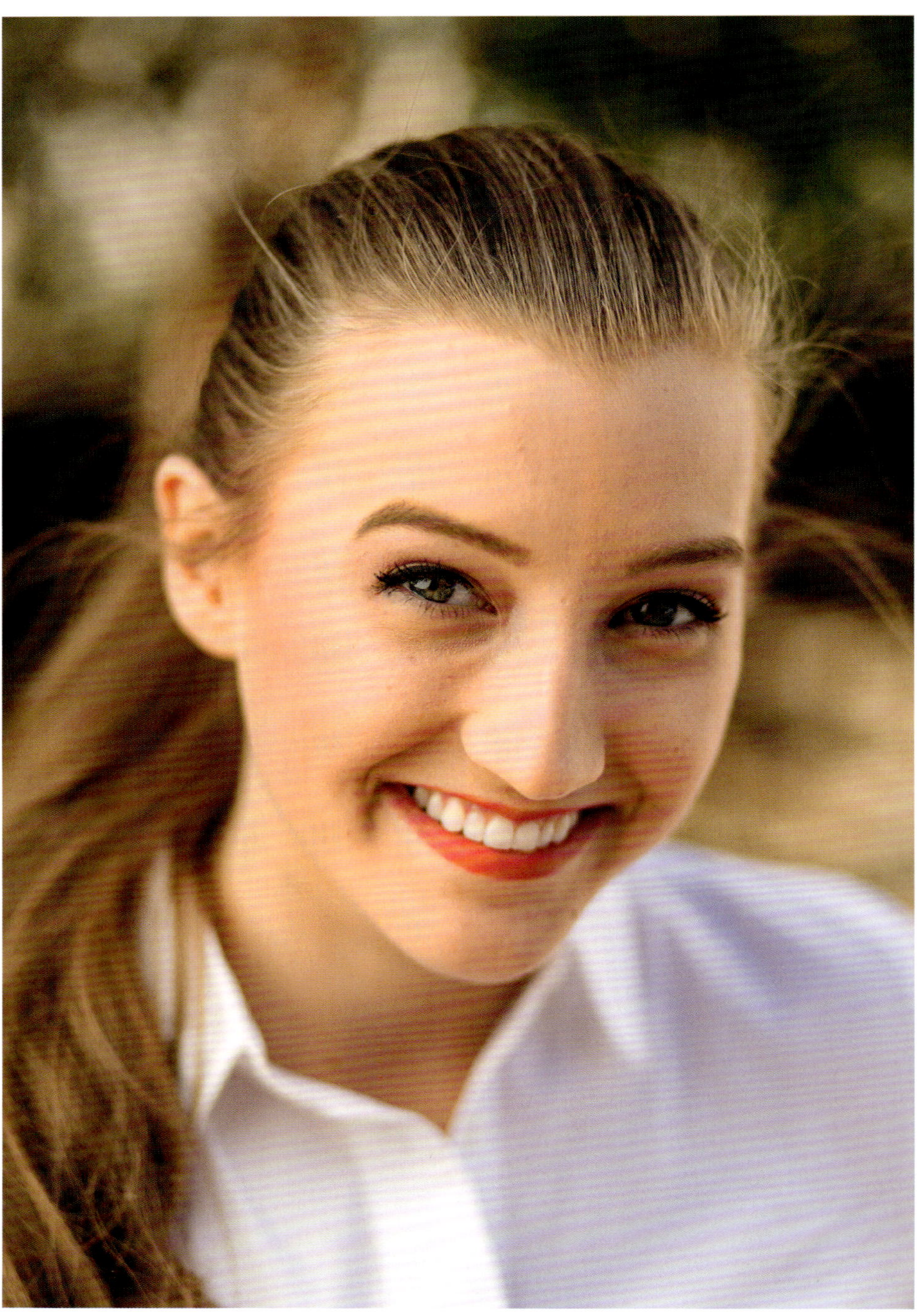

33.4 The camera was intentionally tilted to allow the subject's form to create an attractive, compositionally diagonal line across the frame.
ISO 100; 1/1600 sec.; f/1.8; 85mm

Don't Compose the Horizon Line Behind Your Subject's Head

The title of this sidebar pretty much says it all. Although it's sometimes unavoidable, it's rather taboo to compose the horizon line directly behind your subject's head. This intersection can be distracting, especially if your depth of field is fairly wide. The more in-focus your background becomes, the more it looks like the horizon line is cutting into your subject's head. If you must compose the horizon line behind your subject's head, do your best to mitigate it's potential for distraction. Lower your depth of field all of the way to knock it out of focus (**Figure 33.5**).

However, the most effective alternative to placing the horizon line behind your subject's head is to simply elevate or lower the position of the camera. This will move the horizon line above your subject all together or lower it an ample enough amount to keep it from being a major distraction. Do keep in mind, though, that a horizon line intersecting the bottom of the chin or neck can also be detrimental to the portrait. It's best to have the horizon below the shoulder line.

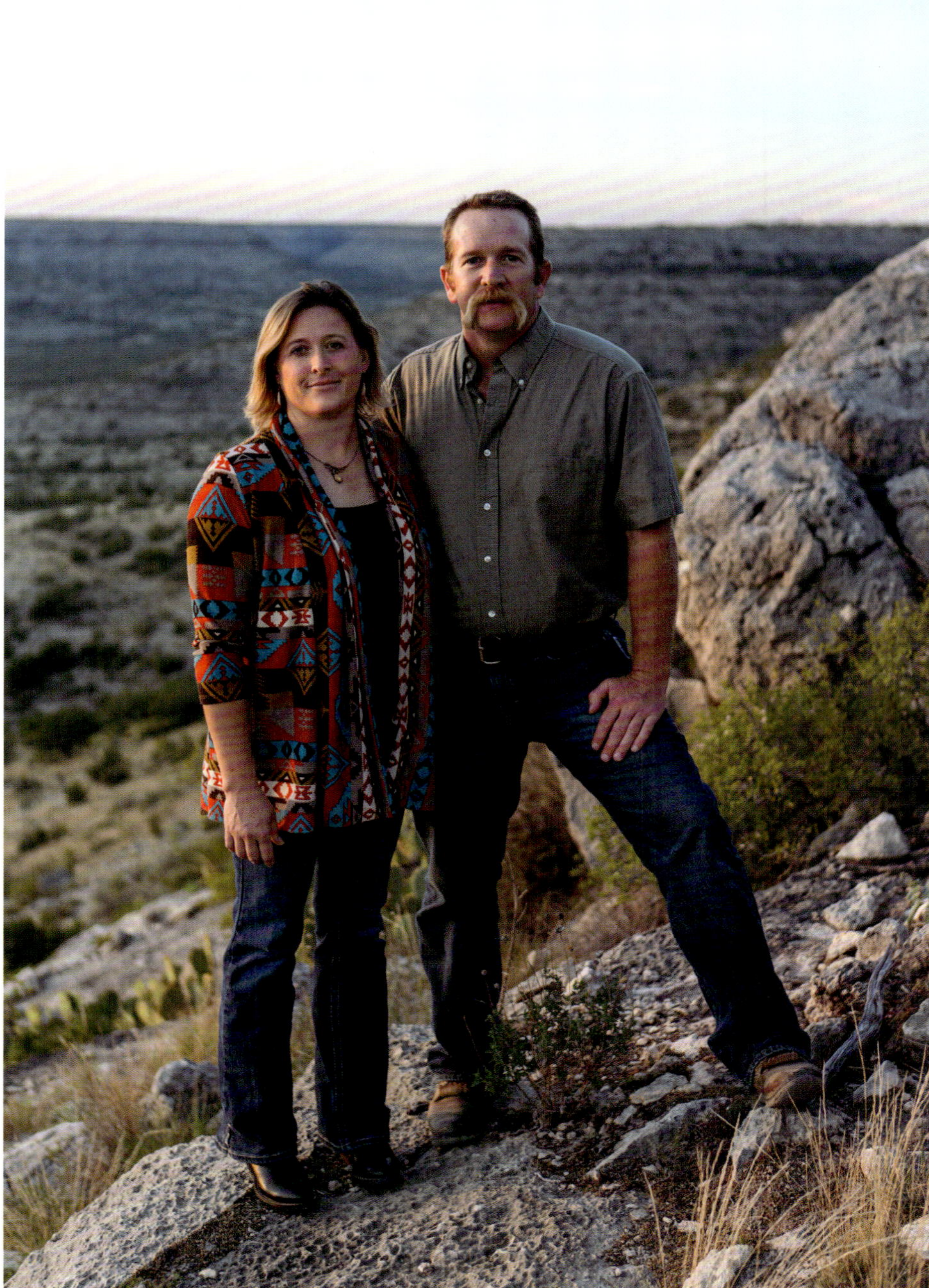

33.5 Although the husband's head intersects with the plateau, the background is sufficiently out of focus for it not to be too much of a visual distraction.
ISO 200; 1/320 sec.; f/2.8; 51mm

THE JURY IS still out on whether or not you can consider a silhouette a true portrait, but since it is a part of so many portrait shoots, so why not give it some thought in terms of composition? There's one guiding principle that should inform your silhouette composition: make sure you show enough of your subject to do her justice.

A successful silhouette cleanly shows the form of your subject, no matter if it's a person, an animal, or a windmill on the horizon (**Figure 34.1**). When a silhouette shot is executed well, the part that *is* the silhouette is black, as well as the ground or structure on which the subject is standing. If the subject is placed too far below the horizon, the subject will be lost in the block of darkness that comprises everything intentionally underexposed in the shot (**Figure 34.2**). To ensure your subject's silhouette stands out, compose the horizon below most of his form. It's acceptable to let the silhouette horizon cut into his legs a bit, but if you intended to get a full-length silhouette of your subject against a dramatic sunset and all you got was his shoulders and head, you have to rethink your position.

Silhouettes can be great fun. They can be very effective, and sometimes some of the most treasured shots of your subject. Consider placing the horizon line lower than the majority of your subject's form; focus; intentionally underexpose the scene; and you'll be set!

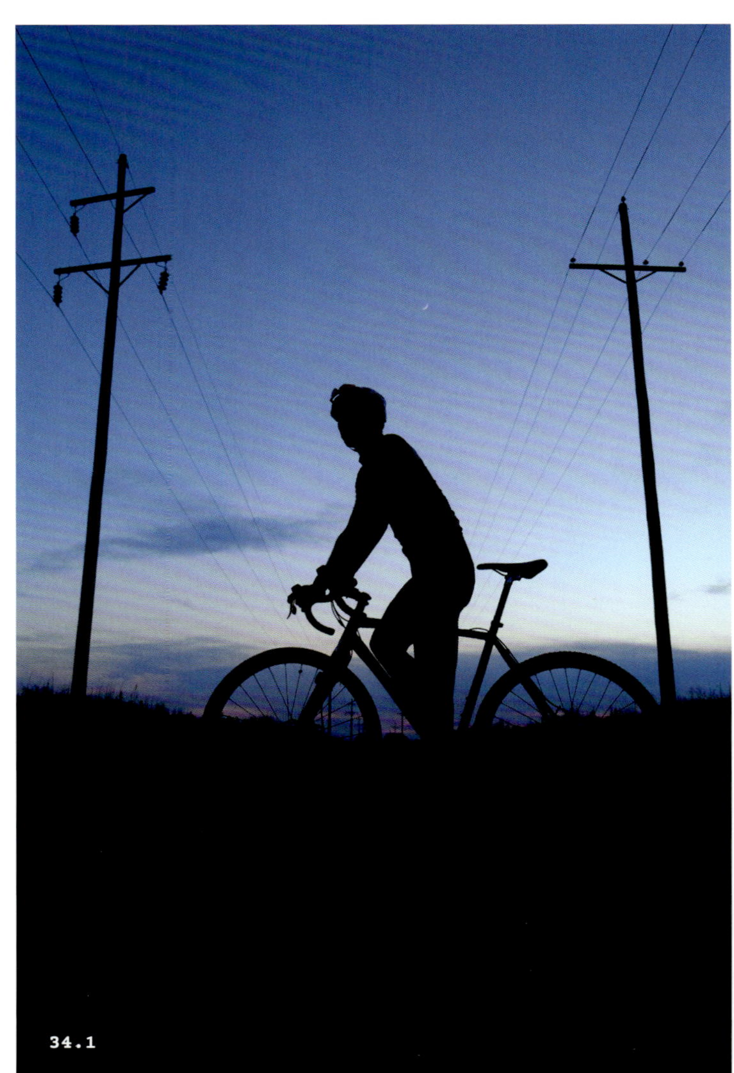

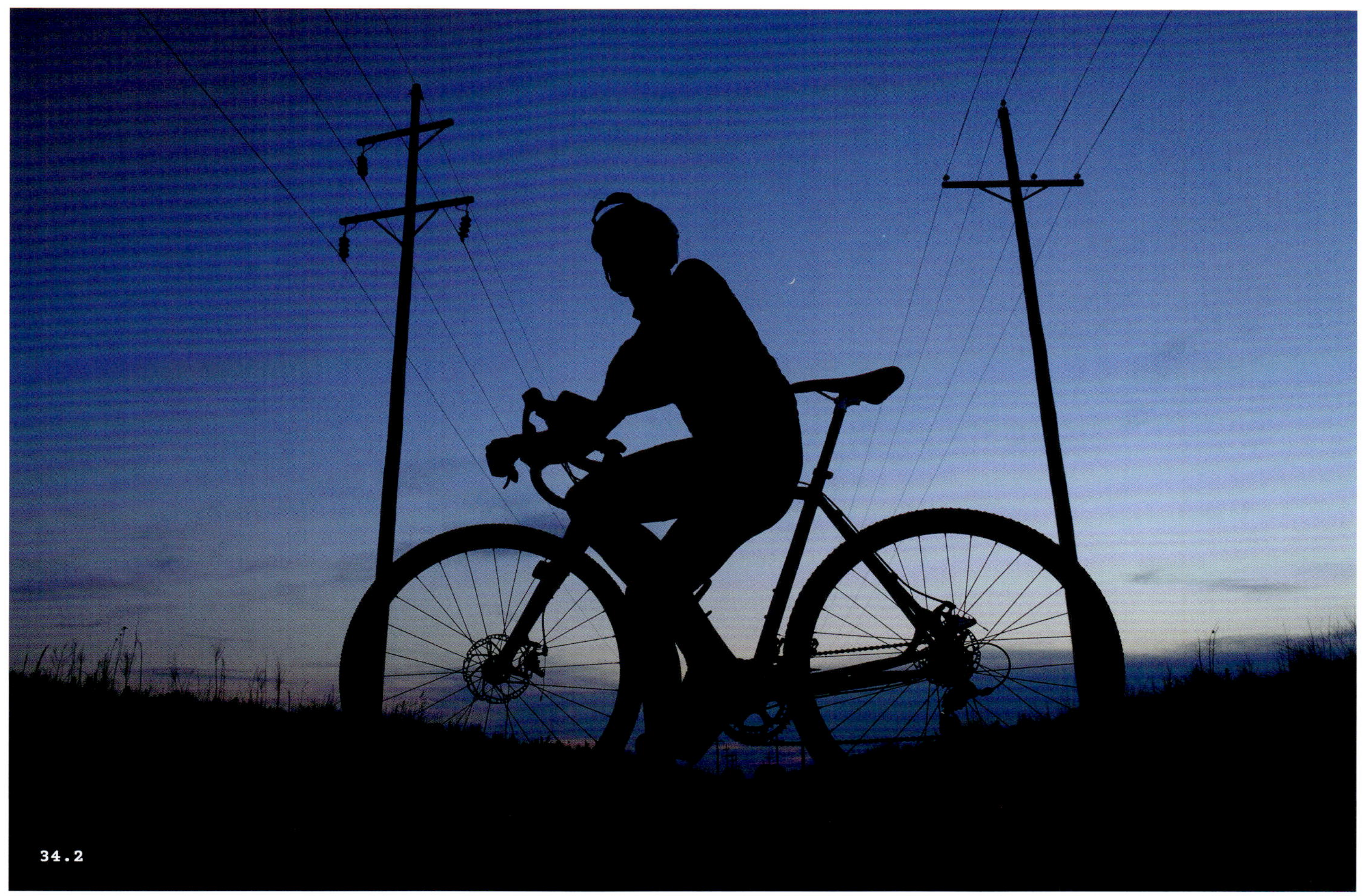

34.2

34.1 Although much of this silhouette works, the horizon line eats into the wheels enough that the subject feels too high in the frame.

34.2 Lowering the camera angle allows the horizon line to drop below the wheel hubs, showcasing as complete a bike form as possible in this dirt road context.
ISO 400; 1/210 sec.; f/5.6; 18mm

Share Your Best Silhouette!

Once you've captured your best silhouette, share it with the *Enthusiast's Guide* community! Follow @EnthusiastsGuides and post your image to Instagram, using the hashtag *#EGSilhouette*. You can also search that hashtag to be inspired and see other photographers' shots.

35. COMPOSE FOR DESIGN

I'LL END THIS chapter with a helpful tip from my experience as a magazine and commercial photographer: compose for design. This is a hard concept to get across sometimes, especially if you're new to photography or haven't had experience working with designers, publications, and agencies. However, I believe working in this particular photography environment has made me a stronger portrait photographer.

Composing for design simply means designing the portrait to move the viewer's eye to your subject, but there's another element: designing with the potential for the portrait to be used with other elements later. For example, each time I'm on a portrait shoot for a magazine, I have to compose at least one or two shots for the publication's cover (**Figure 35.1**). Not only does the portrait need to look great, it also needs to have enough room on top for the magazine's title, and room below and on one side for more text. When I'm working on a campaign with an ad agency, we discuss composition of portraits prior to being on location because I'll need to photograph in a way that meets their needs when they create the advertisement.

Not a magazine or advertising photographer? What about senior portraits that might be used for graduation announcements and invitations?

Many brides and grooms like to use engagement portraits as the background for save-the-date announcements. And don't forget the family photographs that are used for holiday cards and social media invites, etc. Composing with design potential in mind is a great way to create versatile, creative images.

The key to composing for design is managing the portrait's white space (**Figure 35.2**). This design-centric term does not refer to the parts of your image that are strictly white (although white space can certainly be white). Instead, it refers to empty space that can be used for design elements, like text, other graphics, etc. White space minimizes the distraction of external design elements. For example, an out-of-focus portion of the right-hand side of the frame can serve as great white space on which to place the name of your subject and graduation date (**Figure 35.3**). Not only did the composition of your subject and the out-of-focus background drive the eye to your subject, it also left some valuable space for extra designs. Senior portrait and wedding photographers use this space all of the time to create beautiful products for their clients—material that might keep them coming back, as well as bringing them new potential clients.

Now, I'm not saying design should be the only thing guiding your composition. I'm emphasizing its value in making you a more considerate, well-versed portrait photographer. You *are* a photographer first. However, I'll mention two things before closing. First, photography is an art influenced by eons of design, be it architectural, natural, or purely artistic. Composing for design is simply extending this influence and creating artistic possibilities out of your own work. Second (and this relates more to those wanting to enter into portrait photography on a semi-professional or professional basis): composing for design increases your potential to meet the needs of those folks with whom you'll be working. I attribute much of what I earn from various clients to my ability to compose for design, which essentially means I can be a team player in the grand process of a magazine going to print or an ad campaign going to market. We often get wrapped up in the notion that photography is a lone wolf, individual style of work, and in many cases, it can be. However, entering into the industry relies on your ability to work well with other professionals, and composing for design is one of the strongest aesthetic ways of contributing to the work.

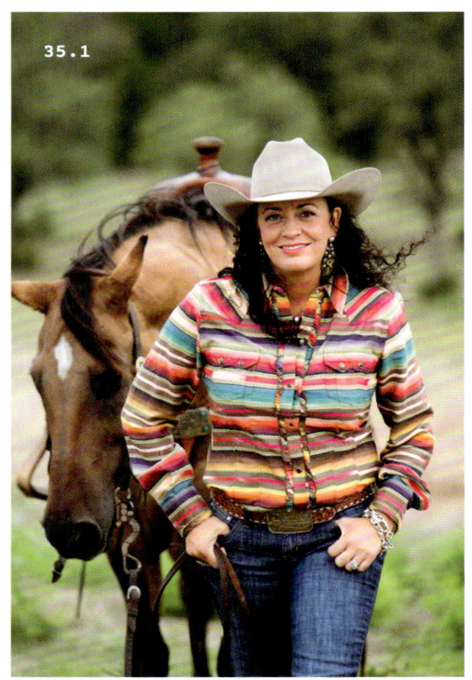

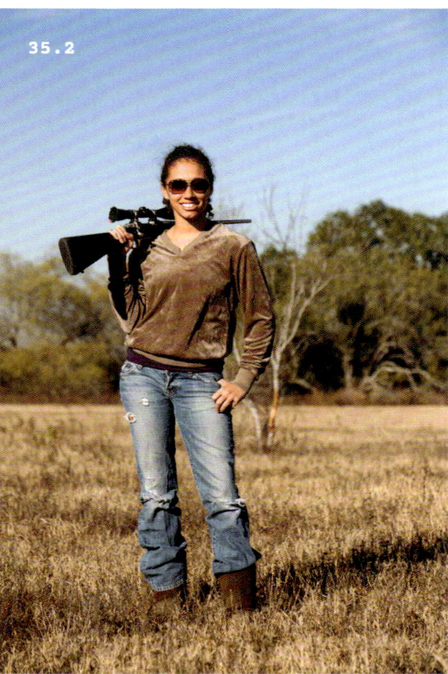

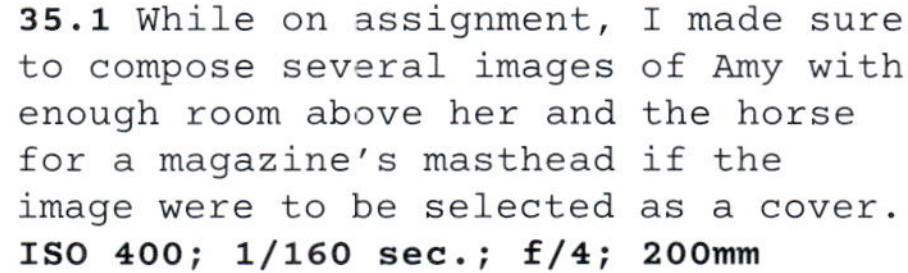

35.1 While on assignment, I made sure to compose several images of Amy with enough room above her and the horse for a magazine's masthead if the image were to be selected as a cover.
ISO 400; 1/160 sec.; f/4; 200mm

35.2 This portrait includes a great deal of design-worthy white space while still being composed comfortably. The sky and the out-of-focus trees and grass to camera right of the subject can easily be used for text or more imagery based on a designer's preferences.
ISO 200; 1/1600 sec.; f/5; 95mm

35.3 This senior portrait may serve well for a graduation invitation based on the attractively out-of-focus background to camera right of the subject.
ISO 200; 1/320 sec.; f/2; 85mm

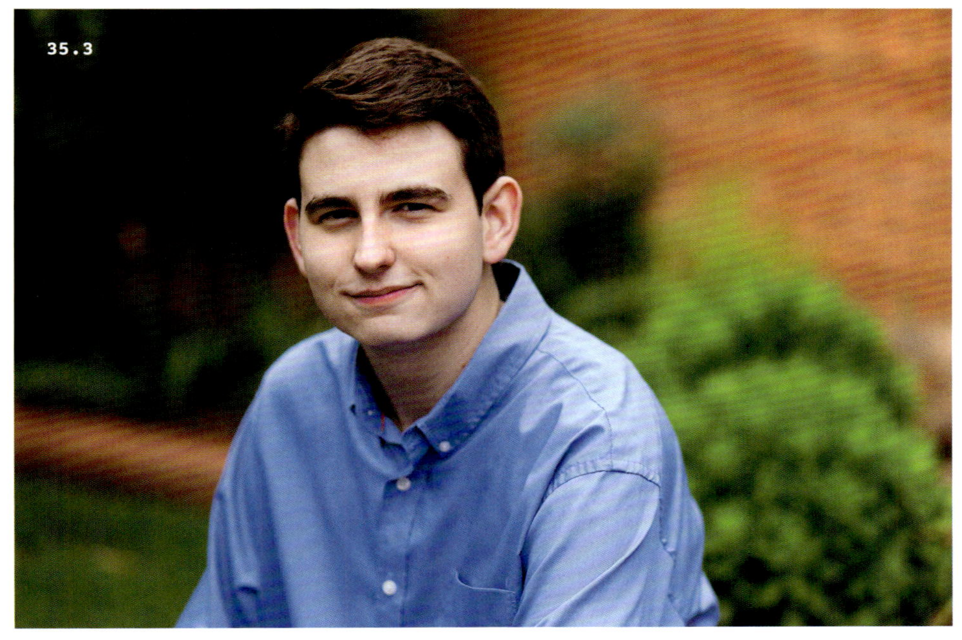

5

POSING AND WORKING WITH THE SUBJECT

Portrait posing is a true art, full of stylistic techniques and aesthetic tastes. Each sub-genre of portraiture has its own inclinations toward posing. For some, it's an extremely essential, creative part of the visual aspect of the photo; others consider it a way to make the subject appear comfortable or to direct the viewer's attention to the subject's face and surroundings. Needless to say, posing is a major facet of every portrait. As such a big part of portraiture, there is no shortage of great resources out there on the topic. However, despite the many books available on how to pose portraits, the majority of them rely on boiling down one key posing principle: *Keep it simple and natural.*

THIS CHAPTER ATTEMPTS to honor this principle of simple and natural by suggesting not only tried and true techniques, but by also introducing considerations based on style and situation. Not surprising, all areas of portraiture have their unique approaches to posing. This chapter cannot cover everything. Instead, it provides a useful foundation on which to base great posing technique.

Lastly, posing should be an integral part of your image's composition. If the posture feels "off" when viewing the image as a whole, then it more than likely is disturbing the image's organization. With every suggestion made in this chapter, don't forget to incorporate good compositional technique to create attractive, engaging portraits. Like composition, the suggested principles need not be used singularly. More than likely, you'll combine two or more posing considerations to create the best portraits possible.

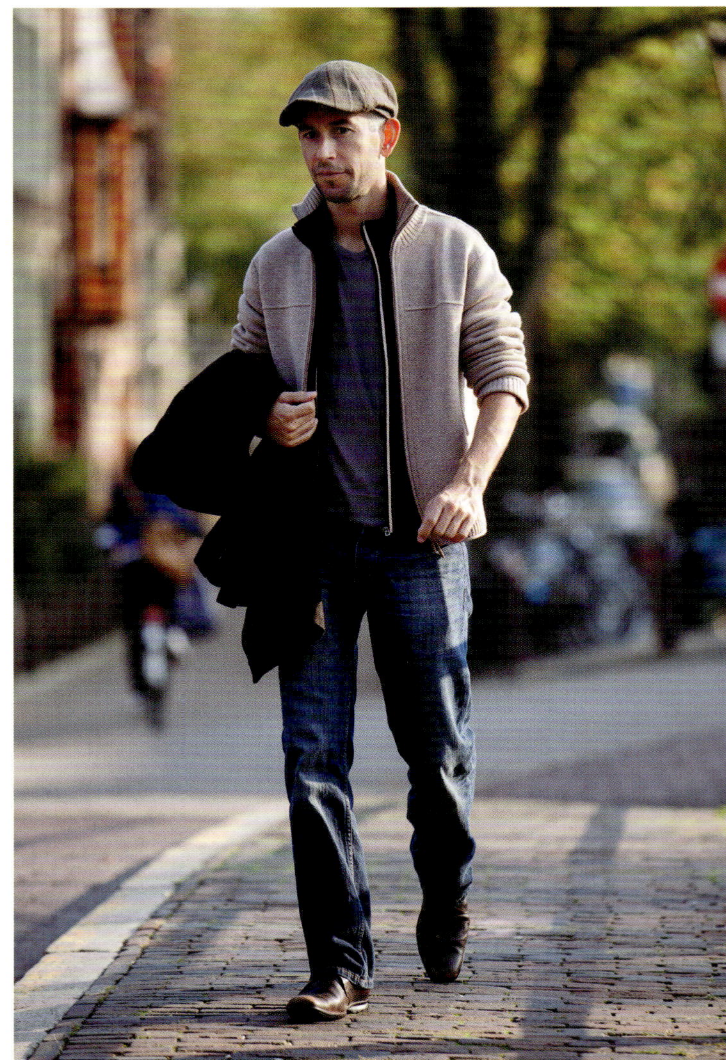

Keep your posing *simple* and *natural*. Although I had the subject walk this sidewalk in Amsterdam several times, I wanted the portrait to look as if he were simply on his way somewhere in the vibrant European city. The jacket over the arm was held naturally and his eye-line doesn't indicate the existence of the camera.
ISO 200; 1/800 sec.; f/2.8; 165mm

RAPPORT IS ONE of those words that simply describes a positive relationship between two people. The relationship doesn't have to be a deep one, but it's one that suggests the people involved are on the same page and they have the ability to work together. If you have ever interviewed for a job, one of the first things you must do is build a rapport with the interviewer. The same applies for working with your portrait subject(s).

Building rapport with your portrait subject is essential. Portrait photography is a social activity, and it can be a bit stressful for both the photographer and the subject. Photographers that are new to portraiture or photographing a subject they don't have a personal relationship with can be a bit tense. Pile that on top of stressing about operating the camera and nailing the shots for the subject—even seasoned photographers experience this anxiety because no two subjects are created equal. Likewise, the subject is probably going to be more nervous than the photographer. Remember that the subject is probably not in front of the camera as frequently as you are behind it. They may be unconfident in front of the camera and unknowledgeable about how to pose (**Figure 36.1**). Having positive rapport can help assuage the social tension between photographer and subject, and it's all based on empathy, authentic interest, and confidence.

Bear in mind that building rapport starts with the photographer. The easiest and most natural way of building rapport is to simply start a conversation before the shoot. This can be when you initially meet at a predetermined location or at a separate pre-shoot visit (see sidebar). As the photographer, you can use this initial conversation to set the mood for the shoot, and more than likely, this conversation will continue throughout the shoot, especially if it's non-commercial in nature.

There's no formula for successfully building rapport, but there are some common techniques that I believe most portrait photographers use to ease social tension:

1 **Shake hands, smile, and be polite.** Need I say more? Shake. Hands.
2 **Ask open-ended questions.** Ask your subject questions to learn about them, who they are, what they do for a living, what they do for fun, etc. This serves two purposes: first, it gets them talking, which is a sure-fire way of breaking the ice and putting them at ease with you (especially if this is your first time meeting); second, it shows that you are interested. As a portrait photographer, you should be. Give them the spotlight. You'll learn more about your subject, and they will know that you care.
3 **Look your subject in the eye when speaking and listening.** Engage them non-verbally to show additional interest and sincerity in your initial conversation. It's not only respectful; it's a natural way of strengthening a relationship.
4 **Discover common ground.** One of my favorite things when meeting people for the first time is finding something that we both enjoy or have experienced. This makes conversation much easier and more interesting. Common ground can arise in just about anything, but I often find it among music tastes, recreational activities, travel, and mutual acquaintances.
5 **Put yourself in their shoes.** Empathize with your portrait subject. Imagine how the experience might be for them. Do they seem nervous or uncomfortable? Consider why this might be. Offer them time to get ready, ask if there's anything you can provide them. This goes for the entire shoot as well. It never hurts to ask your subject how they're doing every once in a while.
6 **Instill confidence in them.** Perhaps a friend referred them to you, or they saw your portfolio online and chose you as their photographer. Either way, they will be concerned about your ability to deliver a product that meets their expectations. Present yourself

comfortably and confidently, and do so in a personable way. Show excitement for the shoot rather than arrogance about your abilities. Tell them about some of your ideas for the shoot; excite them with information about having found a beautiful location for the shoot; etc. Again, this is something you can continue throughout the shoot while you are coaching them and talking about how the shoot is going. Don't let them know if you just shot five out-of-focus shots to get the one that nailed it. Rather, concentrate on how great that one in-focus image looks to you. Additionally, a great way to instill confidence in your subject is to periodically show them some images you are shooting. Some photographers refuse to do this, and some shoots (editorial and commercial) don't afford the time for it, but showing your subject how great they look in an image is a fantastic way of strengthening their confidence in you. It also puts the perception of some control in their hands as well, allowing them some input on the process.

7 **Put your phone away.** Again, need I say more? Rapport should feel natural, and regardless of whether or not you consider yourself a people person who enjoys small talk, you more than likely are already an expert on the process due to past experiences in building relationships with friends. Use this to your advantage. Having rapport with your clients allows for a more manageable, enjoyable experience for everyone involved, and it's definitely one of the facets of the photo shoot that the subject will remember in a positive light and pass along to others (and everyone appreciates a bit of word-of-mouth advertising).

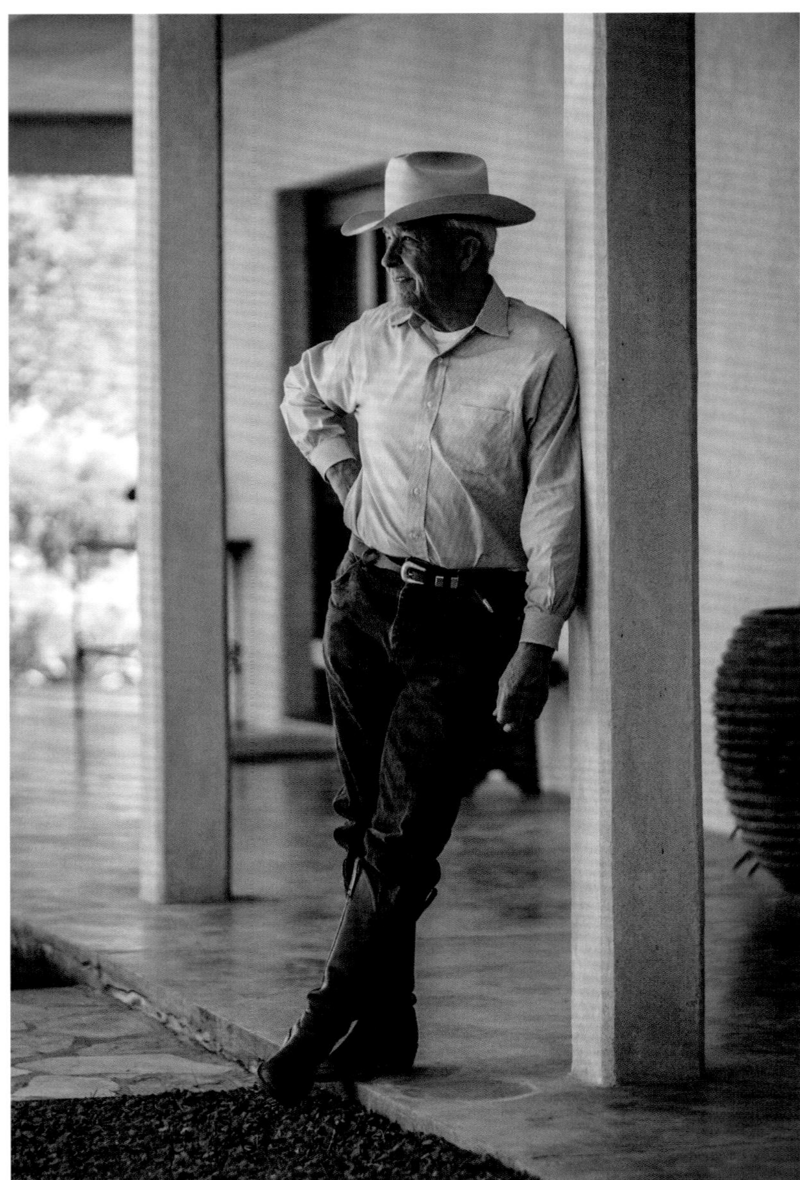

36.1 I spent most of the morning and ate lunch with Ben Love before photographing him for a magazine feature. That time was well spent building positive rapport with him, which resulted in his ease at taking instruction from me during the shoot.
ISO 200; 1/800 sec.; f/2.8; 125mm

Set Up a Pre-shoot Consultation

My good friend and colleague, Linda McMillan, is a great example of a photographer who shows every one of her portrait clients the care and consideration they deserve. Her clients love her, and I believe a lot of it has to do with the fact that she gets to know her subjects days (sometimes weeks or months) before the actual shoot. Linda is an advocate for pre-shoot consultations with her clients. These meetings allow her to become acquainted and familiar with the people she will photograph in the near future.

Linda uses the consultations to get to know the clients in several ways. The one-on-one facetime is incredibly valuable and allows her to break the ice with her client before meeting them with a camera in hand. She gets a feel for their personality and lifestyle, and she gets to talk to them about potential locations. Linda also gives them a questionnaire to fill out, which asks, among other things, about their clothing style. She uses this information to pre-plan the locations and times for the shoot.

Linda also uses the pre-shoot consultations to set expectations for the client—what they should prepare for, establishing the importance of being on time and ready, and easing any anxiety about the photographic process. This is probably the most important part of the consultations, and Linda suggests that having a flexible routine for these meetings is a way to make sure everything is covered adequately.

So, the next time you set up a portrait shoot, consider meeting with your subject(s) beforehand. Choose a meeting area such as a local coffee shop or park—any place that seems upbeat and puts you and the subject on neutral ground. Visit with them about their life, and be genuinely interested (you are a portrait photographer, after all). Walk them through a typical shoot and what you might have planned for them. Use this time with them to brainstorm about the shoot. This meeting will ease nerves for both of you. You won't be able to do this with every subject, especially if you are more interested in shooting editorial portraits. However, I have to agree with Linda that it is an invaluable part of the portrait process.

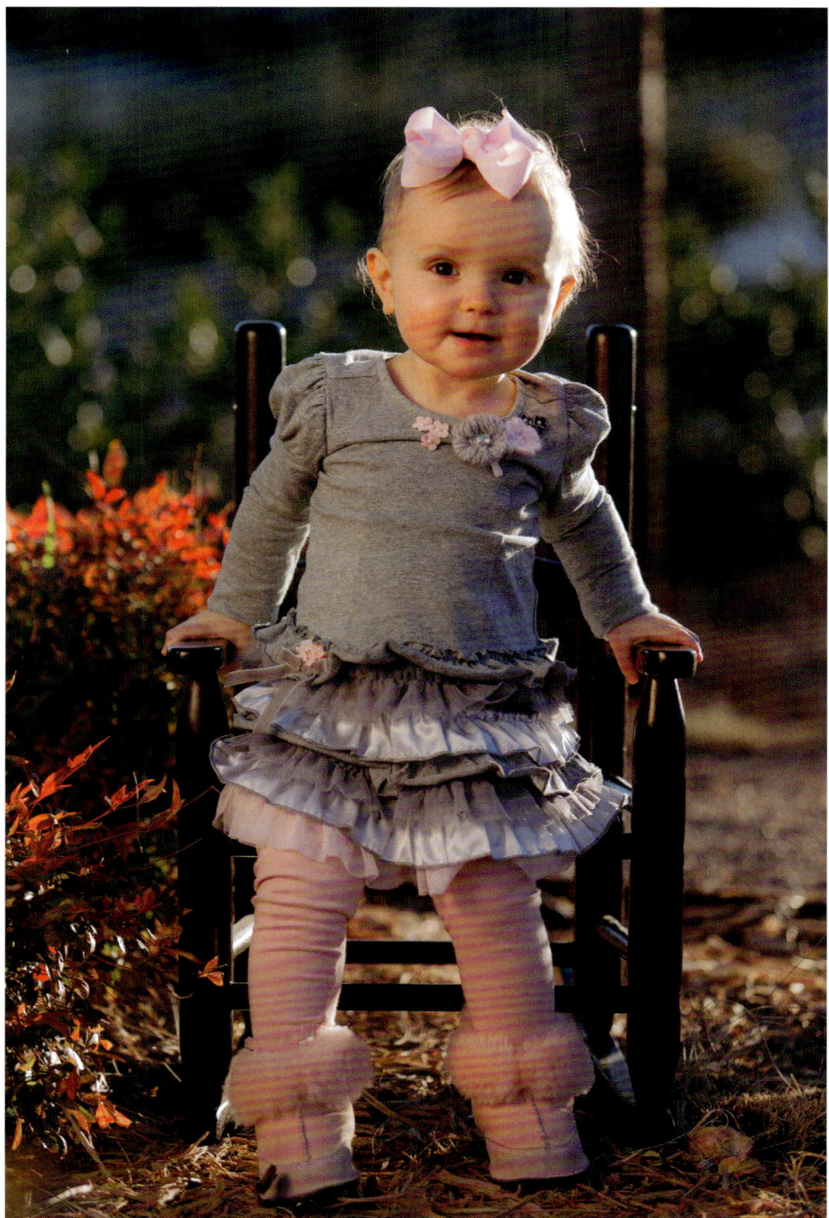

In the pre-shoot consultation for this photoshoot, the family and I brainstormed ideas for images of this little girl about a week before I clicked the shutter.
ISO 100; 1/500 sec.; f/2.8; 130mm

37. COACH YOUR SUBJECT

IF ONE PURPOSE of building rapport is to make your portrait subject more comfortable with the photographic process, proper coaching helps, as well. Whether you are shooting a straightforward corporate headshot or a loose and fun family session, you'll no doubt need to rely on your ability to guide your subject into the right pose and placement to create the shot you both will enjoy.

Coaching is simply a way of guiding the subject throughout the portrait process. Again, since many portrait subjects are relatively unfamiliar with how to effectively pose for these shots, it makes sense that they might need instruction on what to do (**Figure 37.1**). They may also need emotional reinforcement along the way. Some subjects will certainly need more coaching than others, but all will need at least a bit of direction to move the shoot along.

For the photographer, coaching is also a great way to maintain a level of control during the shoot. Most shoots don't necessitate that you instruct the subject on everything, but when shoots feel like they may be going in an ineffective or wasteful direction, coaching the subject to redirect the process can be useful. It's also a great way of reinforcing your expertise in the situation without being blunt, especially for those subjects that, like it or not, are a bit close minded about the portrait process and experience.

The more you photograph in this genre, the better you'll get at being aware of opportunities to help the subject, such as when you are posing them and explaining what you would like to capture in a particular environment. Less obvious, but still valuable, opportunities to coach the subject are those times when you notice subtle changes, such as in their smile or the way the light hits their face as you reposition them for another shot (**Figure 37.2**).

Here are a few good coaching techniques for a wide variety of subjects:

1 **Always remain positive.** Keep the shoot upbeat, even in circumstances that are seriously troublesome for the subject or yourself. Your attitude affects the entire context of the situation, and your rapport will stay stronger with a positive attitude toward anything issue that may arise during the event.

2 **Instructions and communication should be clear.** Avoid confusion by communicating effectively. If you need your subject to back up a couple feet, tell them so in a loud enough voice to be heard (and be specific: consider saying "back up two steps" instead of "back up a couple of feet"). If you need to pose the subject, sometimes showing them your intention rather than describing it verbally is helpful. Additionally, communicate direction to them from their point of view. Instead of referring to your right and left, tell them to move to their right or left. (And, unless you are photographing a farmer on his own land, don't tell your subject to move a few feet to the west, or any other direction for which they'll need a compass.)

3 **Provide feedback and reinforcement.** Throughout the shoot, the subject will ask you for verification that they are posing effectively. This is a coaching moment where you should provide feedback. If everything is going well, let them know. If something needs to be changed, give honest feedback (but remember to keep it positive) and clearly communicate the change that needs to happen. Likewise, it doesn't hurt to give your subject positive reinforcement at any point in the shoot. This can be as simple as letting them know they are doing great. You can try more creative approaches, as well; such as having them imagine they are in a calming place, or telling them to embody a lion or other appropriate animals.

4 **Notice changes in emotion.** You'll be a stronger photographer if you can read people well. Noticing subtle changes in emotion can allow you to steer the shoot in different, potentially more productive directions. This comes in handy if you notice your subject getting nervous, or if they seem intimidated by how close (or far) you are to them. Respond accordingly by providing an alternative plan of action that might be more positively received. You might never be able to tell if a shoot is about to turn awkward, but part of your job is recognizing when it does and coaching the subject into a better emotional space. The last thing anyone wants is an anxiety-filled shoot.

5 Stay alert. A good coach is one that pays attention to the subject. Being aware of your subject's appearance (after all, you are making photographs of him) while he moves through different light, postures, and compositions will very likely offer other photographs you didn't visualize before starting the shoot. For example, as you're walking with your subject from one environment to the next, keep a close eye on how she actually walks and how the light hits her. While you are getting set up, glance at your subject and see how she naturally stands. There might just be a shot there—one that gives you the opportunity to provide positive reinforcement on how they look naturally, and that you'd love to take a few shots in that position. One of my favorite things to catch is how they move from one position to the next in any particular environment. For example, if I like how they held their hands in their pockets before the shoot commenced, I'd say, "I like what you were just doing with your hands. Let's do a couple shots with them in your pockets." You'll never know what you'd miss if you are not paying your subject the attention they deserve!

Photographic coaching helps the subject look their best, but more importantly, it can make them *feel* better about themselves and the process. Taking advice from the photographer involves the subject more intimately in the shoot because it forces them to interact with *you*, the photographer. Most folks are great at following good, clear instructions, especially when it comes with the understanding that it will make them look better.

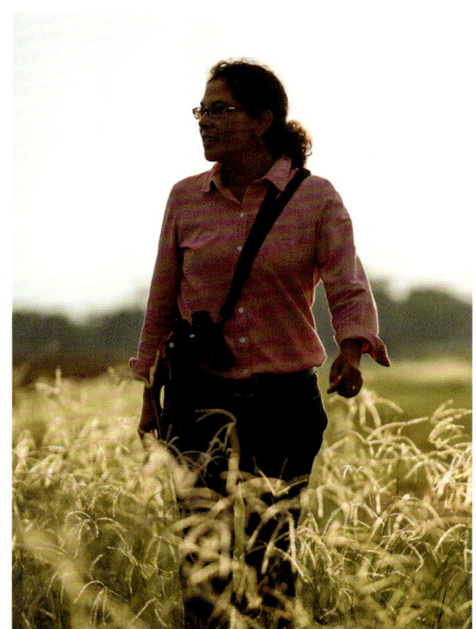

37.1 The subject pictured is a biologist, not a trained model, which meant I needed to be more directive in what I needed her to do as opposed to rely on her to simply know how to look during the shoot. I coached her with simple verbal cues, such as, "Just walk toward me while looking to your right."
ISO 200; 1/2000 sec.; f/4; 190mm

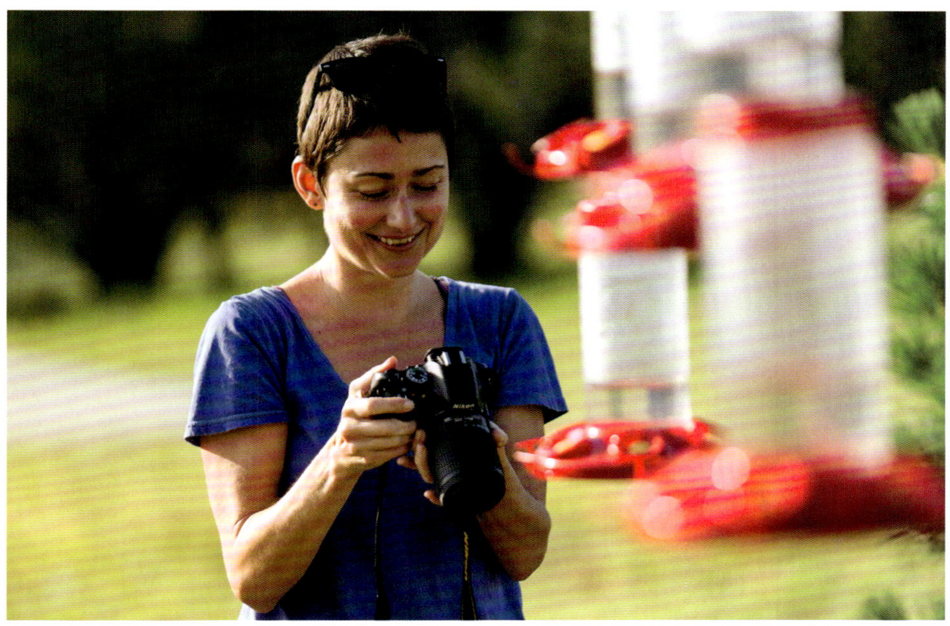

37.2 When photographing a conservationist for a nonprofit, I noticed and liked how she looked down at her camera to review her images. This led to a simple instruction to smile while reviewing her images, which made this portion of the shoot much more effective for my work.
ISO 200; 1/1250 sec.; f/2.8; 160mm

38. WHERE DOES YOUR SUBJECT LOOK?

YOUR PORTRAIT SUBJECT'S eyes are important. Some might say they are the most important part of their body, and for good reason. Humans use information conveyed by others' eyes to determine emotions and non-verbal cues. It's little wonder we place strong consideration on how they appear in a portrait.

We've already discussed how important it is to focus on the eyes in a portrait, but I'll re-emphasize it since the viewing eye typically lands on the part of any image that is in focus. Since we most often want to look at the eyes of the portrait subject, focusing there is crucial. It's also relevant to consider the direction the eyes are pointed. In this realm, it's common to see two types of portraits: a portrait in which the subject is looking at the camera (**Figure 38.1**), and one in which the subject is looking somewhere else—typically outside the frame (**Figure 38.2**). Although you might gravitate to one over the other, it certainly helps to know why eye direction might be worth considering for your next shoot.

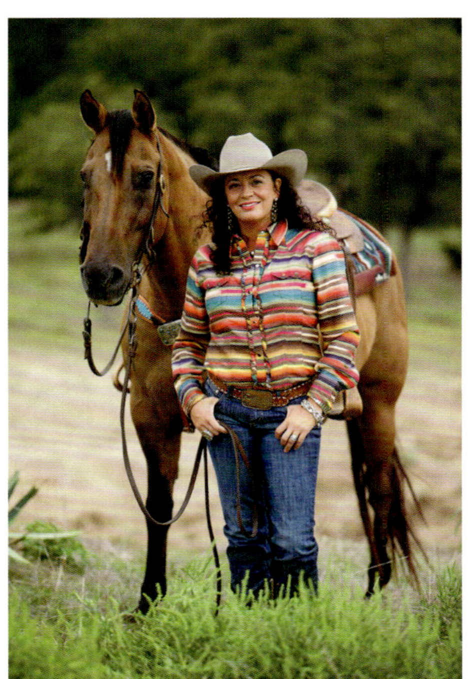

38.1 Eyes toward the camera mean direct engagement with the portrait's viewers.
ISO 400; 1/320 sec.; f/2.8; 160mm

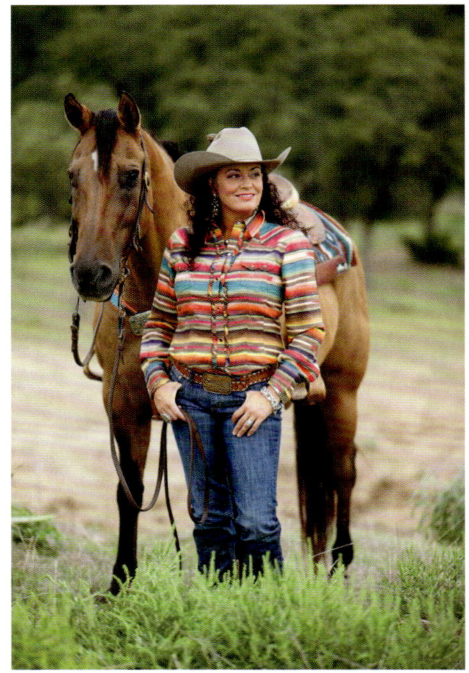

38.2 Eyes directed away from the camera create another level of audience perception. I try my best to get a portrait of a subject looking away from the camera each time I shoot a session.

Eyes pointed at the camera are eyes looking at the image viewer. There's no better way to establish a direct connection between subject and viewer than having them look at and engage the camera. Although both types of portraits make a statement, eyes looking at the camera are more accessible and can cement a more intense relationship between subject and viewer. Viewers enjoy the opportunity to explore the subject through their eyes. Social characteristics are suggested by the eyes; for example, a viewer might quickly determine the trustworthiness of a portrait subject based on their ability to see the subject's eyes. There is also a level of social formality in having the subject look at the camera (**Figure 38.3**). From professional headshots to senior portraits, eyes pointed toward the camera suggest respect, trust, and openness. Depending on the style of the portrait, and how the subject is coached, though, eyes pointed toward the camera can suggest a variety of emotions.

On the other hand, having your subject look away from the camera complicates both the emotional characteristics of the portrait subject. A portrait in which the subject looks away from the camera is less formal. This is popular for lifestyle and family portraits because they offer a carefree, caught-in-the-moment appeal, even though many might not be so candid (**Figure 38.4**). Combined with smiles, distraction-free composition and great light, these types of portraits might come across as being more authentic and personality-filled than others.

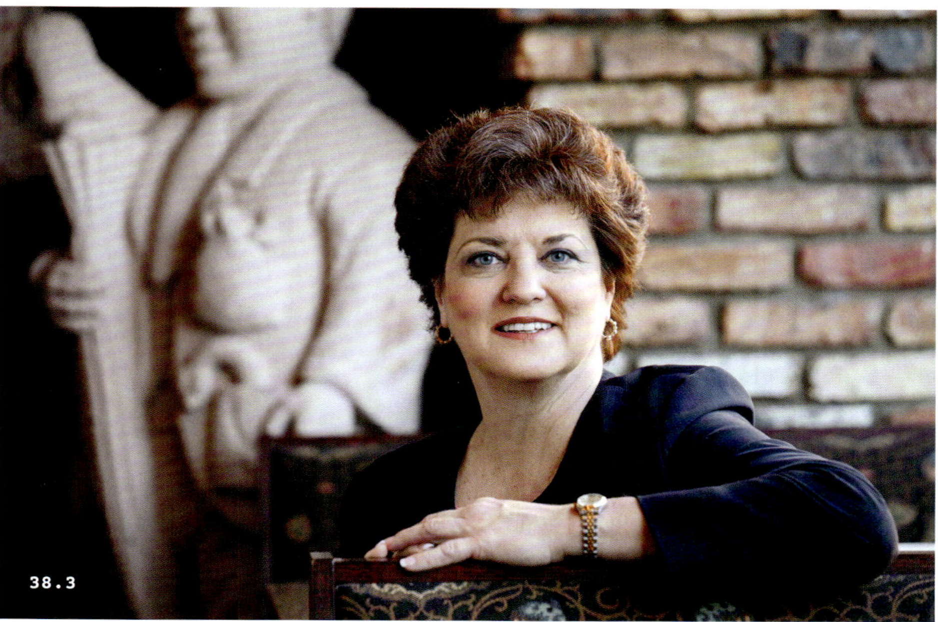

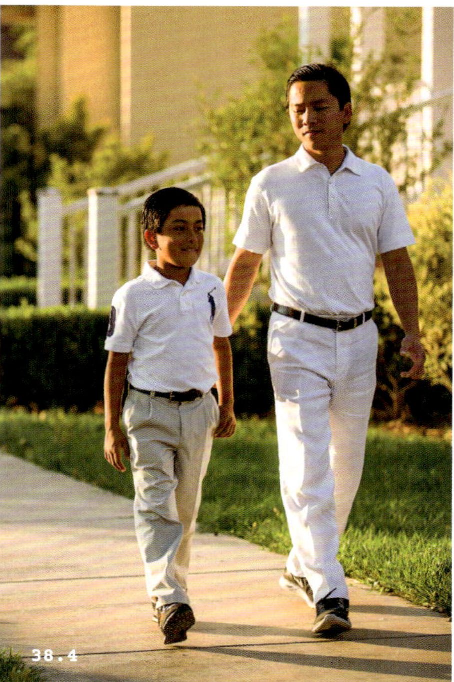

38.3 When I photographed Renee Underwood, she was the vice president of marketing of a regional Mexican restaurant chain. Although I wanted the shoot to be relaxed, I wanted to maintain a level of formality by having her eyes engaging the camera most of the time.
ISO 400; 1/40 sec.; f/4.5; 140mm

38.4 In family portraits, having the subjects engage each other with their eyes is almost more effective than if they were looking at the camera. It also conveys a more relaxed, informal perspective of the portrait and the subjects, even if they were coached to look at each other.
ISO 200; 1/2500 sec.; f/2.8; 125mm

However, there can be an emotionally deeper characteristic suggested by subjects whose eyes do not face the camera, especially when they do not smile (**Figure 38.5**). You can use eyes pointed away to suggest the subject is deep in thought, lonely, full of wonder, or even troubled. Regardless of what you are trying to convey, these types of portraits also make the viewer think—mostly about the subject and their current emotional state. Unfortunately, these types of shots can also cause undue tension in the viewer, so it is best to consider the appropriateness of the subject looking away from the camera or out of the frame. A somber-looking middle-aged man looking out of the frame for an actor's headshot might be useful in landing him a job in a television show or commercial, but the same look might not bode so well for him being photographed with his family.

Like so many things in photography, there is no hard and fast rule on where the subject should be looking within the frame. This is a choice based on portrait style and the subject's story. However, there are a couple of portraiture concepts to keep in the back of your head that refer to the eyes. First, it's a good idea to keep both eyes visible (**Figure 38.6** and **Figure 38.7**). Unless you are intentionally creating a profile-only portrait, being able to see two eyes is comfortable for the viewer. This doesn't necessarily mean that the viewer must be able to see both pupils; for example, in a portrait in which the subject is looking away from the camera, don't make the subject turn her head so much that the camera-opposite side of her face disappears. This reduces the face's dimension, but it also encourages disconnection between the subject and the viewer. Even just an eyebrow or eyelash provides the indication of an eye, the necessary dimension, and a higher level of engagement.

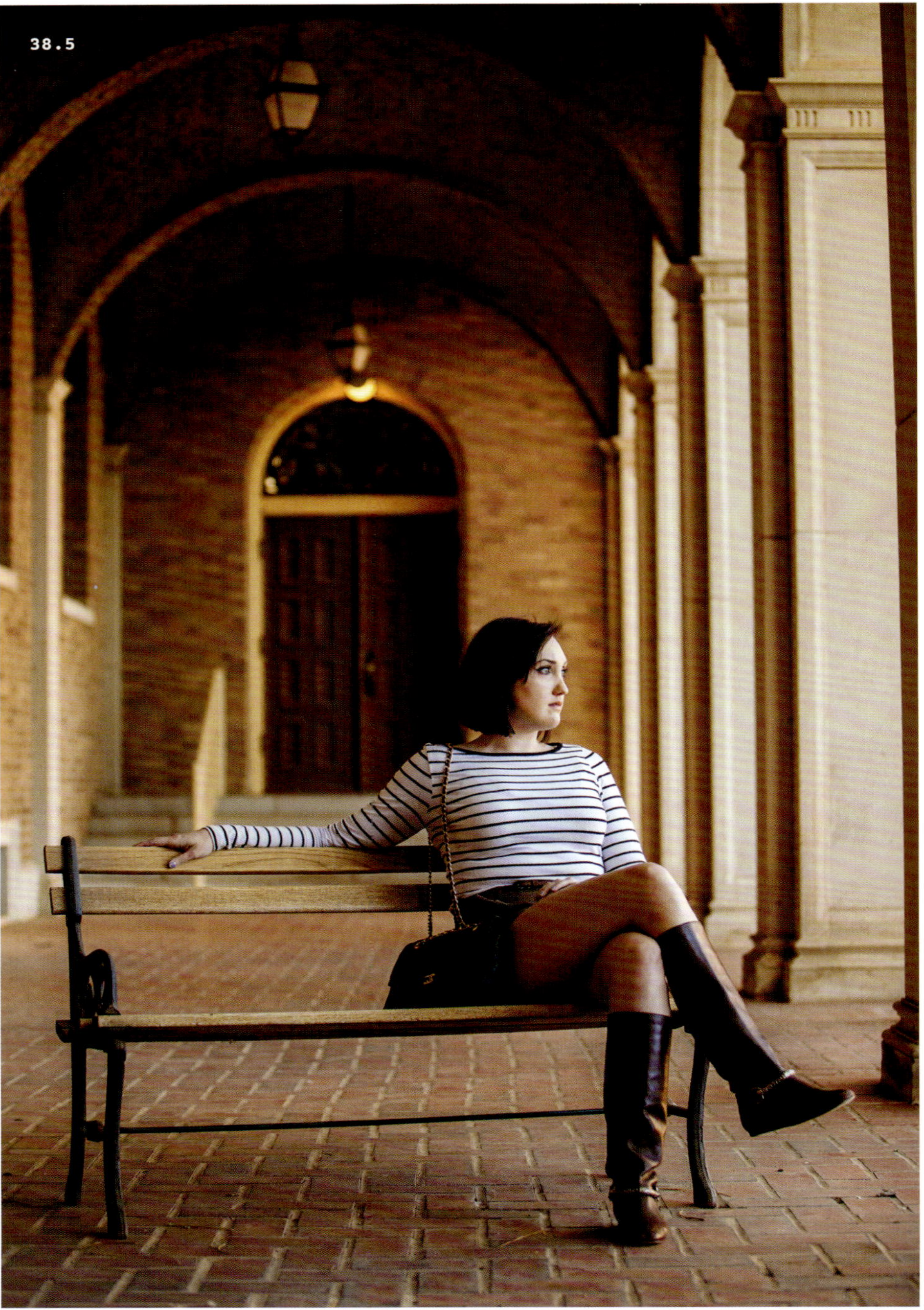

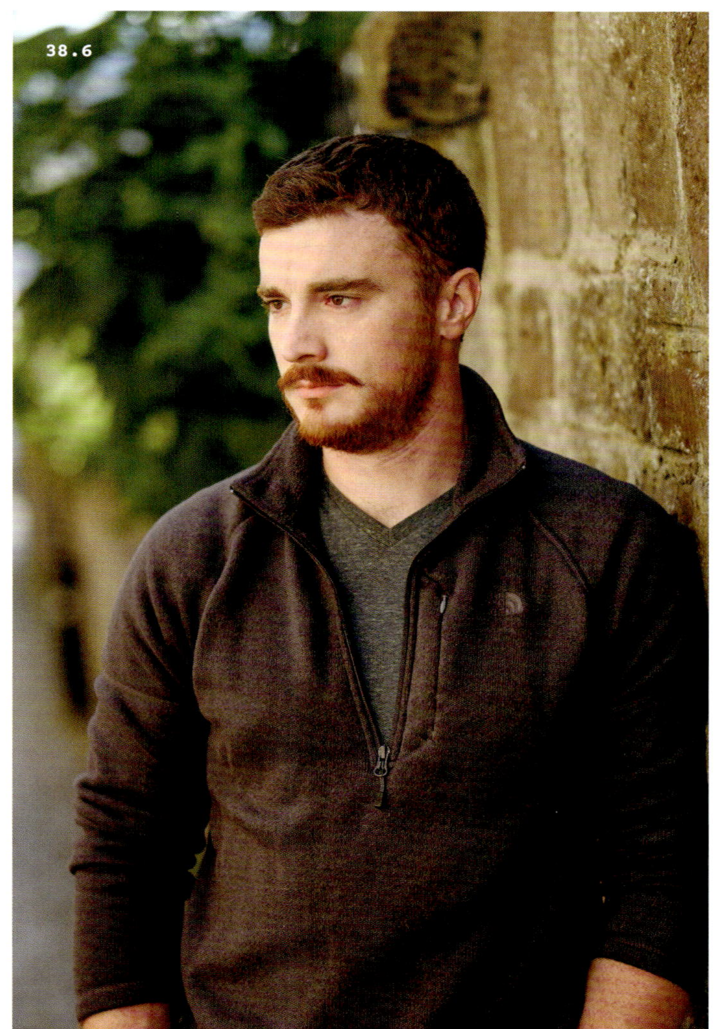 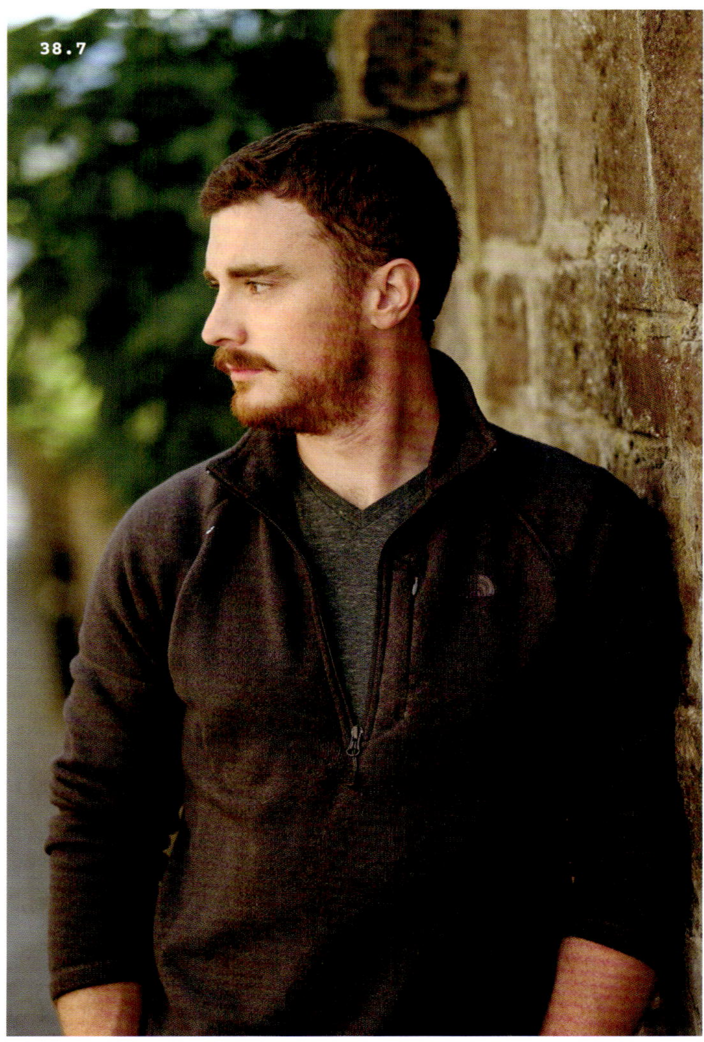

38.5 Often, a look away from the camera and out of the frame creates a pondering feeling for the image's viewer. Abstractly, a portrait such as this one allows the viewer to question what the subject is thinking and/or feeling at that moment.
ISO 400; 1/160 sec.; f/2.8; 70mm

38.6 Allowing the viewer to see both of your subject's eyes mitigates any visual tension in not being able to directly relate to said subject, a result of being conditioned in our lives to see most people by looking at their eyes.
ISO 200; 1/900 sec.; f/2; 90mm

38.7 Although not terribly disturbing to the viewer's perception of the portrait, a face turned profile diminishes dimension and any sense of what the other side of his face looks like.

Second, if you do create a portrait in which the subject is not looking at the camera, make sure to lead the subject's eye (**Figure 38.8**). This means considering having the subject look in a direction that complements the frame's orientation and encourages the viewer to look at more throughout the frame. In a way, you could say it is better for a subject to look *into* the frame, not *out* of it. Compositionally, this provides the photographer more opportunity to use the open space between the subject's face and the edge of the frame, and it avoids unnecessary visual tension.

It's a good idea to give your subject something to look at. Whether the subject is looking at or away from the camera, it never hurts to guide their vision. It might sound funny, but some folks, while looking toward the camera, do not actually look into it. It's easy to miss while you are shooting, but it can become glaringly obvious when the image is on your computer. When shooting portraits in which the subject is looking at me, I tend to say, "OK, just look right into the lens," as if it were a normal part of the conversation that takes place during a shoot. This is especially important for children, but some adults have a hard time with it as well. This instruction keeps the subject from looking at the top of the camera, or even worse, the top of your head! When the portrait subject is not required to look at the camera, I direct them to concentrate on a particular object. I'll suggest they look at something behind me on the ground to their left or right—usually a structure that doesn't force them to turn their head too dramatically. This keeps them looking in a particular spot rather than gazing around in the sky with their eyes, creating that "off into the mystic" style portrait that has become cliché.

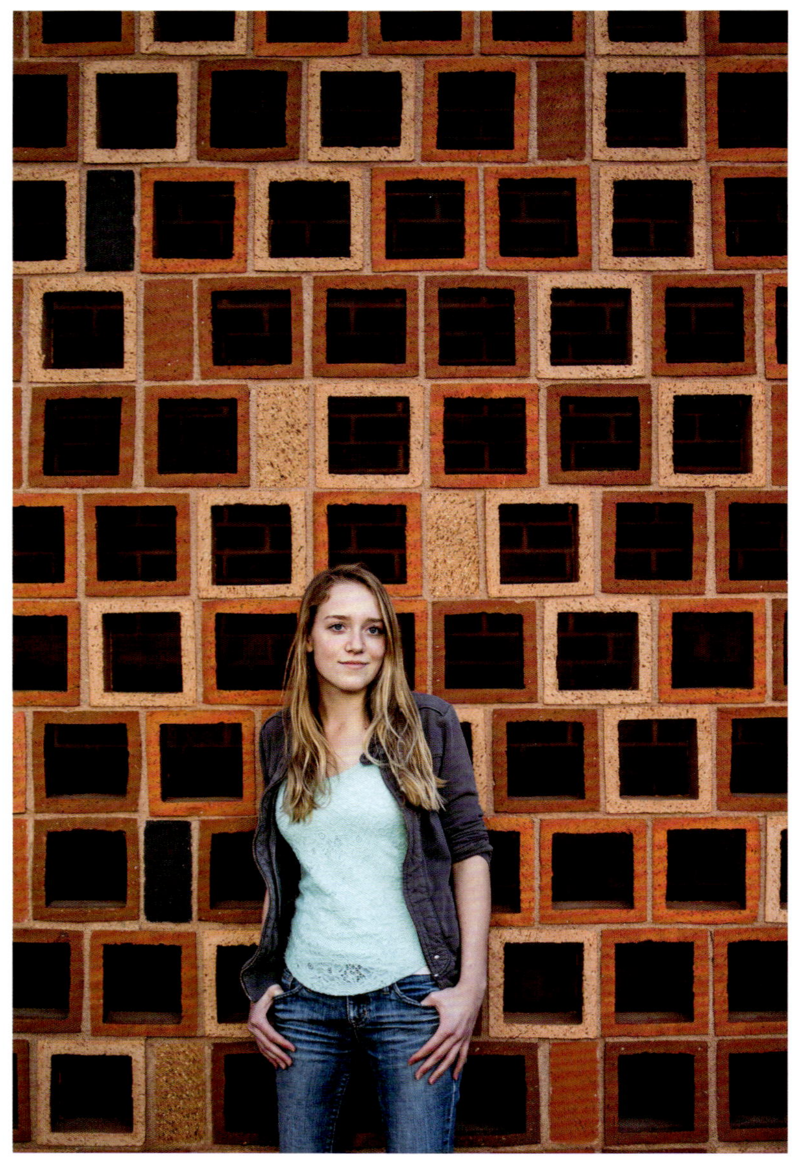

38.8 Although there is no written rule about it, it is thought best to have the subject look *into* the frame, as opposed to *out* of it, leading the viewer's eye into the rest of the image. Since the subject was composed at camera left, I had her look slightly camera right to ensure her vision directed the viewer's into the frame to camera right. **ISO 100; 1/100 sec.; f/2.8; 78mm**

39. "WHAT DO I DO WITH MY HANDS?"

WHATEVER YOU DO, avoid the "fig leaf" pose in which the portrait subject holds both of his hands together over his crotch. Under no circumstance should you use it. Ever.

Alright, so I might be a bit hard on the "fig leaf" pose, but without any instruction, many portrait subjects (especially males) resort to using this very common hand position because they've seen it before or believe it to be the most formal way of posing their hands (**Figure 39.1**). Certainly, it has its uses—it stresses formality, seriousness, and, when combined with a low angle, intimidation—but it can also be a bit unflattering and uninteresting.

So, what do you do with your subject's hands? The simple answer is to try to make them seem natural. For general portraiture, I encourage the subject to relax physically and see where their hands (and arms) fall. At this point, you can coach them to improve the appearance of the hands. Just as the "fig leaf" pose can get a little old, so can arms hanging down at your subject's sides. It's good to give the hands something to do.

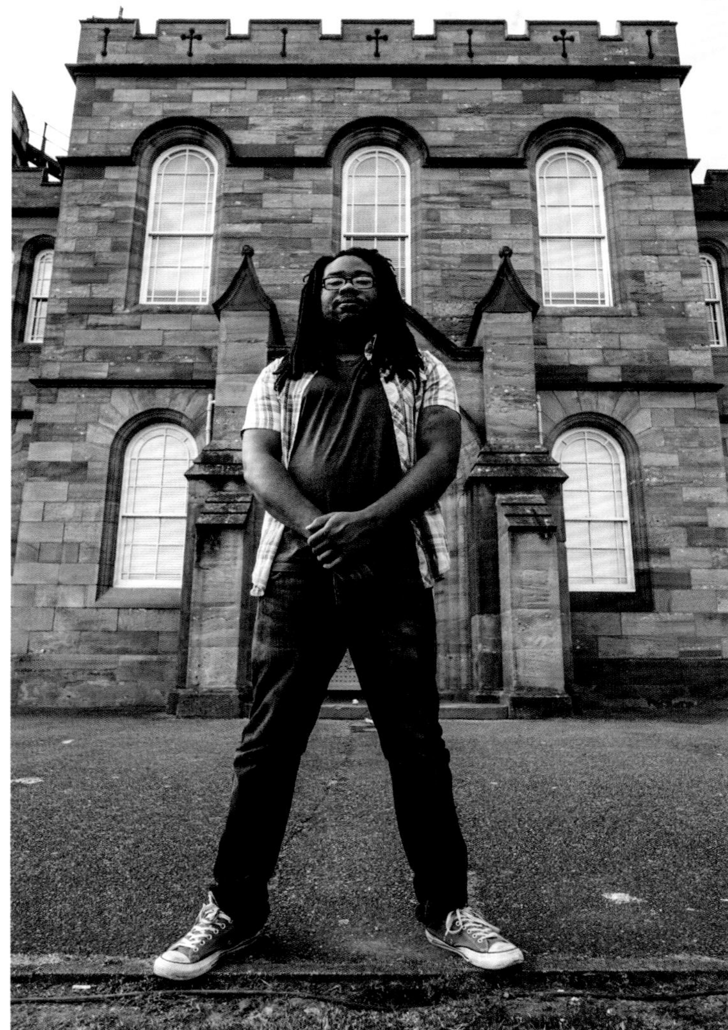

39.1 The "fig leaf" pose is one that, if done well, will probably go unnoticed. However, in many cases, it's a good way to direct your viewer's attention to the subject's midsection and crotch.
ISO 400; 1/550 sec.; f/4; 14mm

My go-to hand and arm positioning is to have the subject cross their arms (**Figure 39.2**). You'll like it or you won't, and that's fine. However, crossed arms are useful for everything from relaxed, candid-like portraits to serious, dramatic-looking images. The thing I like the most about crossed arms is that they make the subject look confident, regardless of whether the face suggests joy or sternness. However natural crossed arms may be for a portrait, one thing to avoid is the subject tucking their hands behind their arms (**Figure 39.3**). Coach the subject to bring their hands out and bend them up into the elbows (**Figure 39.4**). This will appear more relaxed and relieve visual tension created by the missing hands.

For more relaxed portraiture, I also suggest having the subject place his hands in his pants pockets (**Figure 39.5**). This is an especially natural thing to do for male subjects. However, I make sure they don't stick their hands in so far that the hands disappear at the wrists (**Figure 39.6**). Instead, I leave a portion of their fingers emerging from their pockets, indicating that they do have fingers. This also helps keep the subject from looking uptight and nervous.

Speaking of fingers, photographers go back and forth on what to do with them. It's important to keep your subject from holding their fingers too tightly together. Discourage your subject from clenching a fist unless it is an essential part of the portrait. Likewise, avoid hands in which the fingers are spread too far apart. Fingers are best when they appear comfortably spaced from each other (**Figure 39.7**).

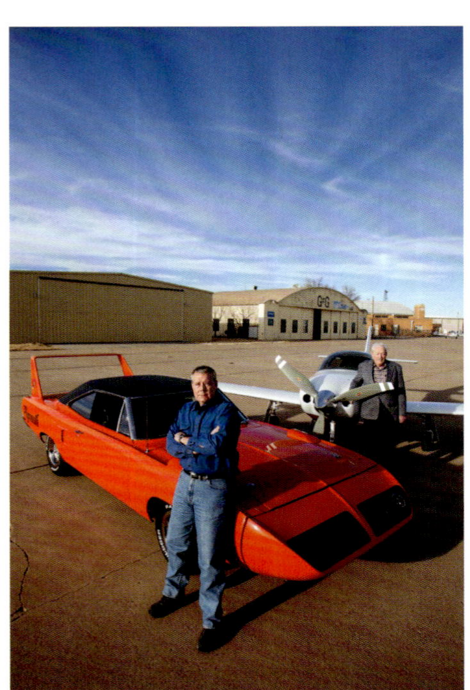

39.2 Having your subject cross their arms gives them something to do and establishes a level of attitude that, when combined with the right content, speaks volumes about their personality.
ISO 100; 1/80 sec.; f/11; 22mm

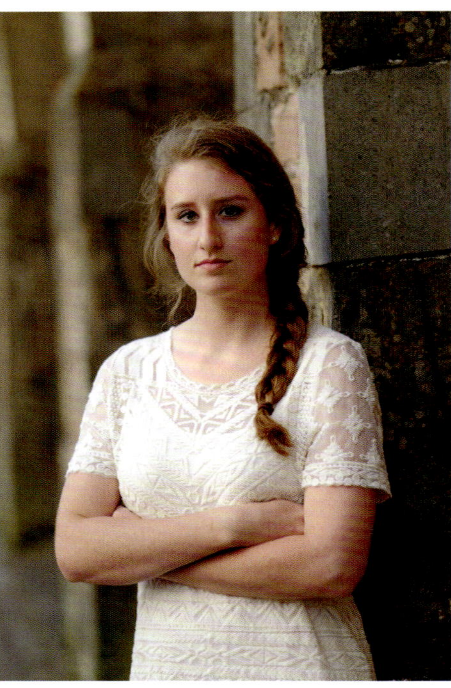

39.3 Avoid allowing your subject to stuff their hands inside their arms when crossing them. Not only does this leave the hands hidden, it also can convey a sense of nervousness or anxiety.
ISO 400; 1/450 sec.; f/2; 90mm

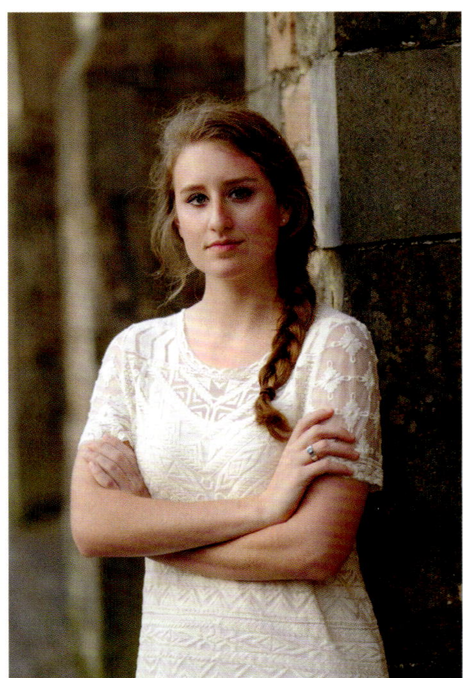

39.4 Instead, coach your subject to bring their hands out from behind their arms, and further give their arms dimension by turning the wrist up so the fingers point somewhat toward the subject's shoulders.

39.5 I wanted this portrait conservation director Jason Wrinkle to convey his personality, so I coached him to put his hands in his pockets. He then hooked his thumbs into his pockets, which reflected his background growing up close to agriculture and as a cowboy.
ISO 100; 1/2500 sec.; f/2.8; 55mm

39.6 It's the little things that count. Coaching the male subject to pull some of his hand out of his pocket would allow him to relax his arm more and separate it from his body.
ISO 200; 1/160 sec.; f/4.5; 175mm

39.7 The subject's right hand seems relaxed in this environmental portrait—it's not clenched, nor are the fingers tightly pressed together— exactly the visual suggestion I wanted to create for the director of an outdoor museum.
ISO 200; 1/320 sec.; f/2.8; 145mm

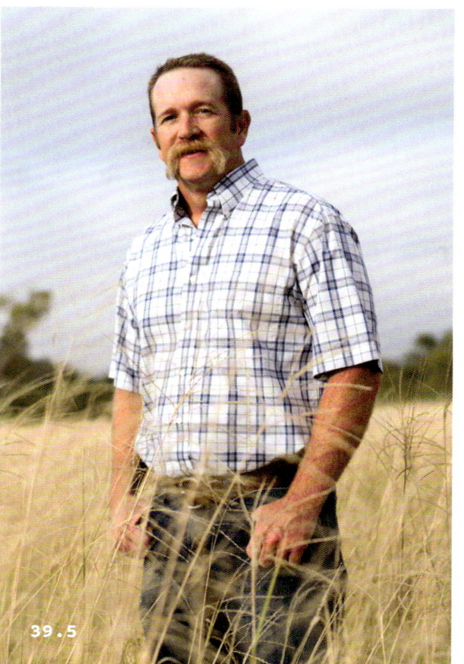

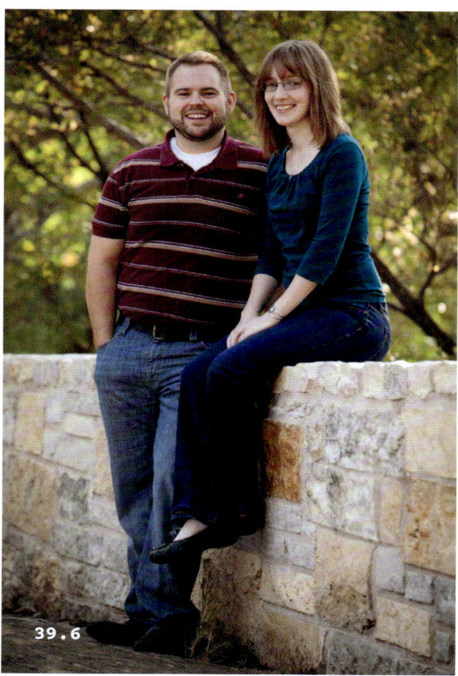

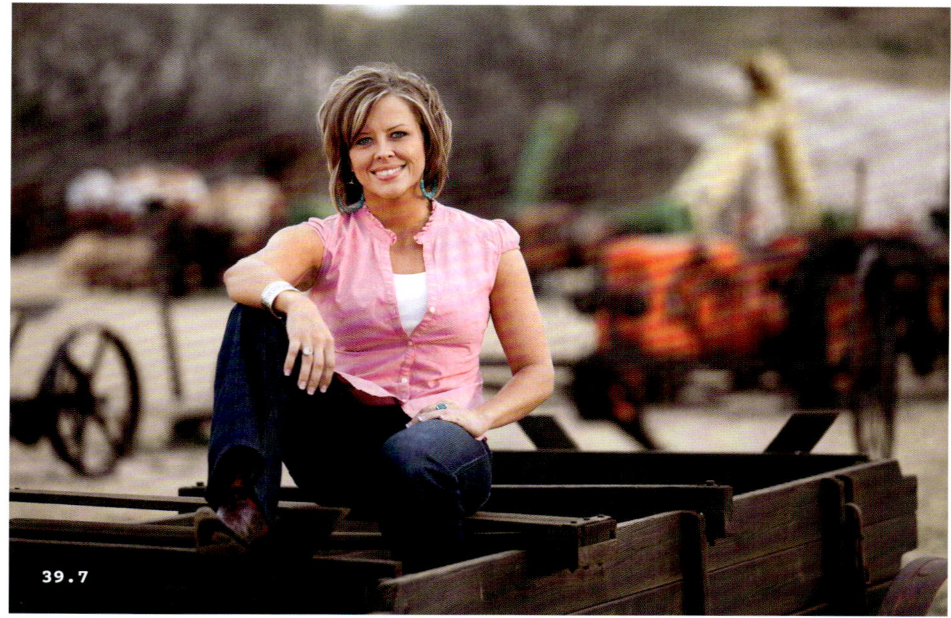

In many cases, you'll more than likely coach the subject on what not to do with their hands, and they'll pick up on it. Regardless of how well they accept that coaching, you'll need to keep an eye on their hands to avoid those problematic issues, including awkward placement and letting them disappear behind other appendages, clothing, etc. One solution that really trumps them all (but, only if the portrait calls for it) is to give the hands something to do. As complicated as it makes other considerations of a portrait, putting something in the subject's hands is a great way to create a natural presence for the hands and convey a narrative about your subject (**Figure 39.8**). Consider a cowboy holding a rope. He knows how to hold the rope,

so it visually strengthens the visual notions presented in the photo. Of course, you don't necessarily have to make your subject hold something *in* their hands; you could place them up against a rail and have them *hold onto it* or drape their arms and hands *over* it, for example (**Figure 39.9**). There's an unending pool of options for this technique. However, be conscientious of how well the prop fits the subject. If it doesn't, you'll know it, they'll know it, and viewers will notice something is awkward about the portrait.

Lastly, all this talk about hands and fingers makes it seem like they need to be in every shot. However, when you need a change of pace, a different shot perspective, or you just keep getting

frustrated with the hands, it's a good idea to switch gears and take them out of the shot altogether. Move from a medium shot to a head shot, using the frame to compose them out (and to provide your subject another "look"). Have your subject hold her hands behind her if the portrait style allows. You're going to have to photograph hands, but it's nice knowing that you can reduce the amount of stress surrounding the concept of photographing them by simply moving on to another type of shot or moving them out of the frame in a similarly appropriate manner.

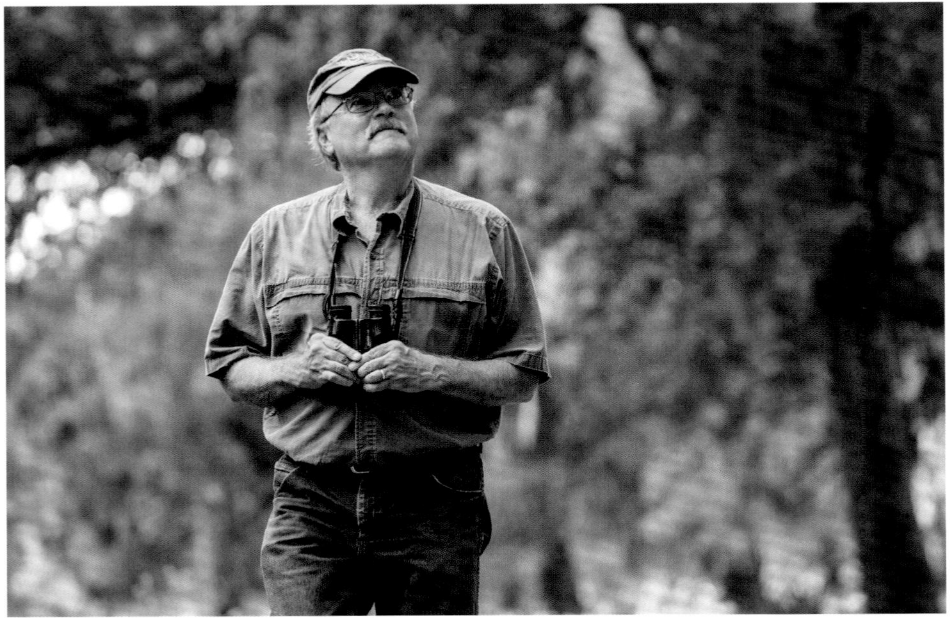

39.8 For this conservationist's portrait, I had him hold onto his binoculars, which gave his hands something to do. Likewise, doing so paired well with the direction he was looking—up, as if he was ready to take a closer look at a bird at a moment's notice.
ISO 400; 1/250 sec.; f/4; 155mm

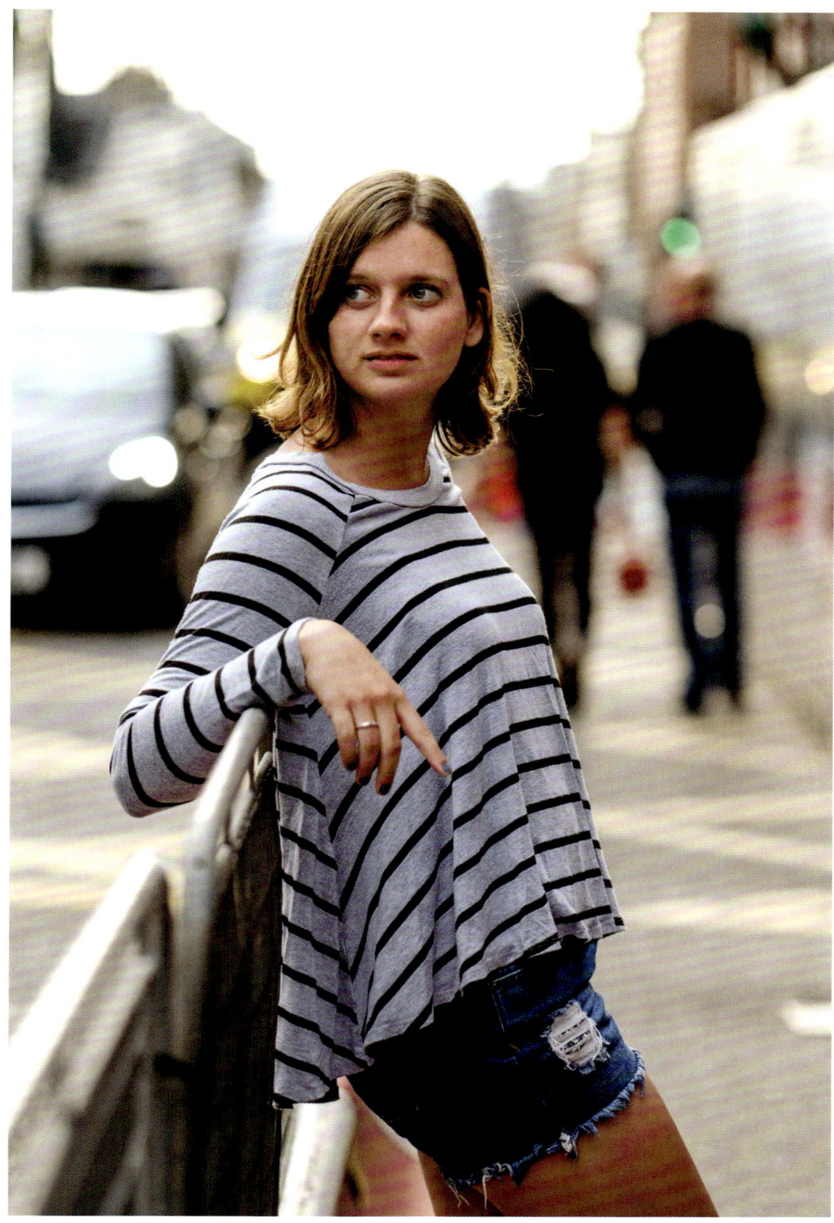

39.9 Draping an arm and hand over a railing offers new composition, new attitude and emotion, and it creates diversity among your shoot's overall take.
ISO 400; 1/950 sec.; f/2; 90mm

LIKE COMPOSITION, POSING the face and body is about creating the visual sensation of depth. This is an important concept to keep in mind as we move through the rest of this chapter. When it comes to the face, two components that create visual depth (and are often the most posed) are the cheeks and the nose.

When the face is turned directly toward the camera, known as a full view (**Figure 40.1**), it showcases the least amount of depth, especially if the lighting is behind the photographer rather than to the side, resulting in shadows that fall behind the subject. As the head turns to one side or the other, the viewer will see better how the face is structured, how large or small the nose is, how round and how high the cheeks are, and so on (**Figure 40.2**). Although many portraits are made with the portrait subject directly facing the camera, I also encourage you to turn the head a bit to create this sense of depth. How much do you need to turn it? That depends on the face, and everyone is different in this regard. However, it is an unwritten rule to not turn your subject's face so much that the nose moves past the camera-opposite cheek (**Figure 40.3** and **Figure 40.4**). This introduces the nose as being more prominent than it should be and it breaks up the nice line of the cheek. Furthermore, turning the head too far might make the subject look relatively strained in an awkward position.

Additionally, one posing consideration to make for cheeks is how they are horizontally angled in the portrait. Imagine a headshot of someone directly facing the camera

(**Figure 40.5**). If she held her head level, her cheeks would be even across, from one to the other. Now, imagine she slightly tilted her head to one side, raising one cheek higher than the other (**Figure 40.6**). Doing so might have added just a bit of emotional and visually suggestive power to the portrait, depending on whether the tilt was combined with a smile or a somber expression. Of course, dramatically tilting the head to one side can be awkward (picture an owl turning its head upside down), so it's best to coach your subject to tilt their head with moderation. This slight tilt can be extremely useful in evoking whimsy, playfulness, and joy, just as much as it can be to suggest sternness and malevolence. It's also not relegated to just portraits where the subject is looking straight at the camera, so be ready to employ this simple but powerful technique in a variety of shots and perspectives.

One of the most noticeable parts of the human body is the nose. Everyone's nose is different, and it is one of the visual characteristics that we use to identify others. Despite all the great things noses do for us, they're often the issue of contempt for some portrait subjects. Folks with large noses or short, upturned noses tend to be more sensitive about how their nose appears in portraits, and while nothing is necessarily wrong with their face, it's an understandable concern. When a subject is worried about their nose, it's best to seriously consider how best to approach easing their anxiety.

40.1 A full-view of the face, in which it is turned directly toward the camera, is largely dependent upon shadow to showcase any dimension the face has.
ISO 200; 1/125 sec.; f/1.4; 50mm

40.2 Rotating the face allows the viewer to see exactly how the face is constructed, it's depth, and an overall sense of how dimensional it is relative to everything else in the frame, especially the subject's own form.

40.3 It's a best practice to avoid photographing a subject's nose extended past the camera-opposite cheek. The face loses quite a bit of dimension and depth in doing so, and it can sometimes make the nose seem unnecessarily larger than it really is.
ISO 200; 1/1250 sec.; f/2; 90mm

40.4 Keeping the nose within the confines of the subject's two cheeks is often considered more flattering for the subject. It reduces the size of the nose without sacrificing how it is situated relative to other parts of the face.

40.5 A tight headshot in which the cheek bones are kept level with the top and bottom edges of the frame.
ISO 400; 1/250 sec.; f/2; 90mm

40.6 Slightly tilting the head to one side creates an unlevel line from one cheek to the other, helps enhance the diagonal line moving from the lower left to the top right of the frame, and slightly boosts the image's personality.

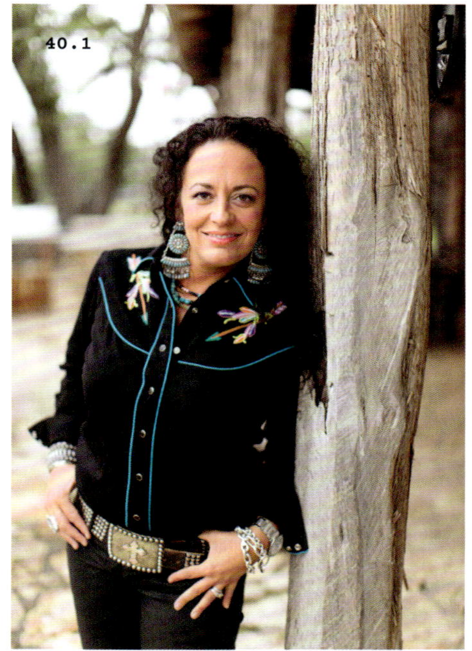
40.1

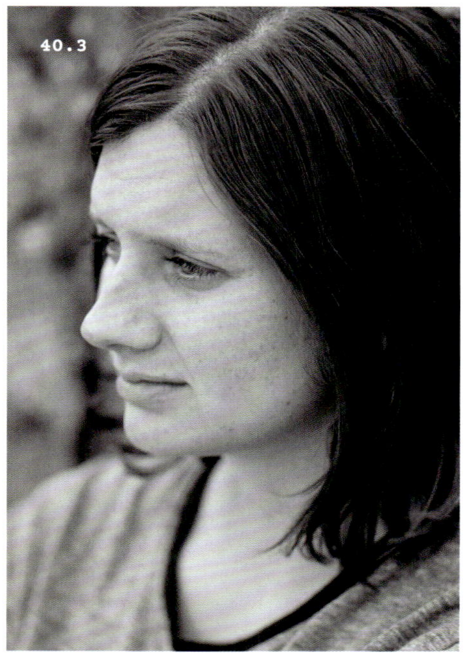
40.3

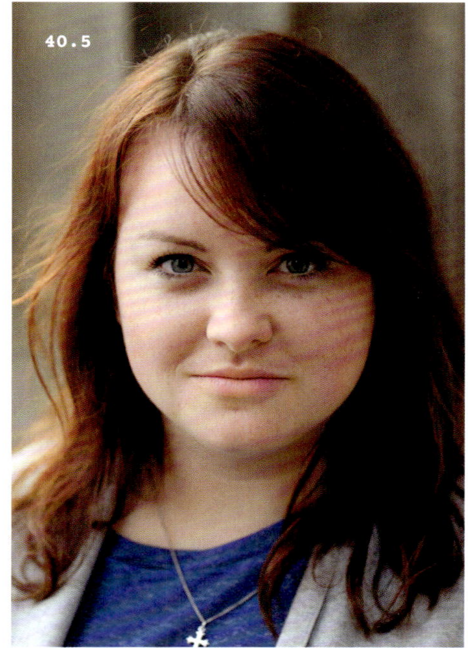
40.5

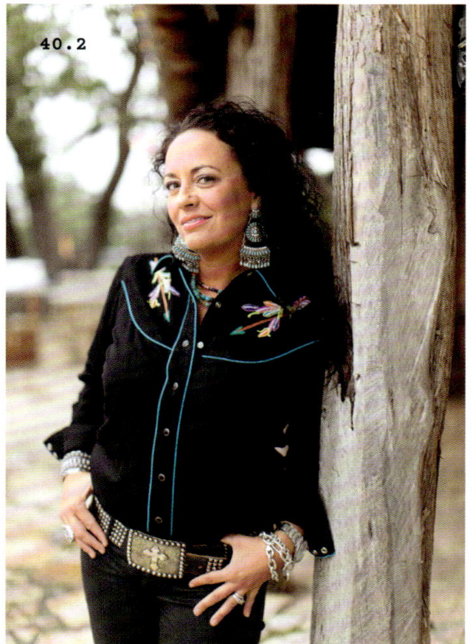
40.2

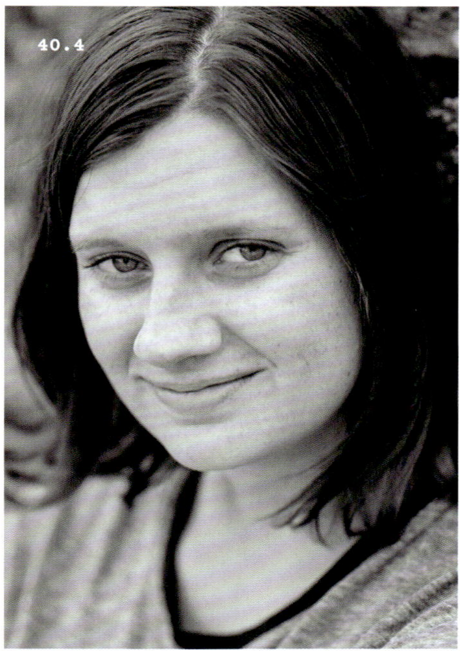
40.4

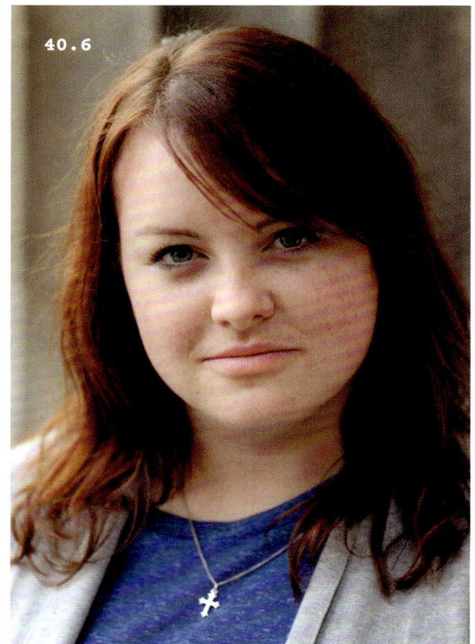
40.6

Although there is no definitive rule or approach to solving every perceivable issue that might arise when it comes to noses, it is to your benefit as the photographer to ensure the nose is not distracting from the portrait itself. Have your subject turn his head to one side and the other to see how light plays on the face (the nose in particular). Also, see if there is an especially useful angle for tighter shots (portraits in which the nose is a more prominent structure). Here are remedies that portrait photographers regularly employ:

1 **Use a longer focal length.** We've already covered how wide focal lengths (anything wider than 50mm) distort your portrait subject. The nose is especially susceptible to distortion. The closer you push a wide focal length in, the worse the distortion will be. Even 50mm can be too wide in some cases. For tighter shots, I favor longer focal lengths like 85mm or even 200mm (**Figure 40.7**). Not only are these great portrait focal lengths, they help compress the nose into the face a bit—flattening it, so to speak—and reducing how pronounced it is compared to the surrounding facial features.

2 **Have subjects with longer noses turn their face toward the camera.** Doing so will reduce the visible length of the subject's nose, something many people are sensitive about (**Figure 40.8** and **Figure 40.9**).

3 **Have subjects with larger, wider noses turn their face slightly away from the camera.** In doing so, you end up using the end of the nose to cover up small or large parts of the camera-opposite nostril (**Figure 40.10**).

4 **Don't shoot from too high or too low of an angle.** If your subject is sensitive about his long nose, then shooting from a higher angle down on him will make the nose appear even longer since the tip of the nose will visually dip down into the upper lip and mouth, depending on how drastic of an angle you take. Consider photographing your subject from their eye level instead. Inversely, portrait subjects with shorter, more up-turned noses are best photographed from slightly above, reducing the amount of the bottom side of their nose is in view (**Figure 40.11**).

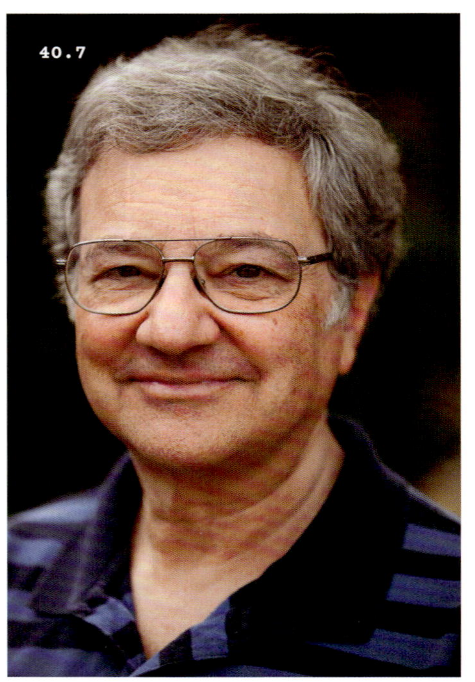

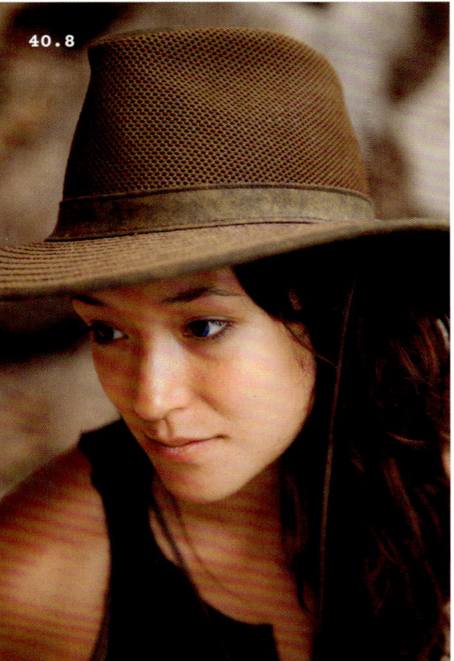

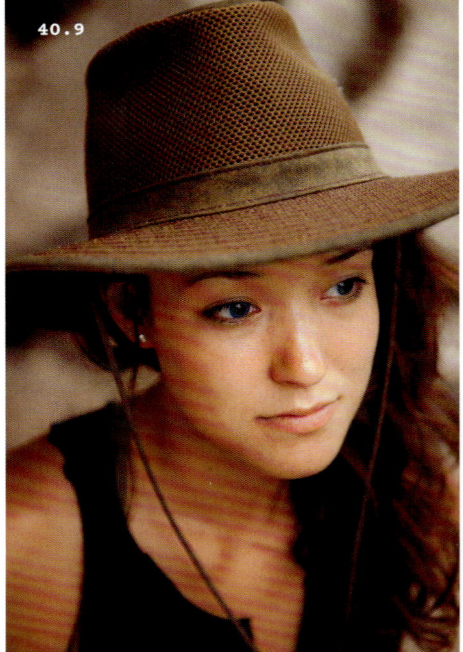

40.7 Using a telephoto focal length, I was able to avoid visual distortion of the subject's face, as well as compress his features a bit, one being his nose, which appears smaller due to the angle of which his head is turned, the flatter lighting, and the optical perspective.
ISO 100; 1/400 sec.; f/2.8; 125mm

40.8 The further a subject's face is turned away from the camera, the longer her nose will appear.
ISO 100; 1/160 sec.; f/2.8; 70mm

40.9 Although this subject does not have a uniquely long nose, turning her head more into the camera (yet still angled off a bit), diminishes the size of her nose, allowing it to recede into the face simply due to her face's orientation to the camera.

40.10 The subject's nose is a bit wider than average, so I turned his face slightly to one side, which subtly moves one nostril farther away from the camera and more into the shadow side of his face, thus mitigating any distraction his nose may cause in the shot while still maintaining his face's characteristic appearance.
ISO 200; 1/250 sec.; f/1.4; 35mm

40.11 Shooting your subject from below, among other things, allows the viewer to look up his nose. Although the angle might work well with some subjects, some might not enjoy the viewer having a peek up their nostrils.
ISO 100; 1/1000 sec.; f/2.8; 51mm

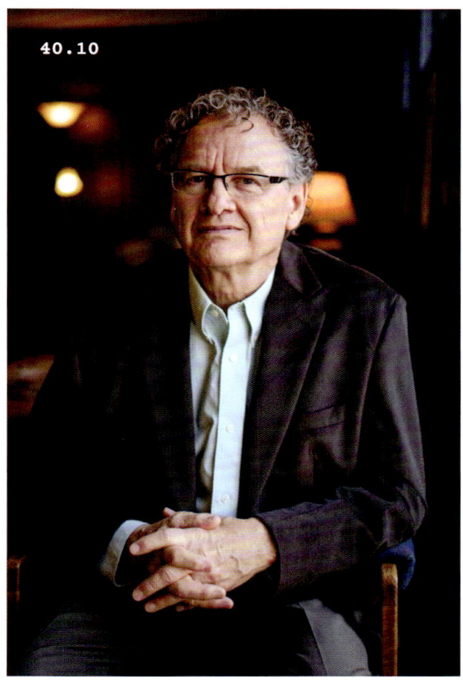

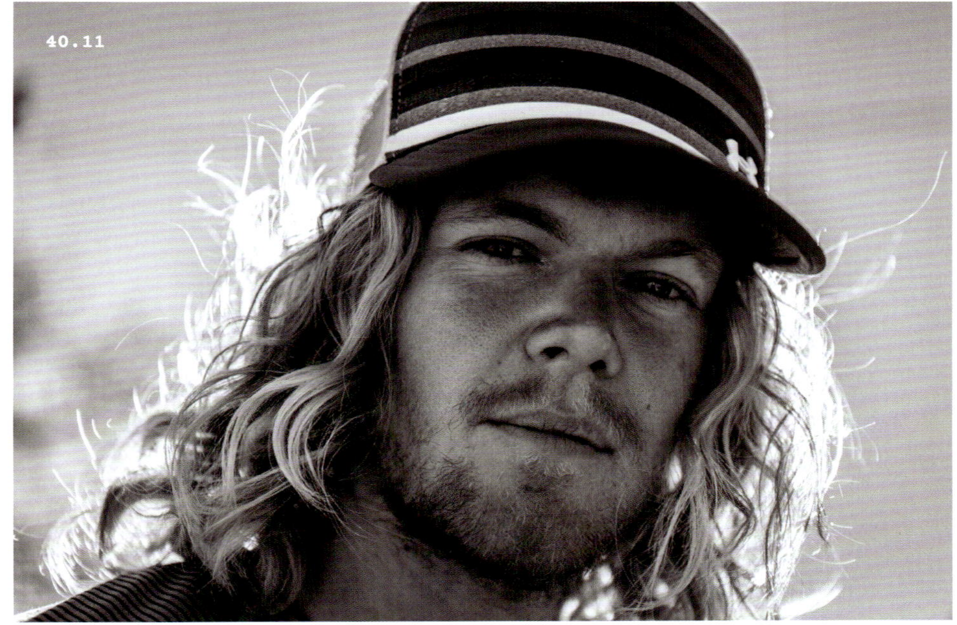

5 **Use non-dimensional lighting.** Shooting with direct front, directionally diffused, or diffused lighting reduces the visual dimension of the nose due to lack of shadows. (**Figure 40.12**) Diffused light is very effective for this since there are essentially no shadows to speak of with this type of light. Direct front lighting works well if the subject, again, is turned more toward the camera than away.

Keep in mind that all noses are different, and aside from the generally unacceptable wide-angle, up-the-nose shot, portraiture aims to make the subject look as good and comfortable as they can possibly appear. It's important that you remain conscientious of how your subject feels about their nose and how they might feel about it after seeing their portraits. It's best not to point out any issues that your trained eye might see; rather, coach them into posing for your shot according to these tips and the experience you pick up after photographing several people with varying nose structures. This goes for all human anatomy, but it is particularly important for noses.

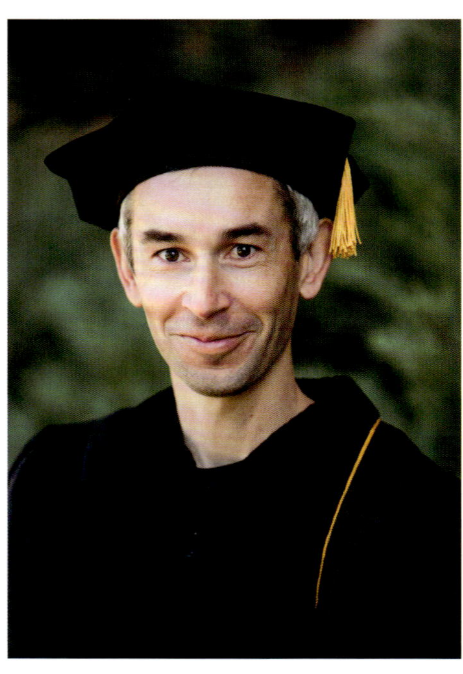

40.12 Soft, diffused or directionally diffused lighting reduces the amount of shadow the nose throws across a subject's face, further diminishing its size.
ISO 200; 1/500 sec.; f/2.8; 155mm

Avoid Double Chins

The chin, arguably, is not the most important part of the human face. It is, however, a visibly recognizable part of the body. We all know folks that have fairly strong, defined chins, as well as those that have "no chin" at all. Most folks exist somewhere in between, and many are aware of the ill effects of the dreaded double chin!

A double chin is sometimes a result of simple head and facial anatomy, especially for heavier set portrait subjects (however, it is most definitely not always a factor of weight). At other times, a double chin appears when one of two things happens. First, double chins have a higher chance of being pronounced when you photograph your subject from below (**Figure 40.13**). Portrait subjects have a tendency to look at the camera, and when the camera is below them, they angle their head down, forcing the chin back into their neck. This increases the potential for skin to fold onto itself around the neck or bunch up and bulge just behind the chin. The solution? Avoid photographing your subject from below, especially for tighter framed shots. Instead, shoot from eye level or slightly above, which forces the subject to stretch the skin behind the chin rather than compress it (**Figure 40.14**).

Having the subject look up at times slims the face as well, which is a welcome approach to posing for many subjects.

Secondly, double chins appear when the subject naturally compresses his chin into this neck (**Figure 40.15**). This is not unlike the issue described in the previous paragraph, but I want to encourage you to stay aware of how the subject naturally poses his chin. Males sometimes stand at attention, which pushes the chin back into the neck. If you see this occurring, coach the subject to relax their chin, slightly push it out (joke about how it might feel awkward at first), and even tilt their head to the side to take their mind off the reason you might be repositioning their chin (**Figure 40.16**).

I've never known a situation where a double chin was desirable by the client. Unless there is a specific reason for tolerating it, be aware of it in your frame, and you'll be able to avoid potentially negative comments from the subject later about how they look in your portraits. As easy as it is to spot a double chin, it's just as easy to reduce them given your position or the subject's posture.

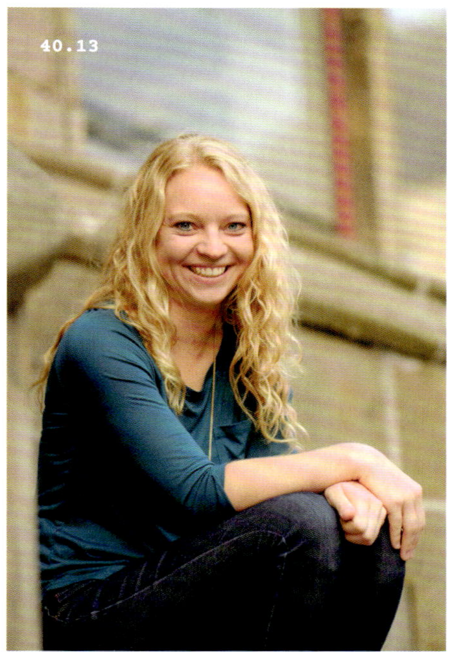

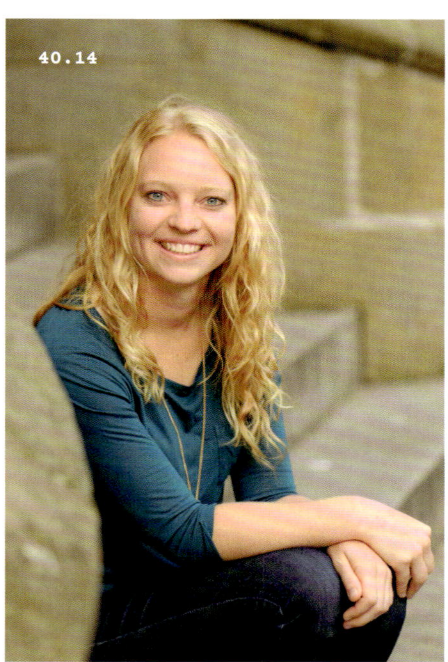

40.13 For many subjects, shooting from a low angle forces them to look down on the camera. This in turn can result in a double chin appearing, even for subjects that would be considered fairly trim.
ISO 400; 1/900 sec.; f/2; 90mm

40.14 Raising the angle of the camera to or just above eye level forces the subject to tilt their heads upward, greatly reducing the presence of a double chin simply because the subject had to stretch their neck out to look up.

40.15 Although this is not a gender-specific issue, some male subjects suffer from a double chin because of how they push their chin back while trying to pose properly or stand correctly during the shoot.
ISO 400; 1/350 sec.; f/2; 90mm

40.16 I was able to reduce the subject's double chin by simply coaching him to elongate his neck and push his chin slightly forward. I also shot from a slightly higher angle than the previous portrait.

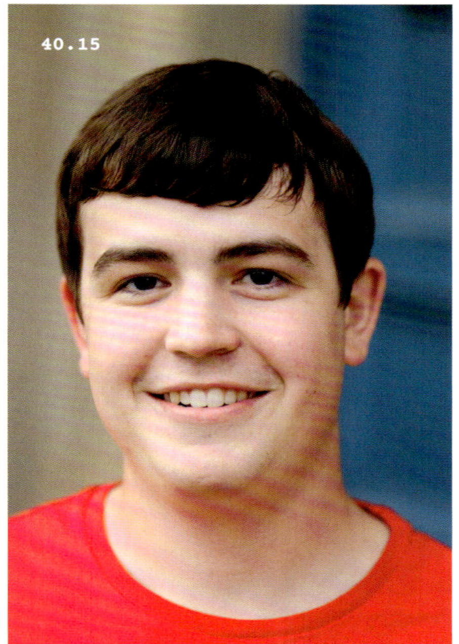

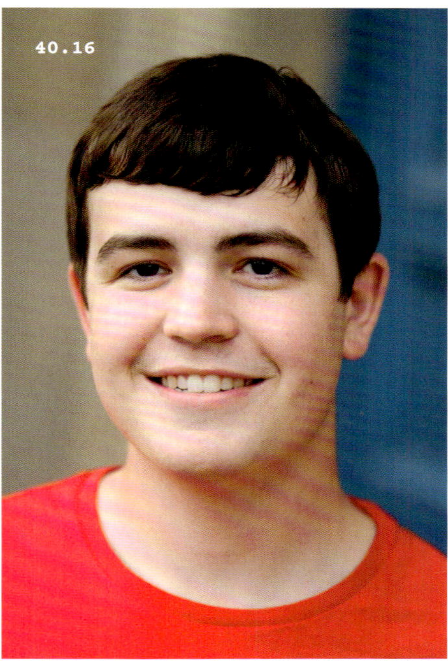

THERE ARE SO many possibilities when it comes to posing bodies that there isn't enough room in this entire book to cover them. There are many large volumes dedicated to this particular art of the portrait genre. On top of that, different portrait purposes dictate the types of appropriate poses available (you wouldn't make a person lay in the grass to make professional headshots, would you?). However, regardless of what type of portrait you are making, there are a few take-to-the-bank considerations for posing the body from the neck down.

I'm sounding like a broken record, but my main concern with composition and posture is whether or not I'm visually conveying a sense of dimension. My primary approach is to position the body so the eye isn't strained to see this value of depth. There is a lot to be said for positioning your subject so that their entire body is facing the camera, especially if the light or portrait style calls for it (**Figure 41.1**). However, rotating your subject slightly provides a hint of dimensional depth to their body, shows off their form, and forces the eye to look deeper into the shot, even if the subject is the only thing in focus (**Figure 41.2**).

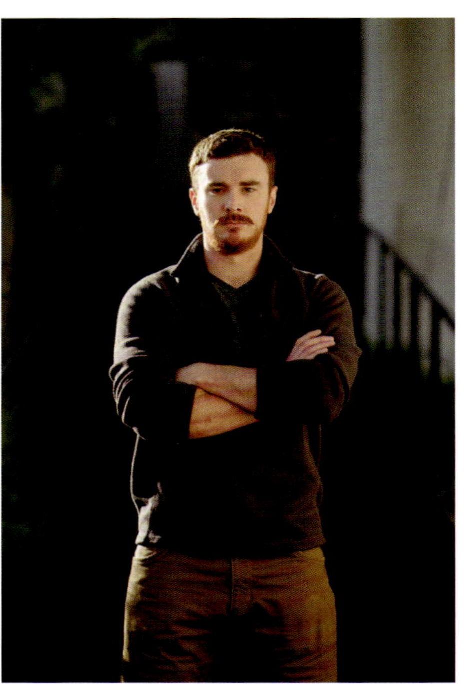

41.1 A front-facing body position can be effective, but only if the shadows cast across or from the subject are apparent. Otherwise, the depth in the image is greatly reduced.
ISO 200; 1/1700 sec.; f/2; 90mm

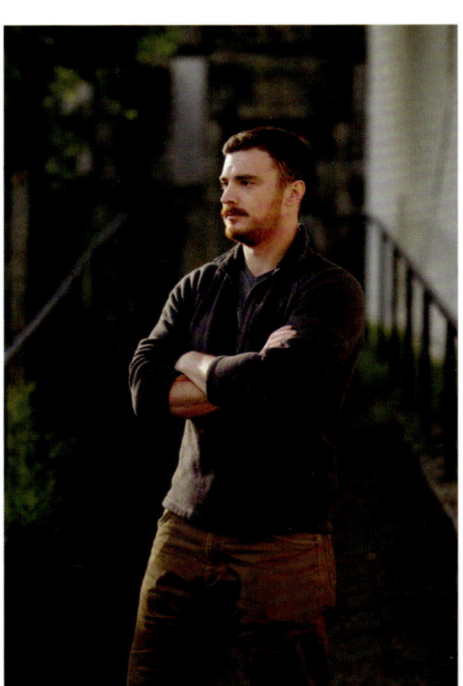

41.2 Turning the subject's body by 45 degrees allows the eye to now view across the body while also looking *into* the shot. Slightly adjusting the angle at which the subject was facing the camera now implies depth into the entire frame.

Creating an angle to the photographic plane of focus also increases the dynamic appeal of the image. If the subject is still looking straight forward, they will not be looking at the camera, conveying a sense of wonder that is popular in portraiture. Turning their face back toward the camera, especially if you tilt their head one way or the other, also creates a nice line (**Figure 41.3**). The next time you are on a shoot (and every shoot thereafter), instead of shooting into your subject's body, consider shooting across it. Turn their body into the light for a brighter portrait, or angle your subject away from the light to increase drama in the shadows (**Figure 41.4** and **Figure 41.5**).

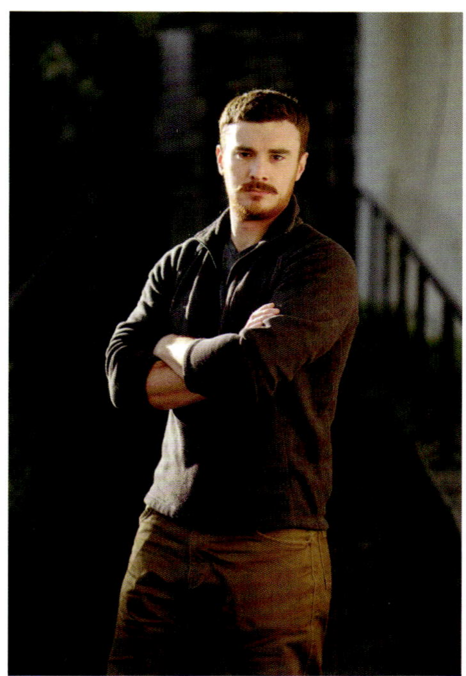

41.3 Turning the head toward the camera and slightly tilting it to camera right adds another compositional element to the frame: an implied diagonal line moving across the frame from bottom left to top right.

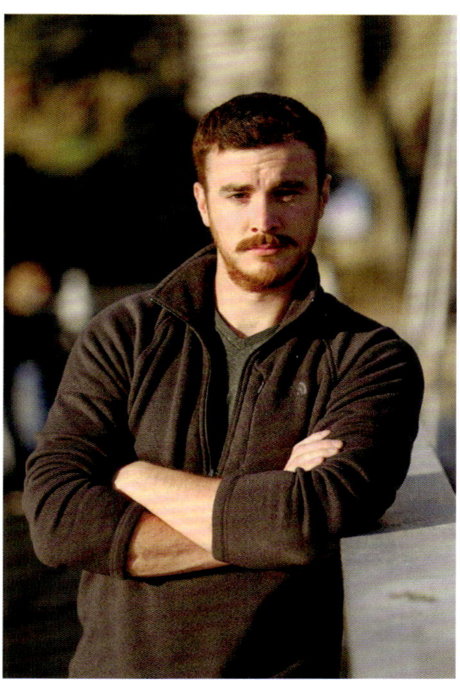

41.4 Turning the body into the sun, even direct light, alleviates the emotional drama created by the shadows in many cases.
ISO 200; 1/4000 sec.; f/2; 90mm

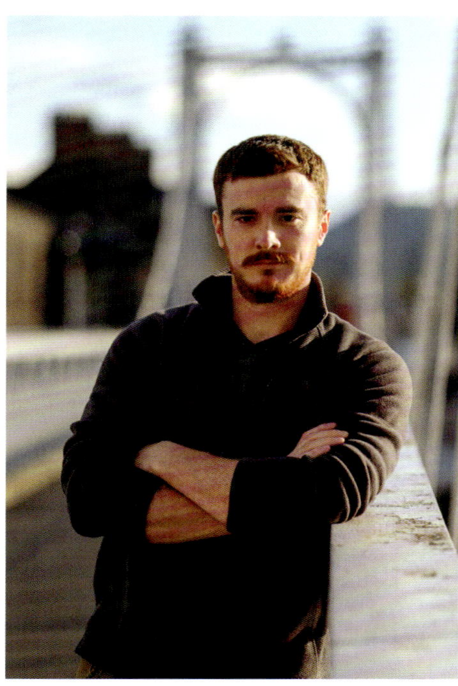

41.5 I often favor angling the body away from the sun to increase the edginess of the contrast between light and shadow. This translates into a more dramatic portrait with deeper, possibly darker, meaning.

Bend Your Subject's Arms

Joints bend. Elbows, knees, fingers, and the like give character to the body, especially when they appear as if they are (or just were) in motion. When photographing your portrait subject, one of the major considerations to make is whether or not bending her arms (or other joints) contributes to the image.

Bending at least one of your subject's arms away from their body contributes to the image's overall composition in creating more lines (**Figure 41.6**). It also creates visual separation from the body, making it seem slimmer. It creates more body dimension, and it looks more relaxed and natural. In the end, bending an arm or two looks more interesting and active.

There are a number of ways to bend arms and other joints to create appealing poses. That being said, you'll know when the pose appears awkward, and the subject will more than likely let you know if they feel odd. It's not a bad idea to ask her if she feels comfortable, and if not, coach her into a better position. Review the portraits you like and see how they incorporate bent arms and joints, and you'll get a feeling of how far to take it in your own work.

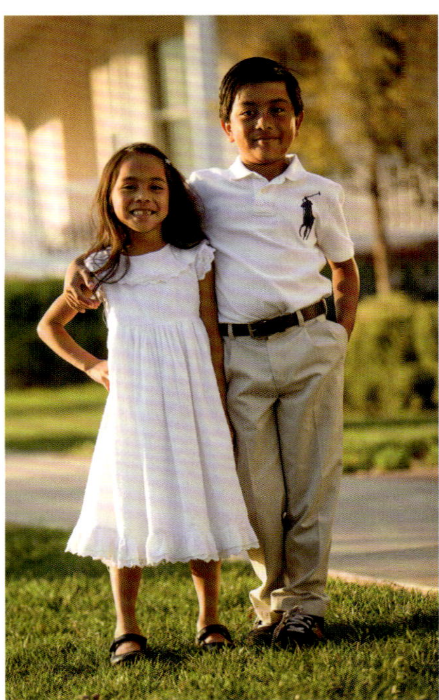

41.6 A bent arm as the result of a hand placed on a hip, creates a portrait that seems more relaxed, and even spunky, especially given the age of your subjects. Since separation is made from the body, a bent arm also allows for a better visualization of the subject's form. ISO 200; 1/1000 sec.; f/2.8; 130mm

Just as some portrait subjects are sensitive about their noses, others can be sensitive about their weight. Not everyone has the anatomical build of a runway model, so it is important to be considerate of your shooting position when it comes to those subjects who can be perceived as heavier than the average person. In this case, avoid shooting them from below (**Figure 41.7**). Photographing from a low angle at any focal length can visually increase their size since you are positioning other parts of their body, namely their midsection and arms, closer to the camera than their head. Keep in mind that the closer you get to your subject, the more dramatic this effect will seem. Unless your stylistic intention is to create an intimidating, overpowering portrait of the subject, it's best to photograph them from eye level or slightly above. Shooting from a higher angle on a larger subject is relatively slimming, largely due to the angle, which forces the subject to raise their head, which helps elongate their neck and reduce a double chin (**Figure 41.8**).

I also try to steer away from photographing any subject from a high angle with a wide focal length. Doing so makes the subject look like an inverted triangle, especially if you're aiming to make it a full-length shot that includes their feet (**Figure 41.9**). This issue will appear no matter the subject's size, and you'll more than likely make this mistake while shooting and notice it afterward during the edit. Shooting from a high angle with a wide focal length distorts the body, and the higher your angle, the more noticeable the effect. In this case, consider using a longer focal length (85mm or longer) to drastically reduce this unattractive effect (**Figure 41.10**).

41.7 Although this subject is no where near being overweight, his height and build make him appear heavier when shot from slightly below his eye level.
ISO 200; 1/250 sec.; f/1.8; 85mm

41.8 Changing up my position to one that shoots down on the subject slims him up a bit from a lower angle.

41.9 Although this is an extreme example, it nonetheless emphasizes why photographing your subject with a wide angle focal length from above is not a good idea. The expansive perspective of the focal length drastically elongates the body and makes the structure closest to the lens (head and shoulders) seem much larger than what is farther away (feet). In turn, the subject looks somewhat like an inverted triangle.
ISO 400; 1/250 sec.; f/2.8; 18mm

41.10 Simply using a longer focal length reduces the expansive perspective and more appropriately exhibits the subject's form.
ISO 400; 1/140 sec.; f/4; 55mm

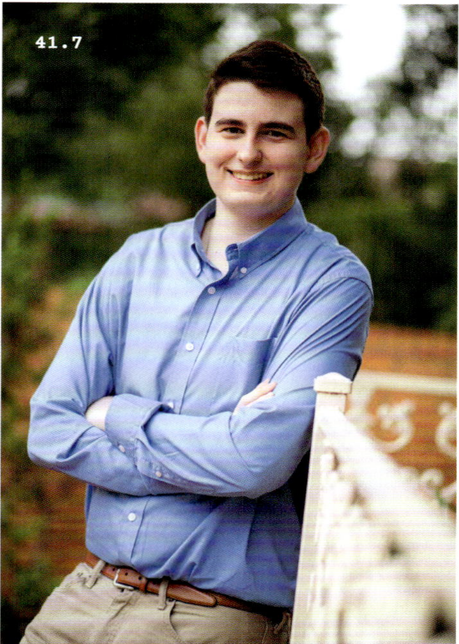
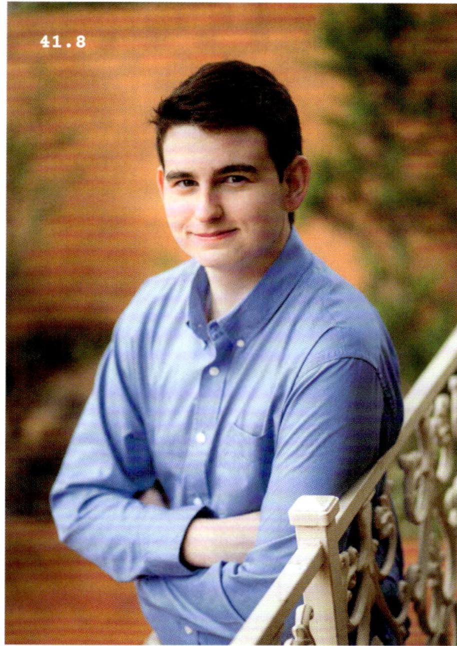
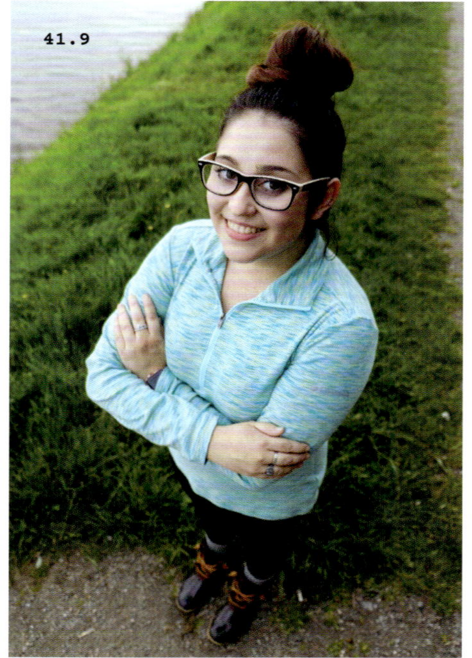
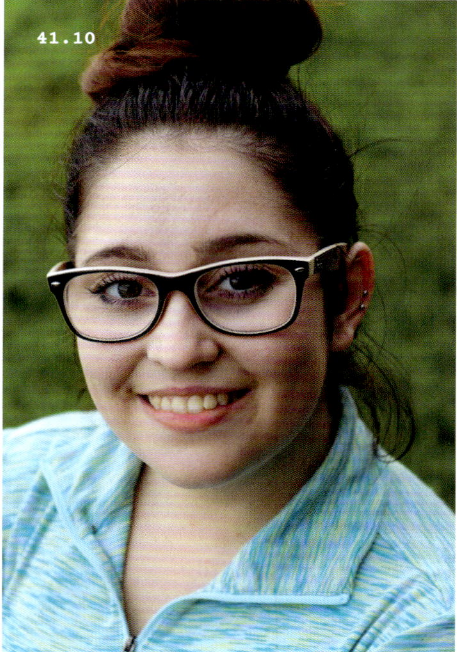

Lastly, I encourage you to pose your subject's entire body, even if the majority of it will not be in the resulting portrait. For example, I'll have a subject turn their body slightly away from the camera, sit up or stand up straight (but not uncomfortably), and cross their arms for some headshots (**Figure 41.11** and **Figure 41.12**). Their crossed arms and feet will not be in the portrait, but in posing the whole subject, the effect will be noticeable in the portrait. The angle will create depth and dimension to the body, and the crossed arms and repositioned feet will provide an overall comfortable look to the subject's shoulders, which creates a visually strong line in the frame. Posing the subject, even if their body is not going to be in the portrait, gives them something to do; it keeps the subject involved in ways other than looking into the lens. It might even give them the inspiration to pull off a certain look you both want in your images.

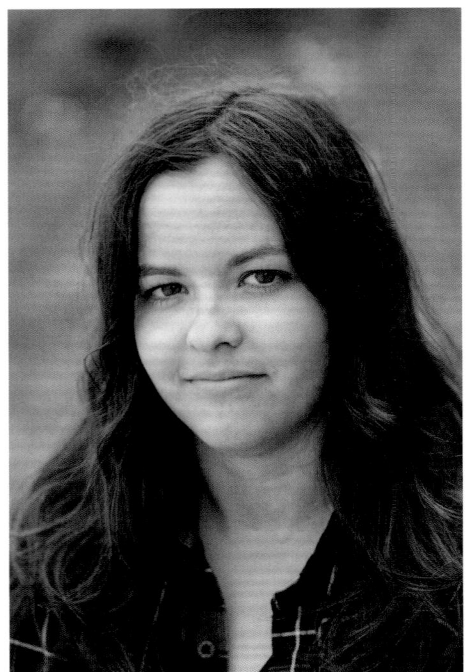

41.11 A simple headshot often does not show just how set up the shot is since it concentrates solely on the face.
ISO 200; 1/800 sec.; f/2; 90mm

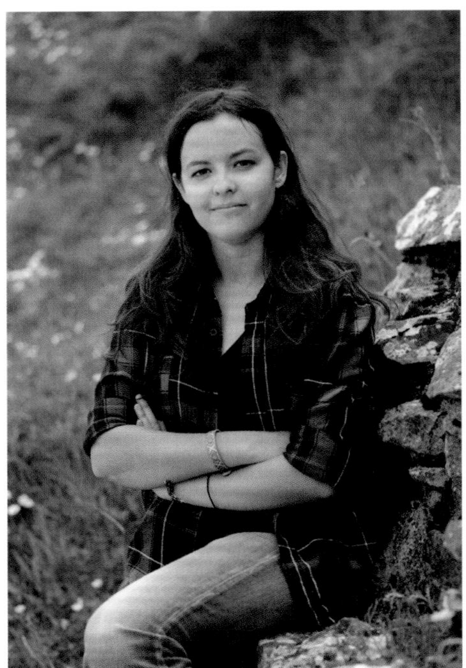

41.12 It's a good idea to completely pose your subject before making a headshot. It often creates a nice angle for the image and a level of comfort for the subject.

BOTH STANDING AND seated poses are great, but depending on the type of portrait you want to shoot, one might be more suitable over the other. For example, corporate headshots are often shot with the subject sitting, while senior portraits involve a mixture of standing and sitting, and environmental portrait postures are often narrative dependent. It's good to keep a few considerations for posing both standing and sitting subjects filed away when on any shoot.

For standing and sitting subjects alike, it's visually attractive to pose the subject so that their shoulders are more or less uneven (**Figure 42.1**). Aside from straight-on shots, angling your subject's orientation to the camera is a great way to do this. For standing subjects, especially males, turning the body slightly away from the camera and placing their hands in their pockets helps loosen up the shoulders (**Figure 42.2**). By creating an uneven shoulder posture, you essentially create a

small (or large, depending on how tight your frame is) line of interest that increases the visually dynamic appeal of your subject. Have sitting subjects position one arm behind them while draping the other across their lap to accomplish a similar line. It might be a simple, very small change you think you're making when you alter poses, but it will render a nice appeal for the portrait.

It's also a good idea for both standing and sitting subjects to lean toward the camera (**Figure 42.3**). It might be natural for some subjects to shy away from the camera physically, but when they lean slightly toward the camera, they become more engaging subjects. They don't have to lean too far toward the camera, just enough to avoid looking like they are afraid of the portrait process.

For standing subjects, take into account the spacing of their feet (generally, it's a good idea to start the feet a shoulder's width apart). You can augment the spacing as you see fit, but you'll

notice the subject may look more awkward the wider their feet are (**Figure 42.4**, **Figure 42.5**, and **Figure 42.6**). It is also a good idea to place one foot more forward than the other. This is especially important when you are orienting your subject at an angle to the camera. Placing one foot more forward than the other allows the subject to relax on the foot in the back, creating a casual, comfortable, and confident-looking posture (**Figure 42.7**). This also contributes to the compositional line of the body, especially in full-length portraits.

For the most part, a seated subject decreases the portrait's formality. Of course, this depends on the intention of the portrait, the environment, and how the subject is dressed (**Figure 42.8**). However, even a man in a tuxedo sitting in a luxuriously appointed room can be made to look casual. So, sitting your subject down can be not only a great way to provide him another posing perspective, it can also increase how relaxed the image feels to a viewer.

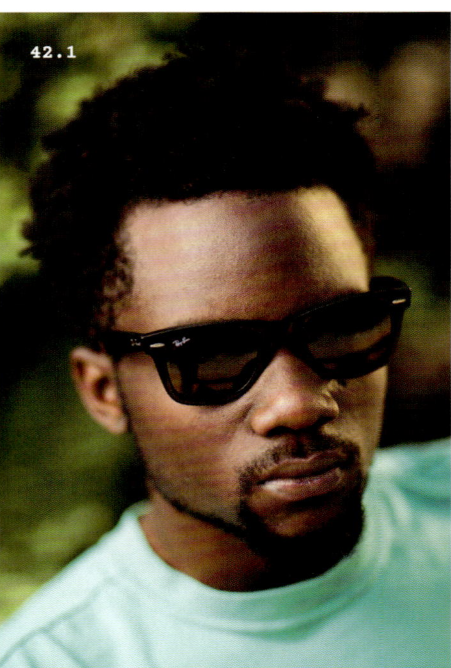

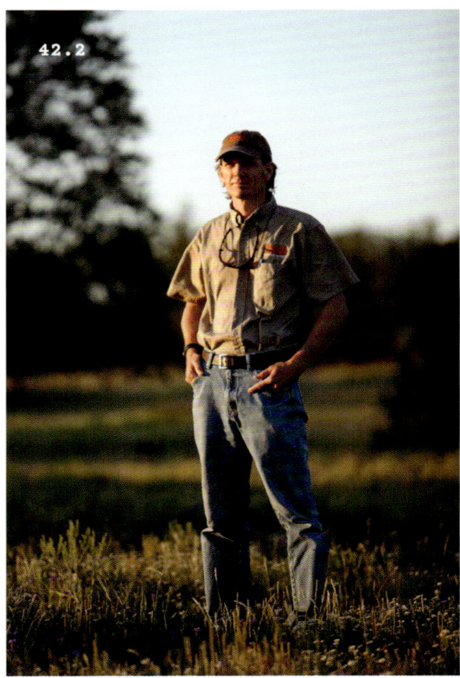

42.1 For this headshot, I posed the sitting subject in a way that his shoulders create an attractive diagonal line across the frame, which moves the eye upward to and across his face.
ISO 200; 1/2500 sec.; f/1.8; 85mm

42.2 Coaching the subject to place his hands in his pockets physically garnered a slight dip in the subject's right shoulder, subtly conveying in tandem with the hands a more relaxed state for this rural resort owner and operator.
ISO 100; 1/640 sec.; f/2.8; 200mm

42.3 A great way to create more engagement with your portraits is to have the subject lean slightly toward the camera as opposed to shying away from it.
ISO 100; 1/2000 sec.; f/1.8; 85mm

42.4 Legs that are placed too close together might convey nervousness.
ISO 400; 1/640 sec.; f/2; 90mm

42.5 A stance wider than shoulder width will increasingly look more awkward for the subject.

42.6 It's often best to place a subject's feet about shoulder width apart, which is both comfortable for the subject and not visually disconnected for the viewer.

42.7 At the same time I encourage the subject to place their feet shoulder width apart, I also suggest moving one foot slightly forward and leaning back on the other. This can visually increase a subject's relaxed mood or personality.

42.8 In a feature on Katharine Love's life in the Texas Big Bend, I wanted to create a portrait of her on her back porch, which opens up to the Santiago Mountains forming the north border for Big Bend National Park. Sitting in one of her favorite places to relax seemed more than appropriate for the shot.
ISO 400; 1/1600 sec.; f/2.8; 85mm

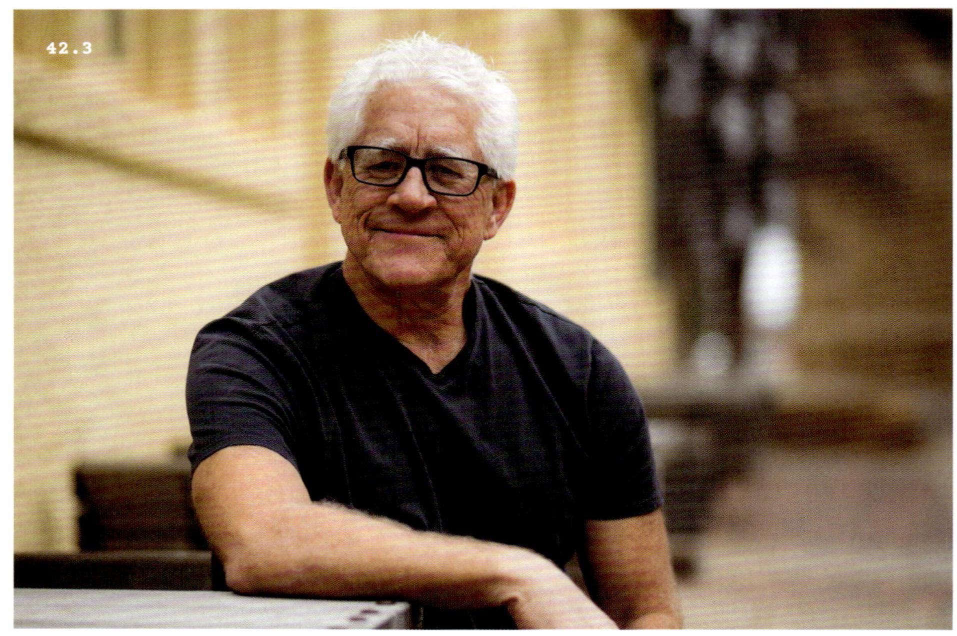

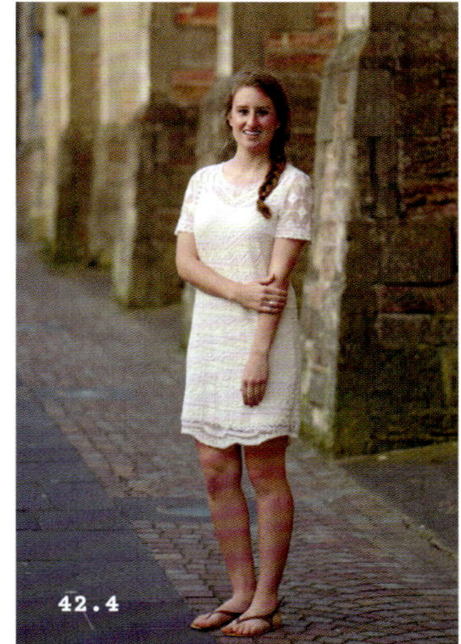
42.4

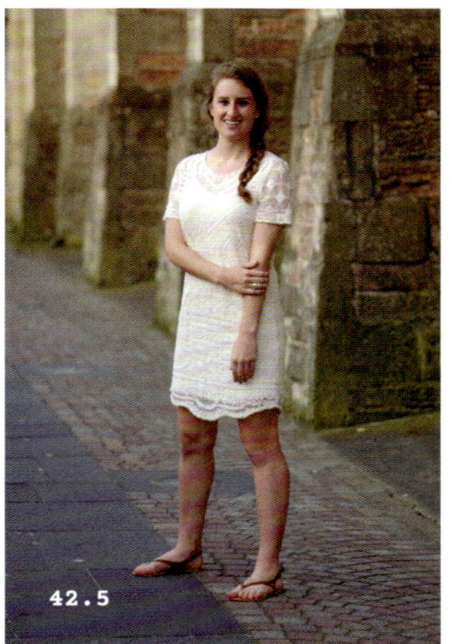
42.5

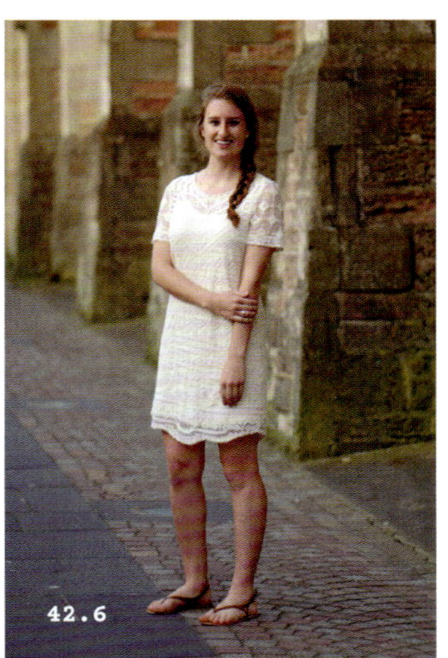
42.6

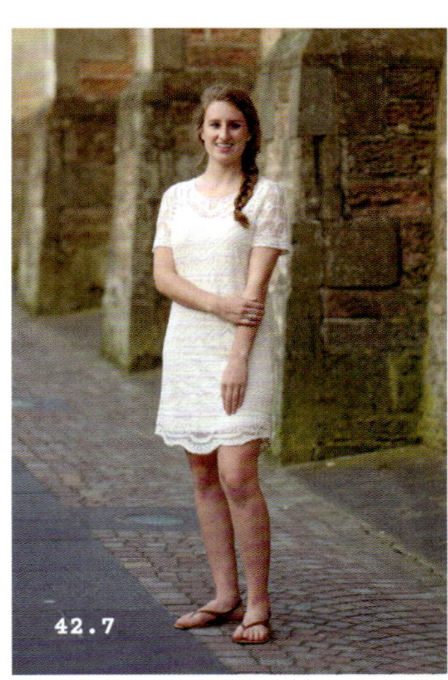
42.7

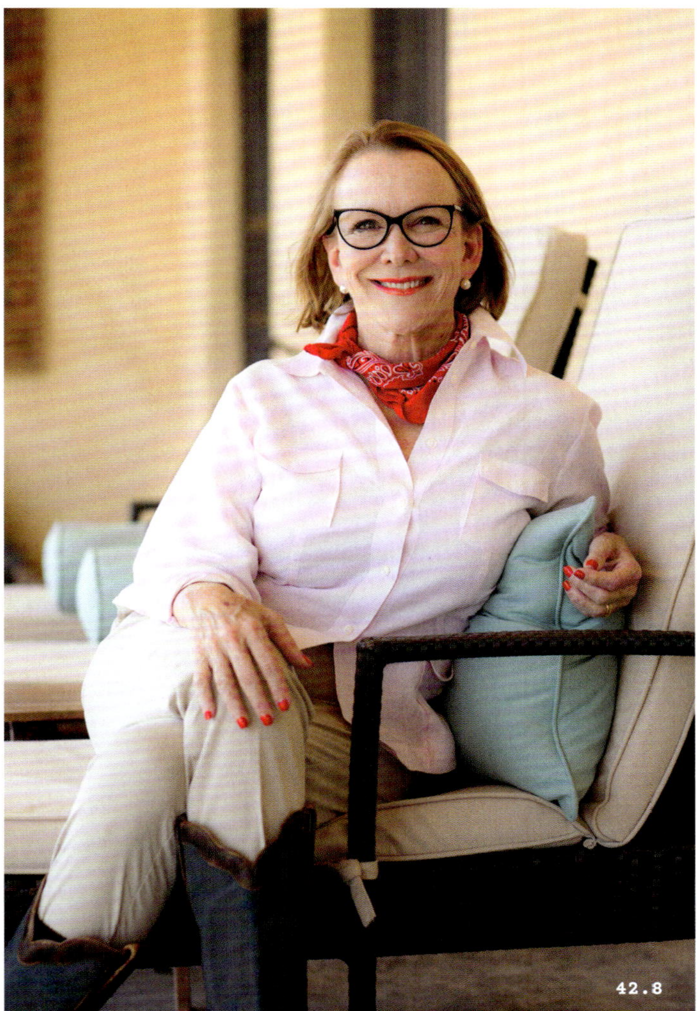
42.8

That being said, there are a few things to avoid when shooting subjects who are sitting. The first thing to stay away from is the dreaded "crotch shot." This occurs when you position a sitting subject so their body faces the camera directly (**Figure 42.9**). When the subject sits like this, we shoot into their legs, which creates an unflattering posture. The solution? Simply angle your subject away from the camera a bit (**Figure 42.10**). For some subjects and camera angles, crossing your subject's legs might also eliminate this issue, as might your subject leaning forward on his legs and holding his hands together (**Figure 42.11**). It is best to cut down on photographing your sitting subjects straight on, or at least when you are framing the shot to include all of their body.

For many sitting shots of female subjects, it is common to pose them leaning back on one or both of their arms. Although this is a very casual, playful pose, it is important to not have them lean back too heavily for fear that their arms and shoulders will flex too much. When a subject in a short sleeve or sleeveless shirt or dress uses her arms to support her when she leans back, her triceps appear under strain. Although this may not be an unattractive visual, this flexing more than likely will make her arm(s) appear larger than they are naturally. On top of that, leaning back with too much weight will also push the shoulder up and forward, potentially covering up the neck and parts of the face (**Figure 42.12**). Instead, coach the subject to ease up on the amount of weight they place on their arm(s) as they lean back (**Figure 42.13**). Tell them why you want them to and they'll more than likely appreciate it. I sometimes joke that it will feel like they're getting a small abdominal workout, but it will most certainly improve their posture and the overall look of the portrait.

On the subject of posture, don't let your subject slouch or hunch unless it is an essential part of the portrait's message. We've all been instructed at one point in our lives that slouching is both anatomically bad for us as well as unprofessional. Slouching should be avoided for both sitting and standing subjects, but it seems to be more prominent in sitting portraits (**Figure 42.14** and **Figure 42.15**). Coach your subject to sit up without becoming uncomfortable. Casual portraits do not look good with stilted posture, but there is much to improve upon the common slouch. For example, when your subject is leaning forward on his knees, ask him to raise his head up a bit. This will correct for an over-exaggerated hunch and make him look more alert, as well as more dominant. Instead of having someone sit slouched into a bench, have them sit up a bit

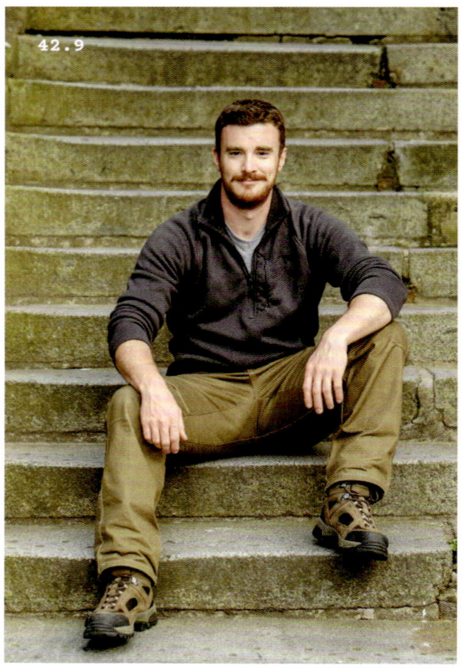

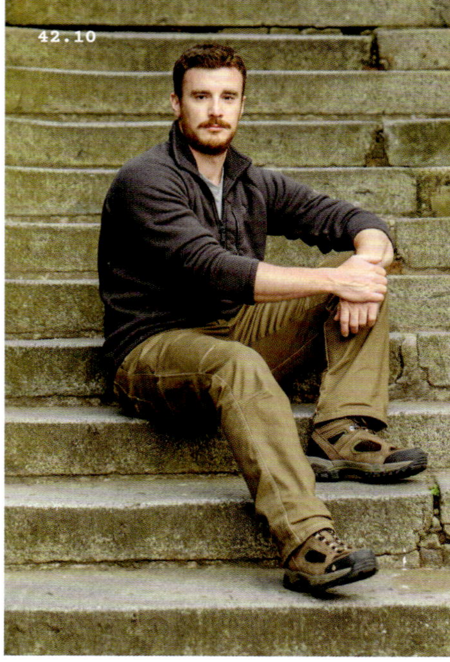

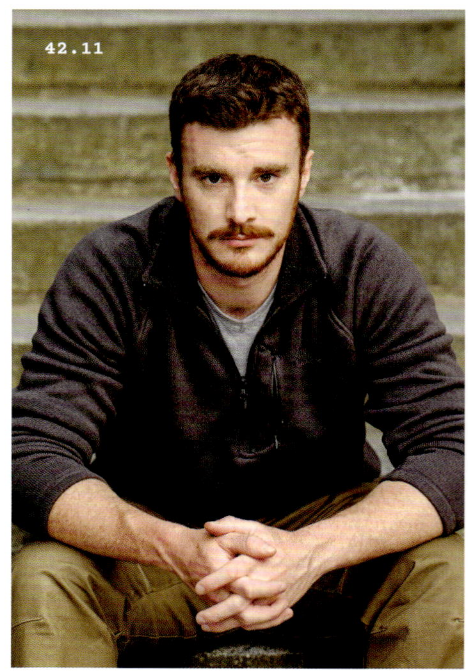

while also putting an arm on top of the bench's back. This will force their posture up and they will lean toward the camera.

42.9 The "crotch shot" is both visually obvious in definition and something definitely worth avoiding. **ISO 400; 1/350 sec.; f/2.8; 90mm**

42.10 One way to avoid shooting into the legs is to simply turn the subject away from directly facing the camera.

42.11 If I want the subject facing the camera while avoiding the "crotch shot," I often coach the subject to place their hands together forward of and in front of the sensitive area.

42.12 Try to avoid having your subject lean back on one or both of their arms with all their weight. It more than likely will force their shoulders up to an awkward position relative to their face and neck, and it will make the subject appear as if they are flexing their triceps. **ISO 200; 1/3000 sec.; f/2; 90mm**

42.13 Coach your subject to ease up on their arms. They will still appear as if they are leaning back, but they will hold their weight off of their arm, moving the awkwardly placed shoulder lower, providing a more defined and trim neckline, and reducing the amount of flex in their rear arm.

42.14 A slouching subject can often sneak up on you in the edit after the shoot. Be cognizant of how your subject naturally poses or holds himself when you start shooting. **ISO 200; 1/420 sec.; f/2; 90mm**

42.15 Coach the subject to straighten up their form. This does not have to be drastically formal, but a more upright position, as opposed to slouching, makes the subject appear more active, professional, and positive.

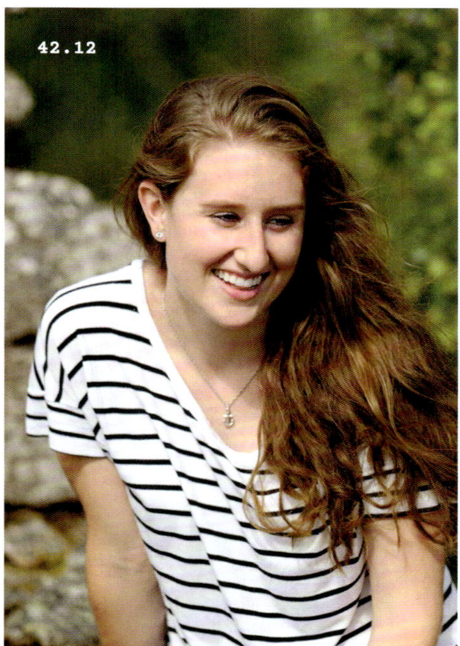

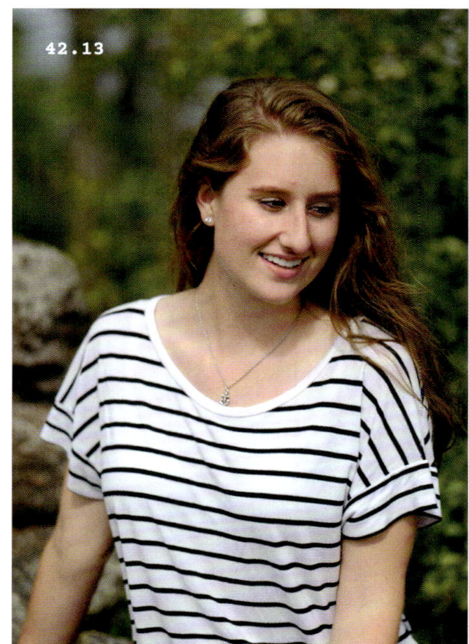

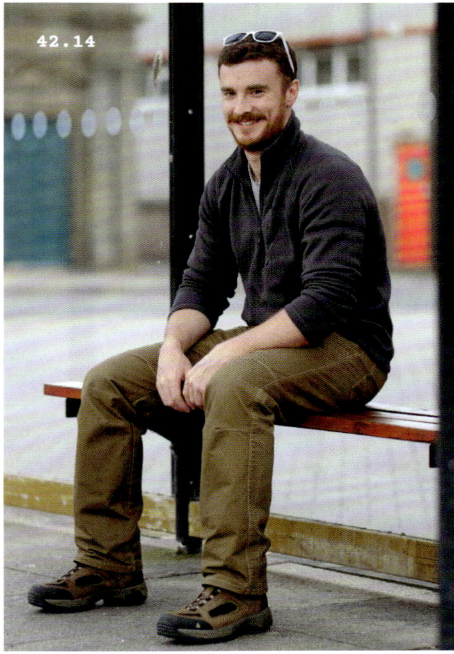

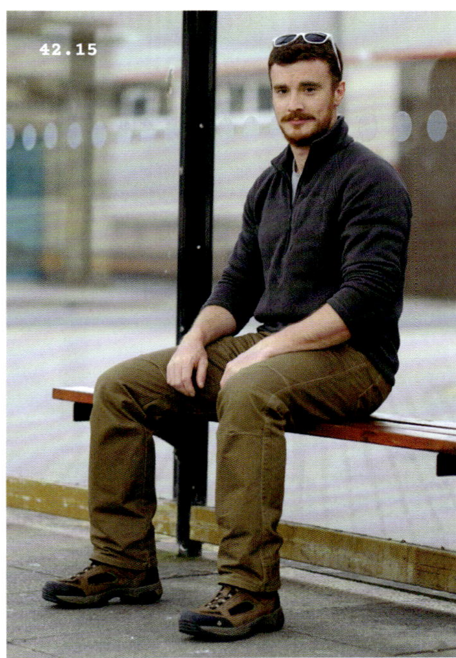

43. TURN YOUR SUBJECT AROUND

WHEN YOU'RE ACTIVELY photographing your subject, it's easy to forget all of your options. Some folks compensate for this by making a shot list, which isn't a bad idea. When it comes to posing, we get so wrapped up in the subject's face and front side that we often forget that there are other sides to her body. I'm certainly prone to focusing most of my attention on photographing the subject looking at or approaching the camera.

Turn the subject around to introduce a new perspective to your portraits (**Figure 43.1**). Photograph your subject from the back using the same framings you would from the front. Have the subject walk away from the camera. Then have her look to her side, providing a thoughtful, less traditional portrait of the subject that, with the right type of light, can convey a whole host of emotions.

Of course, turning your subject around doesn't mean photographing their backside completely; the portrait may gain value just by turning the subject slightly away from the camera and photographing an over-the-shoulder look (**Figure 43.2**). This is popular for bridal portraits, especially if the camera is positioned above the subject. Perhaps your subject has an interesting tattoo on the back of one shoulder. This is a great opportunity to turn the subject around and away from the camera while still being able to include her face. When doing this, however, beware of how creases in the neck are created. If you are photographing someone with long hair, it might not be a bad idea to cover the creases up by laying some of it across the shoulder in front of the neck. Additionally, shooting over the shoulder might not be the best look for male subjects, especially when they are looking back toward the camera.

You won't take all of your portraits of the backside of your subject. However, no matter if they are standing or sitting, lying down or leaning against a wall, it's always a good idea to see what the other side looks like. It gives you something new to work with, and it also gives the subject another perspective to see and present in their portraits.

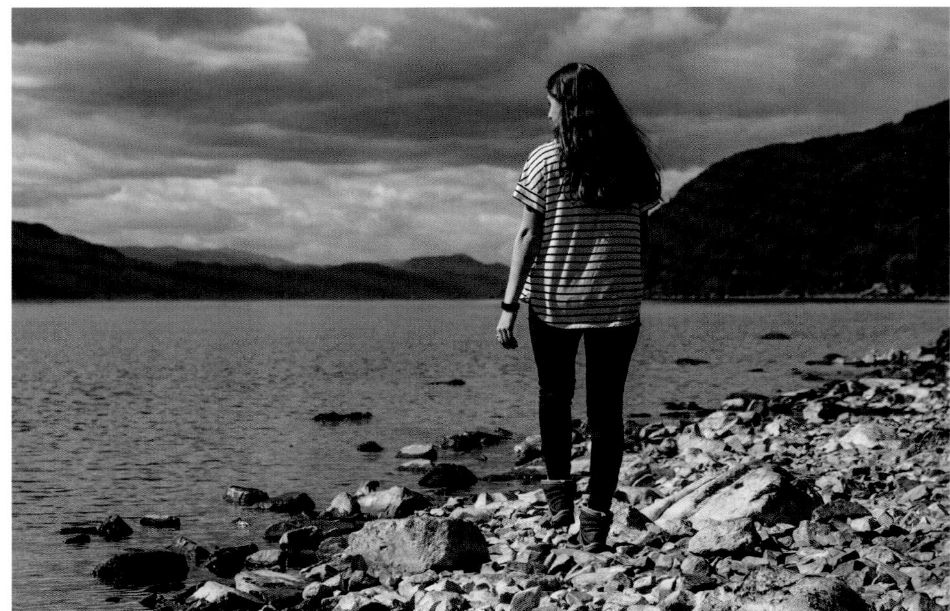

43.1 Although you probably don't want to shoot every one of your portraits from behind the subject, it can be a creative positioning for one or two portraits, especially given the right setting.
ISO 200; 1/2700 sec.; f/4; 55mm

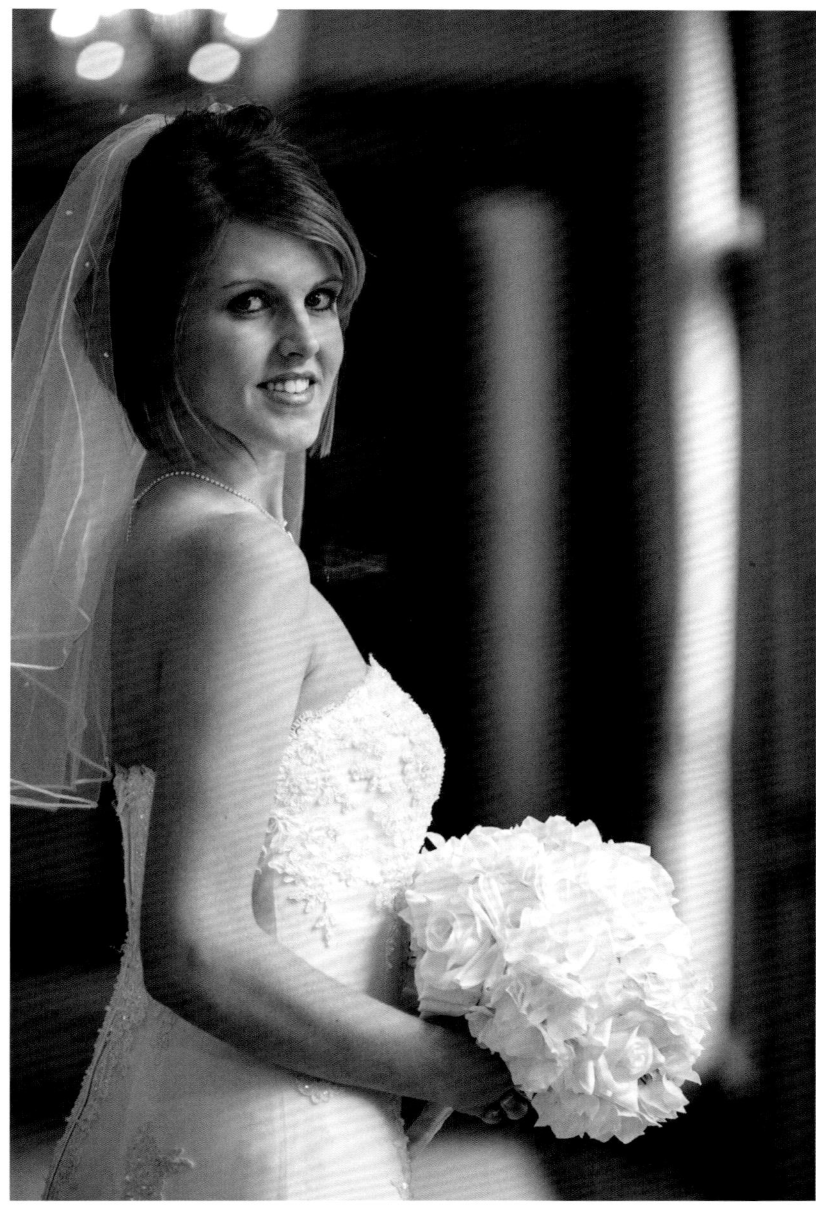

43.2 A classic bridal portrait pose is one in which the subject looks over her shoulder. Although this shot can be made from various angles, the idea is to evoke a fleeting moment, possibly the moment before she walks down the aisle.
ISO 400; 1/50 sec.; f/2.8; 190mm

UP TO THIS point, I've only discussed portraiture as a process between two people—the photographer and a single subject. However, group portraits are also extremely common. All of the tips and techniques discussed so far *also* apply to group portraits: you'll make the same types of considerations for groups in regard to light and composition, and many posing considerations are appropriate as well. However, there are a couple relevant techniques and considerations that are important to keep in mind for group portraiture.

The first consideration is a simple one, though it's often overlooked by portrait photographers. When you photograph two or more people together, it is best to position them so each subject's eyes are on the same parallel plane relative to the camera. Typically, portraits are made with a fairly shallow depth of field, meaning the aperture is very open. Aperture values of f/1.4, 2, and 2.8 usually provide a soft, out-of-focus background on which your subjects are isolated and in focus (**Figure 44.1**). However, the depth of field these aperture values provide is shallow enough that any subject in the group who is not on the same plane of focus will appear soft and out of focus (**Figure 44.2**). This is typically considered a mistake, especially when all subjects should share the portrait spotlight. The simple solution is to position your subjects the same distance from the camera, and when you focus on one of their eyes, the plane of critical focus should apply to everyone in the scene (**Figure 44.3**). This is usually a more pressing issue when working with groups of two or three, since those shots will most likely be tightly framed.

44.1

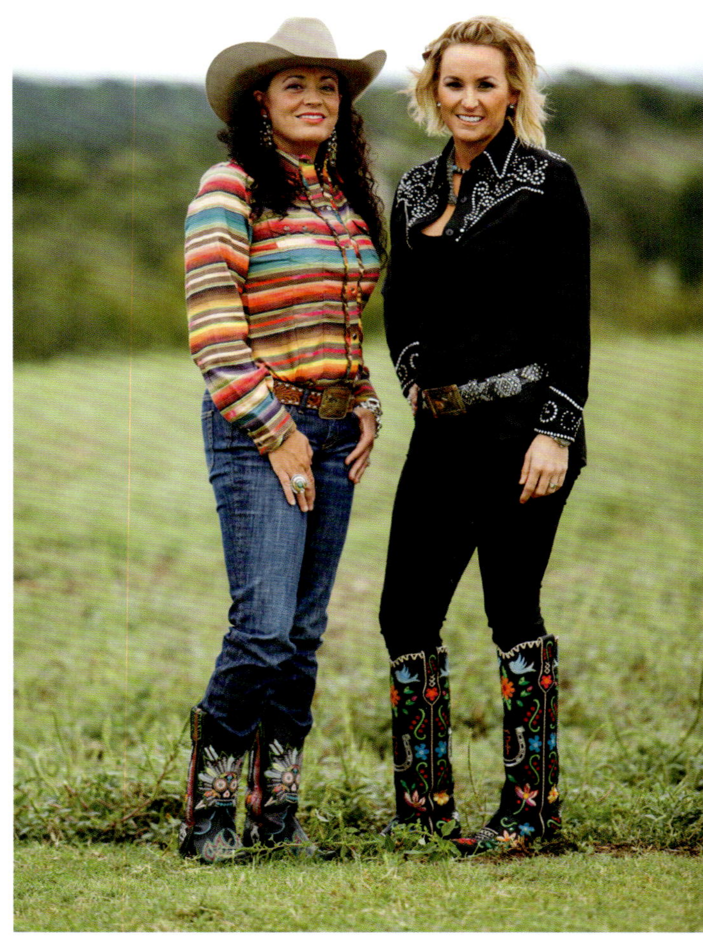

44.1 Even with portraits of more than one person, a soft, out-of-focus background is often desired to isolate the subjects from what can be a relatively busy setting.
ISO 400; 1/1000 sec.; f/2.8; 180mm

44.2 At f/2, the depth of field is so shallow that the camera-left subject is out of focus, even though her eyes are just three inches behind the camera-right subject's head.
ISO 400; 1/550 sec.; f/2; 90mm

44.3 By positioning the camera-left subject to where her eyes are the same distance from the camera as the camera-right subject's eyes, she was brought into focus. This is the only way to maintain focus on your subjects with such shallow depth of field before increasing your aperture value.

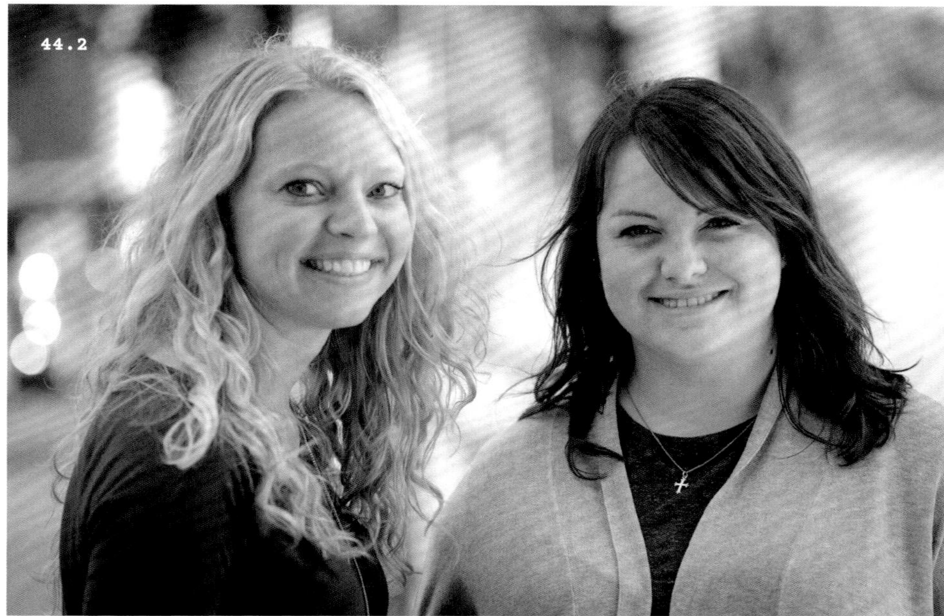

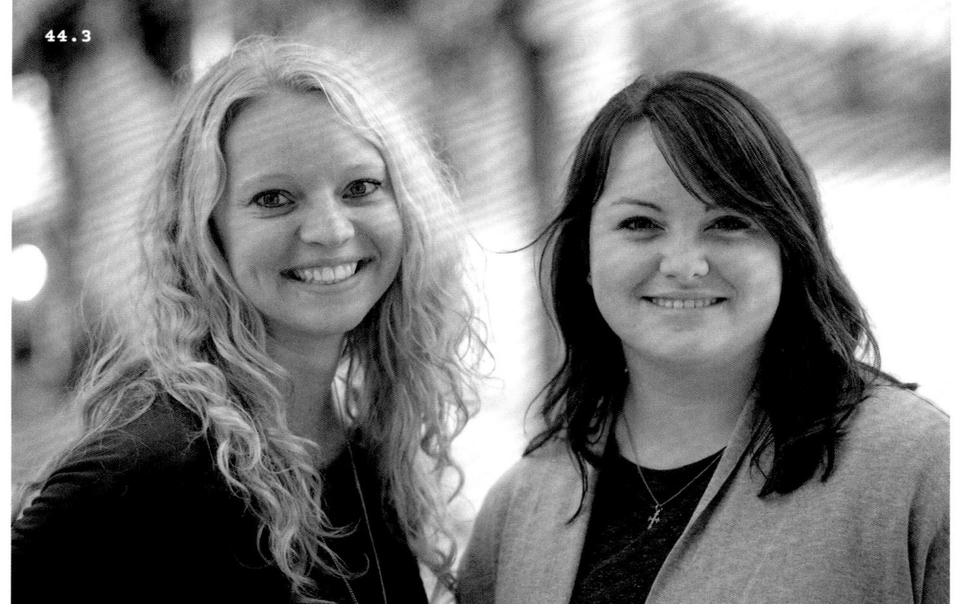

However, what happens when you're shooting a larger group, or you cannot keep even a small group, on the same plane? This is when stopping the aperture down to gain depth of field is essential (**Figure 44.4** and **Figure** 44.5). Gaining depth of field means the space around the plane of critical focus widens in the frame. Although there will be less of that nice, soft bokeh of a background, having each of your subjects in focus is more important.

If your group portrait shows some subjects in focus and others that are not, you can move your subjects so all are positioned on the same optical plane, or increase your aperture value to ensure the right depth of field to ensure sharpness in the frame. Personally, I like to do both. I line everyone up on the same plane, and then instead of shooting at f/2.8, I might shoot at f/5.6 or f/8 (**Figure** 44.6). This usually absolves the issue, especially with a small group. The thing to avoid in this case is a busy background that remains in focus due to the increased depth of field.

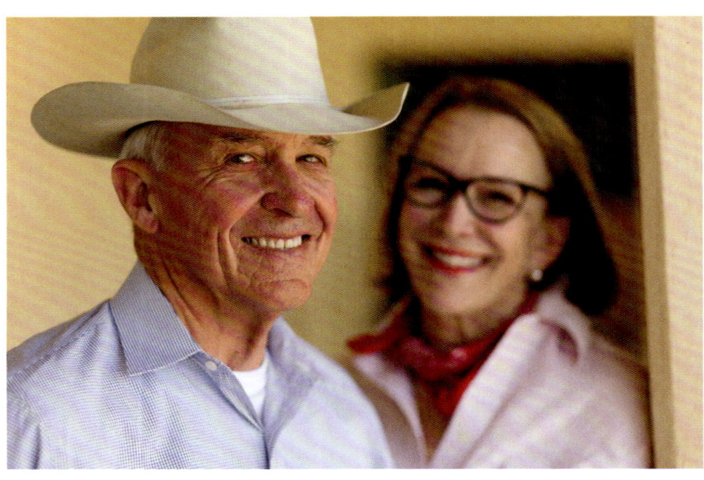

44.4 At f/2, only one of the portrait subjects can be in focus when they are at different distances from the camera.
ISO 100; 1/400 sec.; f/2; 85mm

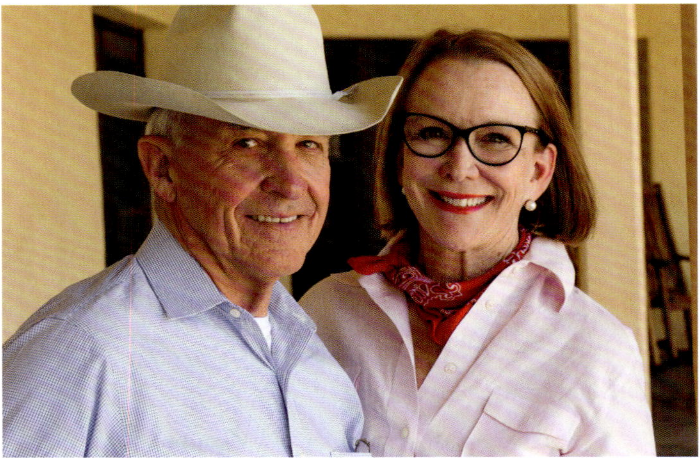

44.5 To gain enough depth of field to have both subjects in focus, I stopped my aperture down to f/11. This in turn brought more of the background into focus as well.
ISO 400; 1/50 sec.; f/11; 85mm

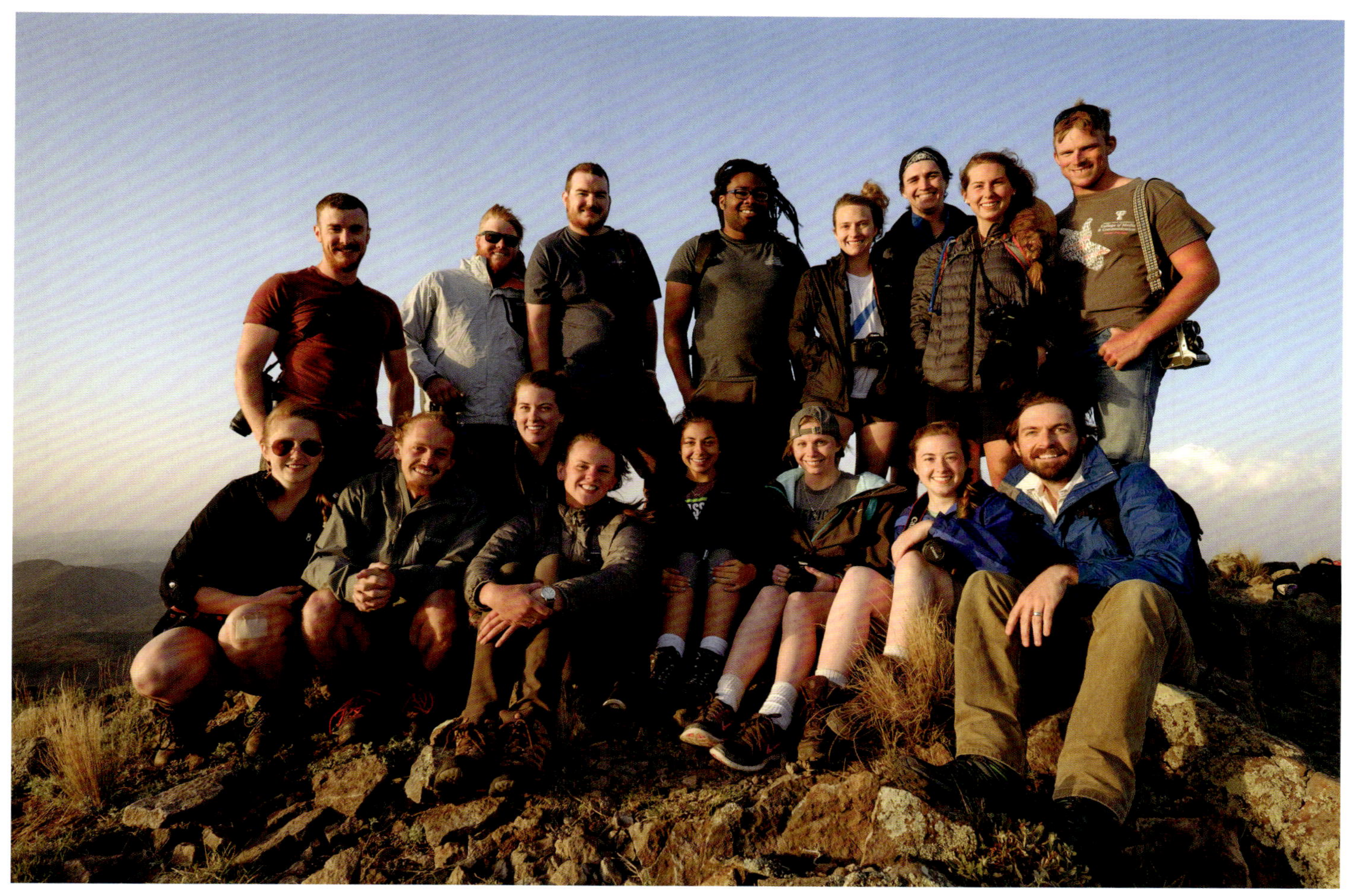

44.6 For this group shot of one of my photography classes in the Davis Mountains, I stopped the aperture down to f/8 on a wide lens to ensure the portrait had enough depth of field for everyone to be in focus.
ISO 200; 1/75 sec.; f/8; 14mm

45. WORKING WITH GROUPS II: THE ISSUE OF HEIGHT

ONE OF THE most frustrating situations for portrait photographers is posing groups. Technically, positioning them so they are all in focus is fairly easy and uncomplicated. However, when it comes to actually posing them, it confounds some photographers, myself included. There are very few rules that one *must* follow when posing groups, but one fairly important suggestion that helps pose a group and maintain compositional interest in the image is to avoid putting all of your subjects' heads on the same level.

Creating a line across your frame of all of your subjects' heads is almost tantamount to placing the horizon line in the middle of the frame. Visually, heads placed at the same level is rather flat (**Figure 45.1**). Instead, create a more dynamic image by visualizing your subjects on varying levels of height (**Figure 45.2**). Have one of your subjects sit in a chair while the other leans on the chair's back, for example. If the hypothetical group here is a family of three, perhaps the child can sit on the ground at the foot of the chair. As long as the heads are not in line horizontally or vertically, this allows for a visual triangle to be created. This way, the viewing eye has an easier time moving and focusing on each individual family member, which is just as important as viewing them as one cohesive unit.

Even if you must pose all of the subjects standing, try to keep those members of the group who are relatively the same height from standing next to each other (**Figure 45.3**). Perhaps place the tallest person in the center of the group and create a sloping line of height to each side of him. Or, better yet, place them apart from each other if the space allows, which will make for easy eye navigation between each person in the frame.

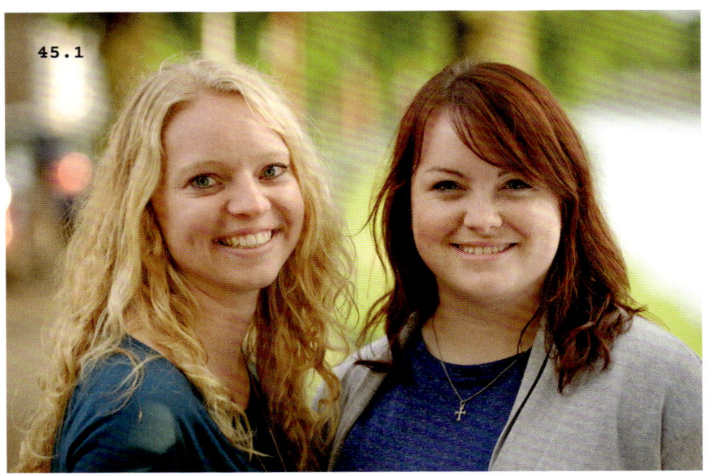

45.1

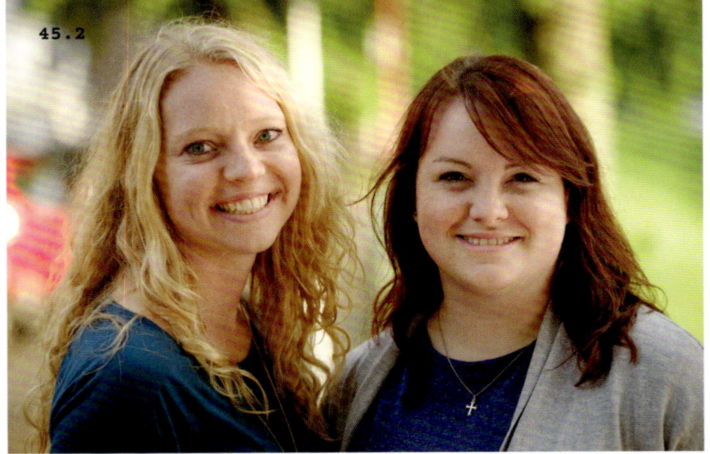

45.2

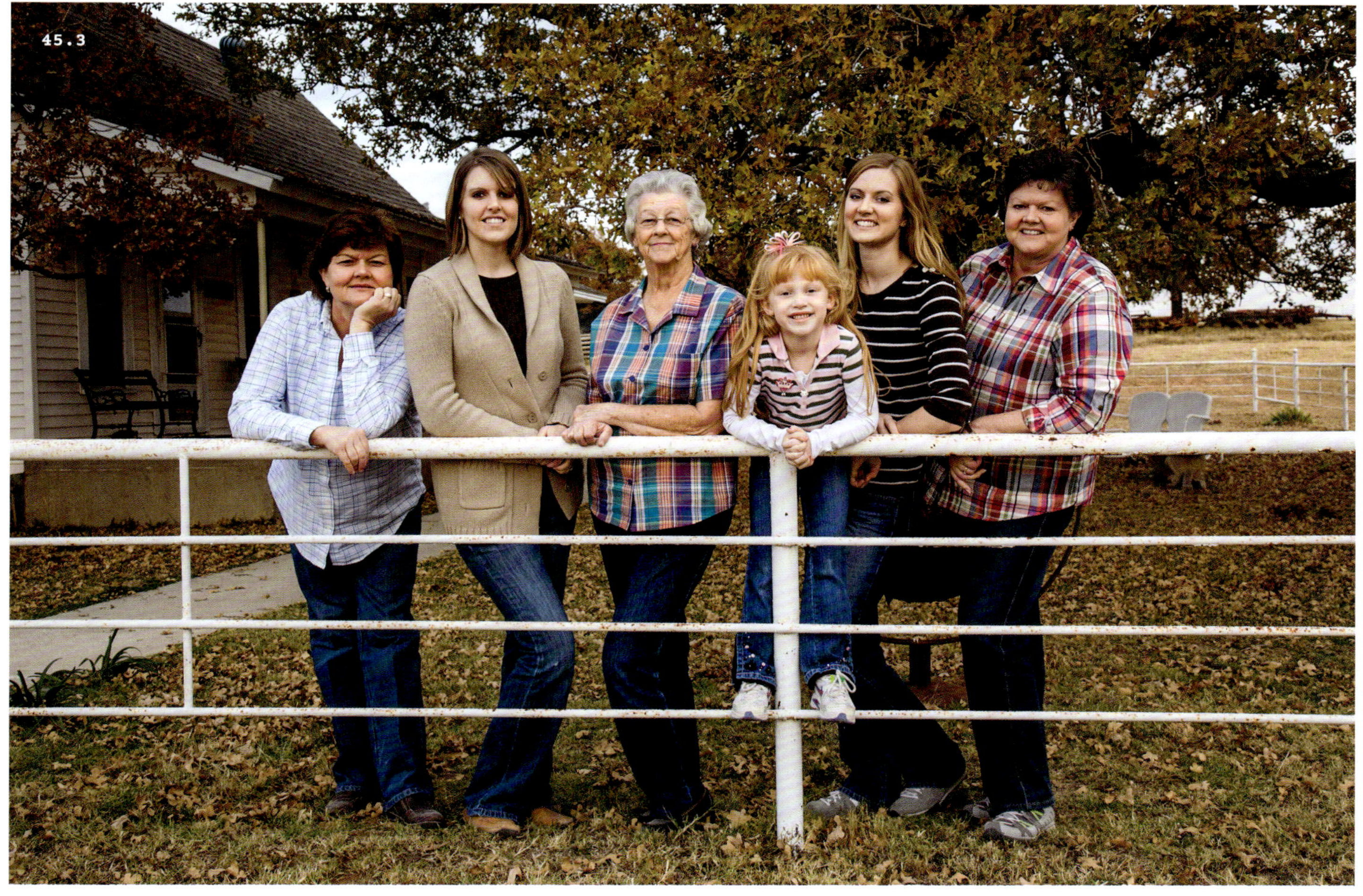

45.1 Often, group shots in which all of your subjects are the same height offer composition with lower dynamic value.
ISO 400; 1/420 sec.; f/2; 90mm

45.2 I coached the camera-right subject to sit a bit lower on a sidewalk railing, not to make her look shorter than the other subject, but rather to add a compositional change-up and value to the simple portrait.

45.3 This portrait includes two pairs of subjects that are roughly the same height per pair. The subjects on the outside are posed at different levels, and the two tallest subjects are not placed next to each other. This is done so in an effort to avoid the eye getting stuck at one height while moving across the group.
ISO 320; 1/100 sec.; f/8; 35mm

While we're on the topic of composition, I also suggest keeping your backgrounds as simple as possible (**Figure 45.4**). The less complicated or busy a background is for a group portrait, the easier it is for the viewer's eye to move to each subject and still acknowledge them as a cohesive unit. Furthermore, it is also easier for you, the photographer, to pose the group without the distraction of a background you would otherwise have to work around. Out of focus backgrounds made up of a simple palette of colors or abstract structure works best, as does a more in-focus structure that can be used to frame the group (**Figure 45.5**).

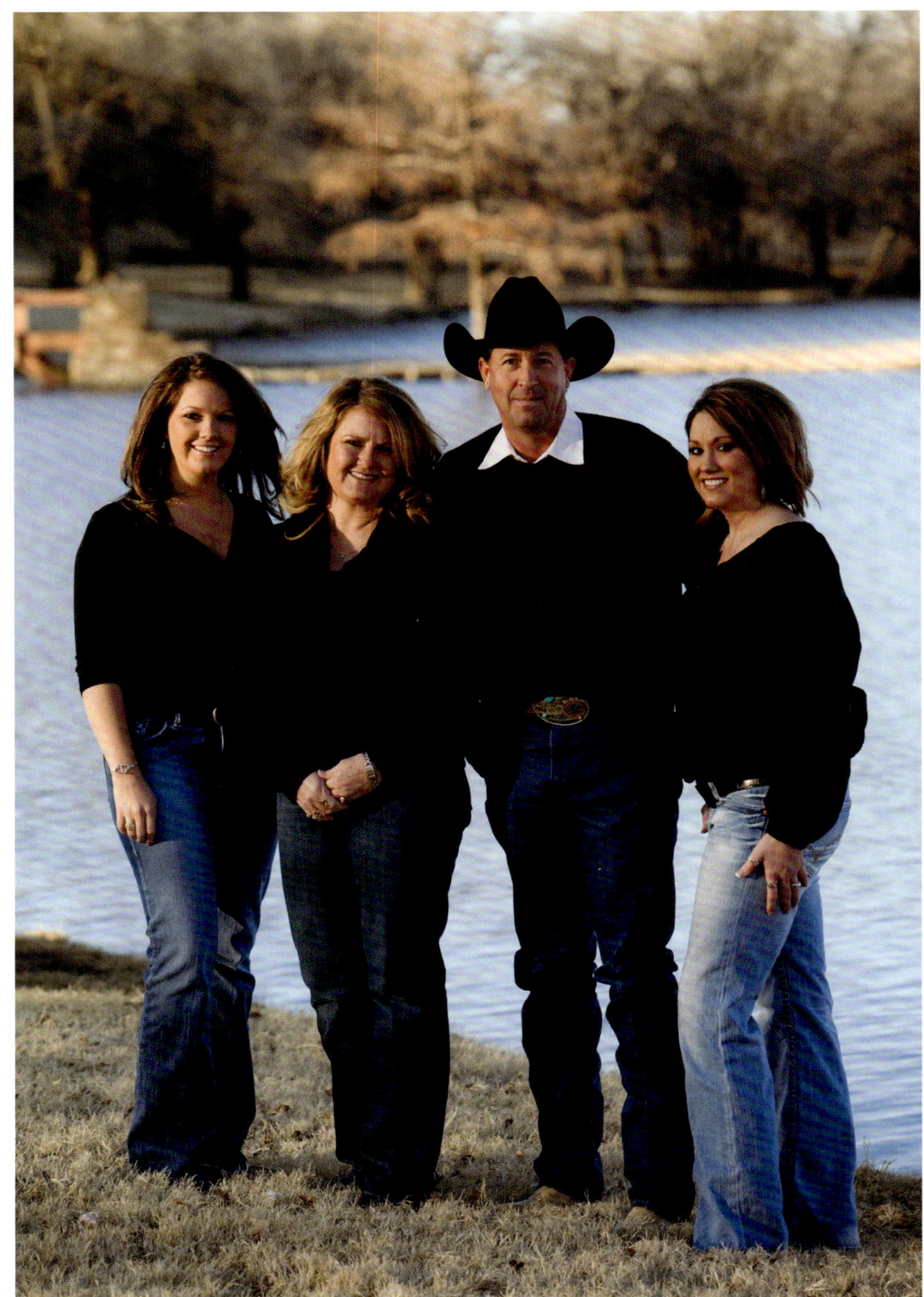

45.4 Simple, often out-of-focus backgrounds, are key to maintaining visual focus on your portrait subjects, and this is probably more true when it comes to group portraits. **ISO 400; 1/600 sec.; f/2; 35mm**

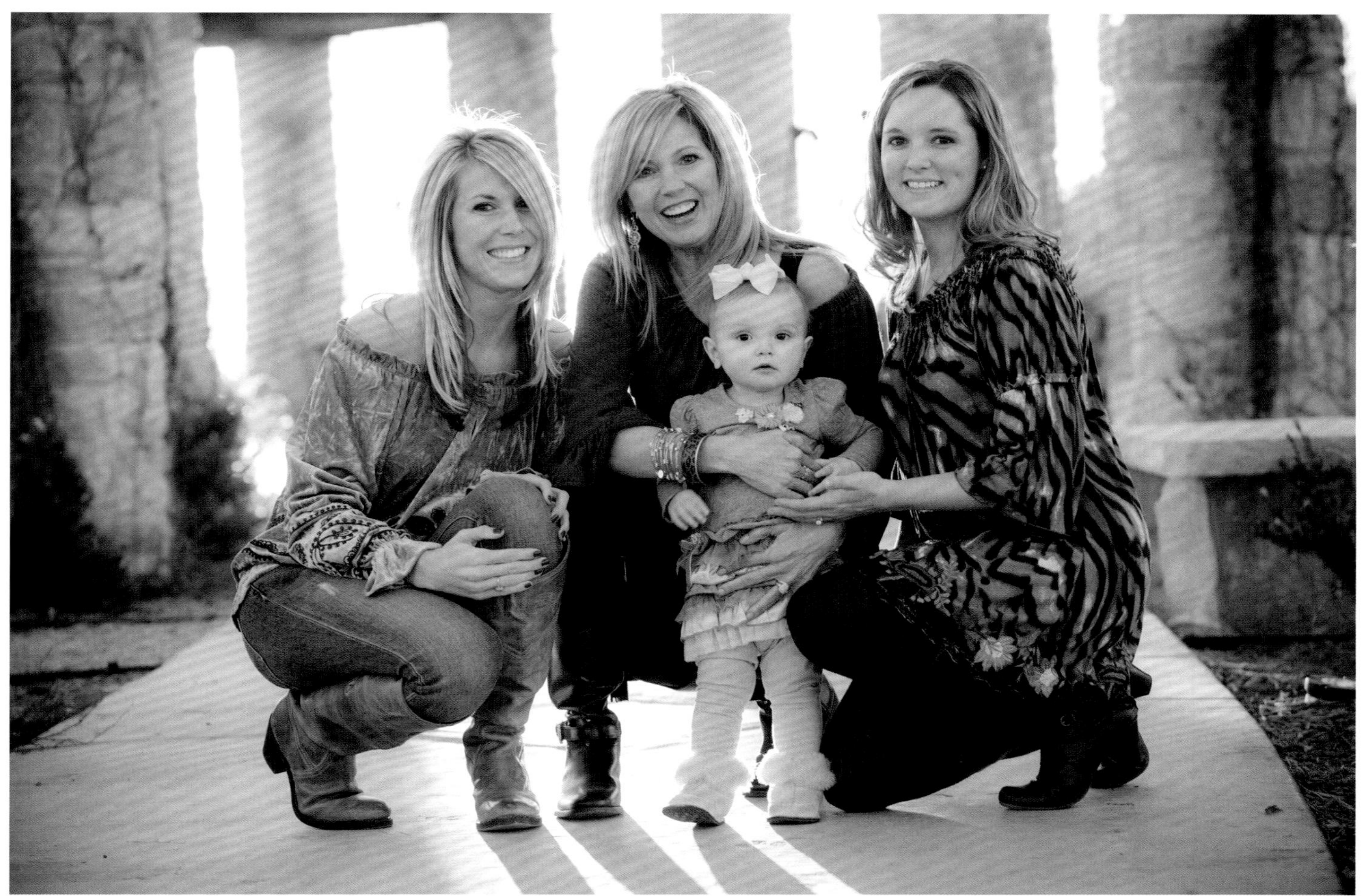

45.5 I placed the subjects in front of a repetitive, out-of-focus background. Although the background is overexposed, the structure helps mitigate the distraction the brighter parts create. Additionally, the direct light hitting the subjects in the back (which is also causing the overexposure), creates a great backlight on their hair and forms, further separating the subjects from the background.
ISO 200; 1/125 sec.; f/4; 105mm

Additionally, it is often easier to compose groups while using longer focal lengths. When you're new to portraiture, you might think going wide when shooting more than two people in a group is necessary to get them all in the frame. However, a wider focal length only forces you to get closer to the group without simplifying the environment in a useful way (**Figure** 45.6 and **Figure** 45.7). You contend with subject distortion more than you need to, and you get so inundated with fixing the problem that you forget that simply backing up and using a longer lens is the real solution. Likewise, not all group portraits *can* be made with a 50mm+ focal length. However, when you can, try shooting with a focal length that compresses rather than expands, and you'll be less concerned with technical matters and more able to focus on posing the group appropriately.

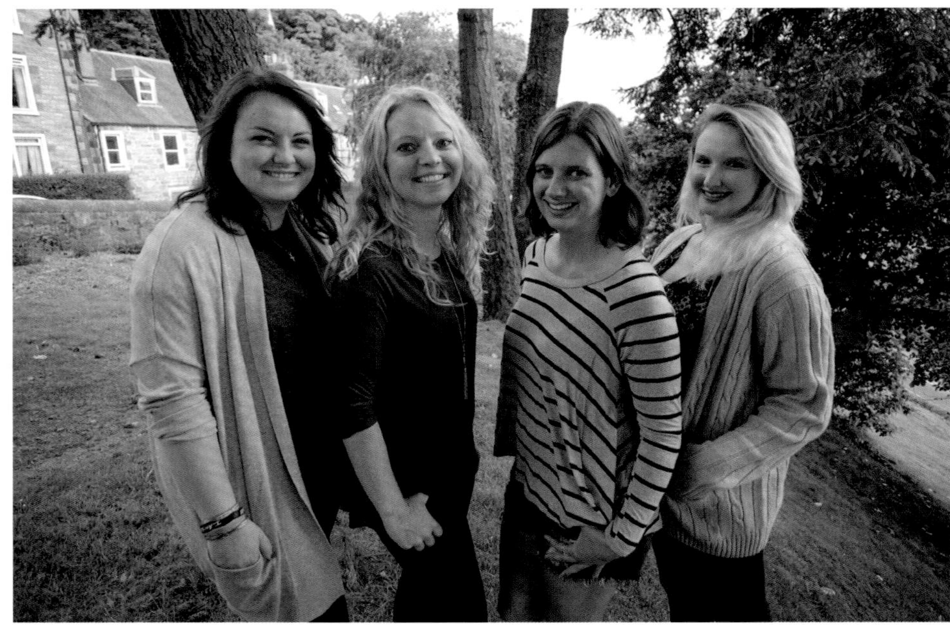

45.6 Although at first it seems appropriate, wider focal lengths distort groups just as much as they do individuals, and more structure surrounding them is brought into the frame.
ISO 400; 1/210 sec.; f/2.8; 14mm

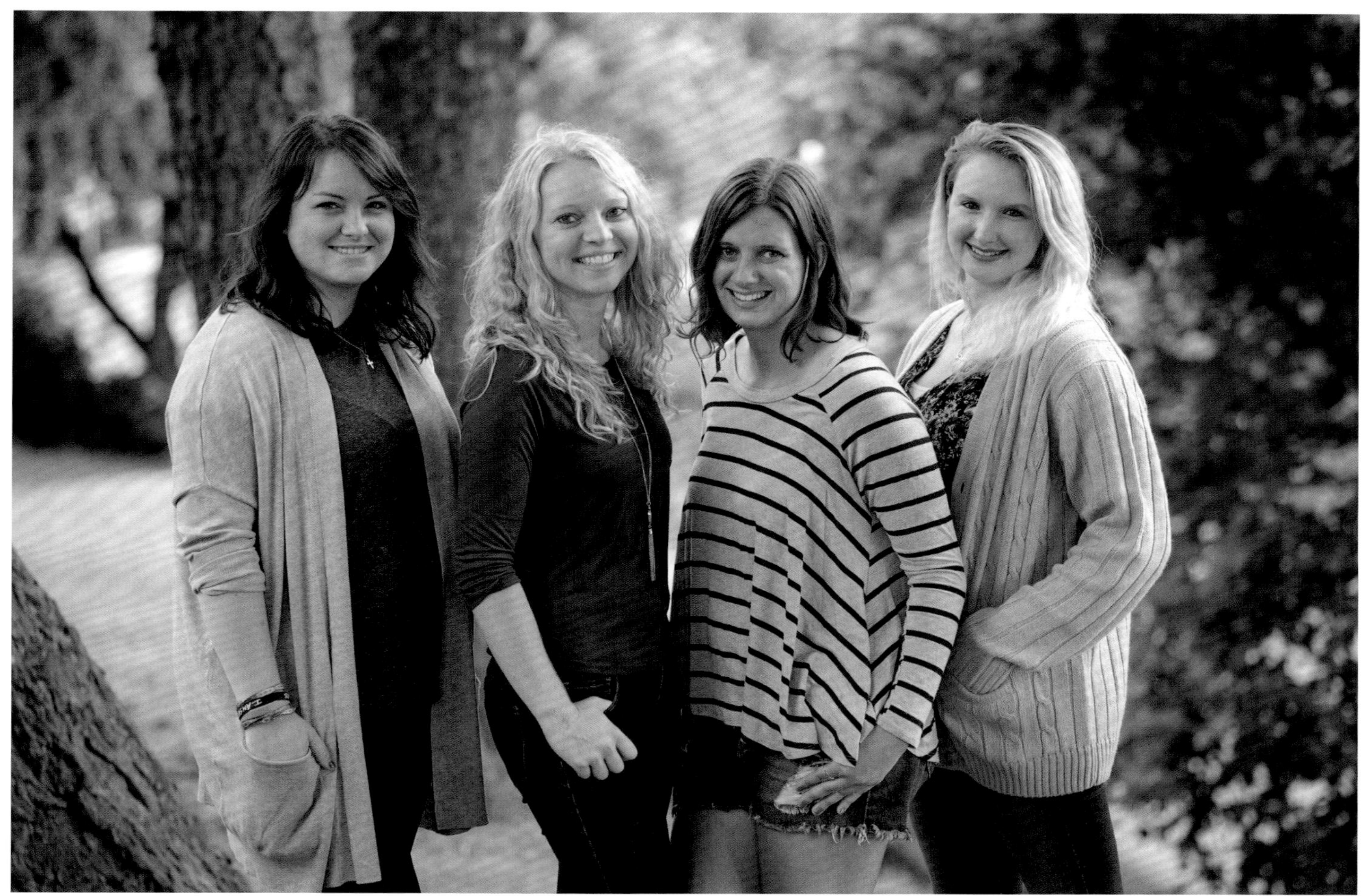

45.7 Using a longer focal length is a great way to reduce distractive backgrounds with large groups. Although you need more distance from the subjects, the reduction in distortion and unnecessary elements in the frame is a big payoff.
ISO 400; 1/280 sec.; f/2; 90mm

6

COLOR

Color is quite possibly one of the most visible yet over-looked elements of photography. We know it's important, but especially for those starting out, it can take a backseat to camera functionality, exposure, and general composition. Yet, color is one of the most malleable facets to consider for all photography, especially portraiture. It's important to take a step back from the hustle and bustle of setting up the perfect light and composition for your portrait subject and consider the overall color of your image.

This chapter encourages you to consider how color applies to your portraits in two different ways. The first is how color appears to us objectively, or theoretically, as a product of the visible electromagnetic spectrum. The second is how we infer meaning from color subjectively: how color can elicit certain emotions and relate to your subject.

I KNOW. YOU shuddered when you saw that word "theory." It's not a word that gets a lot of folks excited, especially when it's tied to doing something creative. Then again, much of what we do in the visual creative fields is informed by theory. For photographers, color is one such element, even if you strictly shoot in black and white. In fact, color theory is behind many of the choices we make strategically and stylistically.

Let's take a look at some foundational color theory that you've more than likely applied before (with or without knowing it)—theory that is sure to strengthen your portraiture work.

There are two primary color schemes to which our eyes are drawn: analogous and complementary. Analogous colors are those that are fairly similar to each other (**Figure 46.1**). Color is a continuous spectrum, and if you imagine looking at a relatively small section of that continuum, e.g., at all the various reds, you would be looking at different colors that are perceived as red. For example, fire engine red and maroon are analogous colors. Analogous coloration is easy to look at, stylistically simple, and can be creatively employed. For portraiture, it allows color to simultaneously stay out of the subject's way *and* stand out as something worth noticing.

Complementary color is often a misused term.

Whereas many folks mistake it for analogous color, it's actually colors that are the exact opposite of each other in value (**Figure 46.2**). On the color wheel, colors that sit across from each other are exact complements. Red and green, for example, are complementary colors, as are blue and orange, and yellow and violet. This type of coloration, like analogous color, is attractive to the eye, but not necessarily because it is comfortable to look at. Rather, complementary colors are dramatically contrasting, and create a great deal of vibrancy when used close to each other. Yet, this contrast can be distracting. When one particular color isn't fighting as hard for real estate as the other, complementary colors work well together.

Being open to color lets you to take advantage of it, whether that be in planning the clothes your subject is going to wear during the shoot, to noticing a great background to complement your subject's shirt. Having an understanding of how colors work together can ensure that you are aware of color in your environment. It's important to understand what most complementary colors are comprised of: dominant and recessive colors. It's also important to remain flexible. Complementary colors usually need to be planned out in terms of your shoot because these types of scenes aren't necessarily common occurrences.

Dominant colors jump out at the eye (**Figure 46.3**). Recessive colors, like the name implies, recede and do all they can to stay quiet. So, colors like red and orange are usually considered dominant, especially when compared to (and when used with) colors like blue and green. Complementary colors, although specifically identified based on their exact relationships to each other, are those that feature this type of contrast.

Dominant and recessive colors, when used together, give photographs great dimensional qualities. Personally, I'm more apt to consider two or more colors' dominant and recessive characteristics than whether or not they are analogous or complementary. Dominant colors "pop" away from recessive colors, which tend to take a backseat to the more flashy colors. When we start to consider this photographically, especially for portraits, one of the great ways to create visual distance and depth between your subject and the background is through color. For example, a red shirt will pop off a background of a less aggressive color (**Figure 46.4**). The key to employing this is to ensure that one of the colors does not take up as much room in the frame as the other. It is common to see much more of the frame's real estate devoted to the recessive color, which lets the smaller, more dominant color shine.

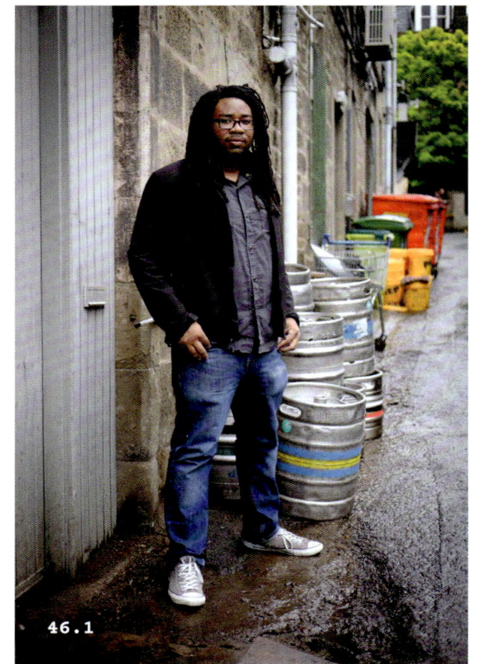

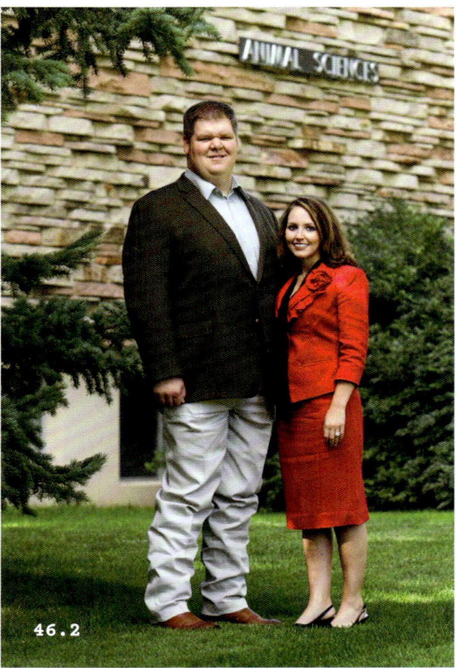

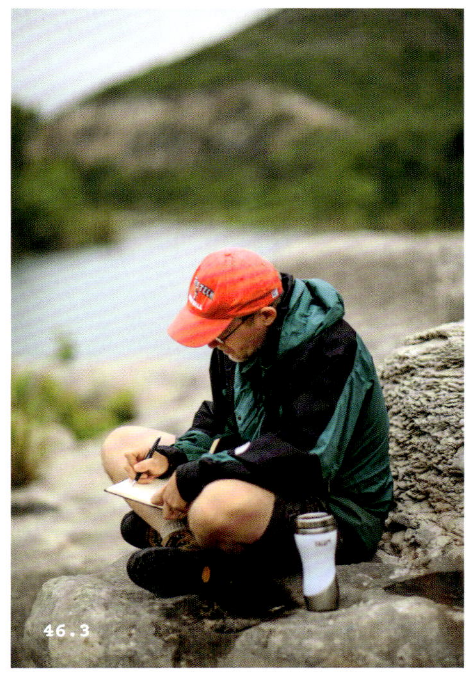

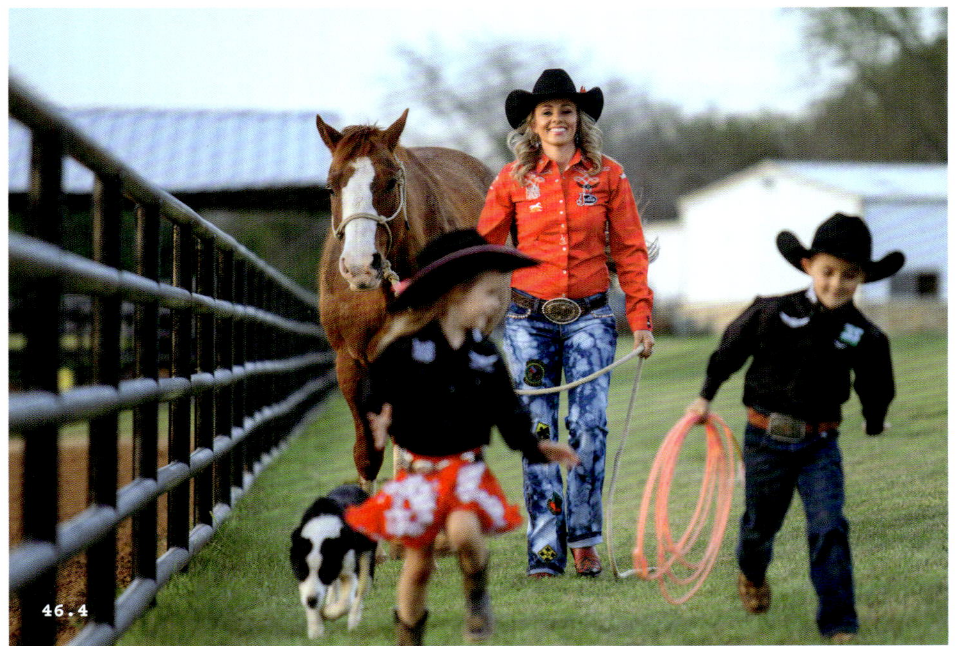

46.1 The subject's clothing is fairly analogous in coloration, and it doesn't depart too much from the other color values in the alley way, lending an almost monochromatic look to the environmental portrait.
ISO 400; 1/600 sec.; f/2; 35mm

46.2 The woman's red dress is a direct complement to the green environment, which makes the couple stand out.
ISO 100; 1/125 sec.; f/4; 108mm

46.3 Poet John Poch's red cap "pops" toward the eye against the more recessive and muted tones around him.
ISO 100; 1/1000 sec.; f/1.2; 85mm

46.4 Not only does Shada's shirt advance off of a muted background, it also draws the eye through the image's composition, which in large part is commanded by her children playing in the foreground.
ISO 800; 1/800 sec.; f/2.8; 200mm

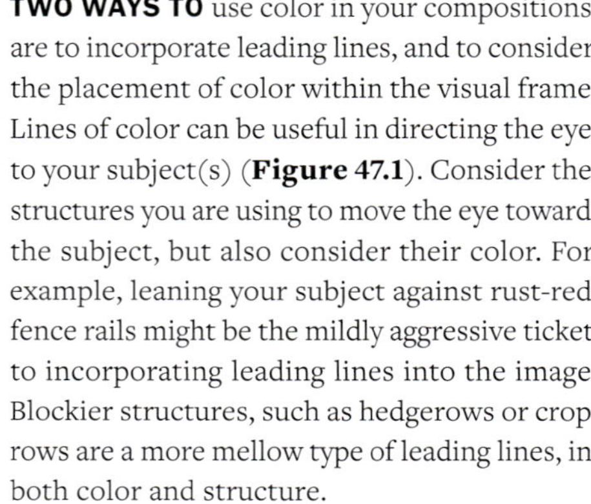

TWO WAYS TO use color in your compositions are to incorporate leading lines, and to consider the placement of color within the visual frame. Lines of color can be useful in directing the eye to your subject(s) (**Figure 47.1**). Consider the structures you are using to move the eye toward the subject, but also consider their color. For example, leaning your subject against rust-red fence rails might be the mildly aggressive ticket to incorporating leading lines into the image. Blockier structures, such as hedgerows or crop rows are a more mellow type of leading lines, in both color and structure.

Color can also be extremely useful in framing your subject. In the previous section, I highlighted how significant dominant and recessive colors are to creating dimension. In addition, if one of those colors is used as the entire background, it can completely encapsulate, or frame, your subject (**Figure 47.2**). This works best when the background color is the more recessive color, such as a blue sky behind a subject wearing a red baseball cap. Walls of color are popular backdrops for portraits, as well. Imagine your subject leaning against a wall of a solid color. In this type of situation, the eye has an easier time getting to where the color breaks—which is where your subject is positioned on the wall.

Color, like it does when used with leading lines, complements traditional framing structures (**Figure 47.3**). The framing structure itself can be a useful color as the background for your subject. The point is to be aware of color and its potential to motivate the eye in a certain direction. Don't use a framing structure without first considering how its color will affect the portrait.

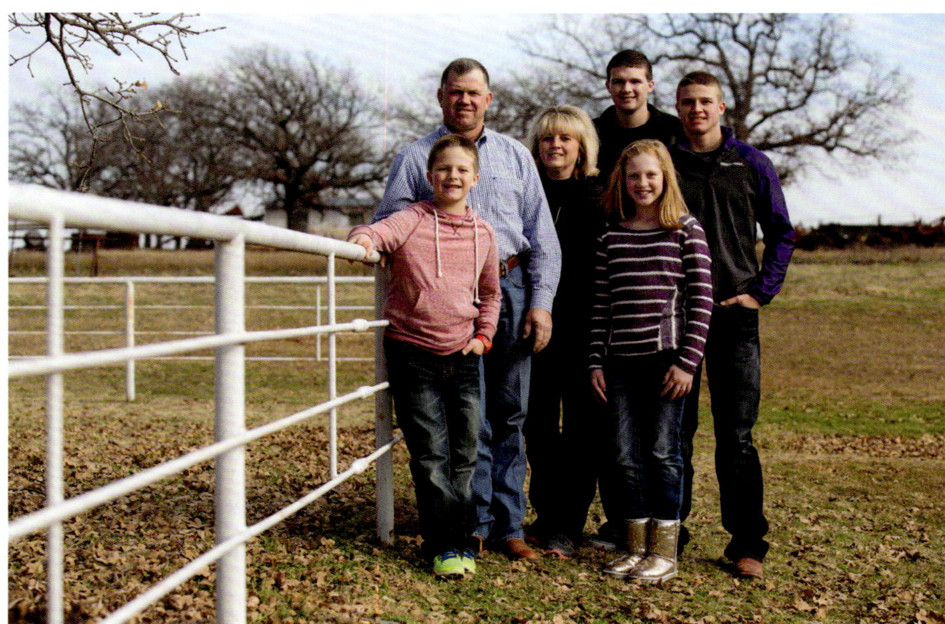

47.1 I used the white fence line to create a clean, attractively bright way of pushing the eye compositionally toward the subjects. A darker color under this type of softer light would not have been quite as effective.
ISO 200; 1/2000 sec.; f/4; 75mm

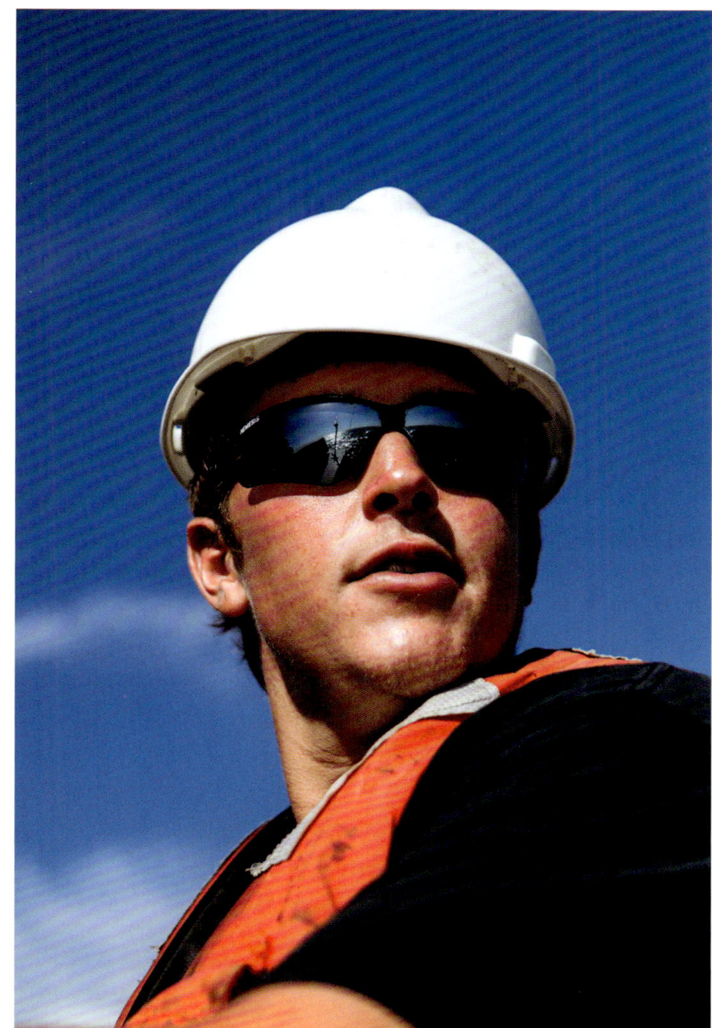

47.2 The blue sky behind the subject does a nice job in isolating his face, allowing the viewer visual comfort in reading the subject. The orange vest is a nice touch against the sky as well.
ISO 100; 1/2500 sec.; f/2.8; 52mm

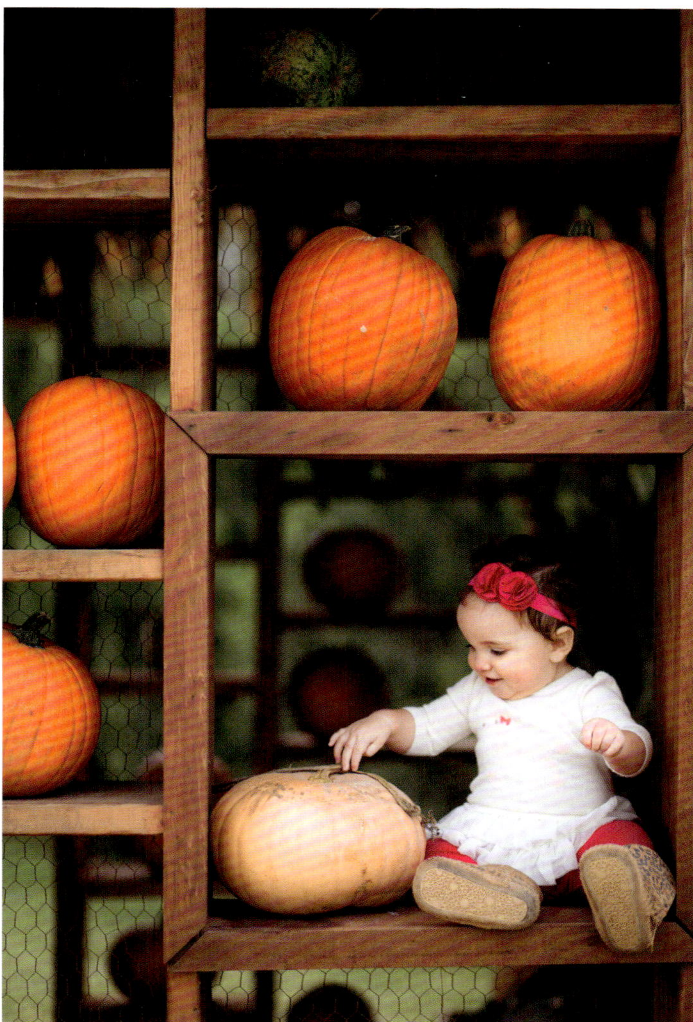

47.3 Not only is my youngest daughter framed by the wooden structure, a well-suited palette of autumn colors also surround the subject.
ISO 200; 1/250 sec.; f/2; 85mm

Look for color in those compositional elements you know are great visual attractants. The human eye is drawn to structures like circles and dots, triangles, parallelograms, and patterns. When color is strategically or narratively valuable among such structure, use it to your advantage (**Figure 47.4**). Abstractly, a red bow is simply a dot of color to which the eye is attracted. Similarly, an out-of-focus pattern of recessive color behind your subject takes advantage of the compositional strength of lines as well as the ability of that color to launch your subject even toward your viewers' eyes.

As great as color can be for your portrait composition, it is worth mentioning that color can also be one of the most powerful distractors in the frame (**Figure 47.5**). Brightly colored backgrounds can steal your viewer's attention away from the subject, especially if the color does not necessarily relate to the other elements in the image. Likewise, the eye can be drawn to a distinctly different color than what is mostly present in the frame or on your subject. This especially relates to your subject's clothing, which we will discuss in the next section. While you are paying attention to how color can *help* you in composing your portraits, also consider how colors can *hurt* you, as well.

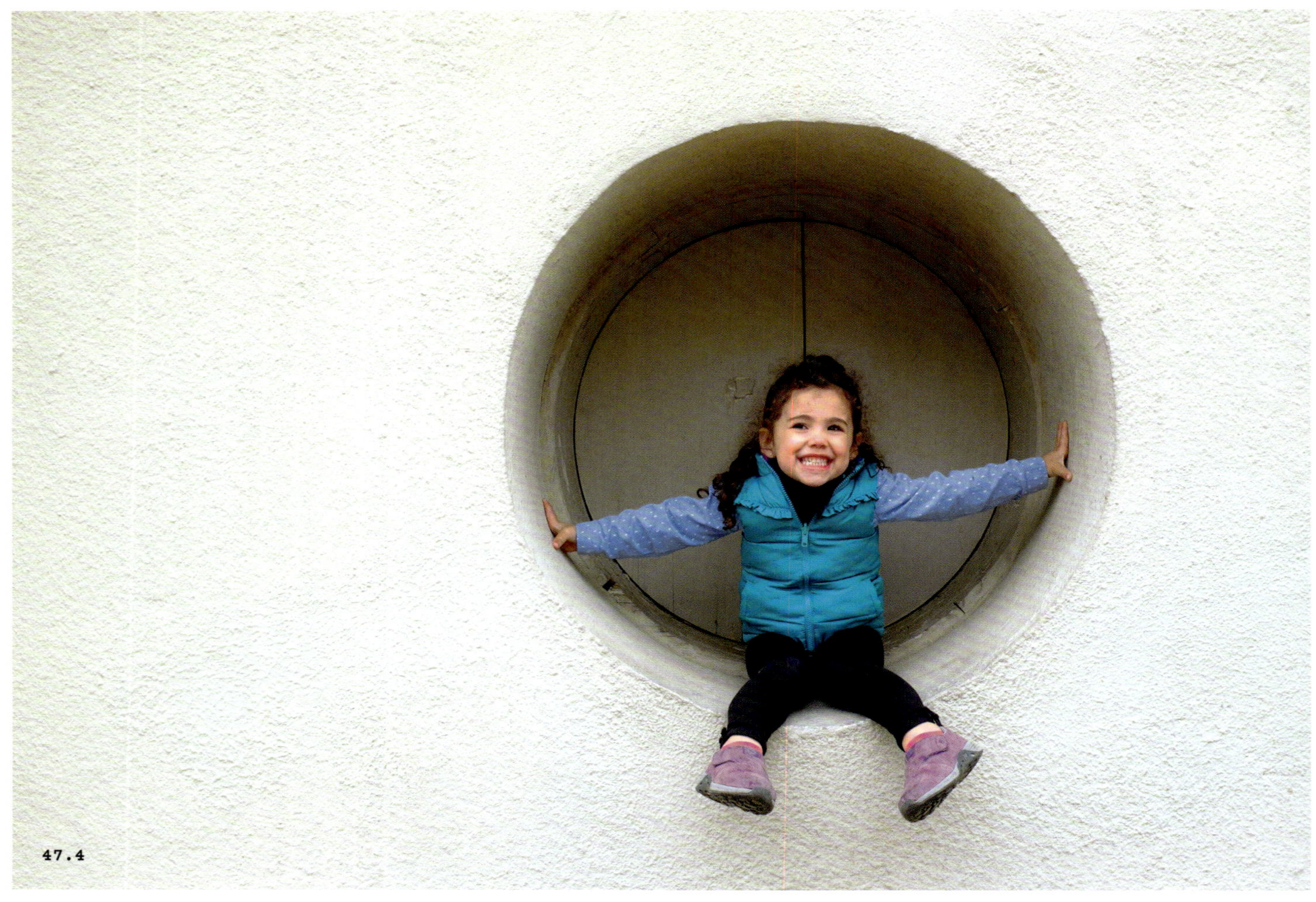

47.4

47.4 I knew the round inset on this taupe wall would be a nice frame in which to place my colorfully dressed daughter. The circle is one of the most attractive shapes, so it catches the viewer's eye (as does the pop of color).
ISO 200; 1/220 sec.; f/4; 23mm

47.5 Although the light and color on the subjects looks nice, the overly bright and yellowish coloration of the background is a great distractor in this portrait.
ISO 100; 1/160 sec.; f/4; 110mm

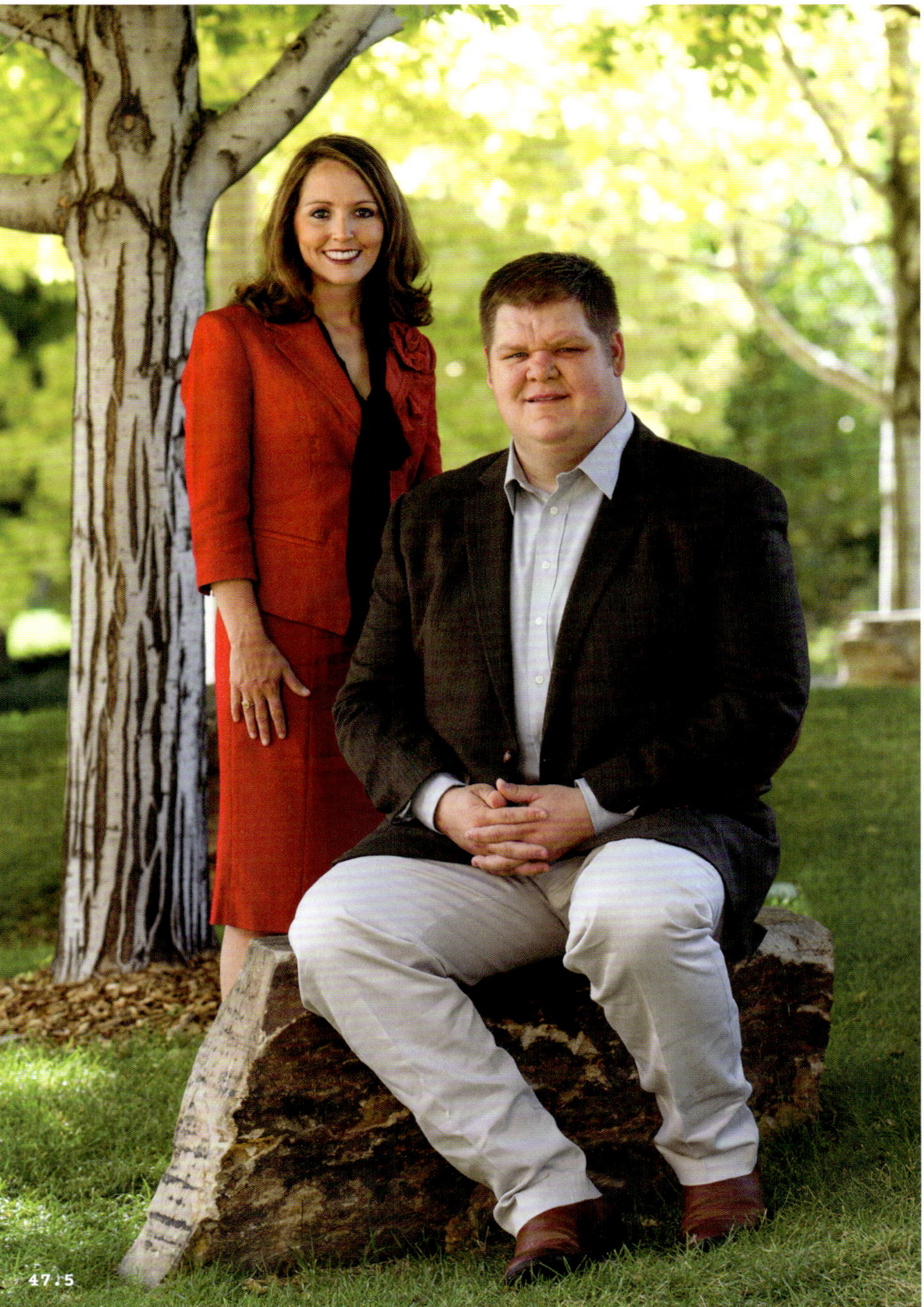

FOR THE RECORD, I am not a fashion expert. However, as a photographer, I do know whether or not the colors my subject is wearing for a portrait shoot are problematic or distracting.

On the technical side, clothing color can present potential distractions or exposure issues in your images. Since aggressive colors attract the eye more than calmer, recessive colors, it makes sense that an overly bright shirt can attract attention from a great face (**Figure 48.1**). Remain vigilant of how much the color of the subject's clothing may distract from their face, especially for tighter portraits (**Figure 48.2**). Extremely bright or popping solid colors and vibrant stripes of multiple colors can compete with what is primarily the main focus of the image. Unless it's a commercial shoot where my creative control is limited, I often tell my portrait subjects to consider simple, solid colors that aren't too "loud." In most cases, this instruction offers the subject control of their style, but it keeps the distraction factor related to their clothes somewhat regulated.

Another technical issue to be aware of is how easy it is to extremely overexpose white clothing or lose very dark or black clothing in a similarly colored background (**Figure 48.3**). Remember that your camera's dynamic range is limited, and blowing out whites when everything else looks well exposed can occur easily. When exposing white clothing, it is best to work in optimum light and contrast conditions, meaning that your timing and situation have to work with the camera's dynamic range (**Figure 48.4**). Shoot when you know the lighting contrast is low, yet can still provide shadow dimension (think about the golden hours); or, shoot in an environment where levels of light contrast are low enough for maintaining detail (such as in open shade or any context where the background does not compete with the subject/foreground). Likewise, black is an easy color to underexpose, and while underexposing black simply accentuates its color, it can be a problem if the background of the portrait is also black or very dark (**Figure 48.5**). Form is lost as a result of the clothing blending into the background. In this case, shooting the portrait in an environment where the background contrasts with the subject or foreground is to your advantage. When I do have creative control over my portrait subject, I often encourage them to select a clothing color other than solid white or black. However, if the subject or client insists on those colors, I (and you should, too) feel confident that there are creative solutions to the potential problems these colors create.

Lastly, as a way of introducing the more subjective perspective on considering clothing in your portraits, it's important that you remain cognizant of how appropriate your subject's clothing in general is to the message of your image conveys. Again, I'm no fashion expert, but we must continually train our eye to notice everything in the image, and color is one of those visual elements that can say much about your subject's personal style (or lack thereof). It is easy to take for granted something so small as the color of a shirt, tie, or ball cap, but you would be surprised as to how many of your subjects need a little help picking out what might work best for their portraits (**Figure 48.6**). This is especially important for traditional individual and family portrait photographers. Although the subject might pick out clothing they might wear any given day, it's part of your job to help them pick out something that will make them look great on the day they are having portraits made. Remember the earlier suggestion about visiting with a portrait subject during a pre-shoot consultation? This is the perfect time to collect fashion-related information on your subject, as well as to have a substantial discussion about their clothing choices and how color can be used to accentuate positive and negative facets of their personality (see the next section).

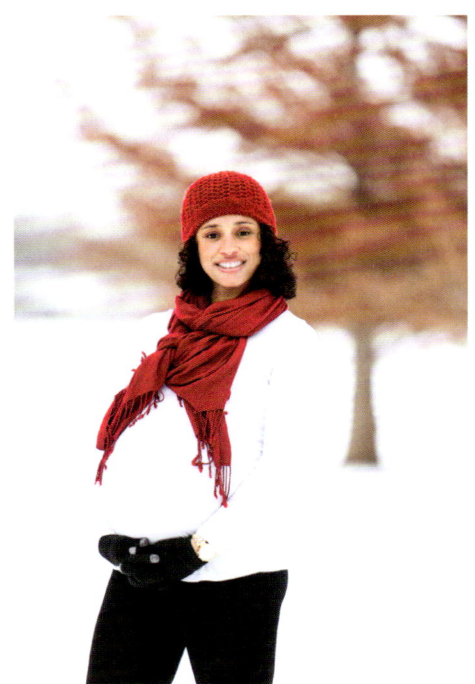

48.1 As much as I like this pregnancy portrait of my wife, my eyes are always distracted from her face to the lack of contrast between her white shirt and the snowy background. **ISO 100; 1/500 sec.; f/2.8; 190mm**

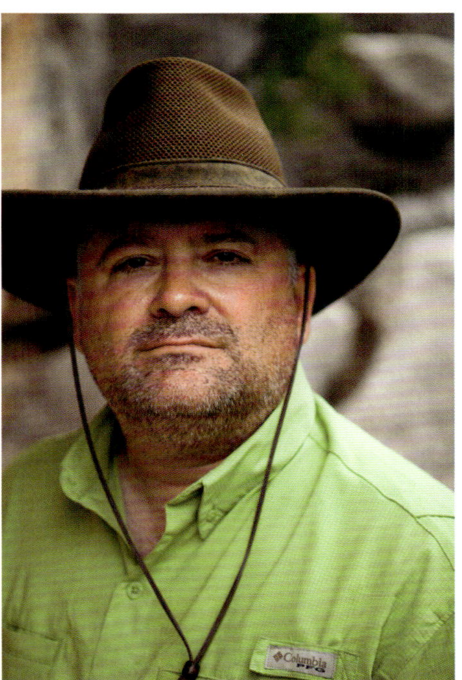

48.2 The chartreuse green shirt seems ill-placed in this headshot of the rugged outdoorsman and aggressively pulls the viewer away from his face. **ISO 100; 1/100 sec.; f/2.8; 70mm**

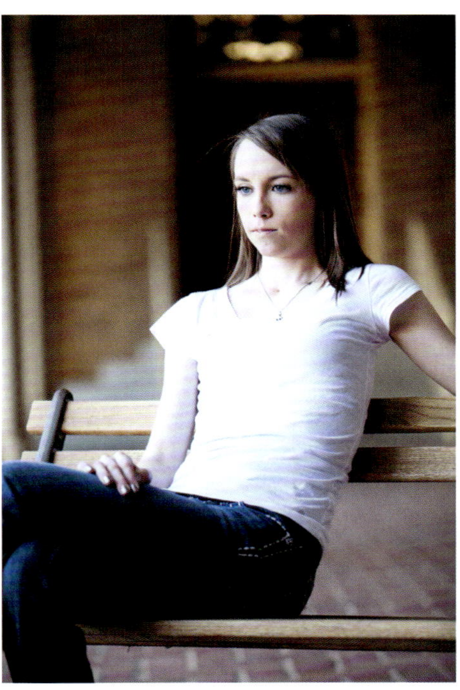

48.3 Technically, the dynamic range of the camera's sensor would not allow me to expose properly for the background and the subject's white shirt. Doing so would either result in an overexposed white shirt (shown here) or an underexposed background. **ISO 400; 1/200 sec.; f/2.8; 120mm**

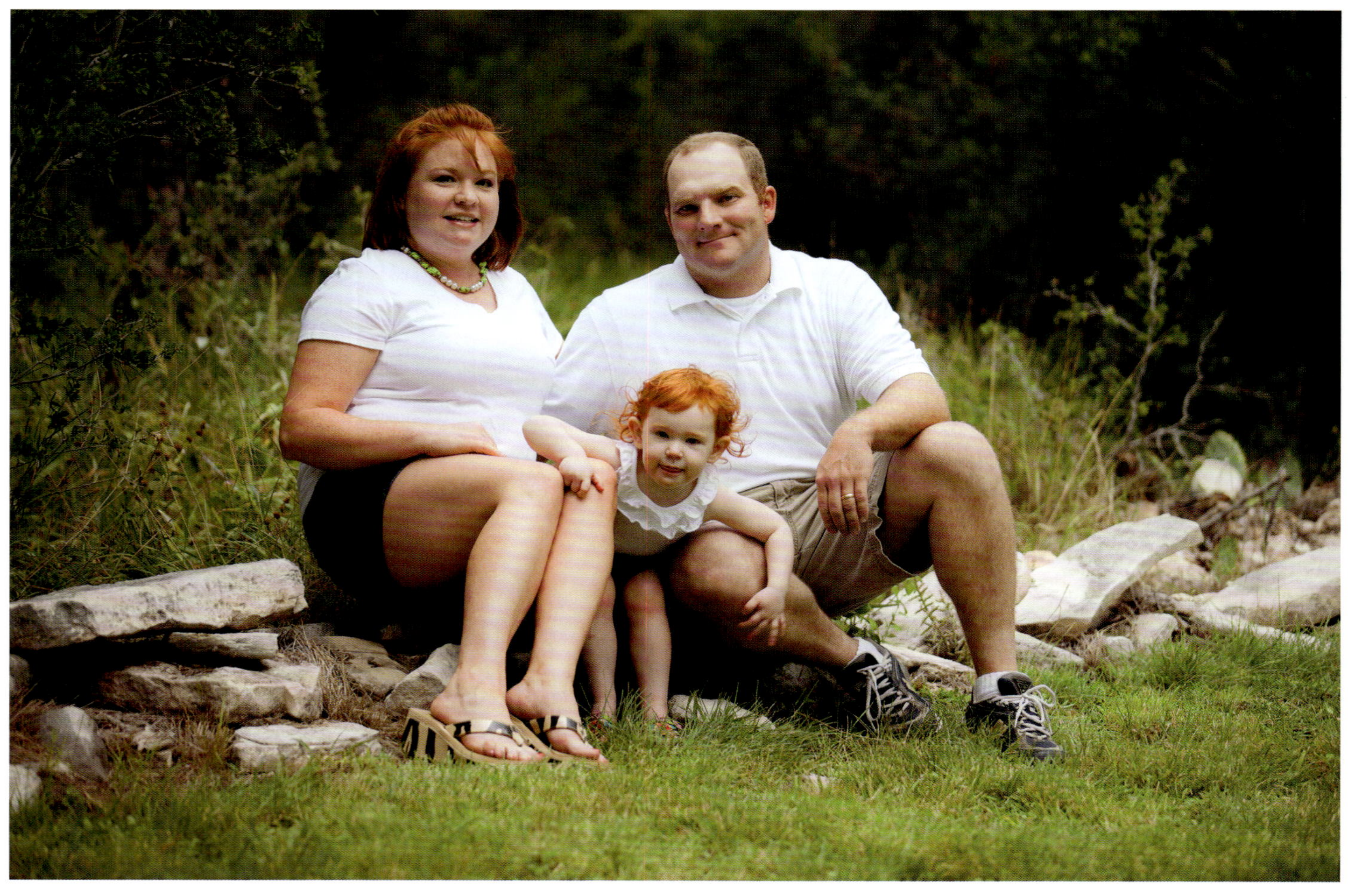

48.4 The family's white shirts were well-exposed as a result of working with diffused lighting and background values that fell within the camera's dynamic range.
ISO 400; 1/320 sec.; f/2.8; 115mm

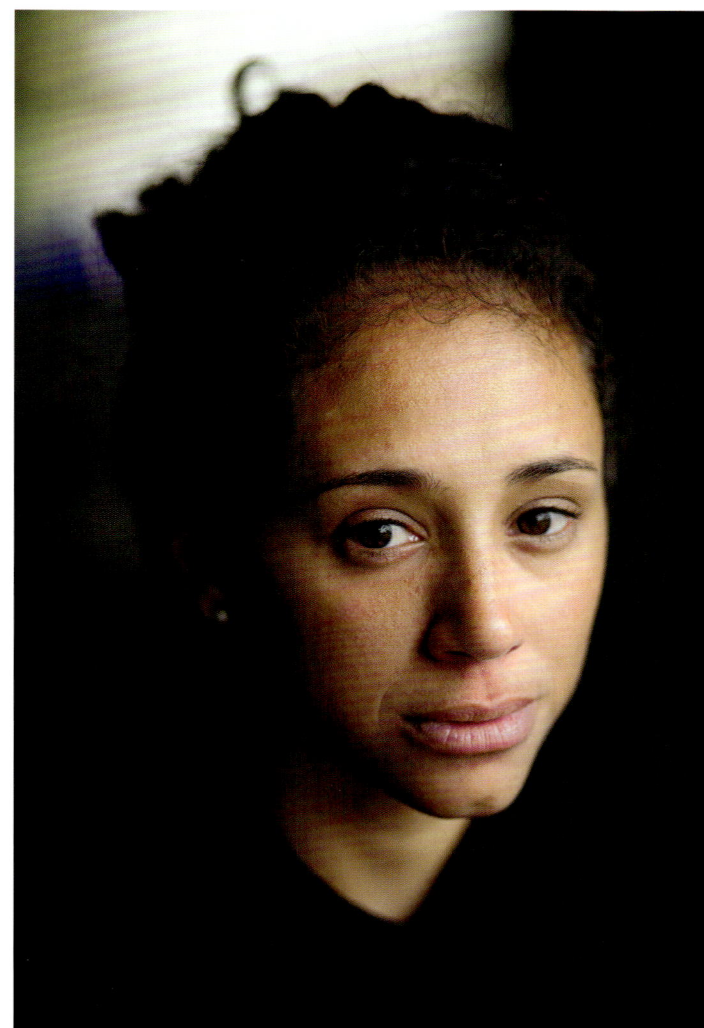

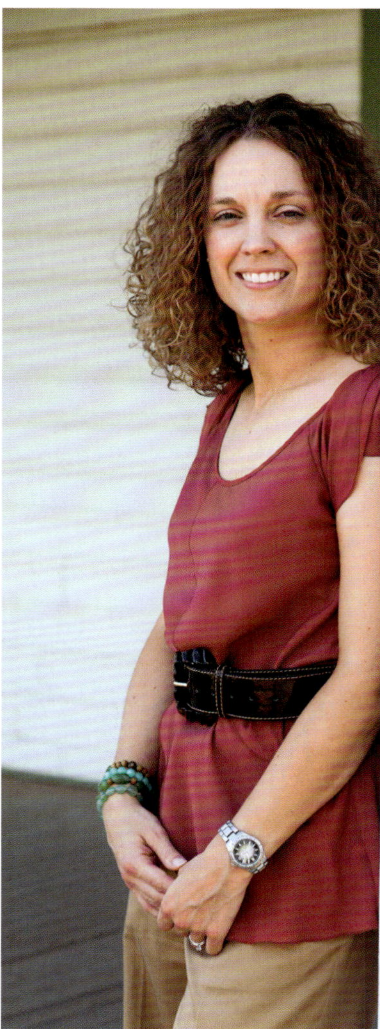

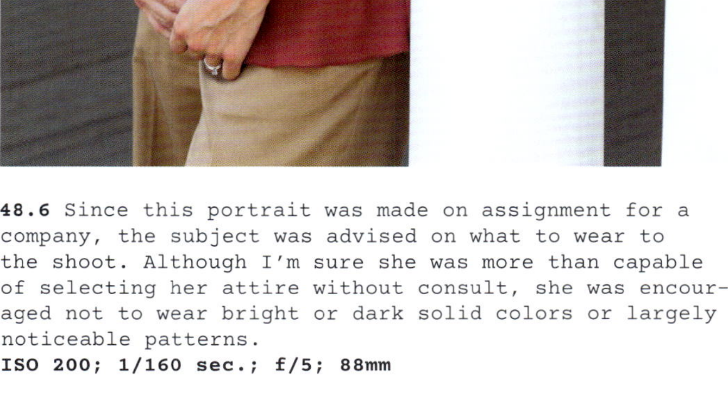

48.5 Again, because the camera's sensor cannot handle the amount of contrast contained in the image, the subject's black shirt appears to disappear in the darker areas of the background.
ISO 200; 1/320 sec.; f/1.8; 85mm

48.6 Since this portrait was made on assignment for a company, the subject was advised on what to wear to the shoot. Although I'm sure she was more than capable of selecting her attire without consult, she was encouraged not to wear bright or dark solid colors or largely noticeable patterns.
ISO 200; 1/160 sec.; f/5; 88mm

49. UNDERSTAND THE SUBJECTIVITY OF COLOR

COLOR IS AN extremely powerful and relatively subjective variable in conveying emotion and personality in your images. When we think about a certain color, it often brings to mind descriptors that are either culturally related or emotionally charged. For example, red is commonly used to describe anger, power, and sensuality (**Figure 49.1**). Green, on the other hand, can stand for life and growth, as well as toxicity (**Figure 49.2**).

Our perception and emotional attitudes toward color are somewhat subjectively understood, but having an understanding about what certain colors can say about your image, your portrait subject, and the environment helps you create highly effective portraits, while also helping you steer away from certain colors or environments in which the color might not convey your subject's story.

Here is a list of some common emotions, descriptors, or characteristics attributed to popular colors:

- **Red:** fast, aggressive, angry, romance, sexy, alarming (**Figure 49.3**)
- **Blue:** loyal, stable, smart, peaceful, weak (**Figure 49.4**)
- **Green:** life, growth, unity, poison, toxicity, death
- **Yellow:** happy, cheerfulness, anxiety (think large amounts of it)
- **Orange:** exotic, earthy, warmth, warning (**Figure 49.5**)
- **Purple:** mysterious, mystical, otherworldly, spiritual
- **Black:** formality, strict, luxury, exclusive, death, depressed
- **White:** innocent, peace, fresh, empty (**Figure 49.6**)

There are many more colors than listed here, and there is no rulebook saying that any one given descriptor is solely tied to any one color. These are general emotional and cognitive reactions to these colors, but how they play out in your portraiture is completely up to you. With these ideas in mind, you can avoid overlooking the emotional significance color imbues in your portraits. Color can manipulate the way viewers see your portrait subject, so you might think twice before photographing your corporate headshots against a bright red brick wall. The wall might be a visual distraction, and also convey aggression.

Of course, the subjectivity of color also means that the implication we infer from them constantly changes. Culture is a major influencer in this regard, and what one color might generally mean to a man from America might mean something different to a man from China. Sub-cultural influence also has an impact on how color is understood and used (**Figure 49.7**). Because of this, it behooves any photographer to remain observant of how this visual element is observed in its environment to see how it might impact the portrait, positively or negatively.

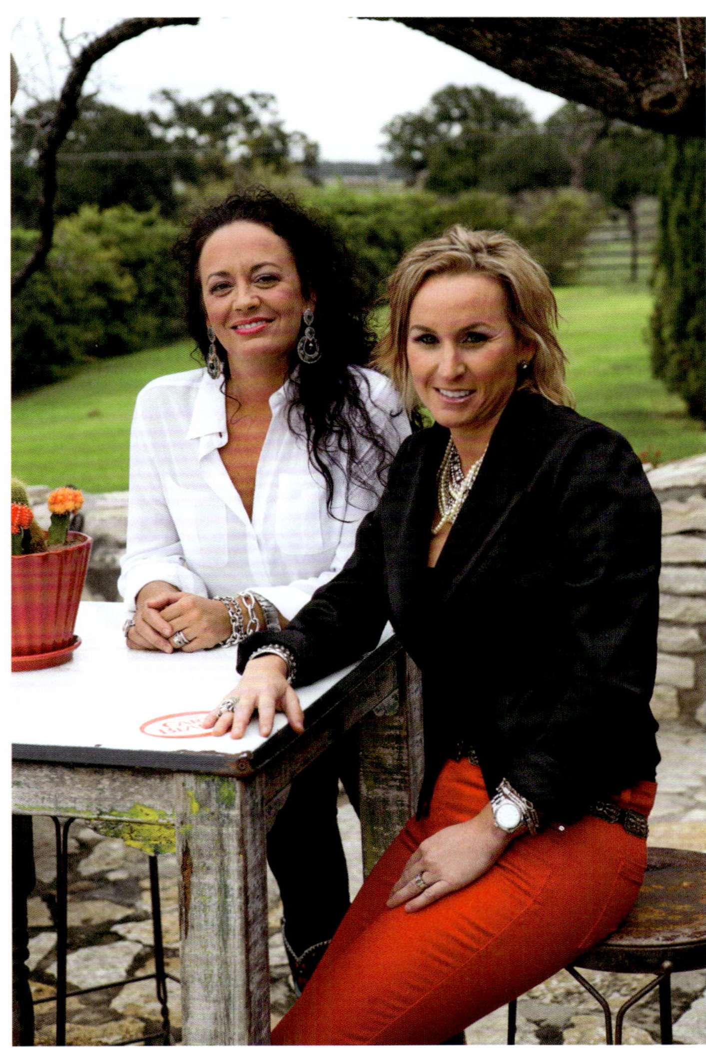

49.1 This subject's red pants attract the viewer's eye, but also shape perception of her personality.
ISO 400; 1/100 sec.; f/5.6; 70mm

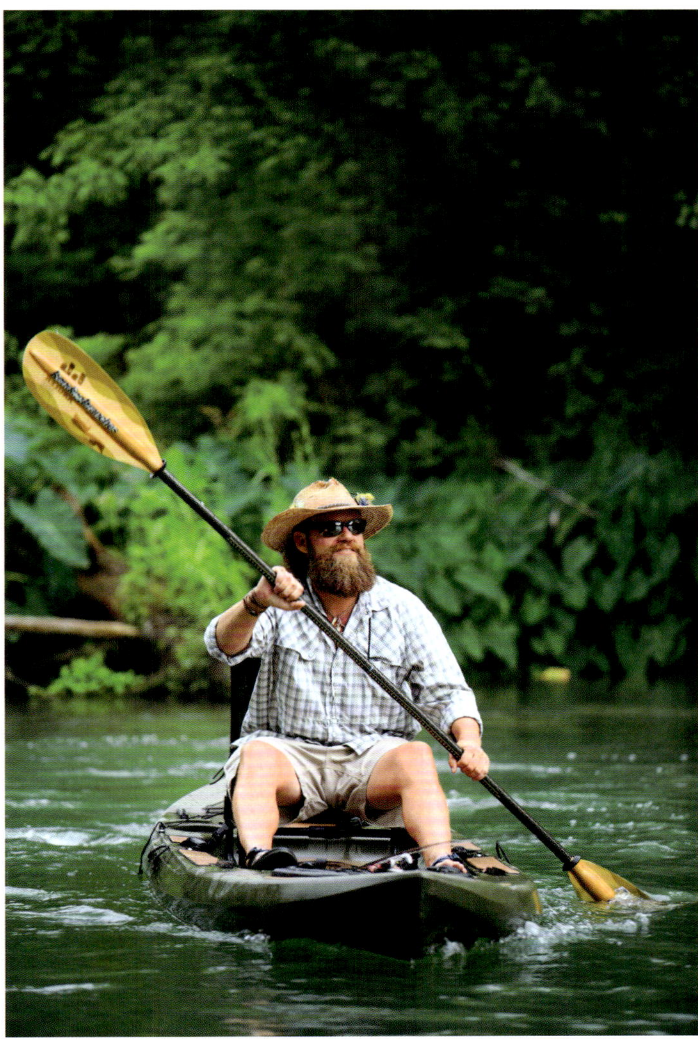

49.2 The completely green foliage background works well for my outdoors friend and creator of Diablo Paddlesports, Thomas Flemons, visually suggesting his passion for the wilderness near running fresh water.
ISO 400; 1/160 sec.; f/2.8; 145mm

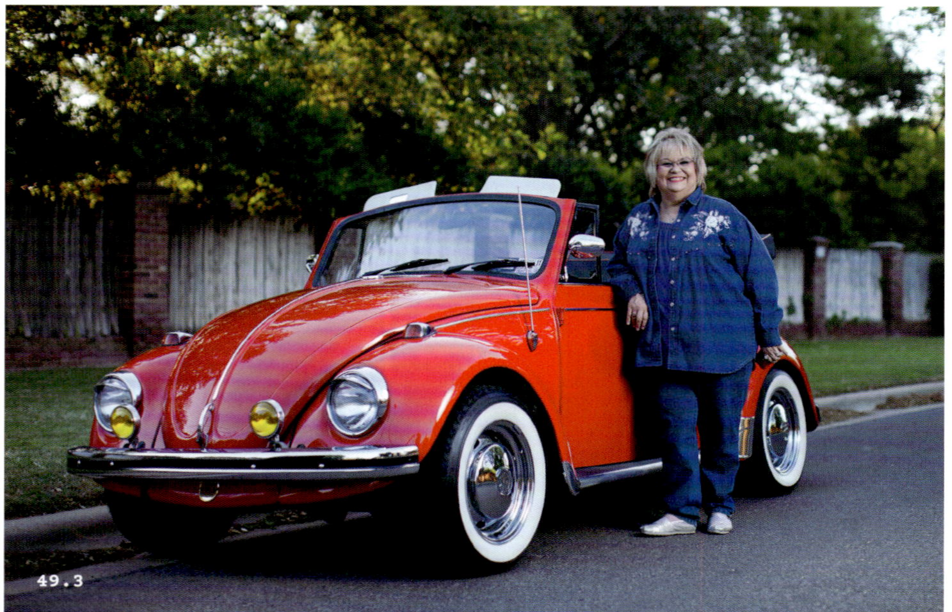

49.3

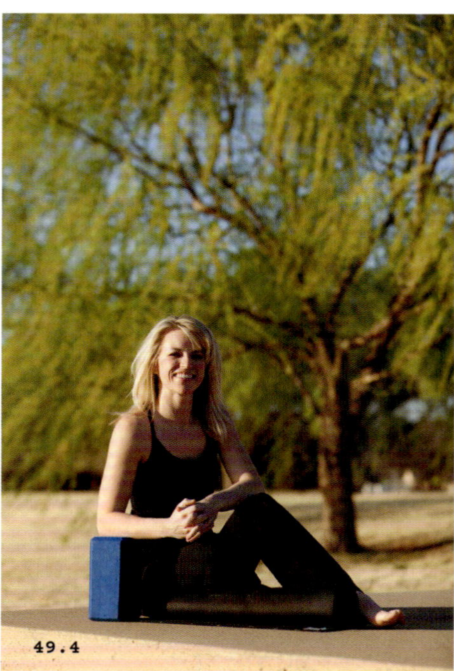

49.4

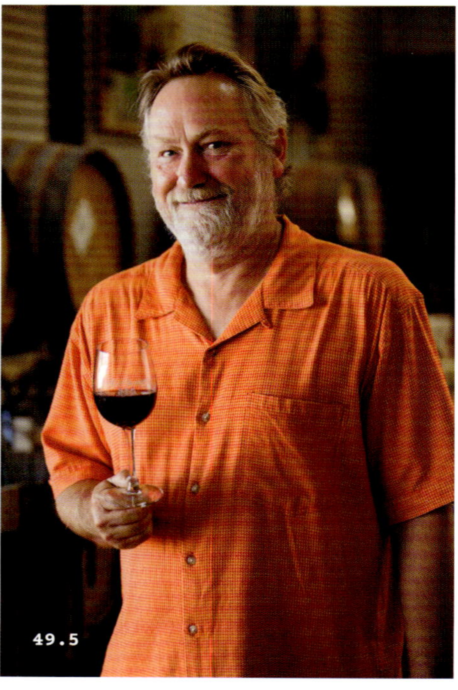

49.5

49.3 The older Volkswagen Beetles might not have been known for their speed, but this racy red one sure evokes that feeling, and it certainly suits the car's owner's personality as well!
ISO 50; 1/125 sec.; f/2; 50mm

49.4 The blue block was a nice addition to this shot of yoga instructor Haley Bevers, characteristically complementing the peaceful and centering facets of the physical practice.
ISO 100; 1/1000 sec.; f/3.2; 85mm

49.5 Orange is an earthy color, which relates well to Texas wine legend Kim McPherson, a product of the red dirt plains of West Texas and the American Southwest.
ISO 640; 1/320 sec.; f/3.2; 80mm

49.6 What can be more innocent than a newborn baby? I took advantage of a portrait when she was wrapped up and surrounded by a clean, white blanket to advance that perception.
ISO 400; 1/280 sec.; f/1.4; 35mm

49.7 I like to tell my university students that they are a part of a sub-culture (Texas Tech University's student body) and they resonate greatly with red and black, the university's colors. A shot of the school's mascot, the Masked Rider, certainly capitalizes on these colors and may evoke strong feelings of pride in current and former Texas Tech students.
ISO 100; 1/160 sec.; f/2.8; 170mm

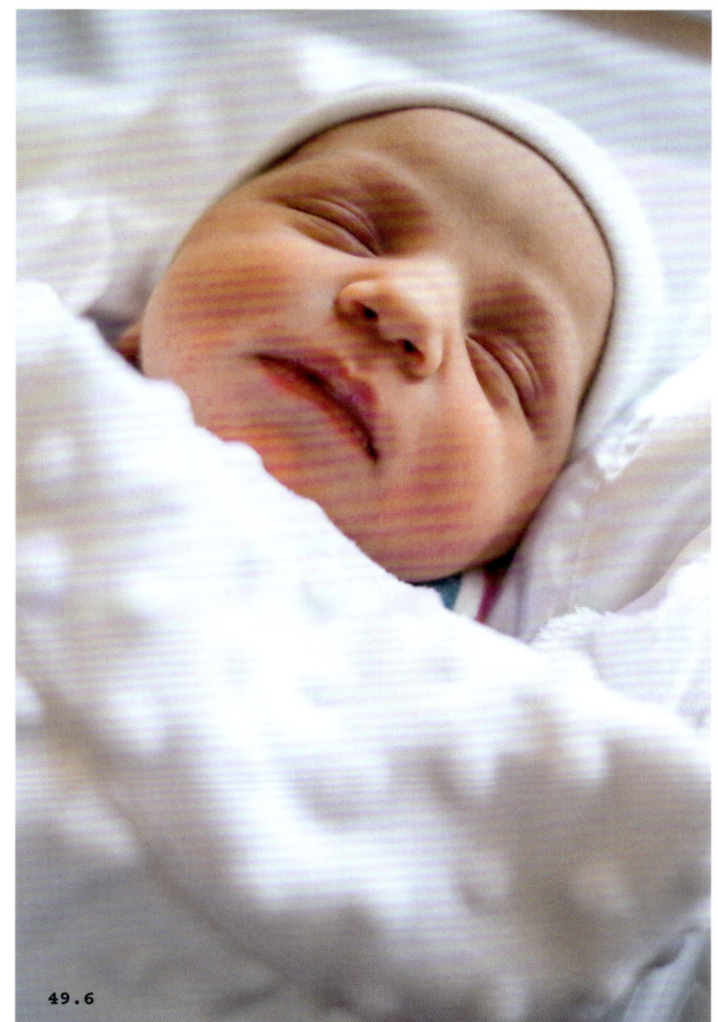

49.6

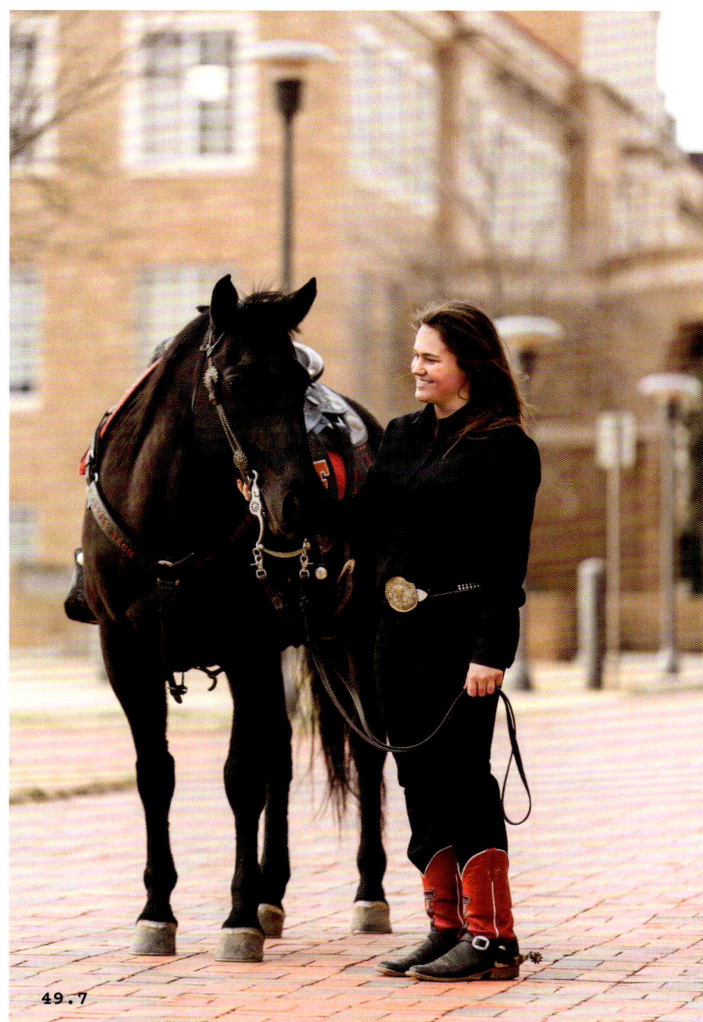

49.7

WHITE BALANCE SHOULD be one of the first things you consider and set up on your camera before beginning any shoot. Setting white balance as close to the available light source as possible is important in photographing accurate color—especially skin tones. In a world where we generally favor warmer colors over cooler ones, you might consider increasing the warmth of your white balance settings to give the appearance that they were photographed under a warmer light source—which is more flattering to your portrait subject (**Figure 50.1** and **Figure 50.2**).

I have no doubt that this will be sufficient enough consideration of white balance for most portraiture. However, if you want something different, you can experiment with color to get out of a creative rut.

What if your portrait subject says something that triggers new inspiration for you that requires augmenting color? Perhaps you could make an intentional move away from a white balance that renders more accurate skin tones (**Figure 50.3** and **Figure 50.4**). By now you have a foundational understanding about how the human eye reacts to color and how the human mind infers meaning from it, so changing white balance intentionally (in a way that affects a global color change in your frame) can change the way we actually see and perceive the portrait. If you want to create an image that feels emotionally more "blue," consider yanking your white balance down to the incandescent or tungsten setting. Too cool for your liking? Go into your custom white balance setting and move through the Kelvin temperature settings until you have it just right. While you're there, you can even augment white balance on both the blue/yellow spectrum and the green/magenta spectrum (bear in mind that not all cameras offer this much control).

Personally, I'm more familiar with making intentional drastic changes in white balance when it comes to landscape photography, but the principle is still the same. You're doing it to effect the visual perception of the portrait. Of course, there's a point where it may seem that the change is too extreme, but you will have to go down that road before you know it. Two things I suggest when considering enacting such a drastic visual change: don't do it all the time, and consider the entire digital process when making such a shift. Everything in moderation is not a bad philosophy when it comes to making this kind of change. However, when you consider your choice as part of a much more extensive digital process, where post-processing is key to your decision in drastically changing your white balance, the change is better justified and creatively intentional.

Lastly, and as a word of consolation for those of you not as apt to take a creative risk like this, remember that you're charged to shoot in the RAW file format. This means that you have the non-destructive ability to revert your choice of white balance back to a "normal" setting while post-processing your images after the shoot. This means you can feel safer in your decision to experiment with global image color in an effort to embrace creativity!

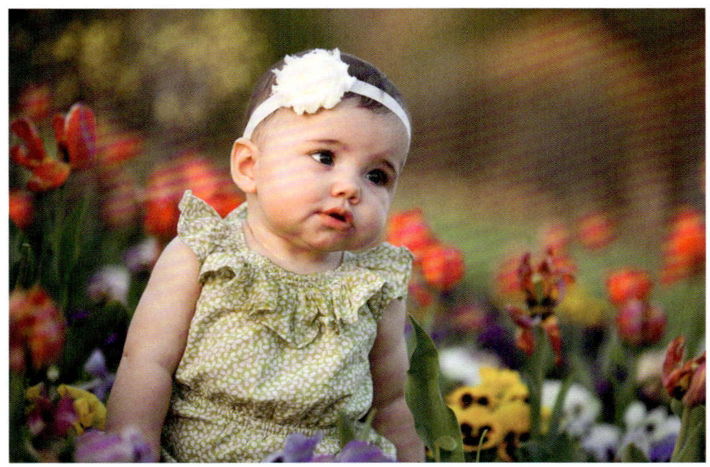

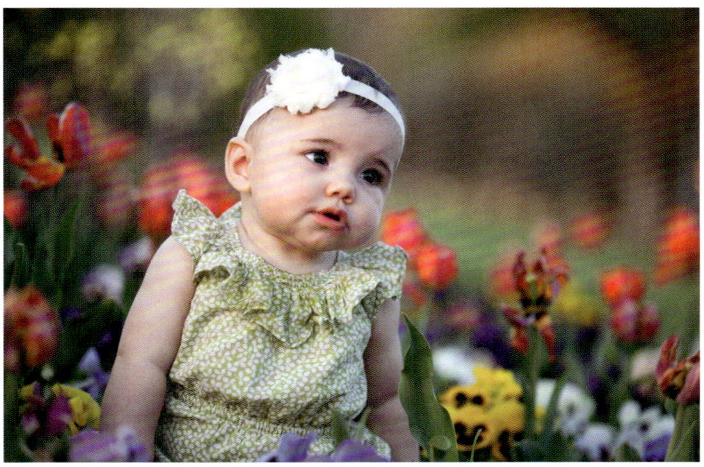

50.1 I intentionally increased the image's white balance from Daylight to Cloudy to warm up the shot overall, but especially in an effort to reduce the amount of blue in the baby's skin tones.
ISO 400; 1/400 sec.; f/2.8; 110mm

50.2 The original image was a bit too cool for my liking, especially in the subject's face shadows.

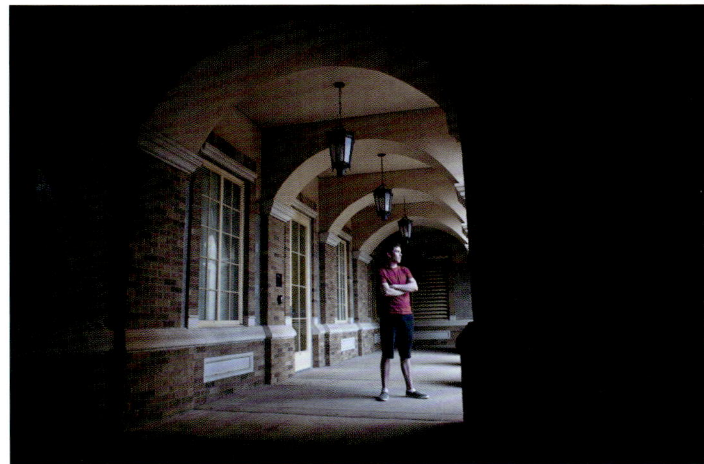

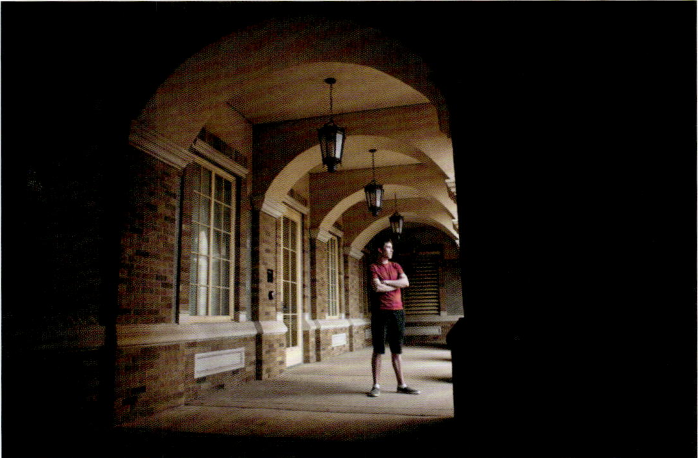

50.3 I cooled this image down to add a more contemplative characteristic, almost as if the subject was being lit by waning daylight or moonlight.
ISO 200; 1/60 sec.; f/2.8; 24mm

50.4 Although nicely colored, the original warmer tonality of the portrait conveys a different emotional appeal based on color than the cooler image.

7

STORYTELLING

Human beings are social creatures, and we desire stories. Images, especially portraits, contain a great deal of narrative information, and it's our job as portrait photographers to convey that story to the image subjects and viewers. Story is a large part of how we know the world around us; it's a large part of our creativity; and it's inherent in how we know and stay connected to other individuals. Portraits allow us to help make these connections. We study faces, facial expression, body language, clothing, and more to form a narrative-driven idea about the person's personality, their occupation, their age, their emotional state, and so on. If you want to create extremely engaging portraits—portraits that captivate your viewer—highlighting story in your images is essential.

The following tips will help put you in the mindset of a storyteller. You know the techniques to making a great-looking portrait. Now it's time to ensure that the portrait is saying something about your subject. Whether you are on assignment for *The New York Times* or photographing a local senior, creating great portraits is ultimately about finding a way to work with the subject to tell their story.

THIS SEEMS PRETTY simple. Get to know your subject. I'm not talking about getting to know them through simple conversation (although, this is an extremely valuable way of learning more about your subject). I encourage all portrait photographers to do their research on their subject and let it show through story-filled imagery. This "research" can vary from relatively academic to purely conversational, but it is essential.

Portrait shoots come in all shapes and sizes and take place in wide ranging contexts, from the journalistic and editorial to the senior and wedding varieties. Each offers an opportunity to learn more about your subject in a way that can make your portraits meaningful beyond great light and composition. The biggest difference in being able to get to know your subjects is the amount of time you get to spend doing your research on them. For example, engagement portrait shoots are sometimes preceded by a consultation or visit with the couple well before the shoot date. The photographer can use this time to ask questions about the couple—how they met, their first date, their life dreams, just to name a few—and use their answers to introduce related visuals to their portraits.

An editorial photographer assigned to shoot a portrait of a CEO of a national company, on the other hand, may be given less than a week to prepare (and at times, less than a few hours). Each shoot will vary, but regardless of the type of shoot, I try to do two things to make sure I know about my subject(s) before I trip the shutter.

The first is a background check. This isn't a job interview, and I don't involve the FBI, but I do try to see what is "out there" about my subject. Since I'm mostly involved in editorial and commercial shoots, my subjects will more than likely have an online presence through either their employer or their own website. Coupled with the information my editors provide me, I use anything I glean from their website to get an idea of who they are (**Figure 51.1**). Even doing an online image search can be informative (and it might be the only thing you have time to do for some shoots), especially for previsualizing light and posing. Depending on how you feel about it, it might be beneficial to also see if your subject is on any social media networks. This might prove fruitful in developing an idea about their personality, especially if you don't have time to meet with

him/her/them before your shoot. Speaking of which, that pre-shoot visit I mentioned earlier is a great way to gather background information about your subject in a face-to-face way (**Figure 51.2**). Each type of photographer and portrait shoot situation will pose a different background check scenario, but the point of doing one is so you do not go into your shoot knowing nothing about your subject. Having done at least a small amount of background research greatly bolsters the second component of my portrait shoot ritual.

Share A Great Photographic Story!

Once you've captured a shot with interesting story-telling elements, share it with the *Enthusiast's Guide* community! Follow @EnthusiastsGuides and post your image to Instagram, using the hashtag *#EGPhotoStory*. You can also search that hashtag to be inspired and see other photographers' shots.

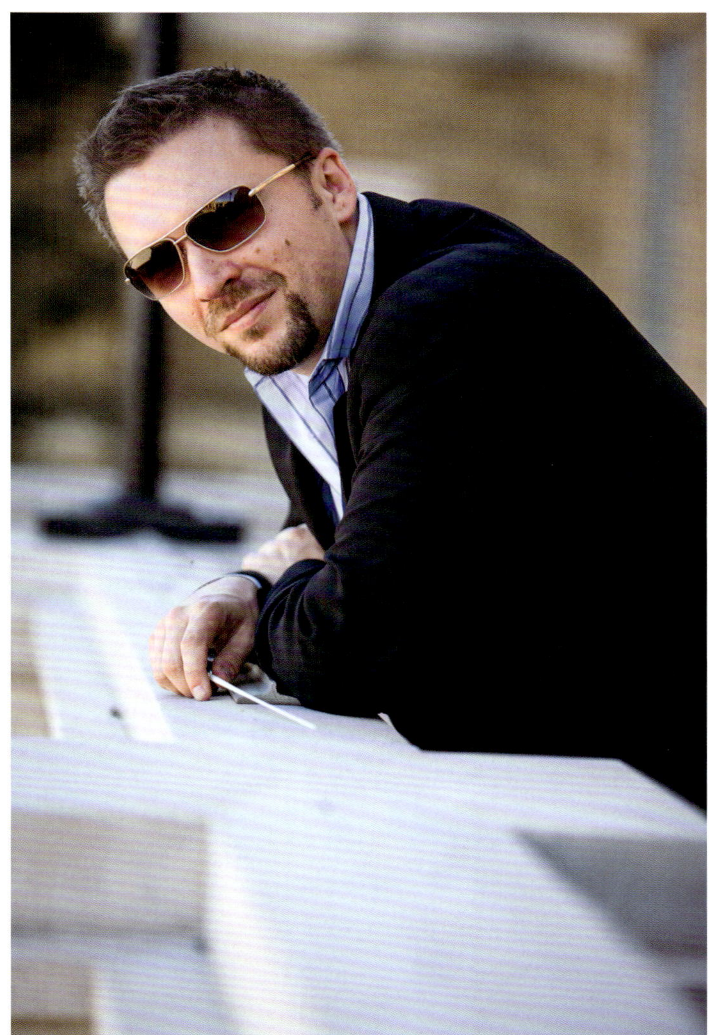

51.1 Before photographing a magazine feature on Tomasz Golka, I spent a good amount of time on his website to learn more about his prowess as a symphony conductor and music composer. I followed that up with online news and image searches to verse myself even more on how he was textually and visually presented in the media.
ISO 200; 1/400 sec.; f/2.8; 130mm

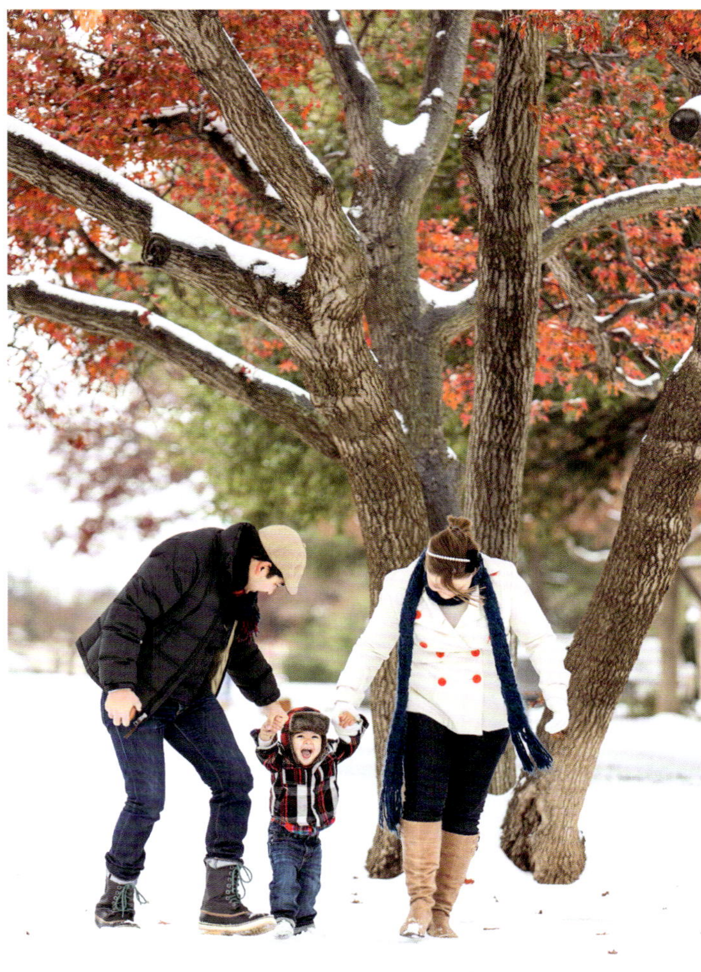

51.2 About a week before we did this shoot, I visited the Luna family to get to know them. I realized that the couple's son was a primary focus in their life, and I wanted to create a portrait that expressed this.
ISO 100; 1/400 sec.; f/2.8; 145mm

In the previous chapter, I wrote about rapport and how it helps put the subject at ease with you. Building rapport, as much as it sounds like small talk, is a way to get to know your subject. More often than not, you will be able to spend at least a few minutes with your subject while you are setting up or walking them from their office to the shoot location, for example. In either case, you can use this time to build rapport with questions that focus on them as a person and as a personality. At times, your subject may not necessarily expect many questions, and it's good to be cognizant of their feelings toward the shoot. However, most subjects are happy to answer questions about themselves and recognize it as an essential part of your work (**Figure 51.3**). For shoots that already included an earlier face-to-face meeting, it is still good to follow-up with questions and conversation to better inform your images so they tell the individual's or couple's story.

Lastly, it's a good idea to take a look around you when you are on a portrait shoot, especially if it takes place in your subject's home, office, or another location in which they spend a great deal of time (**Figure 51.4**). The contents of such a place, be it a desk or a pasture, is relevant to your subject, and can be a conversation starter. Personally, I look around the environment to see if there's anything the subject(s) and I have in common. This makes starting a conversation, especially with a stranger, a bit easier. This particular approach can unearth hobbies, intellectual interests, side projects, and a variety of other particulars that will help you find ways to visually interject pieces of their story in the images. If nothing else, finding something you have in common with your subject certainly helps you establish a great rapport with them.

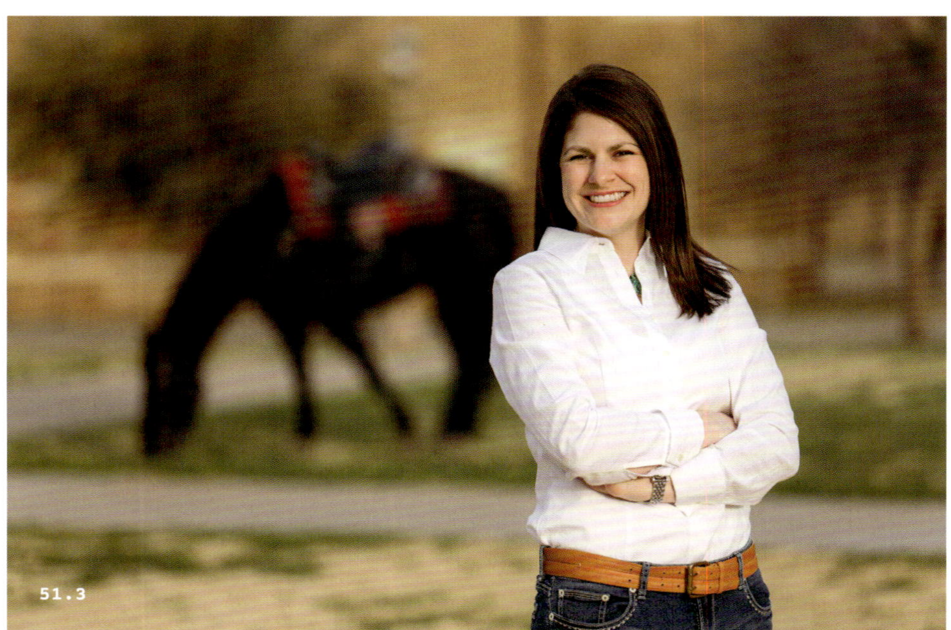

51.3 Asking questions while building rapport is also a great way to evoke genuine emotions from your subject. I asked Stacy, a former Texas Tech University Masked Rider, questions about owning the horse. She beamed while talking about an animal and a personality she loved dearly.
ISO 100; 1/1000 sec.; f/2.8; 155mm

51.4 Jason Wrinkle and I rode around all morning shooting portraits for an article on him and his work as a conservation steward in the Texas Trans-Pecos. Knowing that being in the truck, checking on the land, was an everyday occurrence for him, I got out and shot a few portraits of him through the windshield of his "office."
ISO 100; 1/500 sec.; f/5.6; 70mm

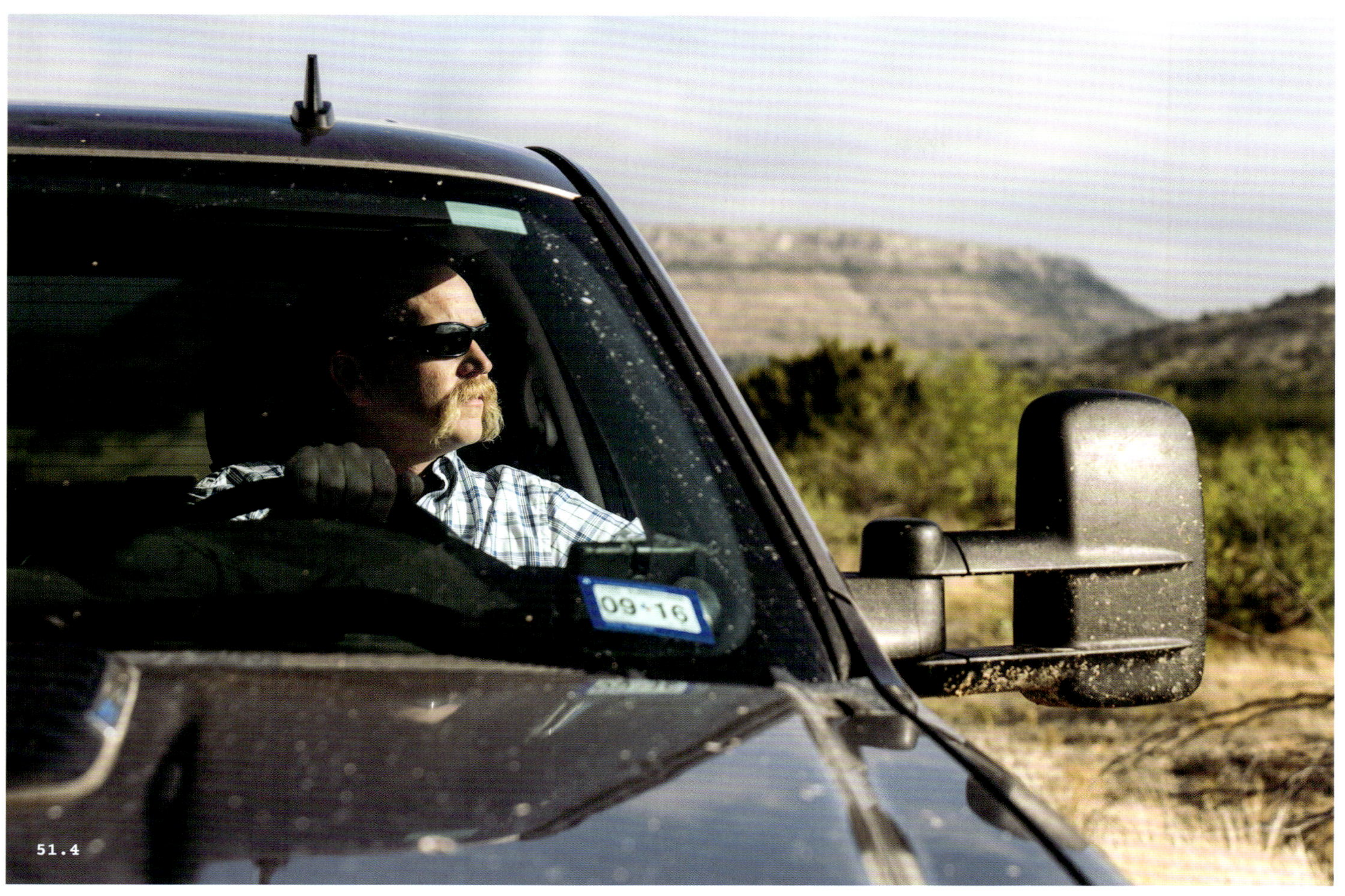
51.4

SIMPLY BY LOOKING into another human's eyes, one is reading a narrative (**Figure 52.1**).

Gesture, in this photographic sense, is that special way a person signals a message or an emotion through body language. Gesture can express joyfulness, sternness, or inquisitiveness, and it can make the subject appear intellectual, confident, or sultry. There's really no end to the amount of information our body language can transmit to another, and it's that special something we're trying to capture in our portraits. No matter if it's a corporate headshot that needs to express professionalism above all else, or the joy and hope in a graduating senior portrait (**Figure 52.2**), gesture will play a large role in how you conduct a shoot—and which shots you end up choosing over others during the edit.

We connect through the eyes. Communicative language is thought to be mostly non-verbal, and our eyes and eyebrows do a great deal of the "talking." Eyes and eyebrows can be used to convey a host of emotions and messages to the viewer (**Figure 52.3**). In essence, it is important that your subject's eyes be the main focus in many (not all, though) portraits you shoot. They are the gateways to a narrative information, be it their color, their size, their placement on your subject's face, or the structure of the face around them. Furthermore, if you lean toward street or travel photography, always be on the lookout for interesting eyes. Knowing that they contain an entire lifetime of story written in them, we can pack quite a bit of information about the subject into a tight headshot (**Figure 52.4**).

While eyes are important in the storytelling process, gesture is conveyed through other parts of the body. Hands are especially expressive. For example, the placement of a rancher's worn hands might be essential to his environmental portrait (**Figure 52.5**). A ballerina's soft hands might look great placed together around her knees in a sitting portrait. Getting a "feel" for the subject's hand by shaking it can be a great way to observe them and consider their importance for his or her portraits. Beyond hands, the way someone holds their shoulders or places their hands on their hips is also narrative-filled body language (**Figure 52.6**). This can be coached out of your subject with a prompt or question, but definitely be ready to shoot if a unique look or posture happens.

The number one rule in capturing great gestures is simply to be observant of your subject (**Figure 52.7**). You'll more than likely come across something that you can shoot or a stance you can tell the subject to re-create. When talking to your subject, always be watching them. This will ultimately result in capturing more great gestures.

52.1 You just can't help but look at the eyes. It's human instinct to look at and *read* the eyes of another living being, hence their significance for photographers.
ISO 100; 1/1600 sec.; f/1.8; 85mm

52.2 Pierce, a recent high school graduate, opens up his elation with his eyes.
ISO 100; 1/160 sec.; f/1.8; 85mm

52.3 The young boy's eyes say a great deal about his excitement, focus, and possibly some restrained hesitancy or fear before his father pushes him faster in the swing.
ISO 100; 1/250 sec.; f/2.8; 150mm

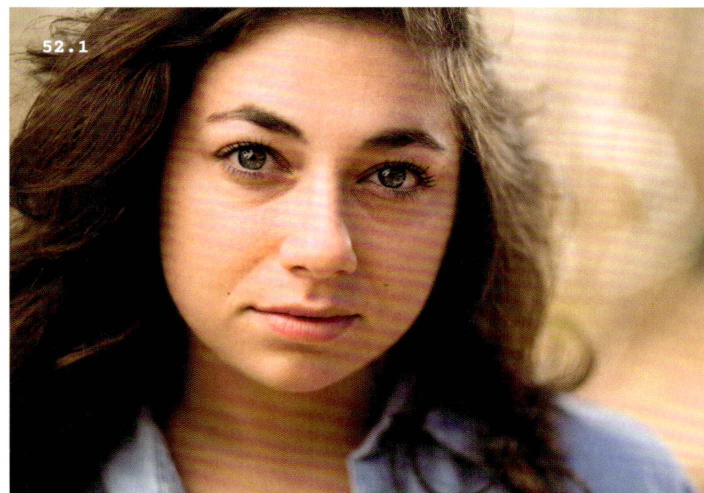

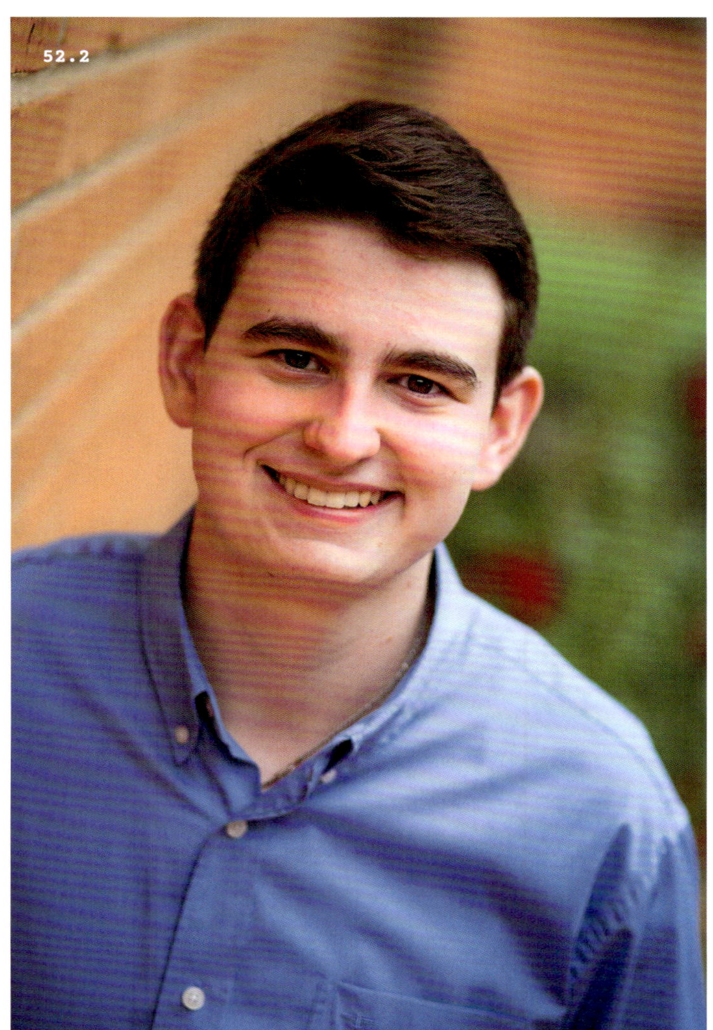

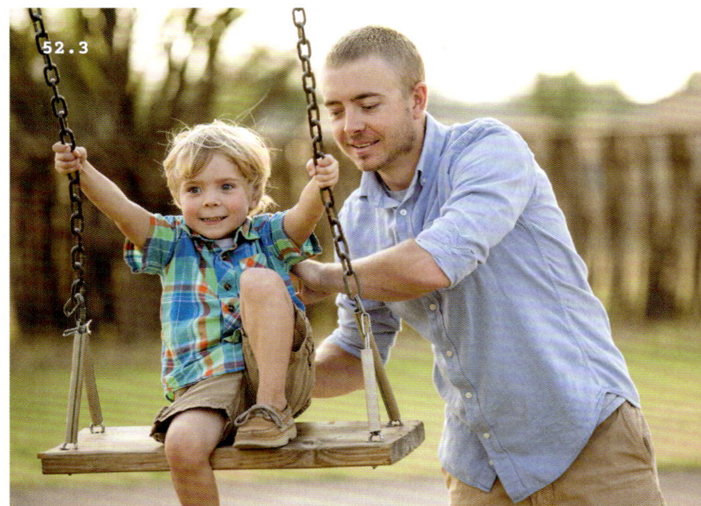

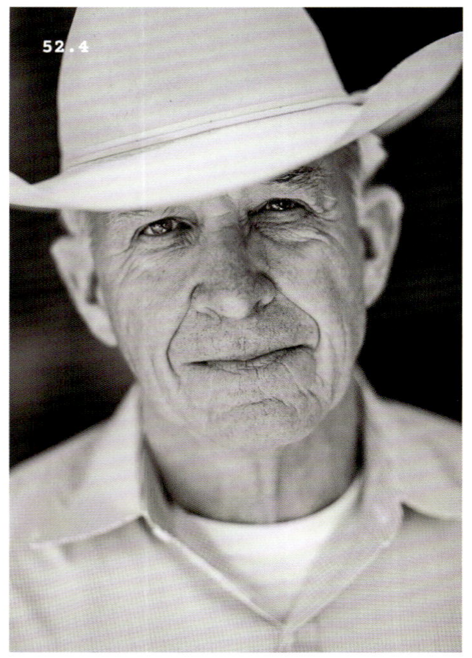

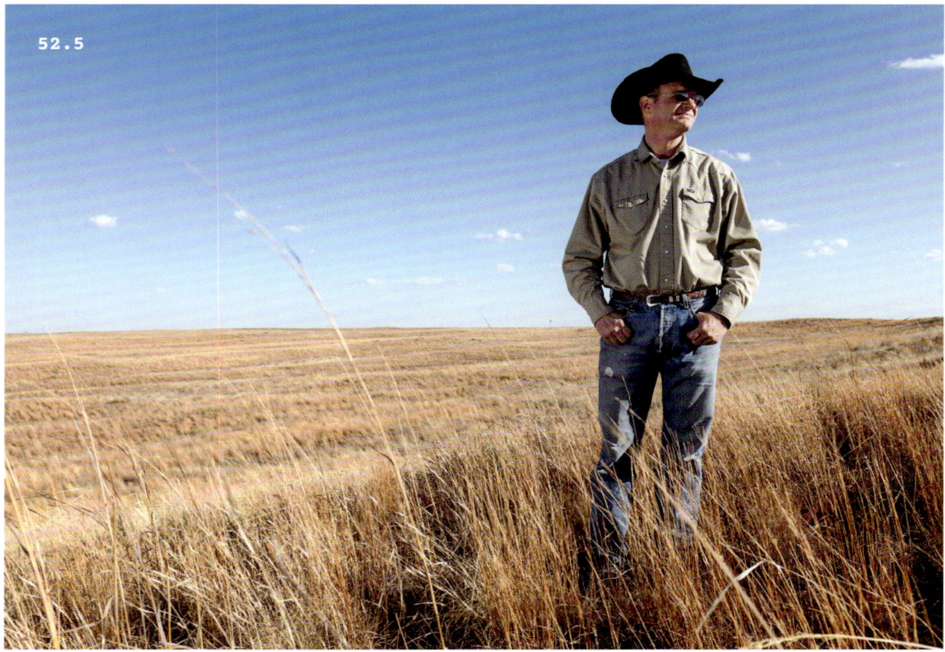

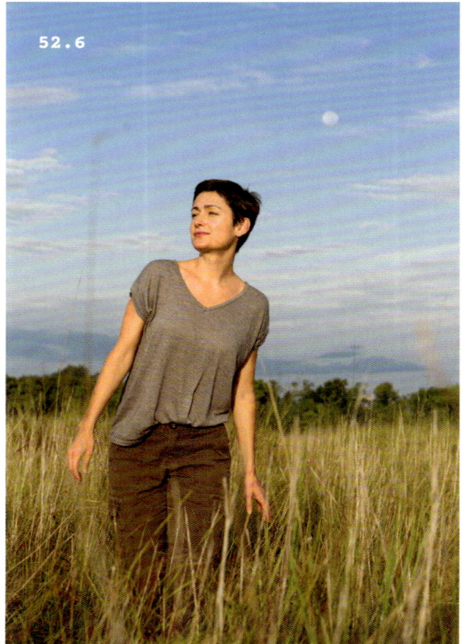

52.4 Older Texas ranchers, who've spent a lifetime staring across harshly lit pastures, have eyes that often speak louder than their voices.
ISO 100; 1/1000 sec.; f/2; 85mm

52.5 The iconic look of a cowboy, beyond the hat and boots, is his thumbs hooked into his jean's front pockets. Although a small gesture, it "completes" the look much like a cherry on top of an ice cream sundae.
ISO 100; 1/125 sec.; f/9; 28mm

52.6 The dip in my friend Jamie's shoulders is more action-filled than any other part of her body, reinforcing the idea that she is moving through the field, brushing her hands on the stems of grass around her.
ISO 200; 1/500 sec.; f/8; 70mm

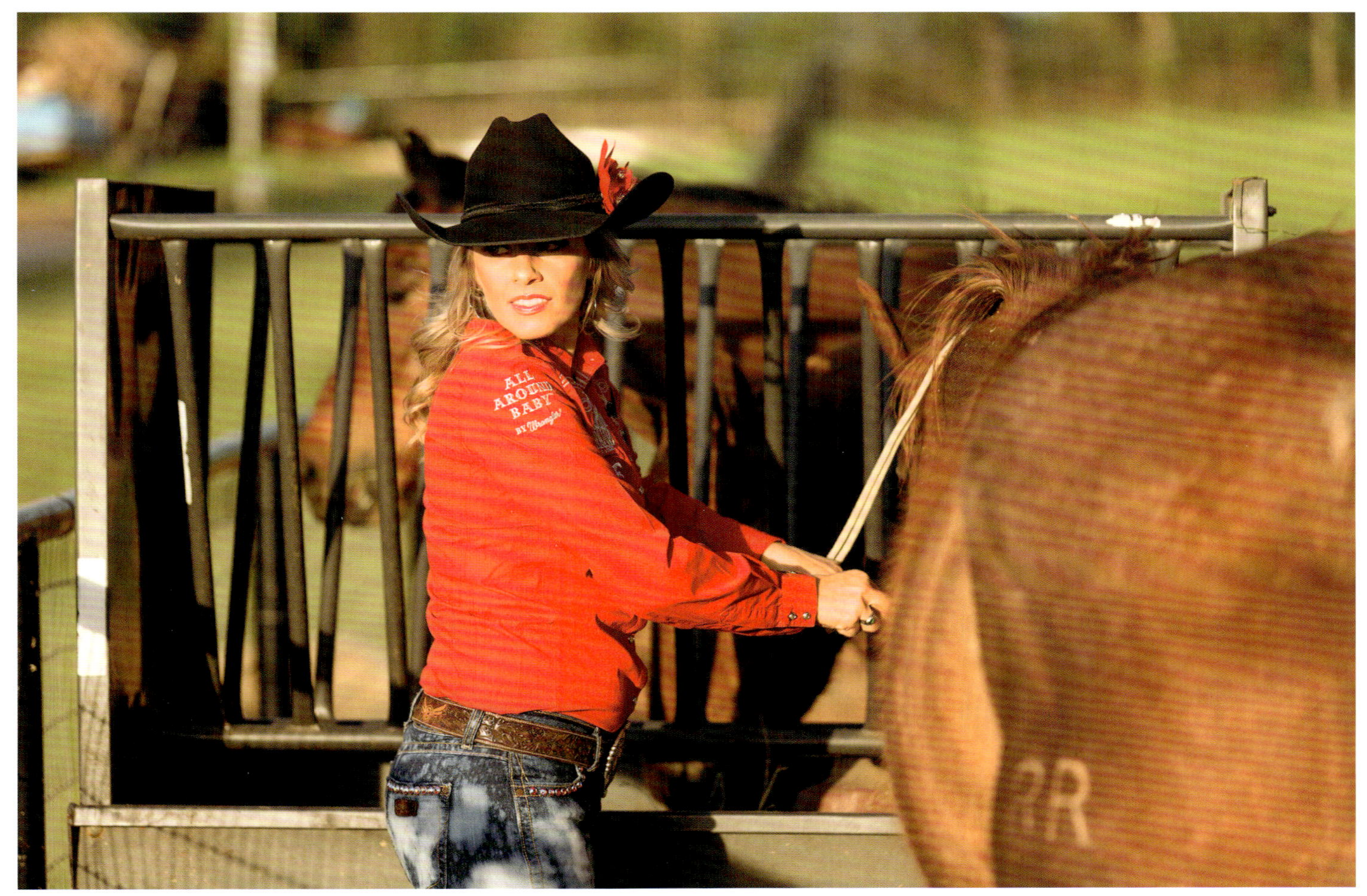

52.7 After seeing the shadow under the brim of Shada's hat, I couldn't resist making a couple portraits. The way the shadow covers just the eyes is a dramatic gesture that would not have been there if she had tilted her head back any more.
ISO 400; 1/3200 sec.; f/2.8; 150mm

53. ON BEING UNOBTRUSIVE

AT TIMES, THE best thing you can do to make your portraits better is to remain out of the way, observe, and grab moments with your camera covertly. This is a departure from our traditional thoughts on portraiture, where the photographer largely directs the portrait-making process, but it can be fruitful, especially for documentary-styled portraits. Of course, being a bit removed, or unobtrusive, can also strengthen other genres of portraiture. The more familiar you are with certain procedural styles, the more often you can identify where else they will be useful.

Below are tips on being unobtrusive. Some are influenced by documentary/journalistic photography practices; others are inspired by simple social norms that keep you both in your subject's good favor and somewhat invisible—the characteristic that might just result in your subject dropping their guard and revealing unique gestures:

1 **Be quiet.** Being a fly on the wall is harder than it seems. Being quiet is sometimes even more difficult. However, when you're quiet, your brain is extremely active, your eyes remain vigilant, and your mental and physical focus is at its peak. If you are on assignment and looking for the ideal candid portrait, being quiet and relatively unknown in a location is advantageous. Perhaps the only signal you give to your subject is a point to your camera and then to them to indicate you want to make a quick portrait (**Figure 53.1**). There may be no need to break your silence. Let the situation develop organically without your interjection. Likewise, if you are shooting an engagement or family session, a situation that you largely control by vocalizing your direction, force quiet moments into the shoot. You never know what chemistry will develop between your subjects (**Figure 53.2**). It might develop into a great memory for your subjects, something unexpected!

2 **Be patient.** It's an art. Sometimes it pays to wait for the shot to occur. Street photographers are notorious for choosing an area in which to sit/stand and people watch (**Figure 53.3**). They wait for a "decisive moment" to happen, something that catches their eye, illustrates something interesting about the environment and/or the people in it, and intrigues a viewer. This same principle can be applied to portraiture. Don't rush a good portrait, especially when it comes to its story. Wait until you become the fly on the wall in a new location—let those around you become comfortable with your presence. On the same note, if you are having a conversation with a stranger or a new subject, don't go straight to shooting.

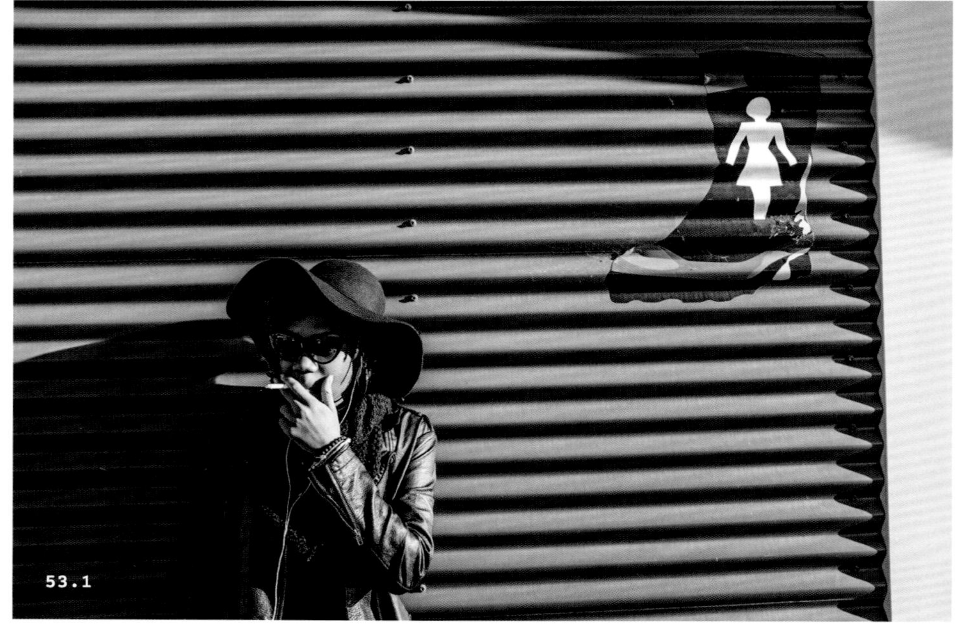
53.1

53.1 I didn't want to disturb the young lady from smoking (in fact, I wanted it in the shot) by verbally asking her if I could make her portrait, so I simply gestured with the camera and was given non-verbal confirmation for this less posed image.
ISO 400; 1/340 sec.; f/5.6; 23mm

53.2 After photographing the mother and son from a more traditional perspective, I just took a step back, became quiet and less apparent, and let their loving interaction come naturally before the camera.
ISO 200; 1/125 sec.; f/2.8; 50mm

53.3 Trains are popular locations for street photographers to photograph life in that context, and waiting for the right face (or two, given the reflection) to appear in front of the camera takes patience and curiosity.
ISO 400; 1/160 sec.; f/2.8; 70mm

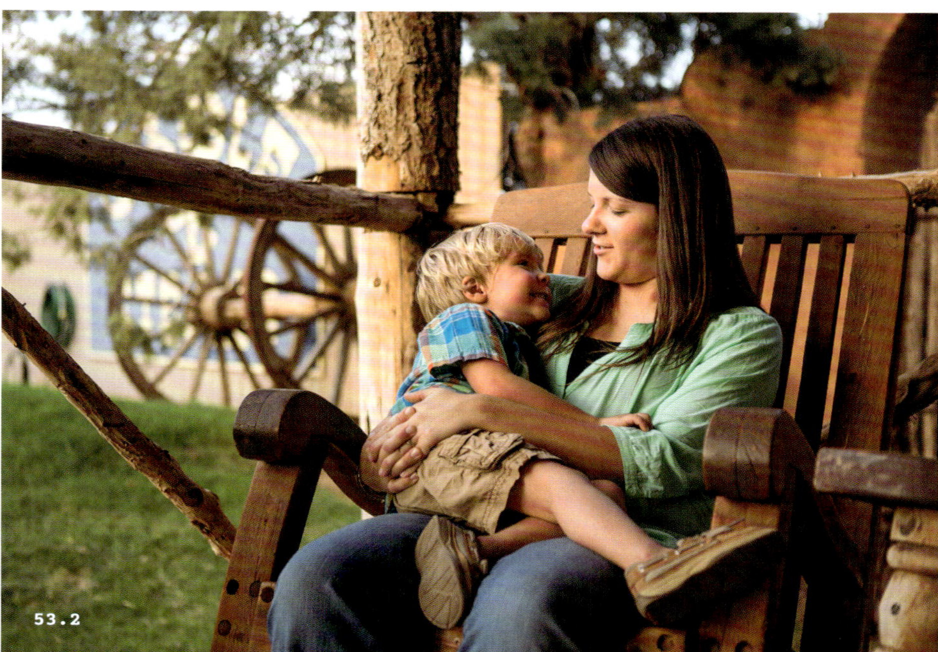

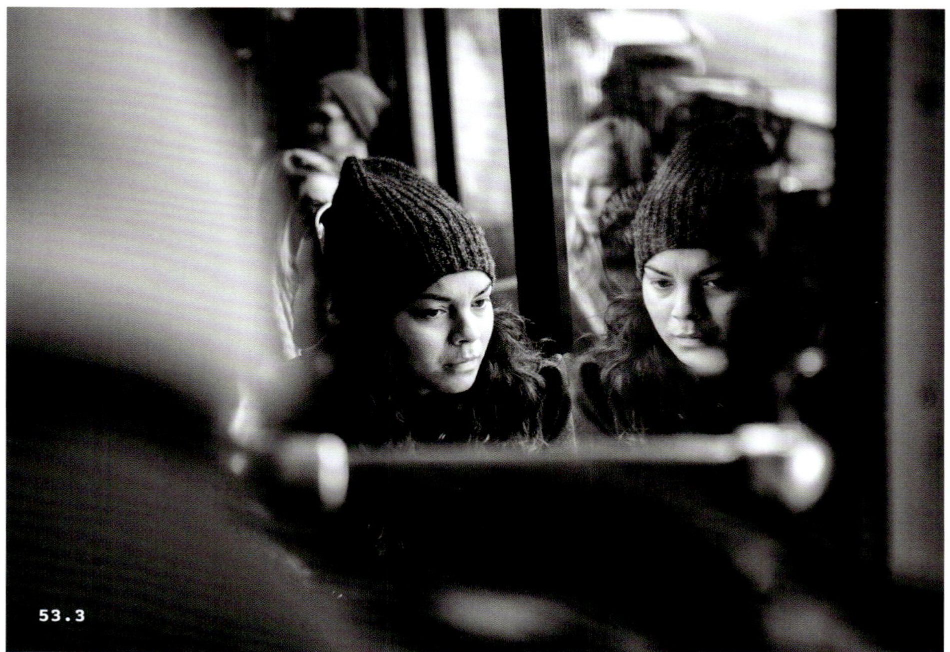

Spend time getting to know them, glean information about them, have a genuine conversation. And, when you feel the timing is right and you're both comfortable, ask to make a portrait or to begin your session (**Figure 53.4**). In a documentary sense, this may mean "waiting" five minutes. It might mean going several days without making a shot. In more set up situations, such as senior portraits, don't rush your subject while they are getting ready, making a clothing change, and the like. Patience with your subject—who is more than likely a little nervous and anxious about how well the images will turn out—pays dividends mere minutes later when you are both in a mental frame of mind to make great shots.

3 **Listen.** This goes hand-in-hand with being quiet and patient. Although your images will always contain your creative DNA, images made with story in mind are largely, if not completely, about the person you are photographing. Being a good listener—not simply someone that just hears or acts like they are listening—means being open to your subject's story. Listening is an active process, and it can lead to the creative introduction of certain elements in an image. For street and documentary purposes, being an active listener can also open up opportunities for portraits of strangers. Otherwise known as eavesdropping, focusing in on a conversation between two people can be used as a way to introduce yourself: "Excuse me, but I couldn't help overhearing that…" It also indicates that you have a genuine interest in your subject. For example, on an assignment in which I

have to photograph the homeless population (**Figure 53.5**), I often spend time listening to someone's story before asking them if it is alright to take their portrait.

4 **Be nice.** Want to know the secret to learning someone's story so you can make a more narrative-filled shot of them? Be nice to them. Indicate that you are truly interested in them, that you are not going to just "take" their picture, but rather "make" an image after learning a bit about them. This applies greatly to strangers, but it's just as important for photographing familiar subjects. A handshake, a smile, and not making it about the image, but rather your subject's story, conveys a great deal of respect and sincerity. Just like with building rapport, the idea here is to gain as much trust as you can from your subject in an effort to make the most informed images of him. People notice and appreciate this level of respect, and I'd rather be considered a nice photographer who was able to learn more about my subject than one that "stole" a portrait from someone on the street. This doesn't mean you have to take each of your subjects (especially for street photographers) out to coffee and ask them 20 questions about their lives, but it does mean you are conveying to them those characteristics we've already outlined thoroughly in this chapter. As a result, your subject will be more open to your image making and to sharing their story with you. Every one of us knows how to be nice and respectful, and believe me when I say everyone of your subjects knows how it feels when someone is the opposite. Make sure you don't fall into this latter camp.

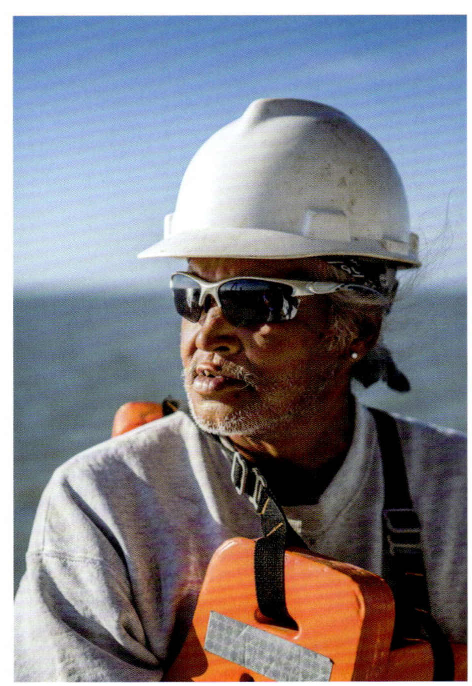

53.4 After visiting with this barge worker for a couple minutes about his travels, he became more focused on the activities at the front of the vessel. He was comfortable enough with me at that time to allow me a more unaffected portrait than if I had just walked up to him and took his picture.
ISO 100; 1/4000 sec.; f/2.8; 70mm

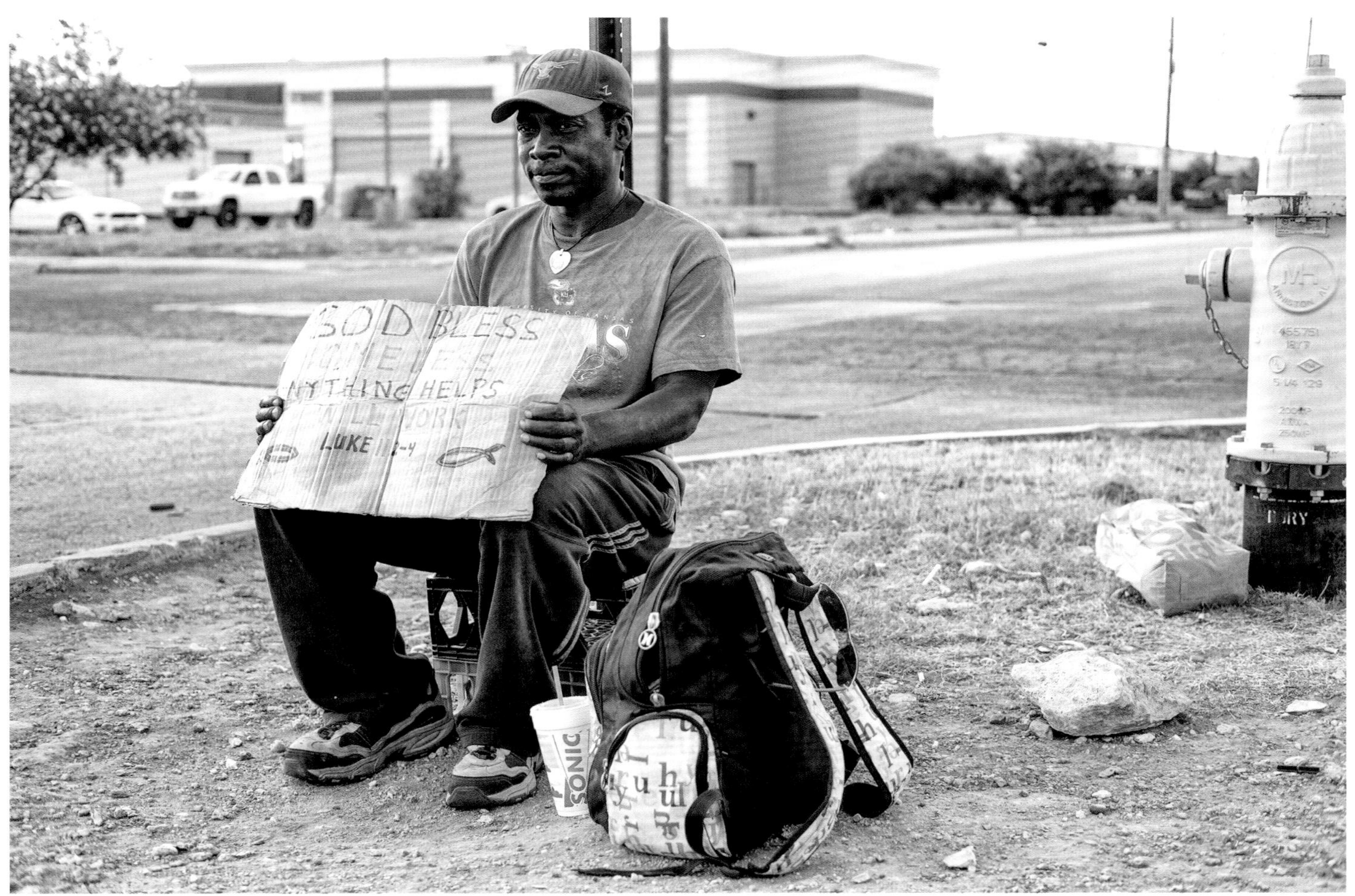

53.5 While on assignment photographing the local oil economy of an oil boom/ bust town, I photographed Mr. Roper. However, I spent much more time listening to him and his story. At a point near the end of our conversation, I asked him if it would be OK for me to make a couple portraits. He readily granted my request. It pays off to use your ears more than your mouth.
ISO 200; 1/550 sec.; f/2.8; 35mm

SHOOTING FOR A story often requires doing some research, be it a conversation, a glance at an online biography of your subject, or an editor telling you a bit about where your subject is located. No matter how you do your research, getting to know your subject is fairly essential to the story-filled portrait process. Another tool that will help you have an efficient, yet creative, portrait session is a shot list.

A shot list is simply a list of images you foresee shooting based on your research and style. It can be jotted down on a small notepad, written up on your phone or tablet, or written alongside your pages of research notes. No matter what it looks like, a shot list is a great way to get ideas out of your head and into some tangible form.

Shot lists are great ways to organize portrait shoots. If you know much about your subject, you may develop a fairly thorough shot list that details where the subject will be placed and in what position, the perspective you want to shoot him from, and possibly even the time of day you'd like to shoot. Other lists may simply be a grocery list of shots, reminding you that you need to get a full-body shot, a headshot, and a shot of your subject with her dog. Either way, you are organizing your thoughts prior to the shoot, which ultimately increases your preparedness for it, as well as the indication of said preparedness to your subject. Shot lists also give your shoots direction. With a list in tow or in your mind, you'll spend less time looking for a new location or lighting scheme while with your subject. Instead, you have a fairly good idea of what you want to achieve, which will move the shoot along efficiently. Lists are also great for communicating with your subjects. It allows you a way to convey to them the direction you've set for the shoot, and give them an idea of what you intend to create. It provides structure to their experience, which boosts confidence and helps them mentally prepare for and proceed through the shoot.

It's very important, though, to keep in mind that a shot list is a skeleton for the shoot. It should always serve as a foundation for a portrait shoot, but it should not in most cases be the only thing moving you from shot to shot. A shot list can often blind you to potential shots not on the list. Some photographers are destination-oriented, hitting the points laid out on a map, but not spending any time looking out the window for other possibilities to explore. A shot list can be a helpful structure, but it's extremely important (especially if you have the time) to remain flexible and observant of other shots available along the way. The last thing you want to do is get home, download your images, start your edit, and realize you missed some great opportunities for more portraits of your subject.

YEP, THAT'S RIGHT. Break. The. Rules.

All of the tips and techniques highlighted up to this point—focusing on the eyes, following the rule of thirds, having the subject face the camera, etc.—are rules that can be broken. While we recognize the benefits these "rules" have in making and viewing images, they can get in the way. What if the most important component of your portrait composition is, say, the feet? Do you focus on them instead of the eyes (**Figure 55.1**)? Do you even include the eyes? Is that even a portrait? Does it matter? Make the shot because you want to, or because you believe it will be a significant representation of your subject. If you want completely undivided attention directed toward your subject, place them in the middle. Use elements around them to further direct the eye toward the middle of the frame. If you want to highlight a quirky personality, follow your subject's lead—cover up their face (**Figure 55.2**). Perhaps having them face away from the camera is a great way to exhibit something eclectic about them (**Figure 55.3**). Ultimately, the point is to tell a visual story, and breaking these rules we've been conditioned to use is sometimes a nice jolt to our creative process. It also gives the viewer a better understanding of your subject.

The rules, however, are still worth "following" and using as constructive guidelines within which our creativity can flourish. So, although breaking the rules can be a nice change-up, it might not be beneficial on a frequent basis. Find the appropriate moments, composition, or lighting to make a break really work for you. Doing so will make the times in which breaking photographic rules is creative and narratively necessary.

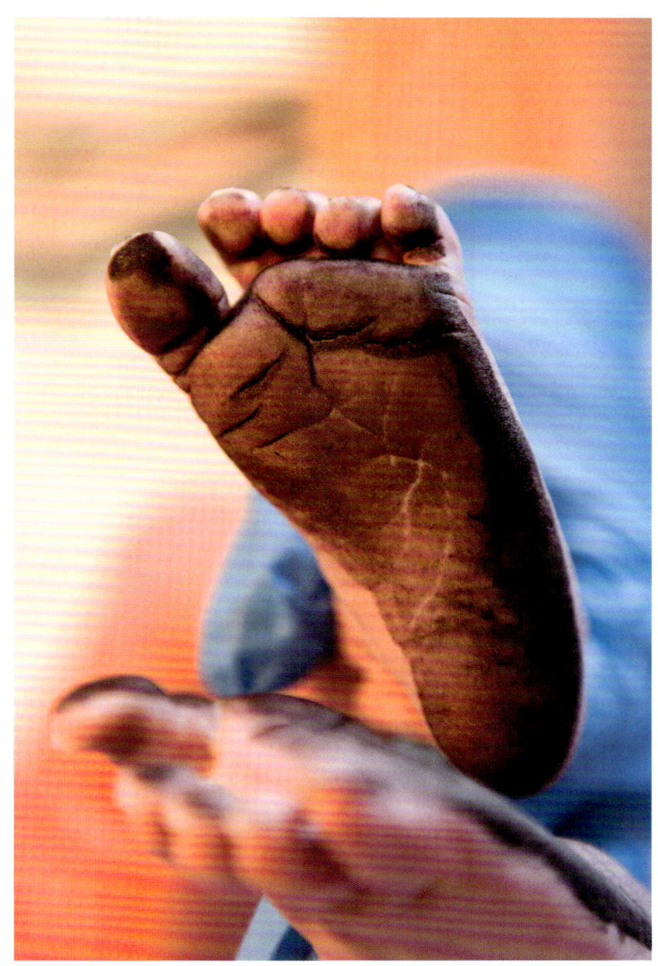

55.1 One of my favorite portraits of my youngest daughter is of her tiny feet after her footprint was taken, minutes after she was born.
ISO 1600; 1/100 sec.; f/2.8; 70mm

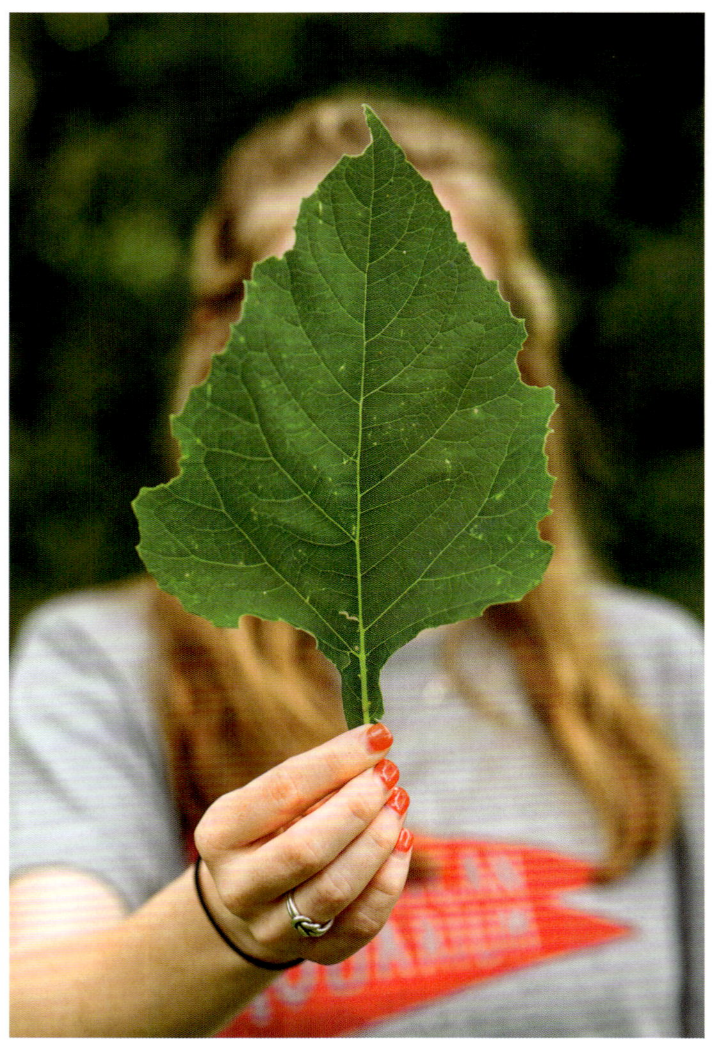

55.2 Placing the leaf in front of the subject's face was all her idea. Sometimes the face isn't the strongest indicator of a personality; sometimes it's what serves in its place.
ISO 200; 1/80 sec.; f/3.5; 85mm

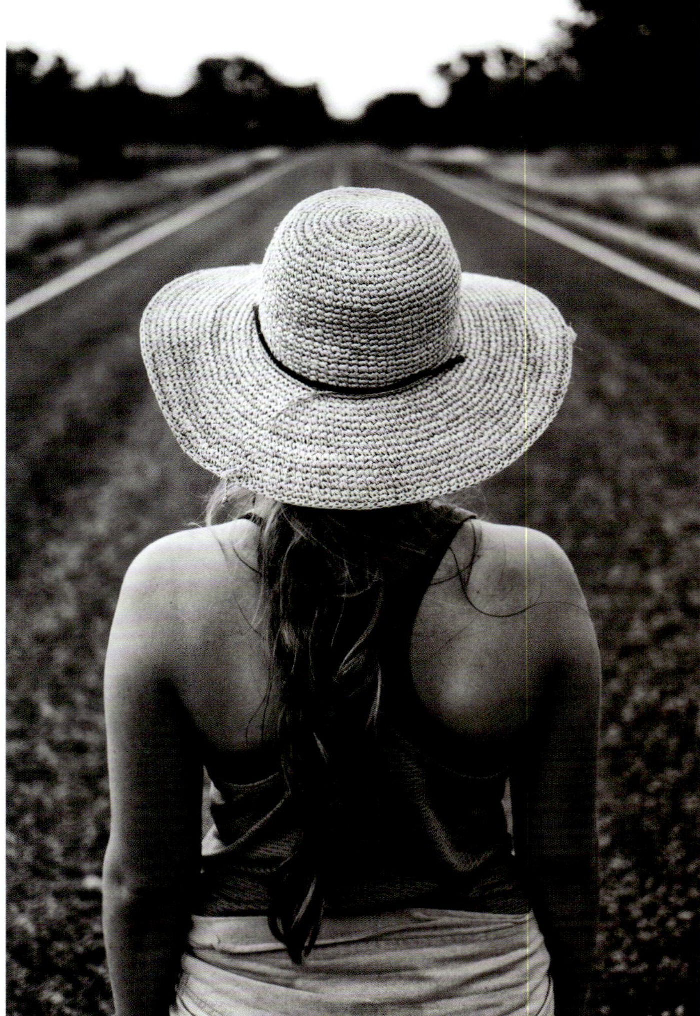

55.3 Anna Claire is one of the most focused and driven young adults I know, with great aspirations for mission work and travel. Having her face away and down the road seemed appropriate for a couple portraits, indicating her curiosity and intention to move forward in life.
ISO 200; 1/120 sec.; f/2; 35mm

Content Over Technique

When we get down to it, the content of an image ultimately trumps all of the visible technique. Non-photographers (which happen to comprise the majority of people taking pictures in the world) often don't know, and frankly, probably don't consider how a great-looking portrait is made. They are drawn to the image because of that special something that we, as photographers, must capture and exhibit. Sometimes the best thing to do is to let our technique take a backseat to our subject.

The best shot in a session may be an accidental image, a candid laugh, or a deeply interesting facial expression. Perhaps the best image is slightly out of focus, yet captures something so unique in the subject's face that it could never be naturally re-created. It never ceases to amaze me when I show clients images, and they often gravitate to images that I would not necessarily choose as a favorite. They are usually focused on content, how they or someone in the image looks, and what they are doing in the shot instead of in how difficult it was to create a particular portrait.

This, however, is no excuse to slack on your technical skills and portrait techniques. Rather, it is a directive to strengthen your skills in order to always be prepared to make an image that really capitalizes on the content (**Figure 55.4**). Again, let the technique go quiet. It's still there, helping "make" the image.

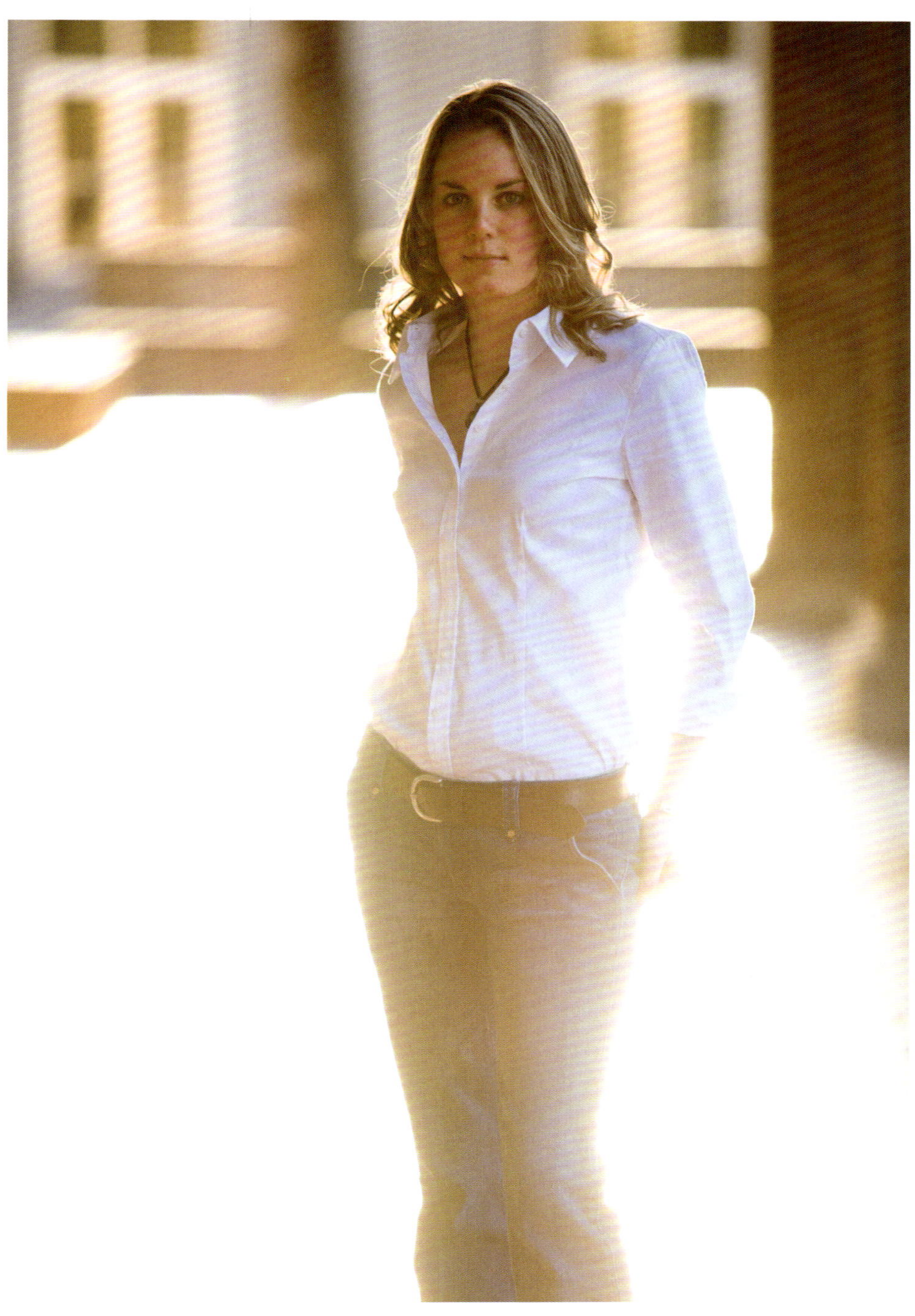

55.4 Upon reviewing the first image leading up to this portrait, I worried about the overexposure and wrap of light around the subject's body. However, I was drawn to the light and how she held herself in that location. In the end, the technical "flaws" of the image only heightened the significance of the subject.
ISO 100; 1/200 sec.; f/2.8; 200mm

8

POST-PRODUCTION

What do you do after you finish a shoot? Immediately upload the images to a gallery so your subject or client can see and download them? If you're anything like other portrait photographers, finishing a shoot is not the final step in your workflow. There is a certain level of post-production work that needs to take place.

IF THERE IS one genre of photography that sees more post-processing than any other, it is definitely portraiture. I dare say hundreds of books have been written on the subject over the years, and thousands of instructional videos and blog articles have been posted on the various techniques that comprise the vast world of post-processing portraits. This chapter cannot begin to approach the depth in which entire volumes reach on specific techniques, such as portrait re-touching (a topic that this chapter does not highlight). However, it can provide a foundational frame of thought when it comes to post-processing your portraits.

This chapter approaches post-processing from experience and capability, and it hopefully grounds your future education of the topic. You'll see where I mention using Adobe Lightroom in parts of the chapter, but it is not to indicate how to push around the settings, but instead to give you practical examples of certain techniques or approaches in action. There are many software applications out there that help you digitally work up a portrait—Adobe Lightroom and Photoshop just happen to be the most popular, and the industry standards.

Quickly, before moving on from this introduction, I want to leave you with one very important component to your entire photography workflow: stay organized. Know where your images are at all times and become familiar with exactly how your workflow software manages your images. Asset management is a vital part of your work as a portrait photographer, and it's extremely important during the post-production phase. The software does not necessarily make staying organized difficult. Organization is a complete mindset, and it behooves you to embrace it when it comes to your photographs. Keep this keystone of your workflow in mind, and you'll create and work within a great digital workflow experience!

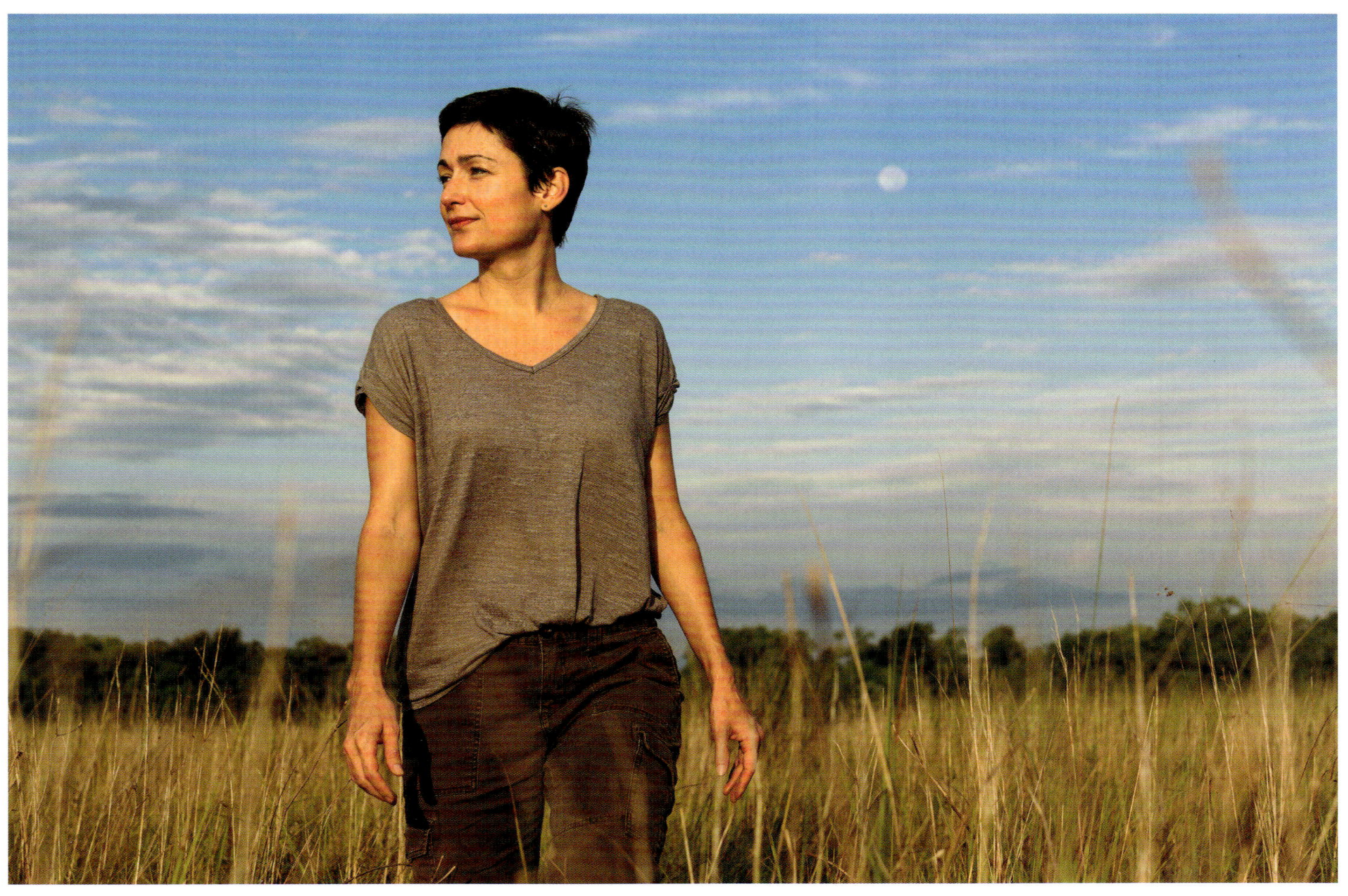

Being as prepared and organized with your shoots before post-processing is the best approach. A prior creative meeting with the client, model prep, and an organized workflow are necessary to keep the touch-up work and turnaround time at a minimum.

IN THE SECOND chapter, I mentioned how shooting in the RAW file format affords you great control over adjusting your image's white balance in post. Indeed, one of the strongest reasons to shoot in RAW is to quickly and effectively adjust white balance, but the RAW format has many more advantages. There's no doubt that if you've been behind a camera any amount of time, you've heard other portrait photographers mention shooting only in RAW. They do so for good reason:

1 **Hold on to the details.** The RAW file format lets you capture all of the detail the digital sensor is capable of, so when you begin your post-processing workflow, you are always working with the complete capabilities of the camera. The idea is that you shoot in RAW to "cook" later in post. Although there is certainly nothing wrong with shooting in high-resolution JPEG file format, it's good to know that when doing so, the camera does the "cooking" for you and compresses the RAW file into the JPEG format. In essence, the camera keeps what is necessary (per the manufacturer's specifications) and trashes the rest of the information captured by the sensor. This can sometimes result in throwing away certain digital values that can be useful later in post, and it certainly limits how much you can push the JPEG file later in post. If you want as much control as possible over your portrait files, it's best to shoot in RAW (**Figure 56.1** and **Figure 56.2**).

2 **A world of interpretation.** Since the RAW file contains all of the data the sensor is capable of capturing, you are able to manipulate a great deal of the portrait file in post-processing. Want to adjust the exposure? Contrast? Cleanly open up the shadows a bit? Or, how about taming those extremely bright and distracting highlights? The RAW file allows you to easily make these adjustments, as well as a host of others (**Figure 56.3** and **Figure 56.4**). Honestly, the extent to which you can make post-processing adjustments is based on the RAW processing engine you are using (such as Adobe Camera Raw, which is found in Adobe Lightroom, Bridge, and Photoshop).

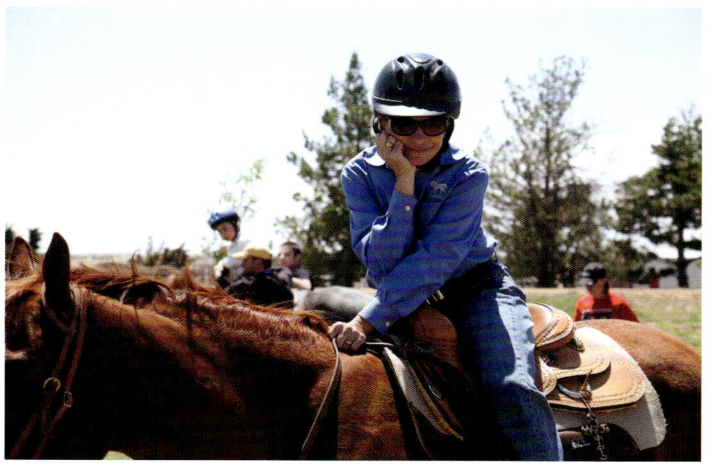

56.1 The shot straight out of the camera features Dr. Brady during a hippotherapy class with a distractingly bright sky.

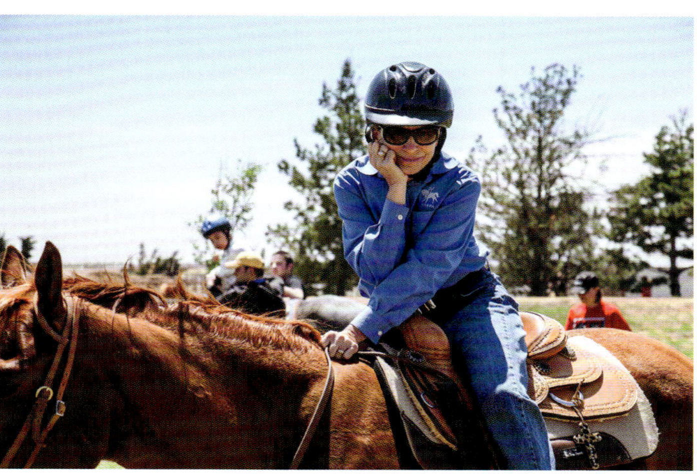

56.2 Since the portrait was shot in RAW, I was able to tone the sky down and open up the shadows on Dr. Brady with much more tolerance than a JPEG would have allowed.

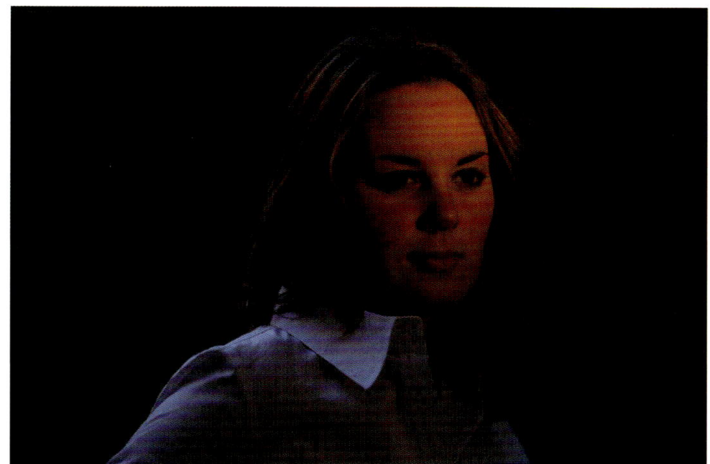

56.3 The original portrait took advantage of some interesting light, but I underexposed it quite a bit and the background was just bright enough to be a distraction.

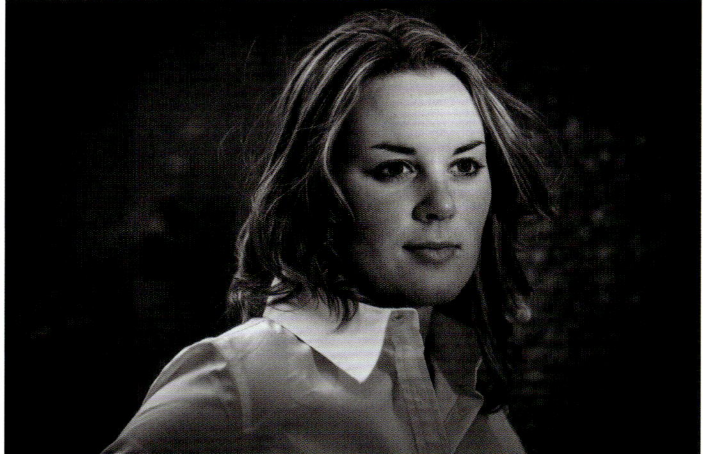

56.4 Shooting in RAW opens up a great more interpretive power. Instead of leaving the image in color, I chose to make it a black and white, enabling the true evocative mood of the light. Likewise, I opened up the shadows a bit more, which allowed for the background to play a larger role in the frame.

You can certainly make many of the interpretive adjustments to JPEG files, but the JPEG file is not configured to handle this extra "cooking" as easily (**Figure 56.5** and **Figure 56.6**). The structural integrity of the JPEG file will begin to fall apart more quickly and the result is more visually apparent if you push the JPEG manipulations too far (which isn't very far at all). Likewise, some of the adjustments that you can make to RAW files even look functionally different than the same adjustment to JPEGs. Again, in the end, the RAW file format is the most functionally and creatively interpretive file format, and when making adjustments to portraits means working in post to make the subject appear their best or most accurate, it's the file format I encourage you to use.

3 **Non-destructive workflow.** Quite possibly the most important reason to shoot in RAW is the fact that it is the foundation for establishing a non-destructive digital workflow. This means that your original file will never be compromised. Aside from completely deleting them from your memory card and/or your hard drive, the RAW file cannot technically be tampered with. Your workflow software, instead, creates a file to which any manipulations to the image made are written to an adjacent file, not directly to the RAW file. Again, with the advancements in software technology, JPEGs can also be used in non-destructive workflows, but it may suffer further compression depending on how you export the files from your applications. The RAW file, however, is an uncompressed image file to begin with and undergoes compression for the first time when it is finally exported into a completely different file format, leaving the original file untouched on your hard drive.

If there's a running theme among all of the preceding reasons to shoot in RAW, it is *control*. Take as much control over your workflow as possible. Although JPEGs make shooting a finished product an efficient workflow, the RAW file gives you complete control over how the image is processed. One downside to shooting in RAW is that it comes with a bit of a learning curve (a curve that may be steep depending on your workflow software) (**Figure 56.7**), and it is a slightly more inefficient file format than the JPEG (you have to actually process out a RAW file to a globally usable file format—think JPEG and TIFF—while a JPEG is technically ready to go). Did I mention it's a much larger file, placing more demand on storage space?

Still, the amount of file information and the amount of control you gain when shooting in RAW far outweighs shooting in and working completely with JPEGs.

Lastly, the portrait you want to achieve is more easily actualized when shooting in RAW. Many photographers begin a shoot with an idea of what the finished portraits will look like after post. JPEGs are limited in how far they will take you toward making your visualization a final product in post-processing. However, the RAW format, for those reasons listed above, allows you to shoot and process for as much of your vision as technically possible.

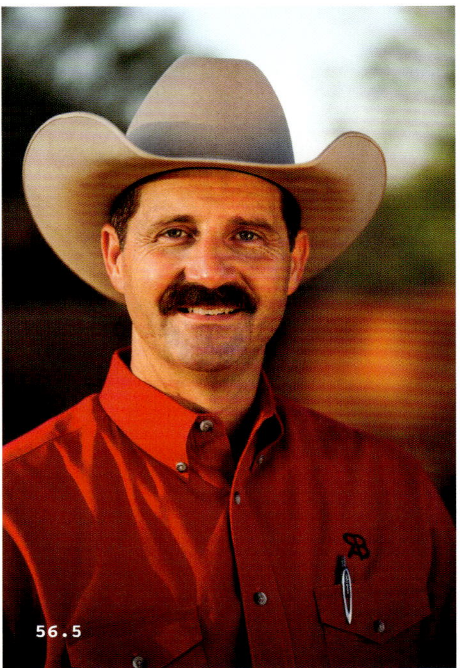

56.5

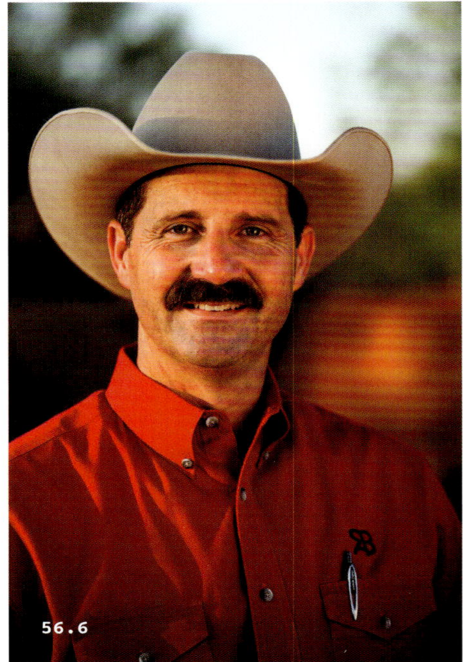

56.6

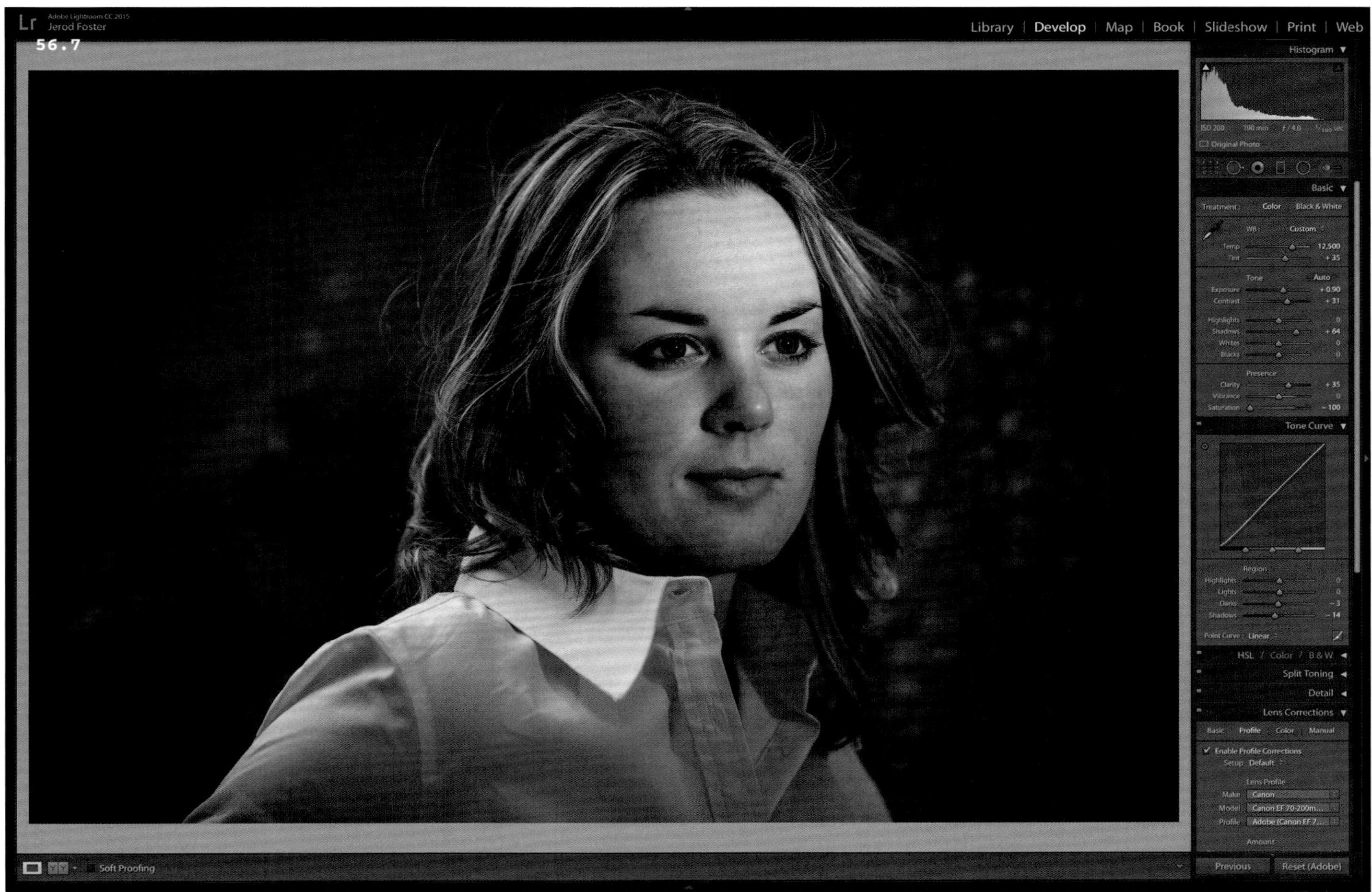

56.7

56.5 This cowboy's portrait has been processed from a RAW file with only minor adjustments to contrast.

56.6 The JPEG version of this portrait, compared to the one worked up from a RAW, does not handle the same adjustments as cleanly. The colors are a bit more saturated, and the shadows are not as open. Furthermore, a JPEG like this would be more difficult to adjust given the relatively low information it contains compared to the RAW image.

56.7 Most RAW image processors, like the one from Adobe Lightroom's Develop module, come with a bit of a break-in period in which the photographer must become acquainted with its tools. However, the results and workflow flexibility they afford you in the short and long term are big payoffs for the investment.

AT THIS POINT, you've seen two discussions about color (given that you've read the book from start to finish). The first appeared in the second chapter regarding white balance, and the second was the full chapter that solely focused on color as a portrait aesthetic. This third iteration of the concept focuses on how to best handle color in post-processing your portraits. More specifically, the following is a set of suggestions on making sure color is as accurate or creative as you need it to be while not overdoing it.

Technically speaking, the first manipulation of color begins with the white balance setting you establish before you push the shutter button. Per the second chapter suggestion, it's to your advantage to try to nail your white balance as close as possible with the camera to keep you from having to adjust later. However, there are times when the white balance we thought was great for the portrait ends up looking off or a bit uninspiring. Luckily, most, if not all, post-processing and workflow software applications provide you a way of adjusting your white balance. Some, like Adobe's Lightroom, which contains their industry-standard RAW processing engine, allow you to adjust it several ways. These include the ability to use the software's white balance or color temperature presets (which are actually fairly good) (**Figure 57.1**), manipulating the manual color temperature controls or sliders (**Figure 57.2**), and using a device such as an "eye dropper" to select a color in the frame on which to establish a more accurate white balance. Presets are fairly straight forward and toggling through them is a great way to become acquainted with their "looks." I suggest using the manual controls when you don't have to make wide sweeping changes to your portrait's white balance, but rather when minor adjustments need to be made. Finally, the eye dropper tool (or whichever tool your own software lets you use to target a specific area of the image for white balancing purposes) comes in very handy when you can readily identify a neutral area of the frame in which the red, green, and blue (RGB) values are all very similar (**Figure 57.3**). This usually exists in a neutral gray area of the image, and once selected with the tool, your image should adjust to a fairly accurate white balance (**Figure 57.4** and **Figure 57.5**). From there, you can adjust with the manual controls where needed. Bear in mind, once again, that manipulating white balance in post is much more feasible when working with RAW files as opposed to JPEGs. The nice thing about the digital workflow is that you can see your color manipulations or corrections take place in real time in front of your eyes. However, this can be somewhat problematic when it comes to seeing consistent and accurate colors to begin with. Although not the first thing many early photographers think about, a calibrated monitor is essential in a well-constructed post-processing workflow. All monitor models are different, and I dare say there is slight variation of color projection within units of the same models. Calibration allows you to more closely obtain accurate color under the lighting conditions surrounding your monitor, as well as gain color consistency for longer periods of time and across multiple monitors. Calibrating your monitor with any number of credible (but not necessarily expensive) calibrating devices, such as the Datacolor Spyder system, will help you realize the benefits of doing so. I don't know many portrait photographers who use uncalibrated monitors, and the benefits of color consistency and accuracy are worth the investment for managing color in your workflow.

Finally, a piece of advice regarding manipulating color: pushing it until it bleeds is not the best thing you can do for your portraits. Over saturation and over vibrance, while at first may seem like a good idea, usually just makes the image look, well, like the colors are too saturated. Typically, if you are working with great portrait light and a good white balance setting, there isn't much need to "punch" the colors. Over saturating colors often results in severe skin tone issues (**Figure 57.6**), as well as color grievances in other areas of the frame, such as color banding in skies (most likely if you shot in JPEG to start with). There is a point where it is quite obvious that driving the colors hard will look excessive (**Figure 57.7** and **Figure 57.8**). Unless the client or subject wants their images pushed in that direction, it is best avoided (see the next section on how to keep your post-processing simple).

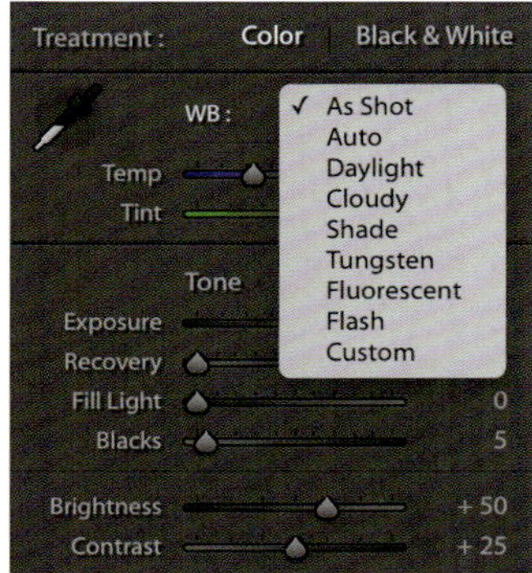

57.1 Adobe Lightroom, like other post-processing workflow applications, offers a collection of white balance presets that can be quite good. Be cautious of selecting the Automatic option if you are batch processing images—each image then has the potential of having a different white balance.

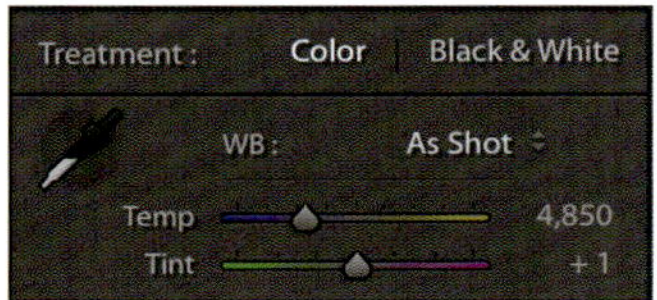

57.2 When a white balance preset won't do, or if it's just a bit off in your portrait, the manual sliders in your software will do a great job of visually getting you close. The color temperature value is especially useful for RAW shooters.

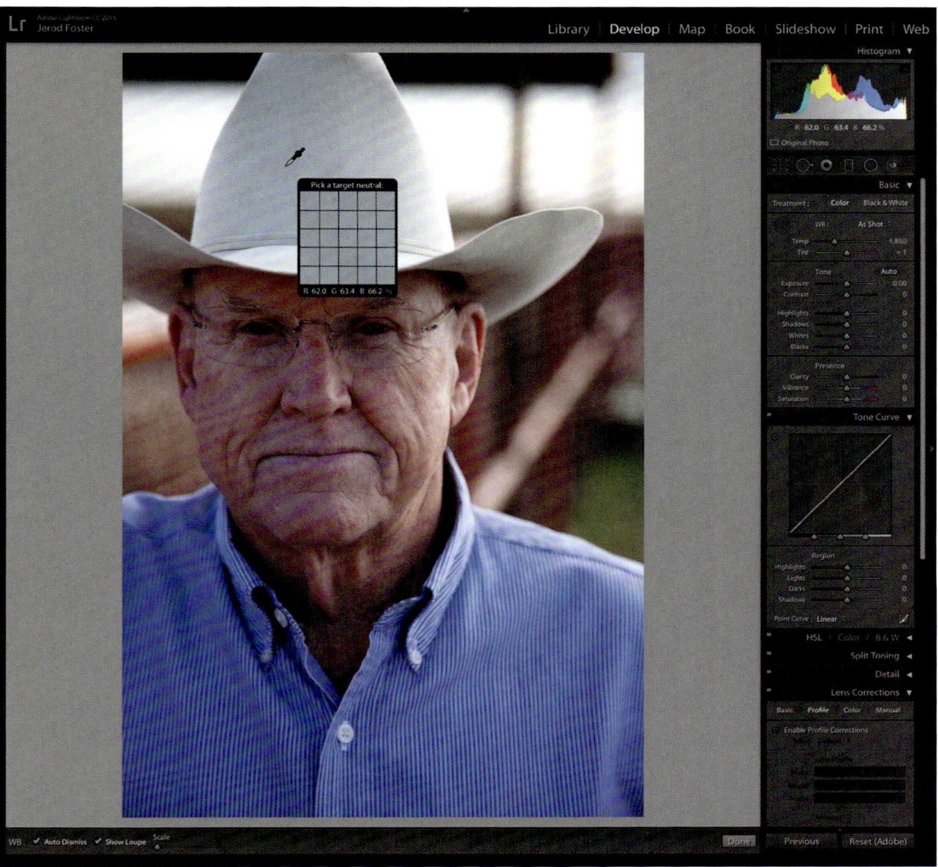

57.3 The most complicated white balance procedure requires that you manually find a neutral tone on which to select an accurate color temperature setting. However, the adjustments are visual, and you'll be able to see if you made an incorrect reference selection.

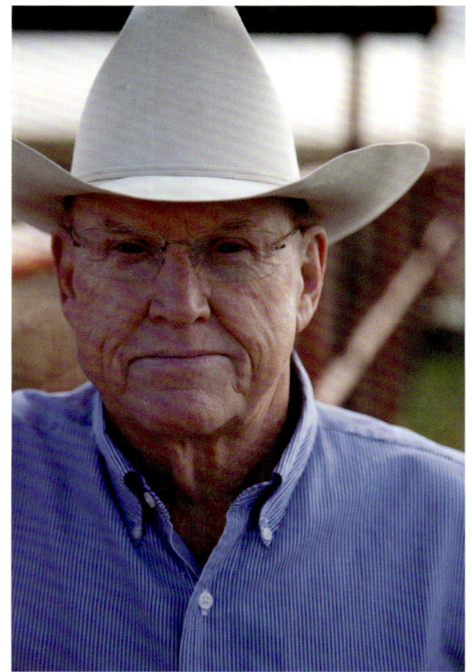

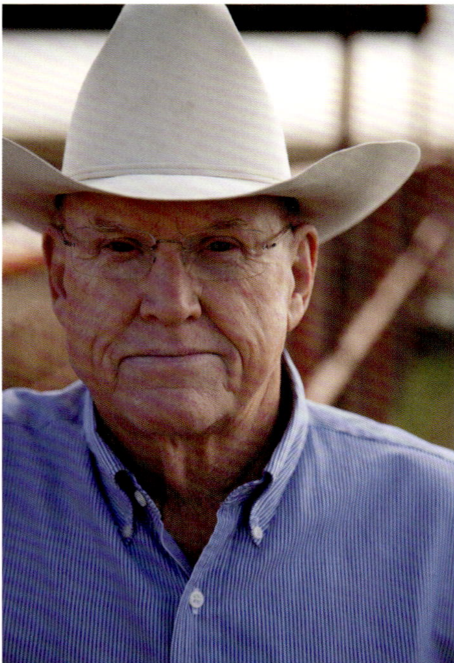

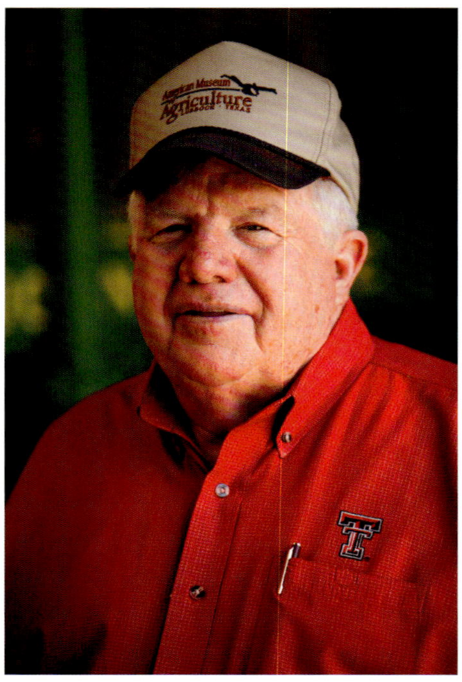

57.4 The image shot was made with the white balance set to Daylight (4,850K), which I thought was a bit too blue and cold for the cowboy's skin tones.

57.5 Using the eyedropper in Adobe Lightroom's white balance tool palette, I was able to make a more accurate white balance setting of 5,450K, which added a more appealing tone to the cowboy's skin without diminishing the blue of his shirt.

57.6 A 10% increase in color saturation in this farmer's portrait might pop his shirt, but it over-articulates the aspects of his face that have had too much exposure to the sun over his career in the field.

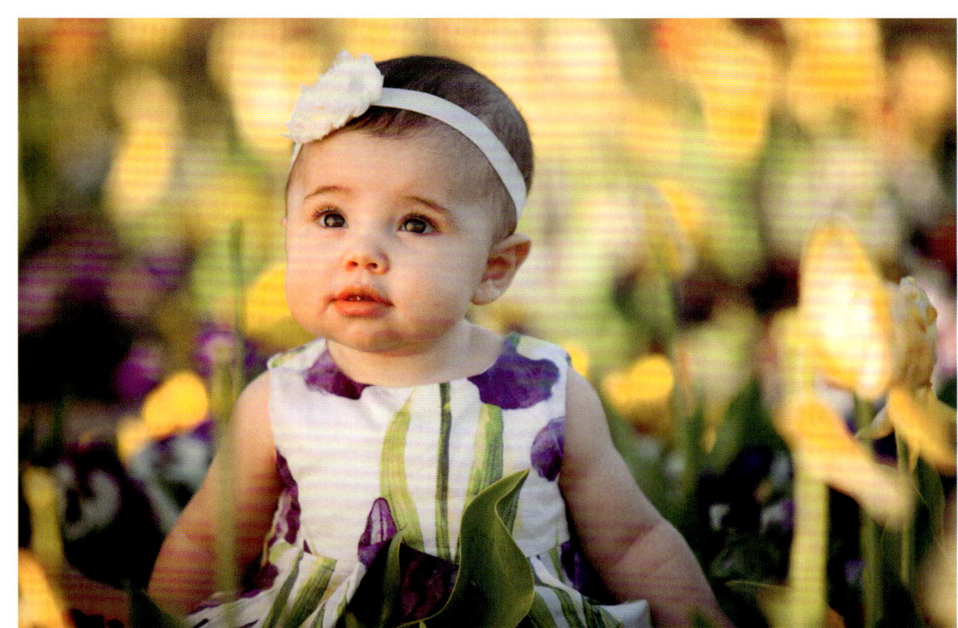

57.7 Great light, a small increase in contrast, and a reduction in clarity is all this portrait needs for the baby to look her best.

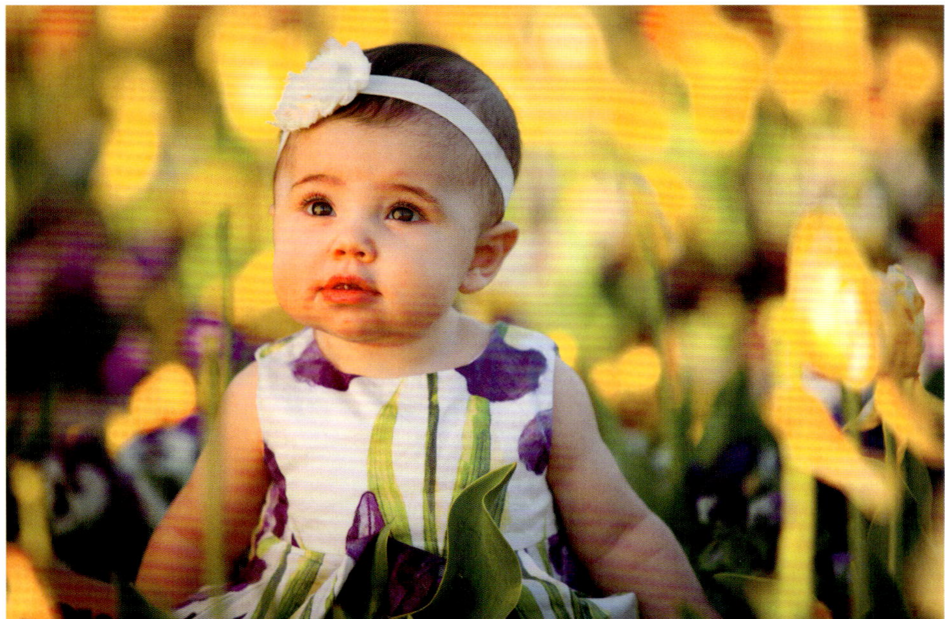

57.8 What might seem like a subtle boost in color saturation is often way too much for many subjects and viewers. Saturation should be one of the last considerations for post-processing portraits.

58. SIMPLICITY, AGAIN

IF THERE'S ONE thing I've learned about my own post-processing and that of many others, it's that the simpler approach is usually the better approach. Post-processing portraits can seem like this large, intimidatingly complex activity (and it can be, sometimes), but many great portrait photographers enjoy shooting much more than they do spending time in front of a computer. Therefore, they work to keep their post-shoot computer work to a minimum.

It is relatively easy to keep foundational post-processing simple. This type of post-processing usually involves correcting exposure, adding or taking away contrast, taming highlights, and opening up shadows. In most post-processing and workflow software applications, these are usually manipulated along a sliding scale (hence the presence of sliders) (**Figure 58.1**). Although you will develop a routine and a familiarity with these controls in time, if you are new to post-processing portraits, it is a good idea to move these sliders 100% in either direction to see the effect their manipulations have on the image. After doing so, you'll more than likely find that backing them down or up to reasonable, middle-of-the-road levels is exactly what you need. For example, on a sliding scale to 100, I don't often increase a portrait's contrast in Adobe Lightroom past +35 (**Figure 58.2** and **Figure 58.3**). Rarely do I ever approach +50, and sometimes all I need is a punch up to +20 (remember to shoot in RAW).

As stated in the previous section, if you are shooting in great portrait light, you shouldn't have to do much with your basic post-processing tools besides correct for minor exposure issues and boost your contrast a bit.

Other processing functions, such as Clarity/Structure, Vibrance, and Saturation, are best handled minimally unless they play a significant role in your portrait style. It is good to become acquainted with them, how they look, and what they do to your image. However, they can get somewhat out of hand quickly, and their effect is often overused. Personally, I steer clear of Clarity in Adobe Lightroom for portraits. It often reduces the image's color, which isn't what I want (**Figure 58.4** and **Figure 58.5**). However, it can be a nice addition to some action-oriented portraits, such as those shot for sports teams, or dramatic black-and-whites (**Figure 58.6**).

A lot of portrait-only photographers even develop automated routines for their computer work in the form of actions and presets they can use for batch processing. However, those that do so usually automate post-processing manipulations that, again, are fairly simple. This discussion does not get into portrait touch-up work, which most definitely can seem intimidating and time consuming. However, again, many photographers that do portraits requiring a fair amount of touch-up work often prepare for making the post-processing simpler

and more efficient.

In the end, you want your images to shine instead of the computer work overtaking your great photography. Post-processing is a viable and often necessary component of portrait photography, but it's largely to our advantage to ensure that it doesn't become a crutch or an overriding factor in the image's ability to tell a story or portray your subject well.

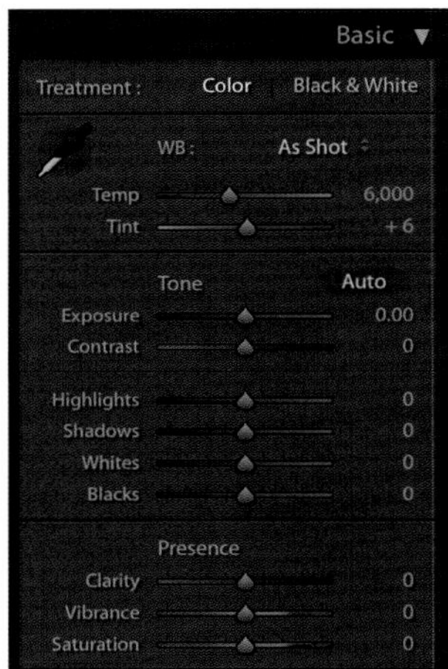

58.1 The basic post-processing tools in all workflow applications are fairly easy to understand and use. In Adobe Lightroom, all you have to do is move the sliders back and forth to get a good visual indication of how the tools will affect your image, both positively and negatively.

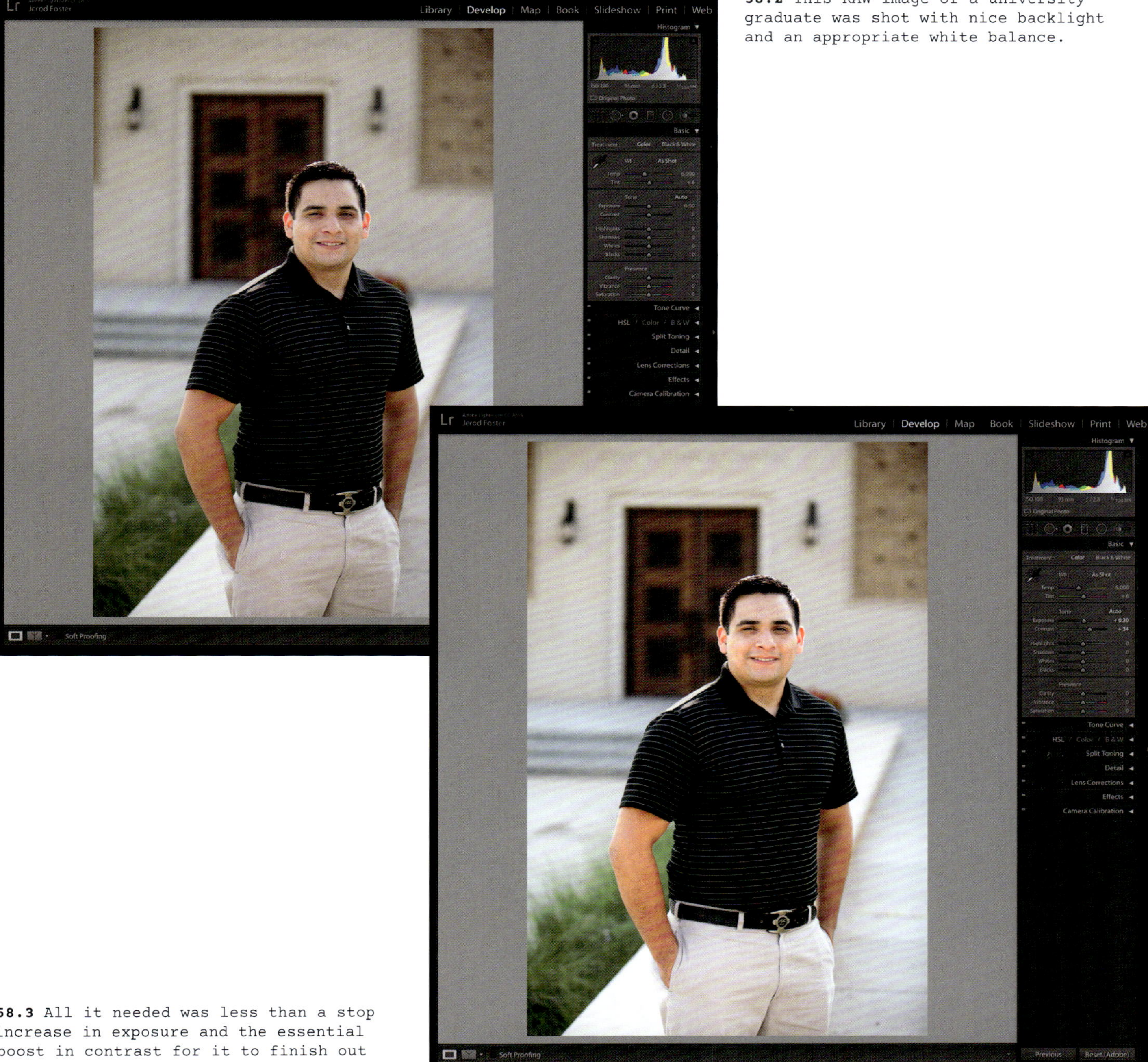

58.2 This RAW image of a university graduate was shot with nice backlight and an appropriate white balance.

58.3 All it needed was less than a stop increase in exposure and the essential boost in contrast for it to finish out well in post. Simplicity at its best.

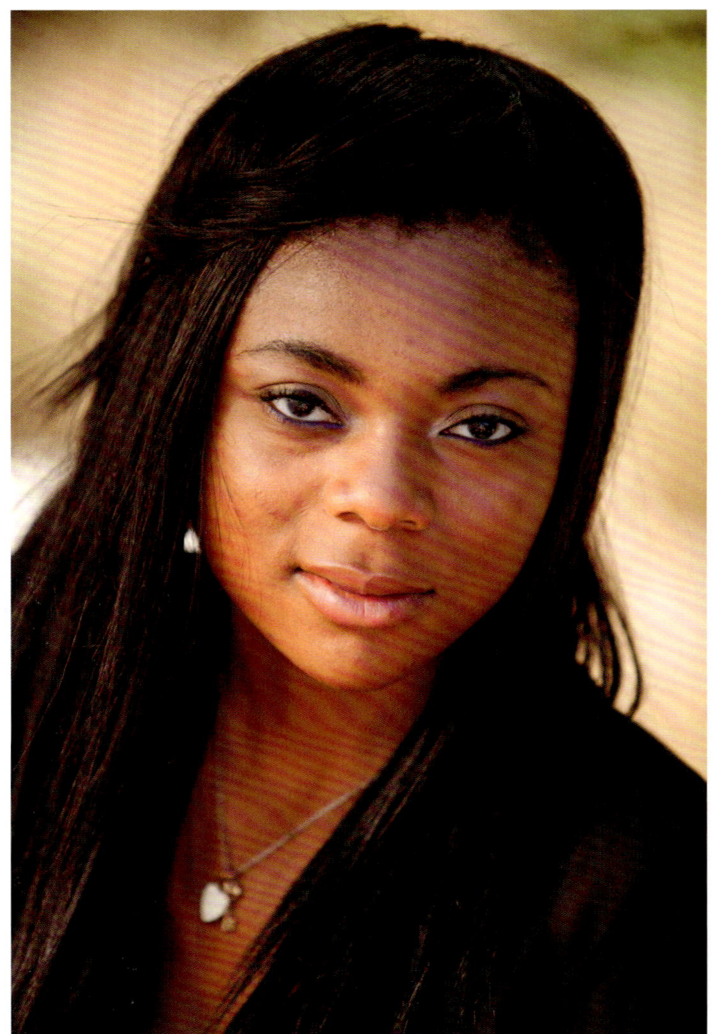

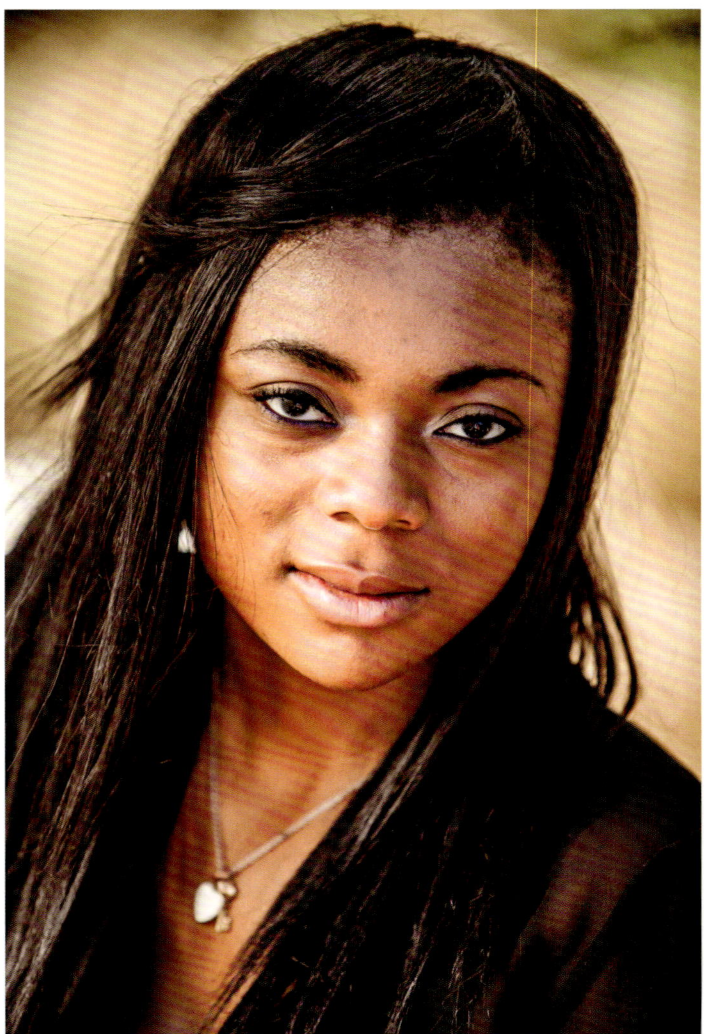

58.4 A cleanly processed headshot for a graduating senior does not require too much dramatic effect to capture her confidence.

58.5 With Adobe Lightroom's Clarity effect increased to 100%, drama is added to the image, but it is out of place for such a portrait. Although in its extreme here, Clarity's visual effect takes place very quickly when added to the post-processing mix.

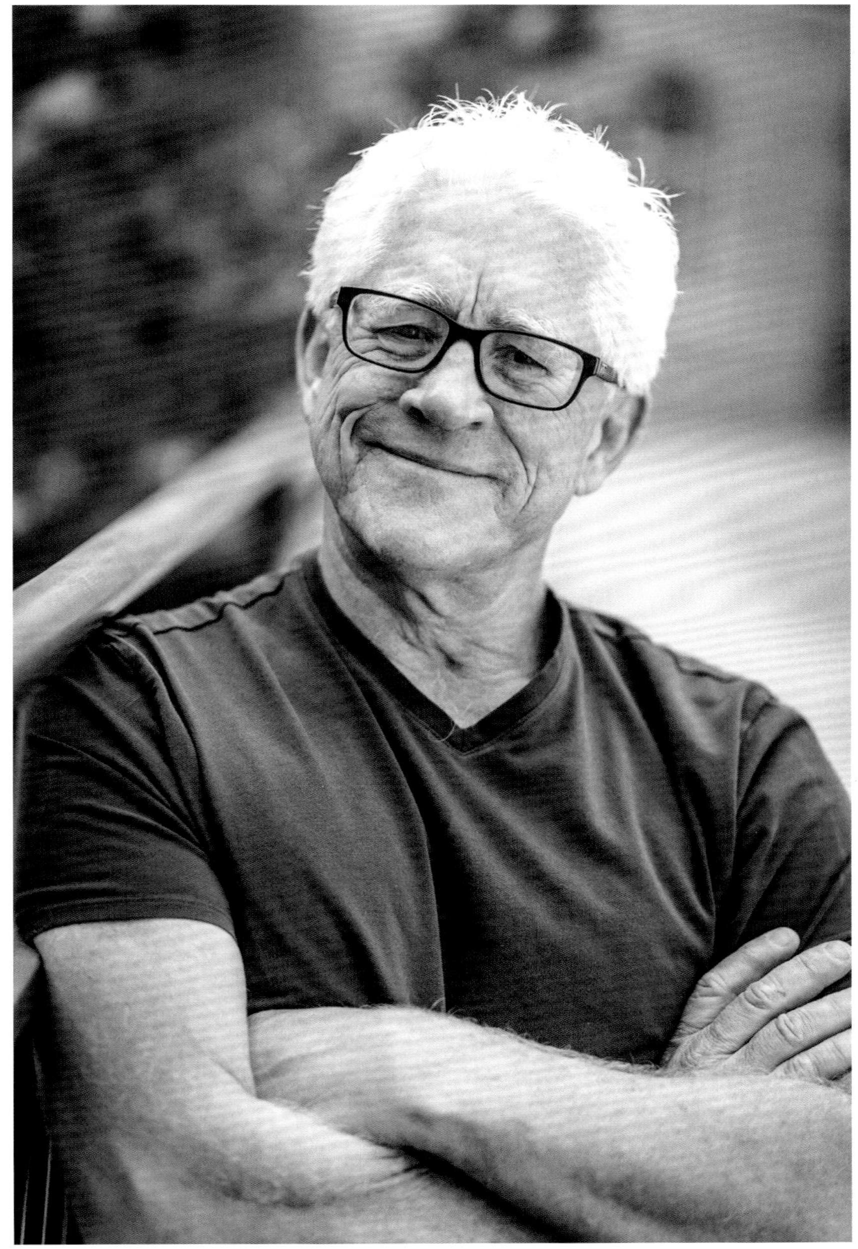

58.6 Portraits processed to black-and-white in Adobe Lightroom often benefit from a slight boost in Clarity, especially for male subjects. Clarity's dramatic effect is subtler after the color conversion.

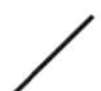

SPEAKING OF SIMPLE, I once watched a very well-known and well-liked photographer present his portrait black-and-white conversion technique to a crowd of about 300 people at a photography conference. Everyone in the audience, who was prepared to learn the "secrets" of Adobe Lightroom's black-and-white functions for the next hour and a half, waited in great anticipation for this artist's technique. When he finally loaded a few color photographs into Lightroom, he went straight toward the Saturation slider and moved it all the way to -100. At that very moment, he was finished. The crowd was flabbergasted. That's it? That's all there was to this photographer's black-and-white workflow? Where was the manipulation of color filters? What about contrast adjustments? What about those tools that translate from the darkroom days for dodge and burn? I saw one person just stand up and walk out, frustrated that she did not "learn" anything. I argue that she learned a great deal, she just wasn't in the frame of mind to receive the lesson that afternoon.

Like the previous section emphasizes, your post-processing techniques don't need to be complicated. The same goes for black-and-white portraits, as proven by the photographer mentioned above. He knew that his workflow only relied on him pushing that one slider all the way to the left in Lightroom. He shot with great light, and that was all he needed for his post-processing.

Black-and-white portraits embody a timeless appeal, and many people (clients, viewers, etc.) prefer black-and-white to color (**Figure 59.1**). Especially for portraits, black-and-white can be very powerful in evoking emotion in the viewer, and there's certainly something to be said for simple, classic styling of an image. And, working up a portrait in black-and-white does not have to be complicated.

I might sound like a broken record in saying this, but the foundation for a good black-and-white digital portrait is the RAW file. A RAW file is always in color, always contains the most information your sensor is capable of capturing, and provides you the most working information for post-processing. Therefore, when you enter into your post-processing workflow, you are not converting, or "cooking," anything but the original. Even if you switch your camera's color mode to black-and-white to visualize how your portrait might look in monochrome, the RAW file will still appear as a color file in applications like Adobe Lightroom. If you are shooting in JPEG, though (and I don't know a single portrait photographer that does), switching your camera to black-and-white just allows the camera to decide how to process the image. You'll certainly have a black-and-white image, but it will be without your post-processing input. Shoot in RAW, shoot in color, and convert to black-and-white in post. This leaves you free to think about the shoot while you are shooting and the post-processing work when the time comes.

Now, when it comes to the actual converting to black-and-white in post, you can make it as simple or as intricate as you would like or need for the portrait. Again, much like portrait touch-up work, converting to and making digital black-and-white portraits can be a rather deep subject, and there are many more book-length resources out there on the topic. However, aside from all of the information available, it's worth focusing on a technique that fits your style, both aesthetically and technically. Personally, I convert most of my portraits to black-and-white much like the photographer mentioned earlier in this chapter, with a simple desaturation of all color in the image (**Figure 59.2** and **Figure 59.3**). Since I use Adobe Lightroom, I'll then adjust my Highlights, Shadows, and White and Blacks much like I would have dodged and burned film images in the darkroom. There are other techniques in software applications like Lightroom that allow you to delve more deeply into black-and-white development (**Figure 59.4**). These provide even greater nuance and sometimes are more suited to landscape and street photographers than traditional portrait shooters. In any case, explore your possibilities and see which fits your stylistic and technical needs.

Recently, I started using the Silver Efex Pro plugin for Adobe Lightroom, provided in the Google Nik Collection of post-processing applications (**Figure 59.5**). This is an extremely powerful black-and-white converter, offering up a variety of not only surprisingly nice presets, but also manual controls that mimic old darkroom and film stock styles. It certainly adds a couple more steps to my own black-and-white converting, but the software is simple and seamless.

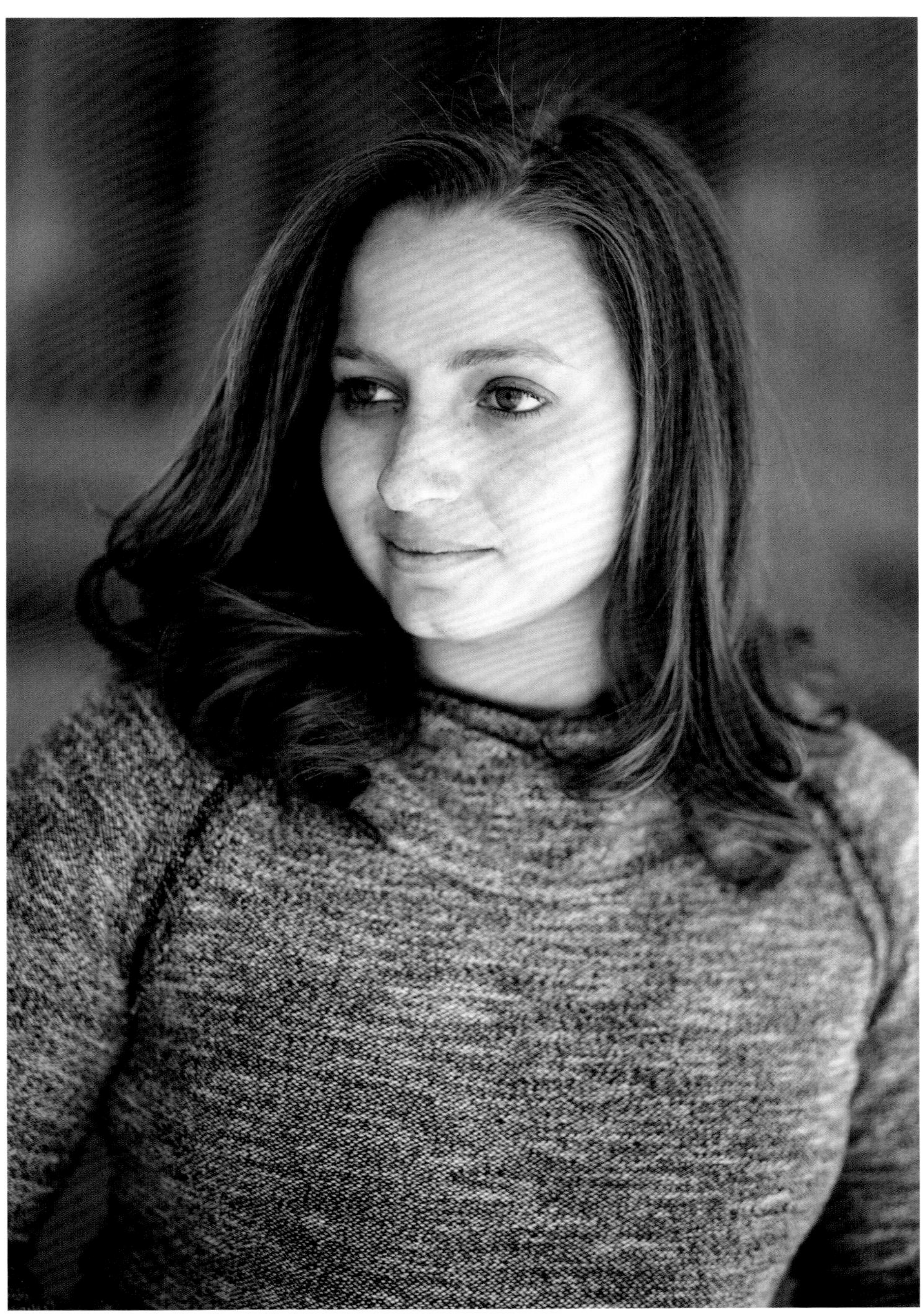

59.1 Many folks, yours truly included, are drawn to black-and-white portraits for their sense of timelessness and depth. Clean, simple post-processing to black-and-white is often the most effective route with your monochromatic portraits.

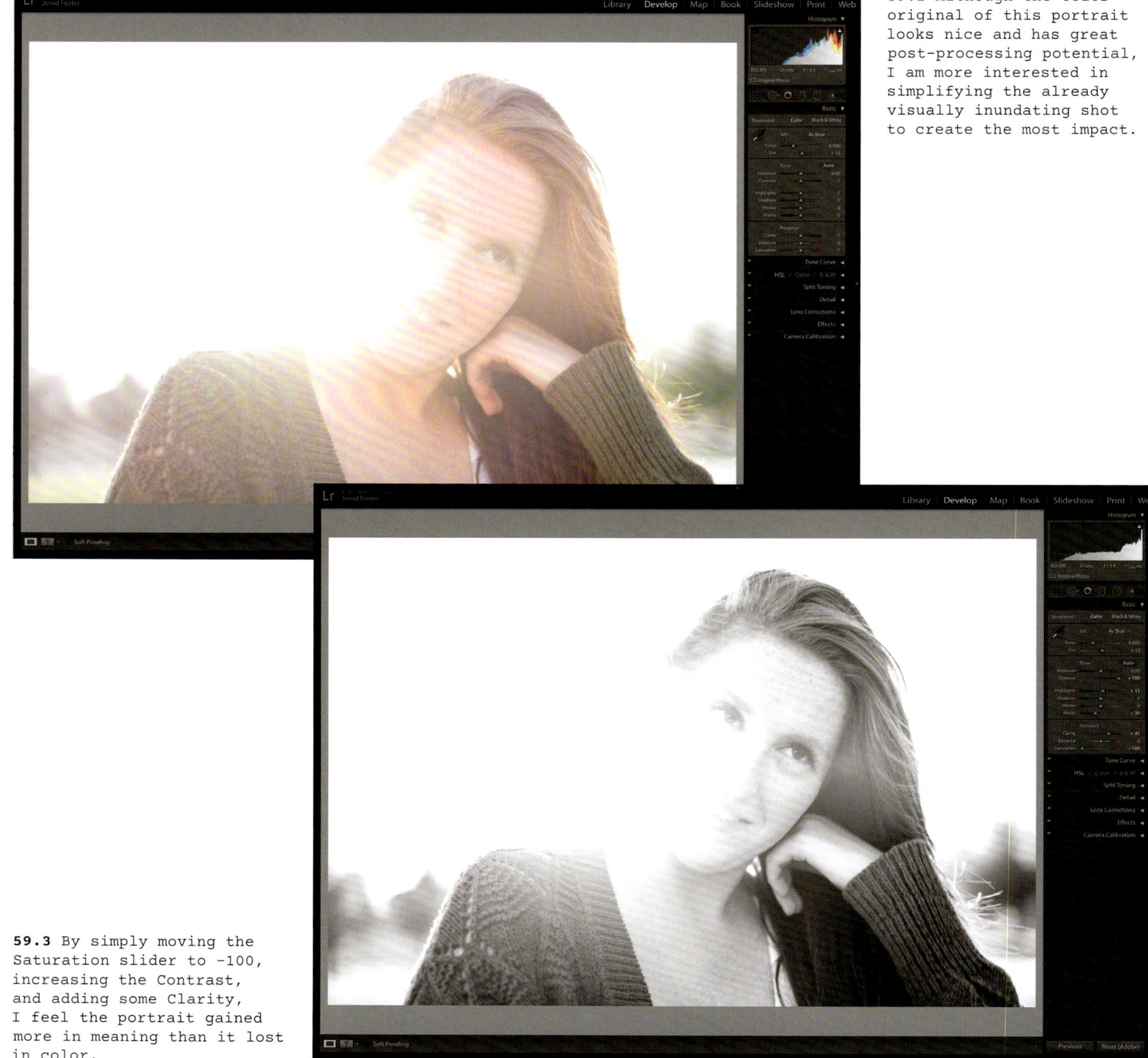

59.2 Although the color original of this portrait looks nice and has great post-processing potential, I am more interested in simplifying the already visually inundating shot to create the most impact.

59.3 By simply moving the Saturation slider to –100, increasing the Contrast, and adding some Clarity, I feel the portrait gained more in meaning than it lost in color.

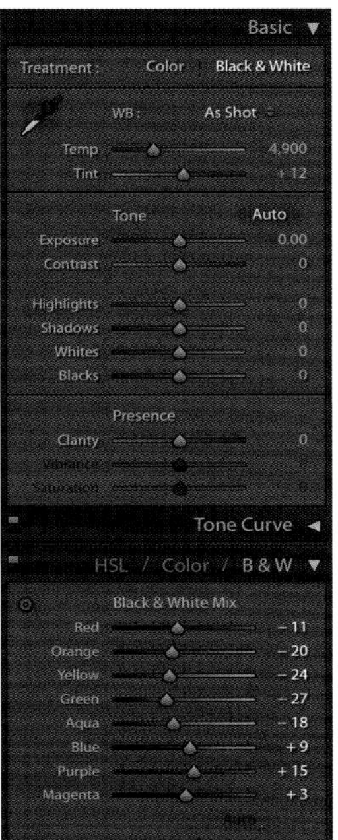

59.4 The Black-and-White (B&W) specific tools in Adobe Lightroom are sensitive to adjustments of the existing colors in the image, functioning the way we used colored filters on lenses when shooting black-and-white film.

Share Your Best Black-and-White Shot!

Once you've captured your best black-and-white shot, share it with the *Enthusiast's Guide* community! Follow @EnthusiastsGuides and post your image to Instagram, using the hashtag *#EGBlackandWhite.* Of course, you can also search that hashtag to be inspired and see other photographers' shots.

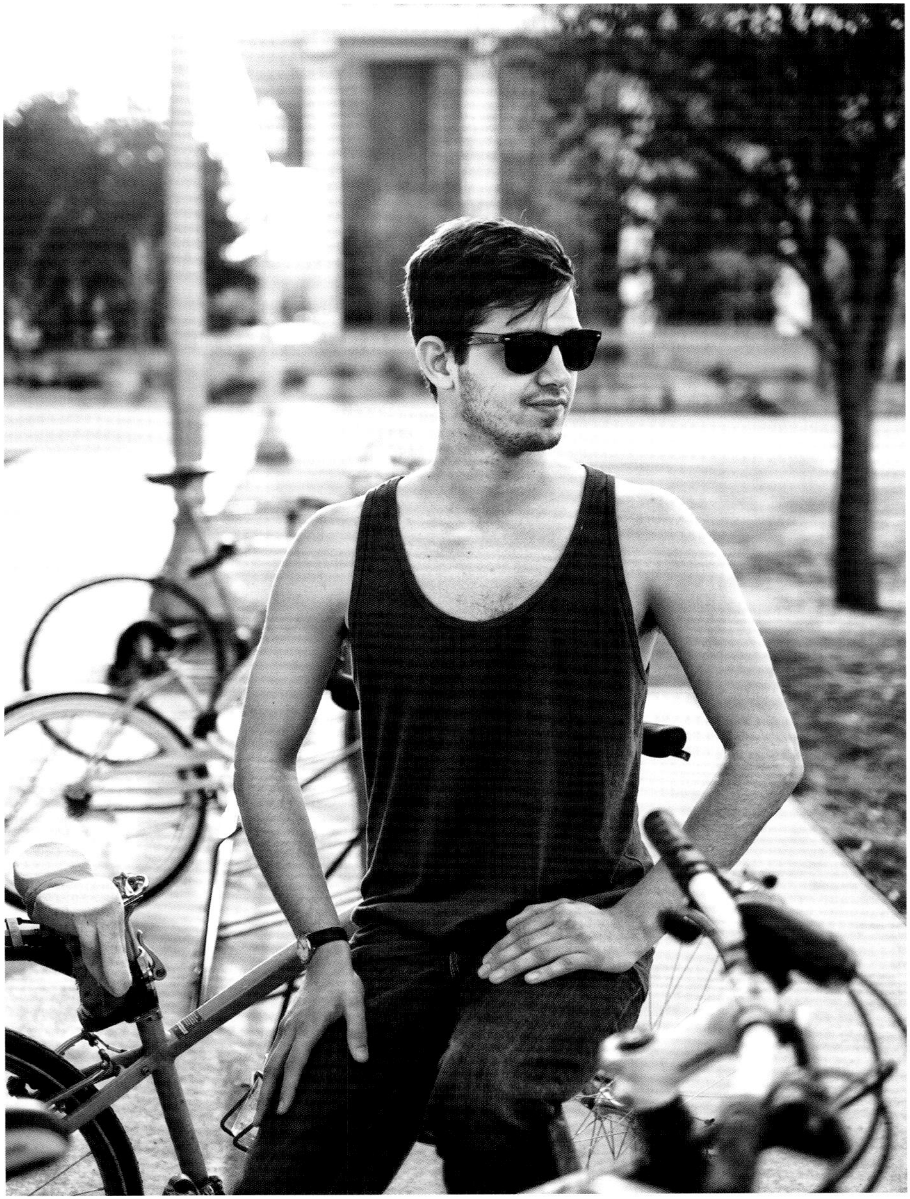

59.5 This portrait was converted from color to black-and-whilte using Nik's most recent version of Silver Efex Pro, a software that offers much more nuanced control on processing black-and-whites than Adobe Lightroom offers. Its especially powerful feature is the film stock simulations of popular black-and-white films. It truly is a digital darkroom.

ONE THING THAT you might have noticed throughout the book is that not every portrait perfectly follows every single tip or technique highlighted. Just as there is no single volume that exhaustively covers all portraiture technique out there, it would be frustratingly inefficient and creatively dull to employ all of the "rules" in order to make the "perfect" portrait. Sometimes, timing gets in the way of taking care of all of the little things. Often, your creative intention or style dictates that you "break" a compositional or posing rule. Most of the time, the portrait just feels good, and you walk away from it and realize later you could have improved it.

In any case, the preceding information is all about guiding, or advising, you toward making better portraits and thinking more deeply about all of the elements that go into making a portrait creative and effective. I hope the information has been useful. I hope some of it was immediately applied and the rest logged away for the long term.

I'll reemphasize the final point I made in the book's introduction: to grow photographically, you must be shooting. This means making mistakes, learning along the way, and every now and then, forgetting to employ a portraiture best practice. Again, portraiture is *intentional*—intentionally creative, intentionally narrative, and intentionally strategic. Be intentional with your portrait photography, whether you are shooting or reflecting on your shoot during an edit. This will most certainly result in your continued growth as a portrait photographer.

With that, happy shooting!

INDEX

ENTHUSIASTS— IT DOESN'T END HERE!

Head over to *The Enthusiast's Guides* site where you can explore the entire book series, download free content, sign up for deals, meet the authors, collaborate with other readers, and more!

VISIT: ENTHUSIASTSGUIDES.COM

 @enthusiastsguides

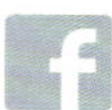 facebook.com/groups/enthusiastsguides

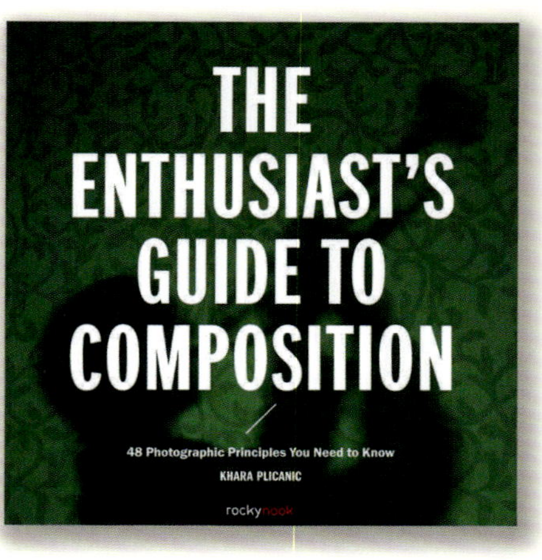

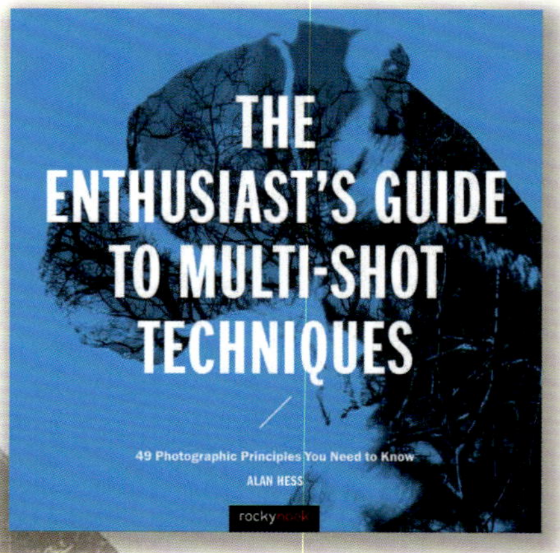

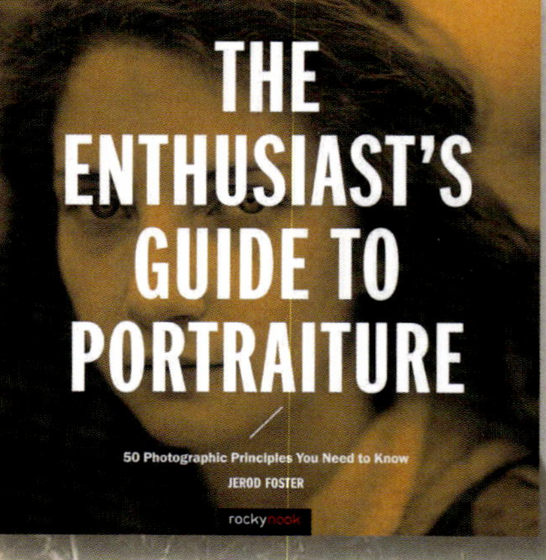